FRACTURED
BORDERS

*Reading Women's
Cancer Literature*

Mary K. DeShazer

University of Michigan Press
Ann Arbor

2008   2007   2006   2005   4   3   2   1

A CIP catalog record for this book is available from the British Library.

Library of Congress Cataloging-in-Publication Data

DeShazer, Mary K.
    Fractured borders : reading women's cancer literature / Mary K.
DeShazer.
      p. cm.
    Includes bibliographical references and index.
    ISBN-13: 978-472-09909-2 (acid-free paper)
    ISBN-10: 0-472-09909-4 (acid-free paper)
    ISBN-13: 978-0-472-06909-5 (pbk. : acid-free paper)
    ISBN-10: 0-472-06909-8 (pbk. : acid-free paper)   1. American
literature—Women authors—History and criticicism.
2. Cancer in literature.   3. Cancer—Patients—United States—
Biography—History and criticism.   4. Cancer patients' writings,
American—History and criticism.   5. Women and literature—
United States.   6. Cancer in women—Historiography.
7. Autobiography. I. Title.
PS169.C35D47   2005
810.9'3561—dc22   2005016627

In memory of Lynda Hart, 1953–2000

Acknowledgments

ALTHOUGH I HAD READ WOMEN'S WRITING about cancer for years as a scholar of gender studies, my intimate acquaintance with this literature developed during five months of the year 2000 that my close friend of nearly two decades, Lynda Hart, was dying of inflammatory breast cancer. A professor of English at the University of Pennsylvania and a renowned lesbian feminist theorist, Lynda had experienced stage 1 breast cancer two years earlier, followed by lumpectomy and radiation therapy. Still, all of us "friends of Lynda," as we came to call ourselves in an e-mail support group, had believed that she would remain cancer-free and had anticipated celebrating her five-year anniversary and subsequent survival status. The shock that Lynda and we, her community, experienced upon learning that she had contracted a new and more virulent breast cancer is one that I now understand has been replicated in hundreds of thousands of friendship networks around the world. When she felt well enough, Lynda read not only the Buddhist teachings that sustained her spiritually but also many of the writings about cancer by the women whose work I analyze in this book. I read alongside her. Sometimes she railed against the sentimental, simplistic, or heterosexist representations she encountered in this body of writing; more often she found solace or humor in its pages. I have written *Fractured Borders* as a way of honoring Lynda's memory and a means of introducing this literature and the feminist theory that contextualizes it to other communities of women confronting this disease.

I must first express gratitude to the friends with whom I shared those difficult months: Catherine Keller and Jason Starr, for providing me with comfort, conversation, and a welcome bed whenever I came to New York; Stacey Foiles, Lynda's life partner, for loving Lynda deeply and sharing her final days so generously with all of us; and Leslie Thrope, Sadie Ghossein, and the late Dominique Ghossein—Leslie's partner and Sadie's mommy, who died of cancer in 2003. Other people close to Lynda I know less well but wish to thank for their camaraderie during the fall of 2000: Una Chaudhuri and her daughter, Sonu Adams; Peggy Phelan; Kerry Moore; Gabrielle Cody; and Kerry Hart. My beloved friend, Anita Helle, flew across country to say goodbye to Lynda and grieve with me; I will always treasure that loving gesture and our years of emotional and intellectual affiliation. I am also grateful to colleagues that Lynda and I met during our years at Xavier University, friends with whom I shared the sorrow of her death and reminiscences about her life: Tyrone Williams, Norman Finkelstein, and Ernie and Nelida Fontana.

I want to thank as well several friends with whom I have discussed the effects that cancer has on individuals and families, especially Jane Mead, whose conversations and poetry have sustained me; Patti Patridge, with whom I have talked about the death of parents; Billy McClain, who shared with me his experience of surgery and healing; Kevin Dettmar, with whom I explored the work of grief; Inzer Byers and Rose Simon, whose insights I have long valued; and Martha Kierstead and her sister, Julie Kierstead Nelson, with whom I conversed about the lessons one can learn from a cancer diagnosis.

My work on *Fractured Borders* was greatly enhanced when Wake Forest University awarded me an R. J. Reynolds Senior Faculty Research Leave in 2002–3. I especially appreciate the support of former English department Chair Gale Sigal and current Chair Eric Wilson; Anne Boyle, director of women's and gender studies; and many other wonderful colleagues at Wake Forest, past and present, with whom I have discussed my writing about cancer literature: Sally Barbour, Jill Carraway, Nancy Cotton, Andrew Ettin, Dean Franco, Gary Ljungquist, Dolly McPherson, Linda Nielsen, Stepháne Robolin, Evie Shockley, Bob Shorter, Sally Shumaker, Olga Valbuena, Sarah Watts, Ulrike Wiethaus, and Isabel Zuber. Gillian Overing, Elizabeth Phillips, and Eva Rodtwitt have been particularly important nurturers of my writing. I also thank my graduate research assistant, April Yount Williams, for her fine work and efficiency; Peggy Barrett, Connie Green, and Linda

Mecum for their thoughtfulness; Scott Claybrook for his technical assistance; and my students for their ideas and energy. Sam and Farrah at the Clemson News Stand helped me locate books about cancer, and Susan Hilligoss helped me escape to the tennis court.

I am grateful to many other friends who have sustained me over the years: Sandra and Alan Bryant in Louisville, Kim Kessaris and Karin Peterson in Asheville, Sarah Lu Bradley and E. J. Essic in Alaska, Susan Carlson and the Mendelson household in Iowa, and all the citizens of Botticelliville. Catherine Paul and Sean Scuras have often treated me to gnocchi and limoncello; I also thank Catherine for reading part of my manuscript and talking through ideas with me.

My family members have been loving and supportive, especially my husband, Martin Jacobi, and my stepsons, Evan and Andrew Jacobi—you're the best! I appreciate as well the support of Sam, Vickie, Ryan, Michele, and Will DeShazer; Kathy DeShazer and Ron Flora; Bettye and Richard Grogan; and Bob and Nan Jacobi. To Sasha and Kent Oberbeck I am thankful for the delightful gift of Jacob. And I remain grateful to my parents, Henry and Marian DeShazer, for all they gave me.

Finally, I thank my editor, LeAnn Fields, as well as Suzanne Poirier and the anonymous readers of my manuscript for the University of Michigan Press for their valuable insights and assistance.

An earlier version of "'Skinnied on the Left Side Like a Girl': Embodying Cancer on the Feminist Stage" appeared in the *National Women's Studies Association Journal* as "Fractured Borders: Women's Cancer and Feminist Theatre." Reprinted by permission of Indiana University Press.

Contents

INTRODUCTION
Women, Cancer, Writing

I am a One-Breasted, Menopausal, Jewish Bisexual Lesbian Mom and I am the topic of our times. I am the hot issue. I am the cover of *Newsweek,* the editorial in the paper. I am a best-seller. And I am coming soon to a theater near you.
—Susan Miller, *My Left Breast*

There are now nearly 10 million cancer survivors in this country, up from 3 million in 1971 and 6 million in 1986. Many live for years or decades, and it is becoming impossible to ignore questions about their lives.
—Gina Kolata, in the *New York Times*

W OMEN'S LITERARY REPRESENTATIONS of cancer provide the focus of *Fractured Borders,* which offers the first comprehensive critical analysis of contemporary writing about breast, uterine, and ovarian cancer. My study takes its title from two lines in Audre Lorde's powerful elegy, "The Night-blooming Jasmine": "death is a fractured border / through the center of my days" (*Marvelous* 52). I examine, however, writers' depictions of the borders women inhabit in living with cancer as well as those they patrol when facing death. My scholarly approach relies on close interpretive readings as well as a variety of theoretical perspectives to illumine the texts and contexts of women's cancers, including postmodern theories of the body, performance theory, feminist literary criticism, French feminisms, and disability studies. Although women published writing about cancer from the 1960s through the 1980s, this body of literature has increased exponentially since the early 1990s as growing numbers of women have faced the searing realities of this disease and given testimony to its ravages and revelations. I aim to analyze the contours of this literary phenomenon.

As playwright Susan Miller's insouciant manifesto makes clear, people of all genders, ages, ethnicities, and sexual orientations are diagnosed each year with cancer, and many of them are "in your face" about it (219). Indeed, living with cancer has become the topic of our times after decades—some would say centuries—of evasion and misrepresentation by many physicians, researchers, and sometimes patients. In an intriguing cultural shift from twenty years ago, breast cancer, once the "silent epidemic," receives the most media emphasis in the United States and the United Kingdom today. "THE NEW THINKING ON BREAST CANCER," screams the 18 February 2002 cover of *Time* magazine, "The Smartest Drugs / The Gentlest Treatments / The Latest on Mammograms." Inside, the article reports that more than two hundred thousand U.S. women learn each year that they have breast cancer, twice the number from 1980; forty thousand die annually from this disease. The article acknowledges that the American Cancer Society's emphasis on mammograms has resulted in overdiagnoses, causing thousands of women who might otherwise live long and healthy lives to undergo invasive radiation or chemotherapy treatments for microscopic cancers and even precancerous conditions. The article further claims that tamoxifen, hailed in the early 1990s as an estrogen-based drug that could both treat breast cancer and reduce the risk of contracting it, may increase the risk of uterine cancer. At the same time the author, Christine Gorman, hails new research methods in the battle against breast cancer and glibly promises readers "a guide to saving lives."[1]

What are cancer patients to make of this complex, evolving, and sometimes conflicting information? What new knowledge has cancer research produced that is available and accessible to people struggling with this disease? Considering cancers of the lungs and breast as examples will help us reflect upon these questions, given that lung cancer kills more U.S. women each year than any other cancer, while breast cancer generates the most new diagnoses. It is widely known that lung cancer is the cause of death for more than four hundred thousand Americans annually, sixty-six thousand of them women; that more than 100 million people worldwide died of this disease between 1940 and 2000; that cigarette smoking and lifelong exposure to passive smoke are the primary culprits; that cigarette manufacturers have increasingly been held legally accountable for decades of dishonest or misleading information about their product's cancer risk; and that while chemotherapy and/or radiation can sometimes prolong life once lung cancer has metastasized, no cure exists for this deadly disease.[2] Regarding breast cancer, it is well known that one in eight women in the United States and one in eleven in the United Kingdom will contract it during their lifetimes, that 75 percent of all breast cancers originate as infiltrating ductal carcinomas in the lining of milk ducts, that 80 percent of breast cancers occur in women over fifty, that genetic factors account for only 5 percent of breast cancers, and that primary risk factors are age-related, hormonal, and environmental.[3] Although no cure exists for breast cancer, the good news is that its death rates are declining; forty-six thousand U.S. women died of it in 1993, forty thousand in 2003 (Casamayou 15; www.komen.org).

How cancer patients can best parse these data remains a complicated issue. Cancer-related Web sites offer a valuable source of information, as do informal support networks.[4] As Gina Kolata's 1 June 2004 *New York Times* article attests, 10 million cancer survivors are living in the United States today, in part because of enhanced diagnostic technologies and early detection, and millions more survivors exist throughout the world. Many of them are speaking out about "how they should be treated, what their psychological states are, and what their medical and social needs are" (A15). "What's new," claims Dr. Julia H. Rowland, who directs the Office of Cancer Survivorship at the National Cancer Institute, "is the recognition and growing attention to the fact that people are living long term" (A15). Although some of these constituents find offensive the widely contested label of "survivor," preferring to consider themselves "cured," "living with cancer," "cancer-free," or free of labels altogether, most cancer patients agree that their lives changed utterly at the moment of diagnosis. For many, notes breast cancer activist Musa Mayer, the fundamental problem is uncertainty about whether the disease is in remission, chronic, or likely to recur: "It's the not knowing that is really the critical issue" (A15). Despite the uncertainties, these cancer survivors have increasingly claimed the authority to ask questions about their lives on their own terms.[5]

As media headlines, diagnostic technologies, and survival strategies have proliferated, so have works of literature by people living with or dying from cancer. Most of this literature is written by women. Although women contract the same cancers men do, a few are gender-specific: breast, uterine, and ovarian diseases account for 43 percent of all women's cancers (Proctor 3).[6] These three cancers provide the focal topic for hundreds of narratives, memoirs, poems, and plays written each year by women in English—works that break silence about this disease, challenge its stigmatization, and retrace its boundaries.[7] The 1970s and early 1980s produced such important examples of "autopathography"—

life writing about illness—as Rose Kushner's *Breast Cancer: A Personal History and an Investigative Report,* Betty Rollin's *First, You Cry,* Susan Sontag's *Illness as Metaphor,* Audre Lorde's *The Cancer Journals,* and Leatrice H. Lifshitz's anthology of poetry, *Her Soul beneath the Bone.*[8] Some of this literature was not especially feminist; rather, it contributed to what Barbara Ehrenreich describes as an "ultrafeminine" cancer marketplace:

> In the mainstream of breast-cancer culture, one finds very little anger, no mention of possible environmental causes, few complaints about the fact that, in all but the more advanced, metastasized cases, it is the "treatments," not the disease, that cause illness and pain. The stance toward existing treatments is occasionally critical . . . but more commonly grateful; the overall tone, almost universally upbeat. (48)

Certainly mainstream approaches to cancer literature and activism have been fruitful; they have brought valuable research and federal budget dollars as well as awareness to the cause of women's health. But early counterhegemonic literary treatments of cancer such as Kushner's, Sontag's, and Lorde's challenged the equation of illness with femininity; questioned the pathologizing of cancerous bodies; examined the politics of mastectomy, reconstructive surgeries, and prosthesis; and documented the power of women's support networks to resist society's discipline and punishment of the terminally ill.[9] These narratives thus provided vital critiques of what Ehrenreich terms "the Cancer Industrial Complex" (52).

Cancer literature came into its own in part for tragic reasons, as studies revealed that while 30,000 U.S. citizens lost their lives to cancer in 1900, 538,000 died of it in 1994; that breast cancer has become the leading cause of death for U.S. and British women between forty and fifty-five; and that women suffer physically and emotionally from the "hallowed triad" of surgery, radiation, and chemotherapy—the breast cancer regimen that Dr. Susan Love has christened "slash, burn, and poison" (Ferraro 27; Proctor 1; Thames and Gazzaniga 5). Shifting cultural landscapes have also contributed to the rise in women's writing about cancer: powerful activism by such leading organizations as the Susan G. Komen Breast Cancer Foundation, the National Breast Cancer Coalition, and Breast Cancer Action; the incursion of feminist values into public policy, institutional practices, and women's daily lives; the rise of women's studies in colleges and universities throughout the world. The feminist emphasis on health care activism, consciousness-raising, and empowerment has facilitated both the initial publication and regularly updated editions of such "sacred texts" as the Boston Women's Health Collective's *Our Bodies, Ourselves* and *Dr. Susan Love's Breast Book*. These books, in turn, have informed women of all ages how to maintain gynecological, reproductive, and breast health and what to know and do if cancer strikes. Post-1960s feminism and a vibrant women's health movement have helped creative writers generate the motivation and confidence to inscribe the cancer experience in dynamic works of literature.

In this project I explore the conceptual themes and metaphors, representational strategies, and feminist interventions offered by five genres of cancer literature: drama, poetry, popular fiction, experimental fiction, and autobiography. Since the ways in which women represent cancer in the first four genres have received little critical attention, my contribution to an understanding of dramatic, poetic, and fictional cancer texts seems timely.[10] Because cancer memoirs that chronicle one woman's struggle have been the subject of significant critical scrutiny, I focus less on such personal narratives than on other types of autobiography, particularly multicultural and environmental narratives.[11] Each literary genre represents the cancer experience through different aesthetic and narrative strategies; I therefore use these differences as an evaluative lens in approaching my subject. As literary scholar Ann Douglas has argued, genres "function prediscursively by forming mental templates" that allow readers room for metaphoric or creative adaptation (i). I aim to examine the new knowledge these generic templates provide about women's representations of cancer. In addition, my perspective foregrounds issues of diversity; thus, I employ a comparative lens to probe the racial, ethnic, sexual, and political differences that characterize cancer literature. Although I emphasize writing from the United States and the United Kingdom, I consider as well works by women from Canada, India, Egypt, and Trinidad to extend the scope of this study.

During the 1990s and beyond, women writers working in all genres devised innovative representational strategies for interrogating how cancer affects women's subjectivity, relationships, and politics of location. Plays by women have employed what Rebecca Schneider terms "explicit bodies in performance" to foreground the cancerous body's materiality as well as its capacity to resist appropriation. (1). Breast cancer poetry has focused on such embodied imagery as the vulnerable nipple, the surgical scar, and the damaged or reconstructed breast tissue. Popular fiction has glorified dying heroines and rewritten the heterosexual romance plot to privilege idealized love between a cancer patient and her female supporters, while experimental fiction has traced the ways that memory measures the power of the erotic at or near the moment of a woman's death. New types of autobiography have emerged: photographic memoirs that chronicle women's deaths from cancer through visual self-representation, ecological narratives that explore links between cancer and lifetime exposure to estrogenic chemicals. Taken as a whole, this body of literature expands women's insights about cancer and pays homage to the power of their voices.

The questions I explore in *Fractured Borders* address issues of experience, representation, difference, and audience. What distinctive contributions to readers' understandings of women's lived experience does each genre of cancer literature offer? How do disability theory and feminist theories of the body enhance any analysis of these textual representations of cancer? How does cancer literature by African American and Trinidadian women differ, thematically and theoretically, from that of white women in the United States and the United Kingdom? With what concerns regarding their experience and representation of cancer do lesbians struggle that heterosexual women do not or do differently? (These questions assume particular significance when we recall that African American women and lesbians are disproportionately vulnerable to dying from cancer, especially of the breast.)[12] Where do women writing cancer literature find common ground across racial, cultural, and sexual differences? For what audiences is cancer literature written, and to what and whom does it ultimately pay tribute?

This project thus entails two primary tasks: interrogating how cancer operates in cultural and literary representation and examining exemplary textual sites that reveal how cancer's multiple meanings are constructed. Chapter 1, " 'The Night-Side of Life': Analyzing Cancer Literature from Feminist Perspectives," establishes the sociohistorical contexts and literary significance of this body of women's writing and discusses the merits of feminist literary, body, and disability theory as methodological tools. Analyzing a wide variety of texts written between 1960 and 2003, I argue that contemporary women's cancer literature has represented ill bodies in five distinctive ways: as *medicalized, leaky, amputated, prosthetic,* and *(not) dying.* I claim as well that, counterintuitively, such representations enhance rather than diminish female subjectivity. Among the theoretical narratives of cancer that I engage in this chapter are Susan Sontag's *Illness as Metaphor*, Audre Lorde's *The Cancer Journals*, Jackie Stacey's *Teratologies*, and Zillah Eisenstein's *Manmade Breast Cancers*. I examine such literary works as Mahasweta Devi's "Breast-Giver," Gini Alhadeff's *Diary of a Djinn*, and poems by Sylvia Plath and Adrienne Rich.

Chapter 2, "'Skinnied on the Left Side Like a Girl': Embodying Cancer on the Feminist Stage," analyzes four plays from the 1990s that represent women's cancer from feminist perspectives: Margaret Edson's *Wit*, Susan Miller's *My Left Breast*, Lisa Loomer's *The Waiting Room*, and Maxine Bailey and Sharon M. Lewis's *Sistahs*. The first three playwrights are white women from the United States; Bailey and Lewis are Trinidadians living in Canada. I argue here that women's performance narratives differ from other cancer narratives by employing explicit bodies onstage to mark cancerous breasts, ovaries, and wombs as transgressive sites of social meaning; by challenging the capacity of a spectatorial gaze or an objectifying stare to appropriate women's ill or disabled bodies; and by fostering reciprocity among playwrights, actors, and audience. To elaborate on these points, I examine diverse representations of body politics and medical politics in these plays and consider how the playwrights integrate such issues as cultural genocide, ethnicity, and lesbian sexuality into their explorations of cancer. For its theoretical orientation, this chapter draws upon the "explicit body" performance theory of Rebecca Schneider and Jeanie Forte and the feminist disability theory of Rosemarie Garland Thomson.

Chapter 3, "Entering 'the House / of Lightning': Resistance and Transformation in U.S. Women's Breast Cancer Poetry," explores sustained, dynamic poetic sequences—from meditative clusters to book-length volumes—that feature breast cancer as their dominant theme. These sequences focus on the shock of cancer diagnosis, the Amazonian imagery of one-breasted warriors, and the symbolic dimensions of the scar that results from lumpectomy or mastectomy. Familiar poetic motifs—the epic journey, the conflict with mortality, the rituals of healing—intersect with newer motifs: the effects of mastectomy on female body image, the ambivalence many women feel toward prostheses. Examining sequences by two African American poets, Audre Lorde and Lucille Clifton, and two Jewish American poets, Alicia Suskin Ostriker and Hilda Raz, I argue that these poets move beyond abjection (emotionally) and beyond elegy (formally) to map vibrant metaphors of resistance and transformation for themselves and other breast cancer survivors. In mounting its argument, this chapter draws upon feminist poetry criticism by Melissa F. Zeiger and Lynn Keller and upon essays by the poets themselves.

Chapter 4, "Dying into the Lite: Popular Fiction, Cancer, and the Romance of Women's Relationships," argues that certain mainstream U.S. cancer novels employ ultrafeminine and sometimes infantilizing themes to forge an updated version of the nineteenth-century domestic novel. Domestic fiction from that century emphasized separate spheres for women and men and a "cult of true womanhood" that required purity, piety, domesticity, and submission. Today's popular cancer fiction revises domestic and romance literature in representing idealized love between a woman dying of cancer and the female supporters who surround her. Analyzing novels by Patricia Gaffney, Elizabeth Berg, Anna Quindlen, and Jayne Anne Phillips, I consider how these writers sentimentalize relationships between best friends or between dutiful daughters and their terminally ill mothers as well as why this fiction is so popular among women readers (as revealed through publishers' Web sites). To interrogate representations of cancer in popular culture, I draw upon Barbara Ehrenreich's analysis of the "pink kitsch" of the U.S. "cancer marketplace." To theorize romance and domesticity, I build upon Janice Radway's criticism of the romance novel, Michelle Masse's study of women's narratives and masochistic desire, Jane Tompkins's insights into sentimental fiction, and Nancy Chodorow's theories of mother-daughter symbiosis.

Chapter 5, "'Floating Out on a Yacht Called Eros': Memory, Desire, and Death in Women's Experimental Cancer Fiction," uses French feminist theories of embodiment to analyze three cancer novels that, explicitly or implicitly, employ such theories in the service of their narratives: Carole Maso's *Ava*, Susan Minot's *Evening*, and Jeanette Winterson's *Written on the Body*. Indebted to Virginia Woolf's stream-of-consciousness technique as well as postmodernism's privileging of textual lacunae, Maso and Minot "write the bodies" of bisexual and heterosexual women dying of cancer at midlife, while Winterson, equally indebted, "unwrites" the lesbian body. In this chapter I analyze the metanarratives, pastiche, temporal ruptures, and fragmentation that characterize this fiction stylistically; I consider as well these writers' tracings of the ways that memory measures the power of the erotic at or near one's moment of death. The primary theoretical lens I employ to examine these texts is that of *l'écriture féminine* as developed in Hélène Cixous's "The Laugh of the Medusa."

Chapter 6, "'Entering Cancerland': Self-Representation, Commonality, and Culpability in Women's Autobiographical Narratives," reconfigures an activist paradigm established by sociologist Maren Klawiter to interrogate three types of cancer memoirs. Personal narratives focus on an individual's diagnosis, treatment, and recovery or decline; multicultural narratives emphasize identity politics and community as critical factors in women's experience of cancer; and environmental narratives argue or imply a causal connection between cancer and exposure to pesticides and other toxins. As exemplary personal narratives I analyze Katherine Russell Rich's *The Red Devil* and Ruth Picardie's *Before I Say Goodbye;* as exemplary multicultural narratives, two works that focus on cancer and sexual orientation: Sandra Butler and Barbara Rosenblum's *Cancer in Two Voices* and Eve Kosofsky Sedgwick's *White Glasses*. Because environmental cancer narratives as a subgenre have received little feminist scrutiny, I examine, as paradigmatic intertexts, the letters of Rachel Carson (who died of breast cancer) and her landmark treatise *Silent Spring*, which posits that cancer and carcinogens are linked. I then analyze two contemporary environmental memoirs: Sandra Steingraber's *Living Downstream: An Ecologist Looks at Cancer and the Environment*, which describes the writer's cancer experience and links cancer prevention to ecological vigilance; and Terry Tempest Williams's *Refuge: An Unnatural History of Family and Place*, which probes the relationship between the death of the author's mother from ovarian cancer and 1950s nuclear testing in the Nevada desert. I argue that taken together, these environmental narratives constitute an innovative, hybrid form of autobiography and construct new knowledge about cancer, ecology, and women's relationships.

In my conclusion, "The Cultural Work of Women's Cancer Literature," I consider what this body of writing *does* as well as what it means and explore a series of synthesizing questions. What has emerged from bringing together these analyses of the various literary genres? How might the themes and theories that illuminate women's writing about cancer be usefully engaged by women—and perhaps men—who actually are living with cancer as they read? How might these texts work against ill women's stigmatization and provide strategies for resistance, healing, and commemoration?

My goal in this project has been to create a scholarly study of women's writing about cancer that appeals to a wide audience of readers, from cancer survivors and their families to health care activists to medical practitioners, from literary scholars and feminist theorists to teachers of cultural studies and women's health issues. I want *Fractured Borders* to make a difference to at least a few people in the real world; thus, I have attempted to write a book that I consider theoretically grounded yet widely accessible. I hope that my analysis of women's representations of cancer will be intellectually and emotionally engaging to other women's studies scholars and that you will find sustenance, as I have, from reflecting upon these galvanizing works of art.

1. "THE NIGHT-SIDE OF LIFE"

Analyzing Cancer Literature

from Feminist Perspectives

Illness is the night-side of life, a more onerous citizenship. Everyone who is born holds dual citizenship, in the kingdom of the well and the kingdom of the sick. Although we all prefer to use only the good passport, sooner or later each of us is obliged, at least for a spell, to identify ourselves as citizens of that other place.

—Susan Sontag, *Illness as Metaphor*

I am a post-mastectomy woman who believes our feelings need voice in order to be recognized, respected, and of use. I do not wish my anger and pain and fear about cancer to fossilize into yet another silence, nor rob me of whatever strength can lie at the core of this experience, openly acknowledged and examined.

—Audre Lorde, *The Cancer Journals*

*I*N *Illness as Metaphor* (1977) THE U.S. PHILOSOPHER Susan Sontag examines the traumatic and transformational power of life-threatening diseases, which force the humans who contract them to face "the night-side of life" (1). Specifically, she compares the nineteenth-century quest to eliminate tuberculosis with the twentieth-century effort to eradicate cancer and discusses the ways in which both diseases are "spectacularly, and similarly, encumbered by the trappings of metaphor" (5). TB and cancer evoke dread and fear of contagion, she explains; physicians typically describe these diseases as *consuming, corrupting, insidious,* and *invasive,* while the culture at large finds them *unspeakable, monstrous.* For cancer patients, portrayed until recently in life and in literature as "humiliated by fear and agony," such metaphors may evoke terror and self-blame; certainly "the people who have the real disease are hardly helped by hearing their disease's name constantly being dropped as the epitome of evil" (17, 84). If cancer can be stripped of negative metaphors and "de-mythicized," Sontag concludes, ill people will stand a better chance of avoiding stigmatization and addressing cancer on their own terms (86–87).

In *The Cancer Journals* (1980) Audre Lorde challenges, from African American and lesbian feminist perspectives, the silences that patriarchal cultures have demanded of women with cancer. Dedicated to "the transformation of silence into language and action," Lorde eloquently describes her diagnosis with breast cancer and subsequent mastectomy as well as her refusal to wear a "grotesquely pale" prosthesis and thereby conform to societal expectations regarding white normativity and symmetrical breasts (18, 44). Although she acknowledges the suffering her illness causes, she refuses to find it humiliating. Instead she determines to mine "whatever strength can lie at the core of this experience," a strength she taps by reflecting honestly on what it means to be a "postmastectomy woman"—black, lesbian, and resistant (1).

While both of these pioneers in the area of women's cancer literature decry the silence and shaming that cancer patients in the late 1970s typically confronted, they differ in their feminist perspectives and thus in their approach to theorizing cancer. In her interrogation of the ways in which militaristic and demonizing metaphors work to stigmatize people living with cancer, Sontag's emphasis is discursive; cultural attitudes toward this disease will shift, she argues, once patients refuse to view their cancerous bodies as "out of control" and physicians abandon their "military rhetoric" in favor of "metaphors featuring the body's 'natural defenses'" (11, 66, 87). Lorde's emphasis is activist; she uses feminist standpoint theory to argue that gender, race, sexual orientation, and other categories of identity and difference are shifting, intersecting, and multiply mediated axes from which one can, with validity, undertake cultural analysis and intervention. Unlike Sontag, who downplays gender, mentions ethnicity only in the context of Nazi disease tropes, and does not acknowledge her own breast cancer, Lorde theorizes directly from her own gendered, racially specific, and embodied experience of illness and recovery. While Sontag locates her narrative authority in philosophy, Lorde locates hers in identity politics. To be sure, these theorists share the sociopolitical goal of destigmatizing cancer and shedding light on how contemporary culture constructs this disease as humiliating. However, each writer has contributed different insights to contemporary feminist understandings of cancer, women's bodies, and representation.

The writings of Sontag and Lorde have influenced an entire generation of feminist theorists of the body whose inquiries drive this chapter's
interrogation of women's cancer literature. Sontag's critique of
metaphoric objectification and the dehumanizing effects of medical discourses of cancer has informed British sociologist Jackie Stacey's postmodern approach to cancer discourse in *Teratologies: A Cultural Study of
Cancer* (1997) and British philosopher Margrit Shildrick's bioethical
argument in *Leaky Bodies and Boundaries* (1997) for a "postmodern feminist ethic" (12). Lorde's emphasis on difference and her view of gender,
race, class, sexual orientation, and ability status as intersecting axes of
identity have influenced theories of embodiment by three U.S. feminists:
Rosemarie Garland Thomson's manifesto on feminist disability theory
in *Extraordinary Bodies* (1997) and related essays; Zillah Eisenstein's pro-
mulgation of an antiracist, anticapitalist "breast-felt politics" in *Manmade Breast Cancers* (2001); and Diane Price Herndl's theorizations of
feminism and bodily hybridity in "Reconstructing the Posthuman Feminist Body Twenty Years after Audre Lorde's *Cancer Journals*" (2002).

In this chapter I use the insights of these and other feminist theorists
to analyze the major themes, tropes, and narrative strategies that govern
literary representations of cancer in exemplary texts by women written
between 1960 and 2003. I argue that feminist theories of the body illuminate cancer literature by providing tools and methodology for scrutiniz-
ing five key ways in which women's ill bodies have been textually represented: as *medicalized, leaky, amputated, prosthetic,* and *(not) dying.*
These five tropes, in turn, serve as a framework for understanding how
stigmatization diminishes ill women's subjectivity and how feminist
writing can enhance it. Medicalized bodies generally experience invasive
treatment and only possible or partial recovery; the women who inhabit
these bodies and/or represent them in literature struggle with issues of
appropriation and agency in the face of medical intervention that can be
traumatic, whether lifesaving or useless. Leaky bodies exhibit an often
disturbing instability, as blood or fluids from the breast or uterus spill or
ooze; women who leak may be represented in exemplary literary texts as
either abject or transgressive. Amputated bodies signify a radical
absence, generally of a cancerous breast or uterus, organs frequently sexualized and culturally constructed as essential to femininity; women who
inscribe the experience of lumpectomies, mastectomies, or hysterec-
tomies strive to confront loss and to redefine themselves or their protag-

onists as strong and erotically powerful. Prosthetic bodies evolve from the surgical reconstruction of amputated body parts; women who write about choosing reconstructive surgery struggle to comprehend a new-found hybridity, while those who reject reconstruction strive to embrace their breastless chests. Surviving, or "not dying," bodies live in a liminal state, vulnerable to the recurrence of cancer and frequent medical scrutiny, while dying bodies typically suffer, shrink or bloat, and eventually fail. Women who record the experience of living with or beyond cancer often express enormous relief yet wrestle with survivor guilt, while women who write about dying may grieve, despair, or review their lives in affirmative ways.

The questions that drive this chapter are discursive, textual, and cultural. What does each of these defining tropes of women's cancer literature mean and do? How has medical discourse, with its language of war, battles, epidemics, victims, and survivors, affected women writers' representations of cancer? What alternative discourses have these writers developed? Since women's experiences of life-threatening illness vary significantly across race, class, nationality, and sexual orientation, how do women's literary representations of cancer reflect these differences even as they trace the common dimensions of this disease?

MEDICALIZED BODIES

Although it was written nearly thirty years ago, Sontag's *Illness as Metaphor* remains an incisive text for interrogating the dehumanization that cancer patients have often experienced at the hands of medical practitioners. In this study she claims insightfully that when "primitive" cells are seen as multiplying wildly, physicians may deny their patients agency, for they perceive that "you are being replaced by the non-you" and that the "natural order" is thus being violated (67). Sontag also critiques the rhetoric of war that characterizes medical discourse about cancer:

> The bromides of the American cancer establishment, tirelessly hailing the imminent victory over cancer; the professional pessimism of a large number of cancer specialists, talking like battle-weary officers mired down in an interminable colonial war—these are twin distortions in this military rhetoric about cancer. (66–67)

Cancer patients rarely benefit from such inflated rhetorical gestures, she argues: their treatments may be invasive, indeed poisonous; their medicalized bodies may strike them as frail and unfamiliar; the stigmatization they face and the pain they experience may be debilitating; the promise of victory may ring false. Sontag applauds the struggle for dignity and self-determination that many people with cancer nonetheless undertake, and she remains optimistic that both the discourse and the treatments of cancer will evolve.[1]

In *Teratologies* Jackie Stacey both draws upon and critiques Sontag's perspective on agency and medicalization. Stacey's postmodern treatise goes beyond Sontag in challenging the gender hierarchies of the medical establishment's discourse, in which "heroic men of medicine," associated with reason and progress, "save women from the horrors of their bodies" (11). Basing her argument on her own experience of treatment for ovarian cancer, Stacey acknowledges the seductive appeal that such "masculine heroic narratives" offered as she moved through the British health care system from diagnosis to surgery to chemotherapy. "Trust the doctors, they know best," she heard repeatedly. "Your body becomes the battleground between good science and bad disease. If you give yourself up to their wisdom and follow instructions, you stand the best chance" (11). But Stacey refuses to "give herself up" to her physicians. Instead, like Sontag, she questions the cultural rhetoric that represents all cancerous bodies as "out of control, governed only by the rules of outlaws," and she further challenges the sexist rhetoric that often objectifies women patients (11). Although she praises Sontag for her astute critique of "metaphoric thinking in matters medical," Stacey ultimately rejects the belief that biomedicine itself will destigmatize cancer. "Sontag's faith in medical science brings her narrative to resolution," Stacey claims; "for her, science is the hero who will rescue cancer patients from their stigmatized status" (47). For Stacey, in contrast, this "retreat into the radical materialism of biomedicine" seems counterproductive, given that the medical establishment has been the primary initiator of such stigmatizing rhetoric. To be sure, Stacey critiques alternative medical models as well—those herbal, dietary, and meditation treatments for cancer that Sontag also interrogates. While advocates of these regimens can be commended for treating patients as subjects rather than objects, Stacey notes, they too often represent patients as heroes who can heal themselves and thereby grow wiser. Thus alternative regi-

mens may participate as actively in "the fantasy of masculine invincibility" as traditional biomedical models do (12).

Stacey further extends Sontag's analysis in her concern with who and
what such heroic narratives exclude—with the ways these narratives
often fail to articulate racial and sexual differences. Throughout *Teratologies* Stacey foregrounds the "political questions raised by cultural
narratives" in part because as a cancer patient she felt isolated due to her
"difference": her ovarian cancer manifested itself in a rare and
"grotesque" form known as teratoma, she is a lesbian who was visited
daily in the hospital by her female partner, she sought alternative thera-
pies as well as conventional medical ones, and she refused to wear a wig
on a ward in which everyone else concealed the baldness that resulted
from their chemotherapy treatments (17). Her medicalized body in effect
spoke its differences, and "in this context my story had a certain freakish
ring to it; no one else seemed to have been here before" (17).

As Margrit Shildrick explains in *Leaky Bodies and Boundaries*, however, many women *have* "been here before"; indeed, she argues that cancer patients have long been "doubly disenabled by their status as female
and patients" (116). Shildrick supports her claim through a critique of the
active/passive dichotomy that has long existed between doctors and
cancer patients of both genders and all races and sexualities. Since the
rise of bioethics in the 1970s and 1980s, the medical encounter has
increasingly been envisioned as "not simply an intervention on the part
of an active participant into the life of a passive one, but a transaction
between two self-determining moral agents" (8). Yet this ideal has not
been fully realized, since patients are rarely accorded self-determination.
With Stacey, Shildrick recognizes that gender bias is a further problem
in both the medical encounter and the ethical theories that evaluate it, for
"both the material body and the female are positioned as other to the
transcendent subject and denied expression in ethical paradigms" (9).
Drawing on Michel Foucault's theory of disease as socially constructed
through the medical gaze, Shildrick argues that as a "disciplinary
regime," biomedicine has long sought to stabilize the corporeal by
endorsing a mind-body split (the split that characterizes all Western religious and philosophical discourse) and thus disembodying the "knowing
subject" (Foucault, *Birth;* Shildrick, "Leaky" 11–13). As a postmodern
feminist she advocates that feminism seek to "reclaim the materiality of
women's bodies" even as she acknowledges that when patients are

treated for life-threatening illnesses, both men and women can be "engendered as female" (115–16). Only by according agency to *all* medicalized bodies, while recognizing the particular objectification of female, racial/ethnic, and gay and lesbian bodies, can the medical establishment practice a just ethic of care.

Sontag's theory and the feminist analyses of Stacey and Shildrick help to illuminate literary texts by contemporary U.S., British, and Canadian/Trinidadian women that examine the intersection of gender and medicalization. For example, U.S. poet Alicia Ostriker's "The Bridge" explores the trauma that occurs during a routine mammogram when the speaker is called back for a second procedure once a potentially cancerous cyst is detected. When "the mammogram technician / Says *Sorry, we need to do this again,*" the poet muses,

> ... you have already become a statistic,
> Citizen of a country where the air,
> Water, your estrogen, have just saluted
> Their target cells, planted their Judas kiss
> Inside the Jerusalem of the breast.
> *Here on the film what looks like specks of dust*
> *Is calcium deposits.*
>
> (*The Crack* 85)

Like Sontag, Ostriker employs the controlling metaphor of illness as a strange country whose "onerous citizenship" humans deplore. However, the poet further defines her troubled "country" in environmental terms—even its air and water are dangerous—and in terms of bodily betrayal: the realization that her own cells and hormones have put her body at grave risk is daunting. "Try saying *fear,*" Ostriker continues. "Now feel / Your tongue as it cleaves to the roof of your mouth" (85). The poet describes vividly how the "the night-side of life"—another of Sontag's metaphors for illness—can overwhelm the day. Entry into the "kingdom of the ill" is disorienting if not terrifying for Ostriker, as for many other women, yet she determines to chart the terrain of her medicalized body on her own terms (Sontag, *Illness* 1).

Sontag's analysis of cancer's militarized discourse can also aid readers in understanding the struggle of Sandra, the protagonist in *Sistahs,* a play by Canadian/Trinidadian writers Maxine Bailey and Sharon M. Lewis. As Sontag points out, cancer cells "do not simply multiply; they are 'invasive'. . . . Treatment also has a military flavor. Radiotherapy uses the metaphors of aerial warfare; patients are 'bombarded' with toxic rays. And chemotherapy is chemical warfare, using poisons" (64–65). Little wonder, then, that Sandra in *Sistahs* represents her uterine cancer in militaristic terms. "Try waking up each morning," she tells her friends and daughter, "deciding whether or not to be drugged up, or sit with the pain all day. . . . I've LOST! This war" (47–48). If metastasized cancer is represented in medical texts as a battleground on which many patients must envision themselves fighting, as Sontag claims, it makes sense that patients like Sandra feel vanquished by so formidable an opponent. Yet Bailey and Lewis do not present Sandra as a defeated victim. Indeed, Shildrick's and Stacey's theories serve to clarify the nature of Sandra's resistance. Shildrick's critique of the "disciplinary regime" of biomedicine, for instance, helps to explain why Sandra ultimately refuses further treatment and takes refuge in her kitchen, disgusted by all the slicing and burning that her medicalized body has endured: "Now *I'm* doing the . . . cutting, chopping, and slicing" (55). Stacey's analysis of medicalized bodies and racial/sexual difference, in turn, sheds light on Sandra's determination to confront cancer on her own terms as a Trinidadian lesbian who likens cancer to cultural genocide and determines to use her own tools: obeah and voodoo and plantain soup and other food from home. "I want a dinner, one dinner with the people that I care about," Sandra explains near the end of the play as she solicits help from the women in her family and community whom she has invited to share what might be her last meal. "It's time. . . . It's time to serve the Mango Chow (47, 56).

Another approach to embodiment, feminist disability theory, draws more upon the methodology of Lorde than that of Sontag to offer insights into the links among cancer, medicalization, and cultural representations of femininity. As Rosemarie Garland Thomson explains in "Integrating Disability, Transforming Feminist Theory," "perhaps feminist disability theory's most incisive critique is revealing the intersections between the politics of appearance and the medicalization of subjugated bodies" (10). Norms of gendered appearance have long been applied coercively in Western culture; witness Victorian women's use of debilitating corsets, disabling body braces developed in the 1930s for women to wear in order to "correct" scoliosis, or the media emphasis today on women's cosmetic enhancement, whether through excessive consumerism or elective surgery (Garland Thomson, "Integrating" 10). In the words of Garland

Thomson, "the twin ideologies of normalcy and beauty posit female and disabled bodies, particularly, as not only spectacles to be looked at, but as pliable bodies to be shaped infinitely so as to conform to a set of standards called *normal* and *beautiful*" (11). Disability theorists' critiques of the cultural enforcement of artificial feminine body ideals as "normate" help readers of the *The Cancer Journals* to understand why as an African American lesbian comfortable with her asymmetrical postmastectomy breasts, Lorde was chastised by her surgeon's nurse for being "bad for the morale of the office" when she refused to wear a prosthesis and thus to pass as a "normal" woman (Garland Thomson, *Extraordinary* 8; Linton 24–25; Lorde, *Cancer* 59). Conversely, Wanda, the straight white protagonist of U.S. playwright Lisa Loomer's *The Waiting Room*, is considered problematic for office morale *because* she sports enormous reconstructed "tits" that are exaggeratedly symmetrical and provoke curious or lascivious stares (17–18). Because Lorde has refused reconstructive surgery, she disrupts established societal norms; because Wanda has undergone repeated cosmetic breast enhancement surgeries, she is disruptive for different (but equally arbitrary) reasons. Thus the oncologists and nurses in Lorde's and Loomer's narratives disparage nonconformist women with a "stare" that objectifies both the sexualized breast and the bodies of people with disabilities (Thomson, *Extraordinary* 26).

The theoretical perspective that feminist disability studies offers on normative femininity also clarifies why some cancer patients, in their journals and memoirs, worry about how their breasts will look after surgery as much as whether the procedure will be successful. In her essay "Titbits," for example, Brandyn Barbara Artis finds equally daunting the technical vocabulary she must acquire and the prospect of confronting her postmastectomy breast:

> Quickly, words, medical words I never thought that I would have a use for proliferate like clouds on a rainy day. Chemotherapy, oncology, carcinogenic embryonic antigen. In the doctor's office for the unveiling, I dub the oncologist Sir James and count the nasal hairs way up in the back of his nose while the bandages fall. I refuse to look at it with the nurses and those assembled because they scan my reaction like an X-ray. The questions haunt me. Will the incision be hideous? What will the skin resemble, some time-ravaged, chipped Venus? Will there be phantom pain? (179–80)

Off-putting medical jargon like "carcinogenic embryonic antigen" coexists for Artis alongside disturbing metaphors of objectification and voyeurism: she resists being *unveiled, scanned*. At the same time, the adjectives she uses to describe her anticipated survey of her amputated breast reveal the depth of her concern about body image: she expects it to look *hideous, time-ravaged*. Artis's effort to reclaim her erotic subjectivity is evident in her comparison of her medicalized body to that of Venus, the sexual and enigmatic goddess from Greek mythology, who in sculptures, even when they are worn by age, appears powerful and desirable. Still, Artis's representation of her postmastectomy body as "chipped" and her acceptance of the designation "phantom" for her missing breast reinforce Garland Thomson's argument that in patriarchal cultures women are socialized to view their medicalized bodies as alien and diminished, even as they struggle to resist such socialization (Artis 179–80; Garland Thomson, "Integrating" 10–11).

LEAKY BODIES

Feminist theorists have argued persuasively that the systemic discrimination and cultural marginalization to which women, people of color, the poor, gays and lesbians, people with disabilities, and the seriously ill are vulnerable has its philosophical roots in a binary logic that posits them as inferior Others: as "pure body" rather than mind or spirit, irrational rather than rational; as necessarily subjugated and in need of governance rather than self-determining and free. The bodies that such Others inhabit, it therefore follows, are characterized either as *lacking* the requisite organs, fluids, sexuality, or autonomy that make them worthy of the designation fully human (i.e., male, white, wealthy, straight, able-bodied, healthy) or as displaying embodiment, sexuality, ego, or debilitation *in excess*. As Garland Thomson asserts, "The gender, race, and ability systems intertwine further in representing subjugated people as being pure body, unredeemed by mind or spirit . . . as either a lack or an excess" ("Integrating" 10–11).

Margrit Shildrick and Janet Price point out in their introduction to *Feminist Theory and the Body* that while all marginalized bodies have the capacity to be unsettling to the hegemonic cultural order, women's bodies are especially so since Western religious and philosophical discourses have long deemed the female body "unpredictable, leaky, and disruptive" (2). Such stereotypical perspectives on female embodiment have maintained cultural credibility through the ages because of the power, danger, and mystery associated with menstrual blood and breast milk, the primary insignia of women's reproductive capacities—capacities that, paradoxically, are both idealized and denigrated in patriarchal societies. "As the devalued processes of reproduction make clear," Shildrick and Price further claim, "the body has a propensity to leak, to overflow the proper distinctions between self and other, to contaminate and engulf" (2–3). This linking of women and bodily excess helps to explain why women were traditionally socialized to experience shame when others saw their bloody underwear on the bathroom floor or their leaky breasts thrust toward a desiring infant.

Women's cancerous bodies are perhaps the leakiest of all, since breast cancer can cause milky discharge, uterine cancer can result in excessive vaginal bleeding, and other inflammatory cancers sometime lead to pus, sores, or open wounds. Although literary representations of the bodily fluids that signify these cancers have been relatively rare because of their taboo nature, writers such as Sylvia Plath, Bailey and Lewis, and Gini Alhadeff have charted this territory in poetry, journals, theater, and fiction. Feminist body theory can enhance our critical appreciation of these cancer narratives by offering tools for analyzing the protagonists' emotional responses to their own leakiness as well as the discursive strategies—from bitter irony to fierce narrative empathy—that characterize the writers' prose.

Plath was ahead of her time in representing women's bodies as terrifying in both their vulnerability and their power. In her poetry of the early 1960s, especially *Ariel*, and in her fiction and autobiography she reveals a fascination with flawed female embodiment. "There is a charge / For the eyeing of my scars," insists the enraged, frantic speaker in "Lady Lazarus," newly risen from the dead,

> . . . there is a charge
> For the hearing of my heart—
> It really goes.
>
> And there is a charge, a very large charge,
> For a word or a touch
> Or a bit of blood
>
> Or a piece of my hair or my clothes.

(*Collected* 244)

Even as she claims to be "your opus, / . . . your valuable," Plath's persona panics at her body's fluidity and fragmentation. The seeds for Plath's disturbing poetic representation of leaky, swollen, and scarred female bodies—bodies often surveyed in mirrors by the self-denigrating or self-aggrandizing women who inhabit them—can be found in her early fiction and diaries. For example, in "Tongues of Stone" the masochistic protagonist fantasizes her own decay as poisonous fluids consume her:

> She imagines the waste piling up in her, swelling her full of poisons that showed in the blank darkness of her eyes when she stared into the mirror, hating the dead face that greeted her, the mindless face with the ugly purple scar on the left cheek that marked her like a scarlet letter. (*Johnny* 270)

Inexplicable self-loathing, an inward-turned misogyny, disgust with the deadly shenanigans of her own internal organs, revulsion at the facial scar and intestinal swelling that threaten to erupt, a sense of herself as dying or perhaps already dead—all of these emotions characterize Plath's narrator in her discursive excess.

A similar concern with the excessive female body and an even greater preoccupation with leaks and liquidity appear in the following self-portrait from Plath's diary. Identifying irrationally, because of acne and a worrisome mole, with a girl her age who has died mysteriously from cancer, Plath peruses her flawed face in the mirror—only to imagine a reprieve from cancer when she fantasizes herself a famous writer, her face miraculously healed:

> Nose podgy as a leaking sausage: big pores full of pus and dirt, red blotches, the peculiar brown mole on my under-chin which I would like to have excised. Memory of that girl's face in the medical school movie, with a little black beauty wart: this wart is malignant: she will be dead in a week. . . . Body needs a wash, skin the worst: it is the climate: chapping cold, dessicating hot: I need to be tan, all-over brown, and then my skin clears and I am all right. I need to have written a novel, a book of poems, a *Ladies Home Journal* or *New Yorker* story, and I will be poreless and radiant. My wart will be non-malignant. (*Journals* 286)

Clearly Plath employs here the same kinds of stigmatizing metaphors that Sontag critiques in *Illness as Metaphor* as demeaning to actual cancer patients (84). Moreover, to use Garland Thomson's terms, Plath's narrator (in the first prose passage) and Plath herself (in the second) identify femininity with both lack *and* excess ("Integrating" 7). Indeed, Plath's speakers have internalized the cultural norms that posit an imperfect, leaky body as both too much and clearly not enough to be valuable or desirable. The fantasy of cancer developing on her porous, pimply face stands in metonymically for Plath's horror at the onerous and unreliable embodied self. Indeed, she views her body as both deficient and excessive: it lacks grace, beauty, security; it has too much pus and dirt. As the body goes, so go the art and the psyche in Plath's emotional landscape: hence her zits will stop leaking, her wart be benign, only if she publishes a story in a well-respected magazine; then she will no longer identify herself with female lack or excess but instead with reason and proportion. Her body will then be ideal, "poreless and radiant." In Shildrick and Price's words, Plath believes that once she publishes she will no longer feel "unpredictable, leaky, or disruptive" (1). Yet she finds authority in art if not in embodiment, in the knowledge that her poems shriek their power: "The blood jet is poetry, / There is no stopping it" (*Collected* 269).

As Sontag has noted, "punitive notions of disease have a long history, and such notions are particularly active with cancer" (*Illness* 57). Ironically, by labeling cancer "the killer disease" and people who contract it "victims," Western culture deems the cancer patient culpable:

> Widely believed psychological theories of disease assign to the luckless ill the ultimate responsibility both for falling ill and for getting well. And conventions of treating cancer as no mere disease but a demonic enemy make cancer not just a lethal disease but a shameful one. (57)

Sontag's insights into Western culture's stigmatization of cancer shed light on the shame that Sandra in Bailey and Lewis's *Sistahs* feels at her inability to control both her temper and her disease. After Sandra has lashed out verbally at her teenage daughter and apologized for having lost her temper, the stage directions reveal this protagonist's shame by foregrounding her leakiness:

> (*A piece of pain hits* Sandra *in the womb; she looks down and sees blood running between her legs*) Blood.
> Rea *comes and helps her change her skirt. Ashamed,* Sandra *unwraps her skirt and hides the bloodstained wrap in the corner* (48).

Sandra is presented here as "humiliated by fear and agony," to use Sontag's phrase, as she confronts the violation of the "you"—her healthy woman-self—by the bloody "non-you" of uterine cancer. But she is also discursively resistant. "Cancer," she tells her daughter and sister in disgust. "Some parasite feeding on my womb. The nerve" (55).

The leaky body of an octagenarian plagued with cancer appears prominently in Egyptian American novelist Gini Alhadeff's *Diary of a Djinn,* which reveals the extent to which the trauma of bodily leaks affects ill women across cultures and across age and class spectrums. A dignified and economically privileged Italian woman who wears Givenchy dresses and studies the art of Leonardo da Vinci—the Princess, as she is called—struggles to control her medicalized body, whose embarrassing excretions belie her dignified exterior. In three separate passages, as the Princess waits in her radiologist's foyer for treatment accompanied by her son's mistress (the novel's retrospective narrator), her cancerous womb leaves its bloody tracks on the seat she vacates, the floor she walks across, the underpants she wears. In the first passage the narrator presents the Princess's leaks as paradoxically reassuring *and* disconcerting:

> Walking to the dressing room, the Princess left two drops of blood in her wake, perfectly round and vermillion—a young girl's blood, just as the doctor had said on being told of her hemoglobin count, which was 13.50. He couldn't believe it could be so high after so much radiation, that she was not the least bit anemic. It was clear he thought she was a human phenomenon in both mind and spirit, not one cell of her willing to concede defeat or to relinquish life. (179)

Here the old woman's mysteriously youthful blood and cancer-resistant body elevate rather than denigrate her: since she participates alongside her physician in what Stacey calls "the masculine fantasy of invincibility," her bloody power can be idealized (1). Indeed, the Princess temporarily experiences authority rather than disempowerment, for she is "distinguishing [her]self in illness" (Edson 53).

In the second passage, however, the Princess's leaks appear more ominous, her radiation therapy less curative, her body less capable of self-control:

> During the "treatment" the Princess's body was no longer hers—it belonged to the illness and to the cure. "Take her to the bathroom and clean her up a little," the nurse said after one of the last and bloodier radiations. The idea of "cleaning her up a little" was preposterous, because the Princess had in no way relinquished care of her body. That would come much later.

Although the narrator continues to invest the Princess with bodily dignity, Alhadeff's narrative strategies make clear that the cancer could eventually strip the patient of this human right. The word *treatment* appears in quotation marks to reveal that the radiotherapy is not working; the nurse objectifies the Princess by not addressing her directly and by suggesting wrongly that she is incompetent to clean herself; and the narrator herself acknowledges, in the final sentence of foreshadowing, that it is only a matter of time until the Princess will be forced to abandon care of her own hygiene.

In the third passage the Princess's bloody leaks become definitive, the narrator's discourse more unsettling. Indeed, readers may feel like voyeurs from whom such intimate bodily malfunctions should be concealed. As her cancer runs unchecked, the patient's dignity is only partially preserved through the nurse's and the narrator's joint subterfuge and the Princess's poor vision:

> When I returned to the waiting room, there was a large bloodstain on the chair where the Princess had been sitting and a trail of blood on the carpet in the hallway and all the way to the bathroom. I thought it was a good thing she couldn't see very well. The nurse was clearly overwhelmed. She came with a container of spray cleaner and a little rag and wiped the stains off the linoleum and the carpet. She dropped a chuck, a sheet of blue plastic lined with quilted white tissue, onto the stained seat. Then she went to the bathroom to help the Princess wash and give her some fresh pads. When the Princess returned to sit on the blue plastic pad I noticed that she had blood on one hand and I fetched a paper towel, ran it under a tap and rubbed off the blood—painstakingly, for it had dried. (184)

Like Sandra in *Sistahs,* the Princess at times responds to her leaky body with shame and anger. "I protest, this is too much," she tells her companion. "I am never coming here again, not for a visit nor for radiation" (185). That the Princess refuses further medicalization to no avail is clear from the narrator's terse admission that the two women returned to the radiologist's a week later. Although Alhadeff does not present in further detail the Princess's decline, the narrator eventually acknowledges her friend's death and decries the uselessness of her radiation treatments. Still, the novelist's representation of the Princess's resistance to invasive technology reveals the protagonist's confident subjectivity; after all, it is not her leaky body that appalls her but the procedure that exacerbates the excessive bleeding.

If leaky cancerous bodies sometimes mortify the women who inhabit them, on what basis can Shildrick argue that "instability, multiplicity, the incalculable, and above all leakiness" constitute the core of a "postmodern feminist ethic"? (12) Feminist theorists have challenged patriarchal allegations that women's leaky bodies are shameful by positing those bodies as resistant to sexist views of femininity and hence dangerous to patriarchy. Indeed, body theorists such as Garland Thomson, Shildrick, and Price view women's bodily eruptions and disruptions as a sign of their agency; in Shildrick's words, the "lived body is acknowledged as a site of subjectivity" (10). In U.S. culture at large, whether they emerge politically from the bowels of the White House or viscerally from the cancerous bodies of women, leaks signals subversion: they reveal secrets, challenge hegemony, and put the lie to the pretense that all is under control. By emphasizing the instability of leaky cancerous bodies, feminist ethicists foreground unpredictability and thereby lay the groundwork for openness and humility (not humiliation) among medical practitioners and for subversive strategies of empowerment among women patients. By stressing multiplicity, moreover, these ethicists privilege gender, sexual, and racial difference, thus disrupting any illusion of sameness among patients to which the medical establishment may cling. And by honoring leakiness, feminist ethicists embrace the blood, milk, pus, urine, and other bodily emanations that render women living with cancer human.

AMPUTATED BODIES

The issue of claiming subjectivity in the face of cancer's unpredictability also informs feminist theoretical perspectives on amputation. A passage from Stacey's *Teratologies* illustrates the complex intersection of bodily contingencies and identity construction:

> The narrative of my body continued to be rewritten at each stage. As I lay recovering from surgery, I tried to find out what had been removed apart from the tumour . The surgeon had taken out the tumour and also the fallopian tube and the ovary on the right side. Overnight my identity was reinvented: I was now a cancer patient; or was I? I was told the disease may or may not still be present in my body. It may or may not return. (4)

The phrase "trying to find out what had been removed" occurs at the point in Stacey's narrative that theory and autobiography most effectively converge; in its echoes we hear the muted voices of thousands of other women in the United States and Great Britain from the 1940s to the 1980s. During the reign of the radical Halsted mastectomy, surgical removal of cancerous breasts generally occurred during "routine" biopsies performed under general anesthesia; although women signed forms consenting to mastectomy if their surgeon found cancer, many believed—indeed, were encouraged by their oncologists to assume— that their signatures were pro forma (Lerner 31–37). In the mid-1980s, when Stacey underwent surgery in London for a rare type of ovarian cancer, it was still possible to enter surgery assuming that no organ would be removed, only to learn after awakening that it had been taken. The fact that women with cancer might awaken from surgery without knowing whether their breasts, ovaries, and uteruses remained raised issues of medical ethics and female agency as well as issues of absence, identity reformation, and healing.

In her narrative Stacey probes the intersection between surgical amputation and female subjectivity, which as a postmodern feminist she defines as fluid and porous. When a woman loses body parts to cancer, Stacey wonders, how might she reconceptualize her "self": as a cancer patient who must anticipate a lifetime of medicalization and anxiety over possible recurrence? As a person living with cancer as a chronic illness, as people live with AIDS? As a woman who envisions herself whole, despite missing organs that society equates with femaleness? As someone struggling philosophically to comprehend mortality? These uncertainties drive her to self-scrutiny: "The past must now be reimagined and rescripted. Life, it turns out, was not what it seemed. The present is not the imagined future it once was. . . . Given the demands of this new bodily evidence, I found myself inventing stories about myself. . . . The body tells a new story and so demands a reinterpretation of recent life history" (5). In a series of jolting questions she acknowledges both the trauma of bodily betrayal and the potential for self-invention: "Can the self be reinvented to cope with the shock? What kind of person does not know they have cancer? What kind of body hides the evidence so effectively?" (5–6).

Lorde addresses similar questions in *The Cancer Journals* by insisting

that "any amputation is a physical and psychic reality that must be integrated into a new sense of self" (16). In this memoir Lorde writes honestly of rage at the loss of her breast. "Somedays," she acknowledges in
her 6 April 1980 journal entry, "if bitterness were a whetstone, I could be
sharp as grief" (13). The silence then imposed on postmastectomy
women, the absence of role models for lesbians and women of color with
breast cancer, the unexplored connections between cancer and environmental degradation—these issues explain in part her bitter moments.
While her grief is born of loss, however, it is tempered by a determination to identify positively as one-breasted—as a gesture of self-invention
and a source of solidarity with other postmastectomy women: "I would
lie if I did not also speak of loss. . . . The absence of my breast is a recurring sadness, but certainly not one that dominates my life. I miss it,
sometimes piercingly. . . . But I believe that socially sanctioned prosthesis is merely another way of keeping women with breast cancer silent and
separate from each other" (16).

Garland Thomson discusses amputation from the perspective of feminist disability theory and analyzes cultural prescriptions regarding normative and nonnormative embodiment, including representations of
amputated bodies in advertising and art. She argues convincingly that
many contemporary feminist narratives "challenge the sexist assumption
that the amputated breast must always pass for the normative, sexualized
one either through concealment or prosthesis" ("Integrating" 12). Subversive power, for example, informs the imagery of "It's No Secret," a
poster used in an advertising campaign by the Breast Cancer Fund that
features a one-breasted woman flaunting her mastectomy scar in the
provocative pose of a half-nude playboy bunny. In this photograph the
amputated breast is not only revealed, it is ironically sexualized in a manner that implicitly critiques soft-porn representations of women's
fetishized breasts, artfully bared.[2] Garland Thomson also employs feminist disability theory to examine the controversy surrounding the artist
Matuschka's sculptures of postmastectomy women. Matuschka, a breast
cancer survivor, has adopted an in-your-face approach to her art as a
means of insisting that the medical and corporate elite as well as the public confront the repeated and systemic "mutilation" of breast cancer
patients.[3] Because the medical establishment has thus far failed to designate enough research dollars to seek humane and effective cancer treatments, much less a cure, Garland Thomson applauds the Breast Cancer

Fund's daring and Matuschka's strategic representation of her amputated breast for political purposes ("Integrating" 12–13).

Stacey's emphasis on rescripting the past after cancer surgery, Lorde's analysis of bitterness and grief, and Garland Thomson's challenge to the mandatory concealment of amputated breasts can help readers analyze Adrienne Rich's 1978 poem, "A Woman Dead in Her Forties." Both a luminous elegy addressed to a friend who has died of breast cancer and a fierce indictment of the culture of silence then surrounding both mastectomy and lesbian sexuality, this poem reveals the physical and emotional scars that such silence brings, particularly the damage of internalized oppression. The speaker's recollection of her first glimpse of her friend's empty chest is stark:

> Your breasts/   sliced-off   The scars
> dimmed   as they would have to be
> years later
>
> (250)

She recalls the breastless woman's discomfort when the two women join their high school friends sitting "half-naked on rocks in sun." For a moment Rich's speaker imagines her friend no longer vulnerable to inquiring gazes—to people who, as Garland Thomson argues, employ an objectifying stare (*Extraordinary* 26). But Rich likewise probes the speaker's own guilt at her failure to gaze lovingly at her friend's scars:

> and you too have taken off your blouse
> but this was not what you wanted:
>
> to show your scarred, deleted torso
>
> I barely glance at you
> as if my look could scald you
> though I'm the one who loved you
>
> (251)

Here the speaker implies that the perverse counterpart of the voyeuristic stare, its eradicating deflection, is equally harmful to the recipient. She further acknowledges her desire to touch her friend's scar, a gesture of shared vulnerability and lesbian desire:

> I want to touch my fingers
> to where your breasts had been
> but we never did such things
>
> (251)

Recognizing her friend's ambivalence toward her body, the speaker empathizes when the breastless woman clothes herself:

> You hadn't thought everyone
> would look so perfect
> unmutilated
>
> you pull on
> your blouse again: stern statement:
>
> *There are things I will not share*
> *with everyone*

(251)

As Melissa F. Zeiger has observed, to the extent that the italicized lines represent the postmastectomy woman's inner thoughts, they serve as an insistence upon her difference and her right to claim it. Rich's poem therefore "foregrounds problems of communication and silence, of connection and separation" between women with cancer and well women (141).

In subsequent sections Rich continues to "rescript the past," to borrow Stacey's phrase, using the speaker's friendship with this woman, which began in adolescence, as a lens for understanding lesbian feminist identity as well as the trauma of breast cancer. In part 2, for example, the speaker relates the cancer victim's physical wounds to her own psychological ones:

> You send me back to share
> my own scars　first of all
> with myself

(251)

In part 4 she recalls the intensity of the bond between her friend and herself until cancer, and perhaps the taboo of lesbian desire as well, drove a wedge between them:

> We cleaved to each other across that space
>
> fingering webs
> of love and estrangement　　till the day
>
> the gynecologist touched your breast
> and found a palpable hardness.

(253)

Diagnosis appears as a landmark moment in many women's cancer texts, and here Rich treats it ironically: her speaker envies the surgeon whose

right it is to touch her friend's breast even as she deplores the fact that he
locates a cancerous tumor. After diagnosis, both women adhere to the
cultural script: the stoic cancer patient feigns heroism through treatment
and metastasis, the speaker pretends that she thinks her friend will
recover. For embracing this lie she feels profound guilt, till now
unspeakable. "You played heroic, necessary / games with death," she
acknowledges. "Of all my dead it's you / who come to me unfinished."
As the poem ends, the speaker honors her friend's amputated breast,
mourns her tragic death, and affirms the love they shared:

> I didn't know your choice
>
> or how by then you had no choice
> how the body tells the truth in its rush of cells . . .
>
> *we never spoke at your deathbed of your death*
>
> (255)

The speaker ends by summoning "more crazy mourning, more howl,
more keening"; with Lorde, Rich evinces bitterness as sharp as grief (255).

More recent U.S. feminist writers have refused to view amputation as
tragic, in part because by the 1990s silence about breast cancer had finally
been broken. In *Manmade Breast Cancers*, for example, Eisenstein challenges the term *mutilation* in recounting her experience with cancer
surgery and recovery: "My breasts were amputated but I do not feel
mutilated. I fought against thinking my body had been disfigured, but I
do not remember having to work hard at this. I built a new chest and
rejected implants. My path was to build my own muscle and create sexual / sensual pleasure on this new terrain" (67). Eisenstein goes on to crit-
icize Matuschka for using the term *mutilation* in documents pertaining to
a lawsuit she brought against the surgeon who performed her amputation. She argues that if Matuschka considers her mastectomy to have
been unnecessary, she should sue for malpractice rather than claiming
mutilation: "I obviously see a breastless chest differently than she does"
(68). In her performance narrative, *My Left Breast*, U.S. playwright
Susan Miller offers a similarly positive perspective on the value, not the
tragedy, of her mastectomy scar: "I cherish this scar. It's a mark of experience. It's the history of me, a permanent fix on the impermanence of it
all" (236). Like Stacey, Eisenstein and Miller recognize that the narratives of their breastless bodies are fluid and contingent; they "continue to
be rewritten at each stage" (Stacey 5). In Eisenstein's case, this rewriting

occurs at the gym and on the track as well as in her text, while for Miller
it takes place on stage—an especially provocative site given that cancer
diagnoses occur in stages and that, in Rebecca Schneider's words, "bodies are stages for social theatrics" (1). Like Lorde, Eisenstein and Miller
confront the physical and psychological effects of their amputations on
an integrated selfhood; like Garland Thomson, they reject society's edict
that "the amputated breast must always pass for the normative, sexualized one" ("Integrating" 12). Eisenstein rejects this edict by exposing her
newly developed chest muscles to the people in the gym where she exer-
cises, Miller by stripping off her shirt and proudly revealing her amputated breast to the audience for whom she performs. Each writer integrates the fact of her amputation into a newly emergent subjectivity.

PROSTHETIC BODIES

In the literature of cancer, the phrase *prosthetic bodies* describes both a
discursive trope and a material condition. Indeed, prosthesis serves as a
complicated metaphor in contemporary disability, narrative, and feminist theory. David Wills, for example, defines prosthesis as "a term that
mediates between the realm of the literary and the realm of the body"; as
a theorist of disability, he claims that prosthetic bodies are actually the
norm, since "all bodies are deficient in that materiality proves variable,
vulnerable, and inscribable" (137). David Mitchell and Sharon L. Snyder
extend Wills's definitions to explore the concept of "narrative prosthesis," which they distinguish from literal prosthesis by suggesting that
whereas prosthetic devices strive to produce an illusion, prosthetic narratives tend to conceal the truth of difference. "While an actual prosthesis is always somewhat discomforting," they explain, "a textual prosthesis alleviates discomfort by removing the unsightly from view" (8).
Prosthetic narratives can therefore be problematic in their (mis)repre-
sentations of disabled people and cultures; indeed, Mitchell and Snyder
determine in their own work "to make the prosthesis show, to flaunt its
imperfect supplementation as an illusion" (8). Eisenstein uses the
metaphor of prosthesis differently in mounting a global feminist critique
of capitalist imperialism, which exploits girls and women worldwide
even as its discourse denies such exploitation. "The cyberreal of racialized gender presents the labor of women and girls in the prosthetic lan-

guage of Microsoft and transnational media corporations," she argues. In challenging such oppressive economic and linguistic practices, she seeks to "refind the bodies *and* their labor to dismantle the mystifying fantasy of the supposed disembodied global culture" (59). These theoretical perspectives on disability, narrative, gender politics, and the global economy illustrate the range of metaphoric uses to which the concept of prosthesis has recently been put.

What, then, do such metaphors signify to women with breast cancer, for whom prosthesis exists as a material issue? If Sontag is correct in claiming that "the healthiest way of being ill" is "one most purified of, most resistant to, metaphoric thinking," then surely both the metaphors and the reality of prosthesis are vexing to cancer patients and to writers who represent illness in their literary texts (3). The choices that surround "the politics of prosthesis" (Garland Thomson, "Integrating" 12) are agonizing for many women but perhaps especially so for second-wave feminists: women writers and activists between forty and seventy years old at the dawn of the twenty-first century. These feminists define the personal as political and view traditional femininity as oppressive, yet they may find themselves, as breast cancer patients and/or chroniclers of this disease, either enraged by or ambivalent toward the changing cultural attitudes regarding reconstruction. After all, in the United States more than 233, 500 women each year undergo breast augmentation or reconstructive surgery, a choice especially popular with women under forty (Kasper and Ferguson 81). Advanced technologies have made this cosmetic practice more feasible, as have attitudinal shifts toward female bodies as no longer fixed or capable merely of minor modification but as endlessly malleable—shifts embraced by some feminists as well as by women with traditional values.

In 1980 feminist poet Deena Metzger spread her arms wide and bared her unreconstructed breast, beautifully tattooed, in the first widely distributed photograph of a postmastectomy nude. Reproduced worldwide in poster form, Hella Hammid's photograph of Metzger, titled "The Warrior," became a landmark insignia of feminist iconography.[4] Indeed, this poster mirrored the dominant attitude among feminists of the era that amputated breasts should be recuperated as beautiful and defiant and that reconstruction should thus be resisted. However, twenty-five years later this view has been contested, as is evident in Amelia Davis's *The First Look*, a collection of recent photographs of women's postmastec-

tomy breasts. The women represented here define themselves as liberated, as is clear from their commentaries and their willingness to have
their amputated and reconstructed breasts photographed. Fully half of
the women depicted have undergone some form of reconstruction, from
silicon to saline to the TRAM flap taken from the patient's abdominal tissue. Although in the accompanying testimonies as many of the women
discuss their decision *against* prosthesis as speak in favor of it, the non-
prosthetic women typically defend their choice while the prosthetic
women (generally younger) see no need to do so; instead, they either
celebrate new technologies or seem to take the benefits of reconstruction
for granted. In addition, among the physician commentaries that conclude *The First Look,* Stanford University plastic surgeon Loren Eskenazi offers a potentially self-serving yet relatively unbiased explanation
of how and why breast reconstruction makes sense for many U.S.
women (75–82). Still, as Susan Ferguson notes in her feminist study of
breast reconstruction, between 1985 and 1998 the Food and Drug
Administration received 127,500 adverse reports regarding silicone-
filled implants and 49, 661 regarding saline-filled ones; during that same
period 118 women are believed to have died from complications related
to their breast implants (in Kasper and Ferguson 79). In light of these
statistics, Ferguson urges women to question the Food and Drug
Administration's position that reconstructive surgery after breast cancer
constitutes "an integral part of cancer treatment"—and to consider why
the medical establishment views amputated breasts as requiring medical
intervention (in Kasper and Ferguson 77).

For Audre Lorde, who died of metastasized cancer in 1992, the
assumptions that underlie the dominant representation of postmastectomy breasts in *The First Look*—that reconstruction is desirable, safe,
economically viable, and liberating—would probably be troubling.
Writing in *The Cancer Journals* in 1980, when reconstructive surgeries
often caused irreparable damage to women's breast tissue and sometimes
produced serious infections or even new cancers, Lorde concludes that
"when other one-breasted women hide behind the mask of prosthesis or
the dangerous fantasy of reconstruction, I find little support in the
broader female environment for my rejection of what feels like a cosmetic sham" (16). Using emotionally laden language to explain her resistance to what she calls the "travesty of prosthesis" and a "potentially life-
threatening practice," Lorde analyzes how race, gender, feminist

conviction, and lesbian sexuality influence her choice to remain unreconstructed (9, 68). She critiques prosthesis on four major grounds: that women who choose it risk losing self-awareness and feminist visibility; that this choice buys into the patriarchal culture's sexist politics of appearance; that women who undergo reconstruction court danger, since cancerous breast tissue can form and be hidden underneath; and that reconstructed women cannot be effective as breast cancer activists, who must interrogate "the function of cancer in a profit economy" (9). Ultimately Lorde concludes that the cultural emphasis upon surgical prosthesis serves as "a way of avoiding having women come to terms with their own pain and loss, and thereby, with their own strength" (49). Having broken silence and examined openly her breast cancer and the choices it necessitates, she determines that "either I would love my body one-breasted now, or remain forever alien to myself" (44). Since self-alienation is unthinkable, self-acceptance becomes essential: "I refuse to have my scars hidden or trivialized behind lambswool or silicone gel" (60). In addition, Lorde contextualizes her decision by connecting it to the antiracist struggles of black women in the United States: "What woman of color in america over the age of fifteen does not live with the knowledge that our daily lives are stitched with violence and with hatred and to naively ignore that reality can mean our own destruction? We are equally destroyed by false happiness and false breasts, and the passive acceptance of false values which corrupt our lives and distort our experience" (75).

For Diane Price Herndl, however, the advantages of breast reconstruction outweigh the disadvantages. In her 2002 essay "Reconstructing the Posthuman Feminist Body Twenty Years after Audre Lorde's *Cancer Journals*," Herndl explains that "my choice to have reconstruction was to leap with both feet into the posthuman, the partial, and the contradictory" (151). She views self-alienation as unavoidable in a postmodern culture; breast reconstruction cannot alleviate this state, but neither does it preclude self-awareness or feminist activism. Lorde thus represents to Herndl a powerful if unyielding foremother whose edicts against prosthesis and reconstruction inspired her until Herndl herself faced a mastectomy; at that point she determined to question Lorde's theoretical perspective, and ultimately she justifies her own decision to opt for reconstruction. In support of her position that remaining "alien to [her]self" is inevitable once cancer has struck, whether or not she chooses a prosthetic breast, Herndl marshals the "posthuman" feminist cyborg theory of Donna Haraway and the admonition of body theorist Susan Bordo that feminism "is not a blueprint for the conduct of personal life (or political action, for that matter) and does not empower (or require) individuals to 'rise above' their culture or to become martyrs to feminist ideals" (quoted in Herndl, "Reconstructing" 145–49). Despite these observations, Herndl admits ambivalence toward her choice: she "warns" readers that her essay may be "a theoretical version of self-justification, a meditation on a fall from one version of feminist politics, a confession" (144). She incorporates into her text a letter to friends in which she recounts "an agonizing weekend of decision-making," yet acknowledges the "silver lining" of "a free tummy-tuck"; in addition, she determines "that feminist relations to the body are different now than they were twenty years ago for Lorde and that feminist relations to breast cancer are different," largely because cancer and mastectomy need no longer remain hidden (144, 148–49). Whereas Lorde condemns "the mask of prosthesis" as a form of culturally imposed silence, Herndl embraces prosthesis *because* "its artificiality is palpable"; she views it as negating, not causing, silence: "I will never be able to pretend this didn't happen to me" (Lorde, *Cancer* 16; Herndl, "Reconstructing" 152).

For Zillah Eisenstein, forgoing reconstruction but wearing an occasional prosthesis represents an empowering middle ground for women in the early twenty-first century: "I am not completely free and I am also defiant. I wear my prosthesis as I wear my jewelry and clothes; often as costume. . . . I have reconstructed my own body while my body is never wholly mine to define" (32). As a breast cancer survivor and a feminist theorist, Eisenstein admits in *Manmade Breast Cancers* that in 2001, society's norms define her postmastectomy body to some extent even as she tries to defy them. Both Lorde's antireconstruction stance and Herndl's acceptance of self-alienation as inevitable resonate for Eisenstein, who lifts weight to develop her chest muscles and often runs bare-chested in the park, her scar proudly on display, yet who also wears a prosthesis intermittently "as costume." Eisenstein admires Lorde, whom she describes in her narrative as having "asserted her one-breastedness in order to make breast cancer visible," yet she wishes she could discuss with Lorde the fact that, twenty years later, lumpectomies have "changed the issue of visibility" and multiple forms of feminist cancer militancy now exist (32). Still, Eisenstein agrees with Lorde that an oppressive politics of appearance at least partially explains the current prevalence of reconstructive surgeries. Indeed, Eisenstein critiques her own oncologist for recommending against lumpectomy because "she thought my breast would look better after mastectomy and reconstruction. . . . I wondered why she was so much more focused on the cosmetics than on the recurrence of cancer for me" (27). Moreover, drawing upon Lorde's theories, Eisenstein develops what she terms a "breast-felt politics" as a form of antiracist and global feminist resistance: "I want to open up politics to the pain and suffering of the body and humanize the world through this journey" (2). Like Herndl, however, Eisenstein acknowledges the advantages of wearing a prosthesis "when I do not want to negotiate the world through my breast cancer" (32). "I have chosen my flesh over silicon or saline," she concludes, "but sometimes this is not enough. So clearly I do not want a breast cancer identity plastered onto me" (33).

Despite their differences or perhaps because of them, Lorde, Herndl, and Eisenstein contribute significantly to feminist theories of prosthesis and to our understanding of its literary representations. For as Eisenstein notes, "the body is an incredible place to build resistant consciousness" (171). Consider once more, for example, the character of Wanda in Loomer's *The Waiting Room,* a woman whose body has experienced such extensive cosmetic surgery that neither she nor the medical personnel evaluating her for breast cancer know how to distinguish the "real" from the "artificial." In act 1, scene 2, when Nurse Brenda takes Wanda's medical history and asks her about prior operations, Wanda at first says none; she does not attempt to conceal her cosmetic surgeries but rather takes her reconstructed body for granted:

BRENDA: Not even for . . . cosmetic purposes?
WANDA: (Laughs). Oh. Well, I had my nose done. (Beat). And they left
    too much cartilage, so I had to do it again. (Beat). And then I had to
    have the chin enhancement to match. (Beat.) And cheekbones. Uh . . .
    lipo—tummy and thighs . . . (Brenda struggles to write it all down.) No
    arms. Just tummy and—
BRENDA: Thighs. I got it. (Stares at Wanda's chest.) Anything else?
WANDA: (Laughs.) Well—my tits. [. . .] They were a present. From my
    father. Okay, So . . . (Counts on breasts.) Tits in, tits out . . . new tits in
    . . . new tits out . . . plus the tits I have now—(16–17).

Although Loomer treats Wanda's prosthetic body humorously in this passage, she critiques the medical establishment for performing breast enhancement surgeries on women with family histories of cancer, as Wanda has, often without telling their patients of the risks. In her discussion with Brenda, Wanda acknowledges recurrent problems with her implants: "The foam broke down. The casing hardened. It's funny, I can keep a couch six years, I can't keep a pair of tits six months" (17) When Douglas, the surgeon she consults, learns of these difficulties and her family history, he asks Wanda, "By the way, did the doctor who gave you those implants ask you any questions?" Her response exposes the industry's irresponsibility. "Yeah," she replies. "What size?" (19)

By bringing Lorde's theories to bear on Loomer's presentation of Wanda, we can recognize "the travesty of prosthesis" when it enables vulnerable women to accept distorting cultural images of what it means to be beautiful or feminine; or when prosthetic implants endanger a woman's health by masking or even causing breast cancer, as they do for Wanda, who later in the play must undergo a mastectomy. By considering Wanda's prosthetic identity from the perspective of Herndl's theories, we can see the extent to which Wanda's "posthuman" body both alienates her from herself and enhances her self-image. For instance, when told by a waitress that she "looks fabulous," Wanda explains that "I saw this modeling expert who said to divide my body in parts and go over it with a magnifying glass. Parts I could improve, I'd work on, and the rest I'd just cover up. So I started from the top" (39). Finally, by using Eisenstein's theories to examine Wanda's increasing outrage at the medicalization of her body, we can analyze her emerging resistant consciousness: as she tells Douglas that his unproven treatment methods for incipient breast cancer "suck" and she's going to Jamaica to seek a cure, for example (65), or as she insists that it's her right to reject chemotherapy because "it's MY BODY!" (70).

Other writers have chronicled their decision to choose or not to choose prosthesis and their feelings about this choice. In her poem "Freestanding," for example, Carol Dine compares her reconstructed breast unfavorably to her natural one:

> I have a breast that's sculpted
> from the skin of my back.
> If there are two pink roses
> on a stem,

it's the one that's faded.

(in Raz, Living, 252)

The image of healthy breasts as "two pink roses / on a stem" recalls
Garland Thomson's analysis of the prescriptions of normative femininity, through which the color pink signals the conventionally feminine
and roses waiting to be picked inscribe heterosexual love. No artificial
breast, Dine fears, will measure up to these idealized "roses." Dine further probes this theme of diminished femininity in another poem, "Cir-
cles," by describing the reconstructed breast not as her own body part
but as her surgeon's technological "rendering":

> Tomorrow, I will remove a bandage
> unveiling
> the plastic surgeon's rendering—
> my tattooed nipple
> that cannot be
> suckled or aroused.

(in Raz, Living, 253)

In contrast to Metzger's celebratory representation of the tattoo that cov-
ers her amputated breast, Dine depicts her tattooed nipple as static, asex-
ual, and diminished. The new breast's artificiality does not empower her,
as it does Herndl; to the contrary, without erotic sensation in her breast,
Dine confronts only loss:

> Then in the mirror
> I will face the body
> and the body's unrequited desire
> for what's been given up.

(in Raz, Living, 253)

In her autobiographical essay, "The Good Mother," Annette
Williams Jaffee interweaves the story of her mother's death from breast
cancer with her own experience of amputation and reconstruction.
Worse than her diagnosis and mastectomy for Jaffee is the struggle she
has subsequently with reconstructive surgery and malfunctioning silicone implants. "I am not going to fake breasts," she asserts ironically,
even as she grows impatient waiting the required three months until she
can undergo reconstruction. When her surgery goes badly, however,
she wishes she had settled for a prosthetic bra: "This time it hurts; I am
not the good girl patient. They carve into the wall of my chest to put the

silicone blobs under muscle. There is an accumulation of blood on one side that needs to be painfully aspirated twice a week, and for a month I live and breathe, sleep, and eat in a bone corset, like one of the women in *The Story of O*" (52). Jaffee both critiques and embraces the culture of femininity that Lorde and Garland Thomson consider responsible for the late-twentieth-century increase in breast reconstruction. Although she refuses to be "the good girl patient" that she had been during her mastectomy, she accepts the painful insertion of "silicone blobs" into her chest and submits to the cruelty of a "bone corset" in a manner she recognizes as similar to that of women tortured by sadists. In a follow-up procedure, when a surgeon fashions nipples from the patient's groin, Jaffee recounts that her "wounds weep" and describes graphically the application of saline compresses to her leaky implants. But that is not the end of her suffering. "The following year the outer rims of the implants pop and I have to replace them. This time they use solid gel that hardens and feels heavier. I have had four surgical procedures in less than eighteen months, but I'm still cracking jokes. Just like me, I say, to spend months and thousands of dollars to replace something I already had" (52). Ultimately Jaffee reenacts the "good girl" role she has disclaimed, as the culture of femininity insists that she do. Her narrative rarely questions the wisdom of her choice, the surgeon's obvious errors, the dangers of silicone implants. Instead, she mocks herself for wanting prosthetic breasts so desperately, even as she admits that "of course, they're really not breasts. . . . There are two round things sticking out" (52–53). In Herndl's terms, Jaffee struggles to embrace her "posthuman" body, but unlike Herndl, she is not successful. For Jaffee, bodily hybridity evokes conflict.

In contrast to those writers who document their choice of breast reconstruction, Alicia Ostriker and Marilyn Hacker recount in autobiographical essays the reasons they reject it. In "Scenes from a Mastectomy" Ostriker outlines her view of the "perils of reconstructive surgery" as well as her desire for openness: "I do not want something stuck on me/in me that will mask the reality. . . . No, I want truth. *My body is sending me pictures. Fish, stabbed fish, healed over, swimming in deep water. Half boy, half woman*" (182). Finding this vision empowering, Ostriker likens herself to legendary one-breasted Amazon warriors, to "the androgynous god Shiva . . . a male chest on his left side and a breast on his right, carved in the living rock of the cave temple on the

Island of Elephanta" (186) Ultimately she views her amputated breast as sacred and determines to revere the surgical scar. In "Journal Entries" Hacker, a U.S. poet living in France, approaches amputation pragmatically. She claims hardly to give a second thought to the option of post-surgical reconstruction, since she considers prosthesis a travesty as much as did Lorde, whom she credits for having raised her consciousness on this issue. When her oncology nurse tries to force a mastectomy bra upon her, Hacker refuses to wear it: "I want my half-flat-chested survivor status to be visible" (212). Hence she demonstrates with pride her resistant subjectivity.

Feminist theories of prosthesis as culturally mandated illuminate Wanda's struggle for autonomy in *The Waiting Room* and Jaffee's ambivalence toward her leaky implants. Lorde's analysis of "the mask of prosthesis" provides insight into Ostriker's androgynous imaginary and Hacker's refusal to wear a mastectomy bra. In turn, Herndl's spirited defense of prosthesis illuminates Dine's effort to embrace her reconstructed breast. As these texts clarify, the choice of prosthesis reflects the lived experiences of countless postmastectomy women in the developed world who either have their amputated breasts surgically reconstructed or wear prosthetic devices. Conversely, prosthesis is anathema to the many cancer survivors who opt for "doing nothing" after surgery, who bear/bare their mastectomy scar with pride. While the terms of this debate are contested, its ethics require that feminists avoid the trap of stigmatizing as "politically incorrect" either decision regarding prosthesis. Clearly Susan Bordo's insight that contemporary women's bodies have become "cultural plastic" signifies to some feminists a disconcerting commodification, to others an empowering hybridity (246).

(NOT) DYING BODIES

As postmodern feminist theorists, Elisabeth M. Bronfen and Jackie Stacey agree that while scientific discourses and medical practitioners often claim to have defined the knowable, many female patients and women's illness narratives acknowledge what is unknowable about life-threatening illness and the process of dying. As the ultimate mystery, "the most unthinkable and unknowable aspect of nature," death defies the logic of science and the men of medicine in a manner that they must find puzzling and frustrating (Stacey 240). Moreover, since Western discourse has linked femininity and death as tropes for what is "superlatively enigmatic,"

> the fear of death translates into the fear of Woman, who, for man, is death. She is constructed as the place of mystery, of not knowing, Freud's "dark continent," as the site of silence but also of the horrifying void that "castrates" the living man's sense of wholeness and stability. (Bronfen 205)

As Bronfen argues in *Over Her Dead Body*, death and the feminine represent otherness, alterity, and instability in Western culture; only through a denial of female power or its eradication can stability be restored. Dying female bodies thus serve as potent insignia in literature and art. Indeed, Bronfen further claims, "femininity and death cause a disorder to stability, mark moments of ambivalence, disruption or duplicity and their eradication produces a recuperation of order, a return to stability" (xii). Over women's dying bodies, therefore, order can be restored; "cultural norms are reconfirmed or secured" (xii).

What happens, then, when dying women, or very ill women who fear dying, inscribe their own experiences? To what extent does their writing confirm the associations of femininity, death, and Otherness, and to what extent does its frankness disrupt this tropic trajectory? Stacey posits that when a woman dying of cancer exerts her subjectivity rather than her objectified status, she gains narrative authority, for "death seems to promise a 'moment of truth'" (243). Yet paradoxically, writing also serves "as a symptom of not dying" and can therefore be a means of conferring order on experience or defying the unknowability that death signifies (241).

A tension between the passivity of imminent death and the agency of likely survival appears in Roberta L. Hacker's essay about her cancer experience, particularly in her rhetoric of unknowability. The theme of luck's arbitrariness permeates "As Luck Would Have It"; Hacker does not understand why she has temporarily survived when so many other women have not, nor does she trust this reprieve, having been fooled by her sneaky disease several times already. "The unpredictability of cancer leaves me unsettled," she explains. "After surviving so much, after having been broken and healed and broken and healed again, cancer has made me question my luck. Yes, I have survived; yes, I am lucky. *But for how long?*" (81). This ambivalent response to survival gives credence to trauma theorist Cathy Caruth's claim that "survival itself can constitute a crisis" and reveals the radical instability of much survivor discourse (10). Survivor dis-ease can produce a conflicted narrative, as Roberta Hacker's is, or a brashly defiant one such as Ruthann Robson's in "not// a story." Here the narrator relies upon the "shock of humor" that can sometimes undermine terror in the face of death (Newmark 242). Robson's narrator, for instance, mocks her oncologist's preoccupation with the tragic and the orderly: "She can't even ask a question without putting me on a trajectory toward tragedy. . . . Am I just paranoid, or is she disappointed if the disease is not progressing on schedule?" (48). Roberta Hacker's account ends on a note of unpredictability and muted crisis: "I have survived. . . . *But for how long?*" (81). Robson celebrates the uncertain future as well as her nonnormative appearance and lesbian sexuality: "If only for today, this bald dyke lives" (53). Whereas Hacker fears the unknowable, Robson embraces it.

As Julia Kristeva explains in *Powers of Horror*, the human confrontation with bodily treachery—"defilement, sewage, muck"—often evokes abjection, a disruptive liminality that can be radically destabilizing (1–3). In the presence of death itself or of that which signifies death—"a flat encephalograph, for instance"—many humans can find a certain equanimity, but in the presence of vomit, convulsions, pus-filled wounds, and actual or imagined corpses, particularly the specter of one's own, most of us pale, for there we confront "the most sickening of wastes . . . a border that has encroached upon everything" (3). When death infects life, Kristeva argues, abjection can engulf:

> Abject. It is something rejected from which one does not part, from which one does not protect oneself as from an object. Imaginary uncanniness and real threat, it beckons to us and ends up engulfing us. It is thus not lack of cleanliness or health that causes abjection but what disturbs identity, system, order. What does not respect borders, positions, rules. (4)

Literary representations of women dying from cancer may confront the abject squarely or hover on its edges, but for many writers the engulfing force of abjection disrupts any possibility of death as "knowable" or transcendent. These writers agree with Kristeva that "refuse and corpses show me what I permanently thrust aside in order to live. These bodily fluids, this defilement, this shit are what life withstands, hardly and with difficulty, on the part of death. There, I am at the border of my condition as a living being" (4). Yet while this border produces discomfort, it can also be a site of counterhegemonic knowledge about gendered embodiment and the disruption of social order during the often messy process of dying.

An analysis of Mahasweta Devi's story "Stanadayini," which Gayatri Chakravorty Spivak has translated into English as "Breast-Giver," will reveal the complexities that attend a postcolonial representation of cancer, abjection, and the unknowable. Although cancer texts from the developing world share certain characteristics with Anglo-U.S.-Canadian illness narratives, postcolonial literature necessitates a particularly vigilant feminist scrutiny regarding the political exigencies of embodiment, representation, interpretation, and knowledge production. In *Third World Women and the Politics of Feminism* Chandra Talpede Mohanty offers a series of relevant questions and a theoretical manifesto:

> Who produces knowledge about colonized peoples and from what
> space/location? What are the politics of the production of this particular
> knowledge? . . . What are the methods used to locate and chart third world
> women's self and agency? . . . How we conceive of definitions and contexts,
> on what basis we foreground certain contexts over others, and how we
> understand the ongoing shifts in our conceptual cartographies—these are
> all questions of great importance in this particular cartography of third
> world feminisms. (3)

As Mohanty further notes, Western feminists often wrongly assume that women from developing countries constitute a monolithic constituency and associate these women with "underdevelopment, oppressive traditions, high illiteracy, rural and urban poverty, religious fanaticism, and 'overpopulation'" (6). Furthermore, when assessing postcolonial women's literature, Western feminists may use the constructs "woman" and "autonomous self" in a universalizing way without recognizing that "questions of subjectivity are always multiply mediated through the axes of race, class/caste, sexuality, and gender" (Mohanty, Russo, and Torres 33). In my analysis of "Breast-Giver" I first contextualize its relation to the embodied tropes and Western feminist theories under consideration in this chapter; I then contextualize it culturally and historically through the insights of Spivak and Mohanty.

Set in contemporary urban India, "Breast-Giver" offers an unsettling representation of a medicalized, leaky, amputated, prosthetic, and dying body through its omniscient narrator's recounting of the death from breast cancer of the protagonist, Jashoda, a Brahmin woman who works for thirty years as a "professional mother" and wet nurse after her husband is disabled. At the same time the story offers an ironic indictment of sexism in the patriarchal family and in the Hindu reverence for motherhood, the caste system, the legacy of colonization, and many other aspects of Indian culture. Issues of embodiment are central to this narrative, however; as Spivak notes in the essay that accompanies her translation, Devi problematizes the issue of agency in her representation of a "gendered subaltern," for Jashoda's "body, rather than her fetishized deliberative consciousness (self or subjectivity), is the *place* of knowledge, rather than the instrument of knowing" (260). Spivak's point about women's bodies as the paradoxical sites of both colonial/nationalistic/cultural exploitation and counterhegemonic knowledge recalls Shidrick's assertion in *Leaky Bodies and Boundaries* that from the perspective of a postmodern feminist ethic, "a resistant feminism must seek to explore the body anew" (9). As a woman who has given birth to twenty children and suckled "twenty, thirty boys in the Master's house," Jashoda signifies objectification but also authority as "the milk-filled faithful wife who was the object of the reverence of the local houses devoted to the Holy Mother" (Devi 234, 237). The arrival of breast cancer, however, obliterates her maternal power, as disease and medicalization render her both object and abject.

An initial sign of Devi's bitterly ironic attitude toward the systemic problems that inform medicalization in India is her omniscient narrator's declaration that hospitals "don't admit people who are so sick" (107). More gently ironized is the desire of Jashoda, who has worked for thirty years as a professional wet nurse, to avoid medical examination: "I can't go to the hospital. Ask me to croak instead. I didn't go to the hospital to breed, and I'll go now?" (235) Also subject to ironic scrutiny is the lack of medical knowledge exhibited by her estranged husband, Kangali, and by Jashoda herself. Devi's narrator wryly reproduces the erroneous hypothesis that excessive breast-feeding increases a woman's cancer risk by having Jashoda explain to the woman who first notices the "flaming red" color of her "left tit" that "I suckled so many, perhaps that's why" (234). Yet because her breasts have been income-producing, Jashoda has postponed doctor visits even after having discovered a large lump in one breast, initially palpable, later hard as stone. Once Jashoda is diagnosed with advanced breast cancer and hospitalized, she becomes "doubly disenabled," in Shildrick's terms, when her physician ignores her and directs his comments to her husband (116). Devi treats Kangali's lack of basic knowledge wryly: "You can get cancer in a tit?" he asks in amazement, having long thought of his wife's breasts only as sources of livelihood and sexual pleasure. Moreover, Devi's narrator evinces little belief that physicians help their patients. Indeed, Jashoda's irritable doctor explodes at her husband for bringing her to his office too late and asking if she will recover—"Get well! See how long she lasts. You've brought her in at the last stages. No one survives this stage" (237). Moreover, in the following passage the narrator unmasks the pervasive illogic of what Jackie Stacey calls "the fantasy of masculine invincibility" in the medical profession (12):

> The doctor understood that he was unreasonably angry because Jashoda was in this condition. He was angry with Jashoda, with Kangali, with women who don't take the signs of breast-cancer seriously enough and finally die in this dreadful and hellish pain. Cancer constantly defeats patient and doctor. One patient's cancer means the patient's death and the defeat of science, and of course of the doctor. (239)

By presenting ironically the anger of this physician and the implicit arrogance that underlies it, Devi's narrative recalls Sontag's challenge of a medical establishment that equates the death of a cancer patient with its own "defeat" (Sontag, *Illness*, 54–57). At the same time Devi's narrative indirectly warns women to monitor their breast health, to be vigilant on their own behalves.

As the narrative progresses, Jashoda's leakiness takes center stage. Indeed, her body exhibits sequential excess as her seemingly endless milk supply dries up and her breasts develop cancerous, pus-filled sores. As a wet nurse Jashoda had frequently experienced a flood of milk; "milk leaped out of her" even when she was not actually lactating (238). During her years as a "suckling-mother" she was deemed "Cow Mother," "Goddess," and "Mother of the World" by the wealthy "second-caste" family that employed her (228). Having reached menopause and become ill, however, Jashoda shifts from "Holy Mother" to "the master's servant" (234). When her once admired breasts develop lesions, Jashoda's loss of subjectivity intensifies; an angry outburst at her estranged husband reveals her lack of agency: "See these sores? Do you know how these sores smell? What will you do with me now?" (236). Because Kangali recalls nostalgically his youthful idealization of Jashoda's breasts, he takes pity and seeks medical help for her, but Jashoda continues to experience her leaky breasts as "mocking her with a hundred mouths, a hundred eyes" (236). Her abjection is most apparent when she bathes, as the narrator describes the smell of Jashoda's sores: "Stink, what a stink! Only if the body of a dead cat or dog rots in the garbage can you get a smell like this. Jashoda had forever scrubbed her breasts carefully with soap and oil, for the master's sons had put the nipples in their mouths. Why did those breasts betray her in the end?" (236). Devi's mocking rhetoric exposes male bias and privilege—Jashoda had cleaned her breasts faithfully because she nursed infant *boys*—and foregrounds the agony of bodily wounds. A subsequent passage describing Jashoda's leaky body again recalls Sontag's analysis of cancer's stigmatizing properties, a perspective Devi exploits through the imagery of putrefaction: "The sores on her breast gape more and more and the breast now looks like an open wound. It is covered by a piece of thin gauze soaked in antiseptic lotion, but the sharp smell of putrefying flesh is circulating silently in the room's air like incense-smoke. This brought an ebb in the enthusiasm of Kangali and the other visitors" (238). The narrator's use of discursive grotesquery and ironic understatement appears to situate Jashoda in the realm of the abject. Emotionally isolated and physically deteriorating, she is "cast out of the field of the social" (Judith Butler, *Bodies* xi). In Kristeva's terms, Jashoda has encountered and forces visitors to encounter "the most sickening of wastes . . . a border that has encroached upon everything . . . what disturbs identity, systems, order" (Kristeva 3–4). Paradoxically, however, an ironic power falls to Jashoda through her location in/as a sphere of dislocation.

Although her breasts are not removed, the dying Jashoda experiences a symbolic amputation, as the mammary glands that pleased her husband and nurtured countless infants give way to nasty, oozing hybrids. As her breasts have betrayed her, so have the boys she once suckled, grown into men who have forgotten her ministrations. Her murky awareness of these betrayals adds to her dis-ease: "When the doctor comes, she mutters with hurt feelings, 'You grew so big on my milk and now you're hurting me so?'" Intuiting that Jashoda is addressing these missing boys, the doctor assures her horrified family that she is not accusing them; instead, he explains, "she sees her milk-sons all over the world" (237). Ultimately Devi will not let readers ignore either the irony of a wet nurse abandoned by her "sons" or the horrors of a woman's death from breast cancer. The narrator's graphic language and dramatic reportage inten-sify as Jashoda's condition worsens and her breasts morph into putrid parasites that defeat their "host": "Again injection and sleepy numbness. Pain, tremendous pain, the cancer is spreading *at the expense of the host*. Gradually Jashoda's left breast bursts and becomes like the *crater* of a volcano. The smell of putrefaction makes approach difficult" (240).

Unlike conventional cancer narratives, which conclude at or near the moment of death, Devi foregrounds the spectacle of Jashoda's corpse as a sign of what Shildrick calls the unstable, the multiple, the incalculable (12). This spectacle marks the erosion of Jashoda's caste and maternal identities, both of which Devi treats ironically: by having this Brahmin "Cow Goddess" cremated by an "untouchable" who was assigned to this task because of impermeable caste hierarchies, and by revealing how Jashoda's family rationalizes its abandonment of her diseased corpse:

> Jashoda Devi, Hindu female, lay in the hospital morgue in the usual way, went to the burning ghat in a van, and was burnt. She was cremated by an untouchable.
> Jashoda was God manifest, others do and did whatever she thought. Jashoda's death was also the death of God. When a mortal masquerades as God here below, she is forsaken by all and she must always die alone. (240)

Although the theological ironies of Devi's narrative pronouncement can be read many ways, from a postmodern feminist perspective it seems that Jashoda's grisly death from breast cancer has restored gender, caste, and religious stability. In Bronfen's words, "Over her dead body, cultural norms are reconfirmed or secured" (1). Yet as "God manifest," this "Hindu female" assumes uneasy power even in her death, for in her "mortal masquerade" she either enacts or enables the symbolic and potentially cataclysmic "death of God" (Devi 240).

Although a Western feminist reading of "Breast-Giver" links it to postmodern cancer theory in a useful way, Spivak's postcolonial analysis of Devi's text offers different insights into the production of the embod-ied knowledge and textual representation of Jashoda as a "gendered sub-altern."[5] What happens, for instance, if we read "Breast-Giver" as a nationalistic parable, as Spivak claims that Devi intended? An interpre-tation of the narrative as "a parable of India after decolonization," Spi-vak explains, foregrounds its allegorical function: "Like the protagonist Jashoda, India is a mother-by-hire. All classes of people, the post-war rich, the ideologues, the indigenous bureaucracy, the diasporics, the people who are sworn to protect the new state, abuse and exploit her. If nothing is done to sustain her, nothing given back to her, and if scientific help comes too late, she will die of a consuming cancer" (244). Devi's view of her narrative's "meaning," as reconstructed by Spivak, emphasizes not the "effect of the real" in the text, which most Western readers would likely foreground, but rather the strategy of fabulism. Devi signifies this fabulist slant discursively, Spivak observes, by such "unrealistic" narrative devices as "the telescoped and improbable list of widespread changes in the household and locality brought about by the transition from domestic to 'domestic,' and the quick narrative of the thirty years of decolonization with its exorbitant figures" (267). Devi thus uses the subaltern Jashoda as a "vehicle of a greater meaning"—a meaning that Spivak describes as follows: "Citizens of the nation must give something to the nation rather than merely take from it"—a frequent slogan of militant nationalism (244). Jashoda's cancer, in this configuration of the narrative, becomes a metaphor for social irresponsibility. Such metaphorization recalls Sontag's critique of Western political discourse for its use of cancerous bodies as stand-ins for a ruptured body politic, but Devi uses this metaphorization for subversive purposes by ironizing the pervasiveness of cultural productions of meaning that blame the victims for their cancer and espouse relief when the offending "host" of the disease is vanquished (Sontag, *Illness,* 80–83). Spivak's interpretation of "Breast-Giver" as nationalist allegory offers an important postcolonial perspective on this cancer narrative. Perhaps the dying Jashoda is less abject than she appears "under Western eyes" to be (Mohanty 51).[6]

CANCER TEXTS AND
WOMEN'S SUBJECTIVITY

Across races, sexualities, and cultures women's cancerous bodies inevitably become medicalized; they often begin to leak blood or milk or other fluids. Many of these bodies require surgery, including amputation, and the women who inhabit them must then embrace or reject prosthesis. Some women with cancer survive to the proverbial ripe old age, while others die far too young. Literary texts by women writers from the 1960s to the present represent these aspects of the cancer experience with empathy or irony, humor or outrage. Considered as an entity, women's

writing about cancer foregrounds the agency of ill women by emphasizing not only their suffering but also their resilience and self-determination in the confrontation with life-threatening disease. To use again the
words of Shildrick, "the lived body [is] acknowledged as a site of subjectivity" in these literary works (10).

The five defining tropes of cancer literature that I have discussed in
this chapter serve as the basis for an alternative feminist discourse
regarding cancer and women's embodiment. Through the trope of medicalization, women writers interrogate how the bodies of cancer patients
are "handled" during surgery, radiation, chemotherapy, and other procedures and reveal how women can reclaim their medicalized bodies
through acts of resistance and agency. In employing the trope of leakiness, these writers suggest that while excessive fluidity may render ill
women's bodies unstable and therefore cause feelings of shame, leaks can
be reconceptualized as a transgressive form of fluid embodiment and ethical knowledge. The trope of amputation, traditionally conceived in
terms of lack or loss, appears in many women's recent cancer texts as a
source of artistic and erotic celebration, as mastectomy scars sport tattoos of flowers and trees, as missing breasts are both eulogized and
caressed. The trope of prosthesis, conventionally used to denote substi-
tution or compensation for a missing body part, becomes for many
women writers the basis for an empowering identity as both gendered
and hybrid, feminist and "posthuman." And through the trope of dying
and its corollary, (not) dying (at least not yet), women writers locate the
cancer experience on a continuum of transformational life events rather
than as a fixed traumatic moment or a site of knowability.

While these defining tropes and feminist theories of embodiment help
readers analyze women's cancer literature across generic boundaries, it is
also important to assess what distinctive insights each particular genre
offers. As we shall see, performance narratives approach wryly the fact
that cancer is diagnosed in "stages" and challenge audiences to respond
to ill women's explicit bodies onstage with empathy rather than
voyeurism. Breast cancer poetry laments the breast's absence but honors
the scar that replaces it, thus mapping new metaphors of resistance and
transformation. Popular fiction about cancer rewrites the nineteenth-
century sentimental novel in its representations of women providing
care for dying friends and daughters attending their dying mothers.
Experimental fiction, in turn, inscribes the bodies of women dying (or

thought to be dying) of cancer but simultaneously aroused (or arousing) through the power of erotic memory. And autobiographical cancer narratives chronicle women's relationship to their communities, cultures, and environment—their ecologies of self and world. In the chapters that follow I will further trace the contours of women's literary representations of cancer since 1990 and explore the impact of this vibrant work on a wide range of genres and readers.

2. "SKINNIED ON THE LEFT SIDE LIKE A GIRL"

Embodying Cancer on the Feminist Stage

Investigating a politics of the body has always been paramount for feminists in addressing the category "women" and the ways in which that category is constitutive of an oppressed class in patriarchy. . . . I think it is crucial for Anglo-American feminism, and particularly for feminist performance theory, to focus on the body at this historical juncture.

—Jeanie Forte, "Focus on the Body: Pain, Praxis, and Pleasure in Feminist Performance"

The explicit body in much feminist work interrogates sociocultural understandings of the "appropriate" and/or the appropriately transgressive—particularly who gets to mark what (in)appropriate where, and who has the right to appropriate what where.

—Rebecca Schneider, *The Explicit Body in Performance*

I have stage four metastatic ovarian cancer. There is no stage five. Oh, and I have to be very tough. It appears to be a matter, as the saying goes, of life and death.

—Margaret Edson, *Wit*

*T*HE FEMINIST PROJECT of theorizing the performing body interrogates the ways in which gendered, racial, and sexual embodiment is rendered invisible or visible, appropriate or transgressive, oppressive or liberating through the vehicle of theater or performance art. As Susan Bordo observes, the body serves as both a medium and a text of culture as well as "a *practical,* direct locus of social control"; it is therefore critical that contemporary feminist theorists interested in interrogating textuality, artistic production, and power examine theatrical stagings of women's bodies (165). In her essay, "Focus on the Body," performance theorist Jeanie Forte analyzes three key reasons for this feminist theoretical focus on embodiment: to reevaluate the "practical aspects of body politics, as a much-needed rebalancing of abstraction in relation to materiality"—that is, to foreground the importance of examining not only *the body in representation* but also *material bodies* in their sociohistorical contexts; to consider the body from a different "register" than the symbolic—as the "useful" body rather than the "intelligible" body; and to "unveil new strategies of resistance or make visible already operating strategies within the performance mode" (249–50). This task of exploring the staged body's materiality, utility, and capacity for resistance is particularly complicated when the "explicit body in performance," to use Rebecca Schneider's phrase, is ill or dying (1).

In offering a feminist analysis of women's performance narratives that thematize cancer, I argue that they differ from other cancer narratives in three significant ways. First, these plays employ explicit bodies onstage to mark women's cancerous breasts, ovaries, wombs, or "wounded" body parts as sites of social meaning. These bodies transgress from the "rules" of normative femininity and convey powerful somatic histories. As Schneider notes, explicit body theater aims to "explicate bodies in social relation . . . to peel back layers of signification that surround [them] like ghosts at a grave. . . . A mass of orifices and appendages, details and tactile surfaces, the explicit body in representation is foremost a site of social markings, physical parts and gestural signatures of gender, race, class, age, and sexuality—all of which bear ghosts of historical meaning" (2). Second, women's theatrical narratives challenge the capacity of a spectatorial, consuming "male gaze" to appropriate, fetishize, or otherwise sexualize women's bodies (Mulvey, 1). As the protagonists touch, flaunt, inspect, or bare their bodies in pain, they enact on stage what Schneider describes as "an in-your-face literality, a radical satiability that thwarts the consumptive mantra of infinite desire" (8). Third, these cancer plays invite empathy on the part of readers/theatergoers by fostering a complex sense of intimacy among playwright, actors, and audience, each of whom becomes a "penetrating witness to extreme rites" (Renner 34). While women read most cancer literature in private spaces, theater offers a public space in which audiences can reckon with the physical and emotional ravages as well as the politics of the disease. Although voyeurism remains a potential response, feminist performance narratives tend instead to evoke reciprocity and foster activism.

The four plays under consideration here—Margaret Edson's *Wit*, Maxine Bailey and Sharon M. Lewis's *Sistahs*, Susan Miller's *My Left*

Breast, and Lisa Loomer's *The Waiting Room*—offer trenchant feminist perspectives on cancer and embodiment. Written and produced in the 1990s, these plays foreground women's ill bodies, express outrage at the disease and its invasive treatments, examine environmental and cultural factors that may cause cancer, challenge the medical establishment, and foreground links between the personal and the political. In the words of Nancy Datan, a feminist psychologist who died of breast cancer, "It is a central tenet of feminism that women's invisible and private wounds often reflect social and political injustices. It is a commitment central to feminism to share burdens. And it is an axiom of feminism that the personal is political" (Wilkinson and Kitzinger 124). Theorist and breast cancer survivor Zillah Eisenstein similarly politicizes her mastectomy through a feminist lens: "Feminism's brilliance is found in this recognition that the body is not simply personal, that there is a politics to sex, that personal and political life are intermeshed. . . . Maybe it is this feminist autonomy of the body that has allowed me to live fully without all my body parts" (3). These plays engage postmodern feminisms and disability theory by interrogating the body's cultural history, exploring such concepts as the politics of appearance, the perils of medicalization, and the privilege of the temporarily able-bodied. Theatrical representations of women's cancer thereby "enrich and complicate our understandings of social justice, subject formation, subjugated knowledges, and collective action" (Garland Thomson, "Integrating" 1).

The saga of English Professor Vivian Bearing's unsuccessful struggle to overcome advanced ovarian cancer in the face of increasingly invasive medical treatments, *Wit* is the best-known play about a woman's cancer. First performed in 1997 at Long Wharf Theater in Connecticut, it moved to New York's Union Square Theater and won the Pulitzer Prize for drama in 1999 as well as many subsequent awards. *Sistahs,* first produced at Poor Alex Theatre in Toronto in 1994, explores the nurturant aspects of soup making and women's friendships for a cancer patient with advanced uterine cancer who has refused further chemotherapy. *My Left Breast,* which premiered at Actors Theater in Louisville in 1994, features a lesbian's account of the effects of her mastectomy on her family and her sense of self. And *The Waiting Room,* performed in Los Angeles in 1994 at the Mark Taper Forum and in 1996 at the Vineyard Theater in New York City, spans history and cultures to join women suffering from foot binding in eighteenth-century China, "hysteria" in

Victorian England, and breast cancer in the contemporary United States. Two of the ill protagonists in these plays are lesbians, one is a woman of color—facts that signify the diversity of feminist perspective and implicitly acknowledge the increased cancer risks for lesbians and African American women. As contributors to the women's movement, and as exemplars of a literary category sometimes called "illness testimonials," such plays constitute "counter-authoritative text[s], a revisionary genre, and a call to activism" (Schmidt 73).[1]

In the sections that follow I explore the diverse representations of *body politics* and *medical politics* in these four plays. An analysis of body politics demonstrates how the protagonists view their diseased bodies, amputated breasts, leaky uteruses, and/or cancerous ovaries; how these women cope with their diseases or disabilities and the accompanying fear, loss, and rage; and how they survive or prepare for their deaths. An exploration of medical politics reveals how the playwrights interrogate the medicalized bodies of the protagonists, the complex problem of debilitating cancer treatments, which may seem or be more harmful than the disease itself, and the behavior and discourse of medical practitioners or other cultural agents of surveillance. In probing how the graphic representations of suffering women who nonetheless claim agency provide these works with dramatic urgency, I examine the source and nature of the plays' narrative coherence. As Laura K. Potts has noted, many cancer texts by women follow a formal patterning of structure that she labels the "proairetic code," shaped by such common points of reference as "discovery, diagnosis, decisions about treatment, confronting possible death and life after treatment" (114)—yet the plays under consideration here tend to depart from this model, and I explore why. Finally, I consider the tension between voyeurism and empathy and the forms of reciprocity that audiences may experience while viewing these plays.

BODY POLITICS: MATERIALITY, PERFORMANCE, AGENCY

Feminist theories of the body illuminate theatrical representations of women's cancers by foregrounding the body's materiality, its subjugation, its erotic force, and its politics. In the 1980s and early 1990s many U.S. feminists theorized these aspects of the body. Susan Bordo, for instance, proclaimed the need for "an effective political discourse about the female body," a discourse that would challenge "the practices of femininity [that] may lead us to utter demoralization, debilitation, and death"; she further argued, after Foucault, that such a discourse should consider how to conceive of power as constitutive rather than repressive and how "to account for the subversion of potential rebellion" (167). In "Notes toward a Politics of Location," Adrienne Rich took a related approach but used a different discursive metaphor in defining the body as "the geography closest in," that territory whose boundaries women have a right to draw on their own terms (212). However liberating Rich's metaphor might seem, her consideration of women's embodiment in geographical terms underscores how often women's bodies, particularly those of women of color, have been raped, plundered, and colonized. For many women writing about the body, agency is impossible until violation and its aftermath have been painfully inscribed. As Bordo and Rich both realize, the hurt and rage caused by rape, incest, and sexual abuse inflame many women's writings, as do issues of anorexia, bulimia, and other forms of bodily denial.[2]

Feminist postmodern theory from the mid-1990s and beyond has demonstrated that raced and gendered bodies are never fixed but ever in process, multiple, contingent, and fluid. This theory posits that since the body is both material and discursive, any feminist understanding of its corporeality must be constantly mediated by its spoken contexts. As Judith Butler notes in "Performative Acts and Gender Constitution,"

> As an intentionally organized materiality, the body is always an embodying *of* possibilities both conditioned and circumscribed by historical convention. In other words, the body *is* a historical situation . . . a manner of doing, dramatizing, and *reproducing* a historical situation. (272)

Butler thus contends that "there is no reference to a pure body which is not at the same time a further formation of that body" (272). How women's bodies have been constructed, politicized, and re-formed therefore becomes a central question for contemporary feminism and its textual representations. Indeed, the constructions of gender and embodiment found in women's performance narratives of cancer draw important links between "the everyday body as it is lived, and the regime of disciplinary and regulatory practices that shape its form and behaviour" (Shildrick and Price 8). Butler foregrounds as well the body's *the-*

atricality, its role in "dramatizing" historicity, a perspective shared by Zillah Eisenstein in *Manmade Breast Cancers:*

> My breast cancer body does not say enough about how other body demands have choreographed my life. Although breast cancer has often suffocated me . . . my body has had other selves. I am never simply my cancer because I have other bodies *and* I am something besides my body struggles. (42)

In her equation of "body demands" with "choreography," Eisenstein, too, emphasizes the performativity that breast cancer enacts.

It is with these theoretical contexts in mind that we must consider contemporary playwrights' strategies for inscribing and staging cancer. As Susan Sontag points out in *Illness as Metaphor,* in traditional literary representations "the person dying of cancer is portrayed as robbed of all capacities of self-transcendence, humiliated by fear and agony" (17). Feminist dramatists' portrayals of cancer bear the weight of such condescending representations even as they attempt to upend them. They depict the bodily betrayal and suffering of women diagnosed with cancer but present as well their struggles for agency, their multiple subjectivities. Furthermore, they often do so with outrageous humor, evoking in audiences astonished laughter, itself a healing force, and employing transgressive discursive strategies to represent cancer. For example, the fact that cancers are diagnosed in stages 1–4 provides an opportunity for self-referential punning. Edson's protagonist in *Wit* acknowledges this when she explains wryly that "there is no stage five" (12). Similarly, the speaker in Miller's *My Left Breast* foregrounds cancer's pervasiveness with comic irony, claiming that women's cancer is "the topic of our times . . . the hot issue . . . coming soon to a theater near you" (219). Such metacommentary reveals the playwrights' ironic highlighting of the fact that cancer is virulent, ubiquitous, and commercialized. In Judith Butler's words, onstage representations of women's cancerous bodies "do, dramatize, and *reproduce*" the "historical situation" of the late-twentieth-century cancer epidemic—its ravages, its commodification, and its potential to generate textual resistance ("Performative" 272).

The medicalized body is clearly on display in *Wit,* as Vivian Bearing appears on stage emaciated, bald, and hooked up to an IV pole. She is eight months into her cancer, hospitalized and terminal; thus, the play begins not with her diagnosis, as Potts's proairetic code would dictate,

but with the inevitability of her death. As a distinguished scholar of seventeenth-century poetry, however, Vivian remains authoritative;
indeed, she couches her cancer confessional in the terms of textual criticism. "*Irony* is a literary device that will necessarily be deployed to great
effect," she tells the audience.

> I ardently wish this were not so. I would prefer that a play about me be cast
> in the mythic-heroic-pastoral mode; but the facts, most notably stage-four
> metastatic ovarian cancer, conspire against that. *The Faerie Queen* this is
> not.
>   And I was dismayed to discover that the play would contain elements of
> . . . *humor*.
>   I have been, at best, an *unwitting* accomplice. (*She pauses.*) It is not my
> intention to give away the plot; but I think I die at the end.
>   They've given me less than two hours. (6)

In contradiction to the predictable opening of many cancer narratives—
a traumatic diagnosis, subsequent despair, and a loss of grounding—
Vivian's initial self-presentation exudes confidence. She banters with the
audience, acknowledges the dramatic dimensions of her struggle, and
employs irony to distance herself from her disease, even as she predicts
her imminent demise. Accustomed to scholarly detachment, Vivian
remains impassive through the first third of Edson's play, as she recounts
the diagnosis of her "insidious adenocarcinoma" by a physician who,
like herself, hides behind a professorial mask. Indeed, they debate the
meaning of "insidious," with the surgeon defining it as undetectable at
the source, the patient as "treacherous" (8).

As the disease progresses and the treatment fails to provide a cure or
eliminate her pain, Vivian uses irony as a shield: "One thing can be said
for an eight-month course of cancer treatment: it is highly educational. I
am learning to suffer" (32). Ultimately, however, she reveals her vulnerability, as she moves from discomfort to agony:

> Yes, it is mildly uncomfortable to have an electrocardiogram, but the . . .
> agony . . . of a proctosigmoidoscopy sweeps it from memory. Yes, it was
> embarrassing to have to wear a nightgown all day long—two night-
> gowns!—but that seemed like a positive privilege compared to watching
> myself go bald. . . . Oh, God. . . . Oh, God. It can't be. (32)

A former health care worker in a hospital cancer unit, Edson refuses to
downplay the anguish of the dying patient. As Vivian's condition deteri-

orates, her doctor's initially inane question—"Dr. Bearing, are you in pain?"—becomes cruel:

> Vivian: (*Sitting up, unnoticed by the staff*) Am I in pain? I don't believe this. Yes, I'm in goddamn pain. (*Furious*) I have a fever of 101 spiking to 104. And I have bone metastases in my pelvis and both femurs. (*Screaming*) There is cancer eating away at my goddamn bones, and I did not know there could be such pain on this earth. (71)

This play is not for the squeamish; Vivian does not mince words about her misery. Indeed, Edson herself has described *Wit* as "ninety minutes of suffering and death, mitigated by a pelvic exam and a lecture on seventeenth-century poetry" (Zinman 25).

Moreover, Vivian's medicalized body experiences psychological as well as physical suffering, since she has privileged professional success over human intimacy and thus faces her cancer alone. By representing her protagonist as devoid of friends, lovers, or family, Edson reproduces the unfortunate stereotype of the sexually repressed English teacher, middle aged, single, and isolated; so obsessive about her scholarship that she fails to connect meaningfully with other humans. As she nears death, for example, Vivian blames herself for being insufficiently compassionate toward her students, for being too absorbed in Donne to nurture them. She recalls a clever exchange by two students after class and critiques herself for her rigidity in not laughing with them: "I admired only the studied application of wit, not its spontaneous eruption" (62). When a student once asked for an extension on a paper because her grandmother had died, the dying Vivian recalls, she responded, "The paper is due when it is due" (63). Such memories cause the teacher self-doubt and an uncharacteristic loss of words: "I don't know. I feel so much—what is the word? I look back, I see these scenes, and I . . ." (65). Although one might argue that Edson develops Vivian as a character who needs to find her compassionate side, the fact remains that she is "made" to suffer not only *from* her cancer but *for* her lack of a capacity to nurture. That the nurturant female body is privileged in this text can be seen in the figures of Dr. E. M. Ashford, Vivian's dissertation adviser and only visitor, who mothers the patient by crawling in bed with her to read Margaret Wise Brown's children's story "The Runaway Bunny"; and Susie Monahan, Vivian's mentally "dull" but endlessly caring nurse, who calls her sweetheart, brings her Popsicles, and embodies the kindness that Edson implicitly presents Vivian as suffering because she lacks (78–80, 64–69). When compared to her sympathetic representation of these healthy maternal bodies, Edson's representation of Vivian's alienated, aching body seems punitive.[3]

Like *Wit, Sistahs* violates the proairetic code by skipping over the cancer patient's discovery and diagnosis. This play, too, features a professor with metastatic cancer who is grappling with her own death; however, Sandra Grange-Mosaku's cancer is uterine rather than ovarian. "I carry my story in my womb," she admits in the play's initial scene. "Most women do, but not all" (4). In contrast to the friendless, sexless Vivian Bearing, Sandra boasts a kitchen full of loving friends as well as an attentive female partner and a concerned, if truculent, teenaged daughter. The presence of these supporters is insufficient, though, to quell Sandra's wrath at the ravages of her disease, a wrath that she unleashes on her loved ones when they fail to adhere to her script for preparing West Indian soup and making peace with one another:

> You couldn't make an effort to get along this one time? A lot to handle? I wanted a dinner, one dinner with the people that I care about. Try waking up each morning, deciding whether or not to be drugged up, or sit with the pain all day. Getting needles stuck in you. It took me three hours to get off the bed this morning. A lot to handle? Fuckery! Pure fuckery running through my blood. (47)

Like Vivian, Sandra rages at the attack of her body by renegade cells and at her subsequent loss of control. As she stirs the soup, blood runs between her legs, forcing her to change her skirt and hide the ruined garment so that her daughter will not see. Although Sandra initially feels humiliated—the female body, after all, has been culturally constructed as "unpredictable, leaky, and disruptive" and therefore shameful—she finds comfort in the soothing touch of her sister (Shildrick and Price 2). Nonetheless, both cancer patients find appalling the invasion of their bodies: having destroyed her ovaries, cancer "eats away" at Vivian's bones; it "runs through" Sandra's blood and assaults her womb—insistent, ghastly.

Both Sandra in *Sistahs* and Vivian in *Wit* employ battle imagery, a conventional cancer trope, and each woman perceives herself as losing the contest. Although Sontag has justly critiqued the oppressive use of battle metaphors in medical discourse (*Illness,* 68–71), in feminist performance narratives such metaphors can be liberatory—perhaps because the spectacle of ill women angrily resisting bodily appropriation has been so rarely visible. Sandra approaches her defeat head-on and blames herself for having misplaced her rage by arguing with and striking her daughter:

> I lost my temper. I lost control. Casualties. I lost control of the situation. . . . I've LOST! This war. Fighting, and trying to control my child. I've hit her. Fighting. This gift from my womb, and . . . this thing in my womb. I have done something terrible. (48)

Both the violence of "this thing in [her] womb" and her own internal violence, unleashed on the child she wants to protect, horrify Sandra. Vivian, in contrast, is a measured combatant who initially claims to be destined for fame, if not victory, by "distinguishing [her]self in illness" (53). Yet she realizes—and reminds the audience—that becoming the subject of a scholarly article in a medical journal does not prevent her objectification:

> I have survived eight treatments of Hexamethophosphacil and Vinplatin at the *full* dose, ladies and gentlemen. I have broken the record. I have become something of a celebrity. . . .
>
> But I flatter myself. The article will not be about *me*, it will be about my ovaries. It will be about my peritoneal cavity, which, despite their best intentions, is now crawling with cancer. (53)

Such are the fears of many women cancer patients on- and offstage: that they have become merely the sum of their body parts—and of parts that fail to comprise a whole. They feel no longer themselves—indeed, no longer human. "What we have come to think of as *me*," Vivian muses, "is, in fact, just the specimen jar, just the dust jacket, just the white piece of paper that bears the little black marks" (53).

Despite this apparent loss of subjectivity, both Vivian in *Wit* and Sandra in *Sistahs* experience a transformation that allows them, at least in part, to reclaim their intellectual and bodily selves. It is significant that Edson and coauthors Bailey and Lewis create characters that are university professors, since in their subject matter lie the protagonists' intellectual passion and life's meaning. In retrospective scenes in which each woman lectures to a roomful of engaged, if mystified, students, these playwrights offer insights that characterize their philosophical vision. Vivian and Sandra embrace very different subjects and pedagogies, however: Vivian idealizes the Christian poetry of seventeenth-century writer

John Donne and purveys this knowledge by interrogating and at times bullying her students, while Sandra as an African historian foregrounds issues of race, colonization, diaspora, and genocide and teaches in an urgent, dialectical manner. Edson has claimed that *Wit* is "about redemption"; for Vivian, the vehicle of redemption is Donne's poetry, with its emphasis on paradox and its intricate punctuation: "And Death—*capital* D—shall be no more—*semicolon!* Death—*capital* D—comma—thou shalt die—*exclamation point!*" (14) As Vivian recalls her professor, Dr. Ashford, having explicated the poem years earlier, life and death exist on a continuum: what divides the two states of being are "not insuperable barriers, not semicolons, just a comma," a belief to which the dying Vivian holds tenaciously (15). For Sandra, the possibility of redemption is cultural rather than individual, the vehicle not literature but history. In her classes she lectures on the horrible realities of slavery—"the middle passage . . . the surgical removal of female reproductive organs"—topics that evoke her racial history as well as the loss of her own uterus to a different invading force. But she also teaches her students about cultural survival by urging them to redefine family, not as a patriarchal unit but as "a recipe to survive genocide" (38).

Vivian and Sandra find a reconciled peace, and in each woman's transformation her body figures prominently. Near the end of *Sistahs* Sandra asks her partner, Dehlia; her sister, Rea; and her friend, Cerise, to care for her daughter, Assata, after Sandra's death. However, the play's denouement focuses not on her demise but on the healing properties of the communal soup. "It's alchemy," claims Dehlia; "it's magic," intones Rea. "It's voodoo," insists Cerise; "it's Obeah," chimes Assata. "It's soup," concludes Dehlia, demystifying the healing brew that Sandra has requested. *Sistahs* is the last word Sandra utters, naming the source of the strength she conjures, even as her body continues to suffer. "Sandra *doubles over in pain,*" proclaims the final stage direction. "*Lights come down onstage*" (61). This stage direction undermines the potentially transcendent discourse of healing potions, since Sandra's leaky body continues to cause her agony. Yet in doubling over—enfolding her wounded belly—she affirms the resilience of still-living flesh, a site of power for African women ravaged by disease or cultural genocide. As Bibi Bakare-Yusuf notes in her study of black women's embodiment, because African women during slavery often perceived their flesh as their own, "hidden from the violations of the body," the embrace of one's own flesh can serve as a liberatory gesture for diasporic women. As a source of "counter-memory" and strength, flesh "retrieves, recovers the memory of the body's capacity for resistance, for transformation, for healing" (321).

Wit ends with Vivian's death and one final violation, as doctors attempt to resuscitate her and in so doing ignore her request that no life-prolonging treatment be administered. Despite this ultimate invasion, Edson preserves her protagonist's dignity. As the doctors recognize their error and grapple with possible repercussions, the dying Vivian rises from her hospital bed, *"attentive and eager, moving slowly toward the light."* The stage directions reveal that as Vivian strips off the cap that hid her baldness and the bracelet that provided her hospital name and number, she is luminous, in control of her body and its movements, whole:

> (*She loosens the ties and the top gown slides to the floor. She lets the second gown fall. The instant she is naked, and beautiful, reaching for the light— Lights out*). (85)

Although some scholars of *Wit* have viewed this final scene as redemptive in a Christian sense, I see the ending as employing a transgressive strategy that is characteristic of explicit body performance, as the nude, ghostly Vivian doubles back to reveal her absent presence.[4] According to Schneider, "the subject returns for a second time in relation to its own death, as if beside itself . . . and exposes the historical mechanisms of a social drama which has parsed its players, by bodily markings, into subjects and objects" (180). As Vivian, newly dead, moves toward the light, she assumes again "the guise of subjectivity," what Schneider deems an uncanny "second sight/site" (180).

My Left Breast and *The Waiting Room*, both of which address breast cancer, also move between anguish and subjectivity, with emphasis on the latter because their protagonists are survivors. In *My Left Breast* the narrator, Susan, has lived for more than a decade since her mastectomy, though she is aware that she might not remain cancer-free. In *The Waiting Room* the main character, Wanda, flaunts her prosthetic body, especially her huge breasts, the products of cosmetic surgery, until she learns that a faulty implant may have caused or hidden an incipient cancer. While her diagnosis is unnerving and several lymph nodes are involved, Wanda grapples with the tough decision of conventional versus alternative treatment, not with the immanence of her death. Controlling one's own body, rather than confronting death, constitutes the dominant motif in these two plays. Both plays disrupt the proairetic code, however, by denying the closure that reconstructive surgery or even death can arguably provide.

The celebratory tone of *My Left Breast* is evident when the play begins, as Susan comes out dancing. Indeed, her liberated movement mirrors her frank speech, as she confronts the audience immediately with the reality of her amputated body through a defiant juxtaposition of a "real" and a prosthetic breast:

> The night I went to the hospital, that is what I did. I danced. (Indicates breasts)
> 　　One of these is not real. Can you tell which? (214)

Later in the scene she shows the audience her prosthesis, using it to expound upon the commercial spectacle and emotional vulnerability of cancer patients:

> Don't worry. It's a spare. When you go for a fitting, you can hear the women in the booths. Some of them have lost their hair and shop for wigs. Some are very young and their mothers are thinking: why didn't this happen to me, instead? (215)

Contrasted with the insistent presence of the prosthesis is the poignant absence of the breast itself, an absence the protagonist notes but refuses to find mournful. Like Eisenstein, who claims herself as "something besides my body struggles," Miller's speaker defines her missing breast as a beloved but an expendable body part. It is not as precious as shelter, language, or love:

> I miss it but it's not a hand. I miss it but it's not my mind. I miss it but it's not the roof over my head. I miss it but it's not a sentence I can't live without. I miss it, but it's not a conversation with my son. It's not my courage or my lack of faith. (215)

In addition to assertions of survivor agency, Miller offers trenchant social commentary about the epidemic of breast cancer, thus politicizing her play more overtly than Edson does *Wit* or Bailey and Lewis do *Sistahs*. Specifically, Miller's narrator challenges two cultural stereotypes that evoke her anger: that women's illnesses matter little in light of the major plague of our times, AIDS; and that women who contract breast cancer somehow bring it on themselves. Regarding the first stereotype, it is useful to contextualize Miller's play in an early 1990s time frame, when breast cancer research dollars were sorely lacking and activists yearned to have physicians and government leaders use the term *epidemic* as a measure of public accountability comparable to that which AIDS was finally receiving. The tensions that occurred between certain lesbian and gay male health activists during this era are also reflected in this monologue:

> A man I know said to me, Lesbians are the chosen people these days. No AIDS. I said, Lesbians are women.
> Women get AIDS. Women get ovarian cancer. Women get breast cancer. Women die. In great numbers. In the silent epidemic. He said, I see what you mean. (218)

In a play characterized by rapid-fire monologues, this passage stands out for its staccato language and strategic repetition. Susan unpacks two false assumptions here: that lesbians are not "real women" and that women, lesbians included, are less vulnerable to fatal diseases than men are.

The second cultural stereotype—that women cause their own cancers by living unhealthily or internalizing their emotions—enrages Miller's protagonist even more than the assumption that women are not dying in significant numbers. Debunking this stereotype lets Miller critique a variety of social ills: violence against women everywhere, racism in nineteenth- and early-twentieth-century America, ethnic cleansing in Bosnia, Somalia, the Middle East, and Cambodia. She therefore offers not the liberal feminist perspective of Edson and Bailey/Lewis, who focus on the individual experiences and rights of women with cancer, but a global feminist perspective that links the women's cancer movement to other struggles for human rights.

> There are those who insist that certain types of people get cancer. So I wonder, are there certain types of people who get raped and tortured? Are there certain types who die young? Are there certain types of Bosnians, Somalians, Jews? Are there certain types of gay men? Are there certain types of children who are abused and caught in the crossfire? Is there a type of African American who is denied, excluded, lynched? Were the victims of the Killing Fields people who couldn't express themselves? Are one out of eight women— count 'em, folks—just holding onto their goddamned anger? (219)

Susan's use of urgent repetition, rhetorical questions, and direct challenge to the audience reveal her outrage at the presumption of a "blame the victim" mentality.

This emphasis on global feminist politics in *My Left Breast* intersects powerfully with the experience of one woman, Susan, a lesbian breast cancer survivor who claims her bodily autonomy. She recognizes, with irony, that her body carries political as well as personal signification:

> This is my body—where the past and the future collide. This is my body. All at once, timely. All at once, chic. (219)

Both grateful for societal recognition and resentful of her commodification, Susan determines to display her body on her own terms. Just as the protagonist in *Wit* bares her body on stage as a sign of self-reclamation at the moment of her death, Miller's protagonist confronts the audience with her bodily vulnerability and transforms it into agency.

The primary insignia of Susan's newfound subjectivity is her mastectomy scar, which serves as an erogenous zone and a marker of survival. The amputated breast thus becomes not a site of marginalization due to its difference from the normate body but instead a site of pleasure and power. Indeed, a prominent theme in both *My Left Breast* and *The Waiting Room* is the effect of cancer on women's sexuality and body image. For Miller's protagonist, the loss of her breast pales next to the loss of her lover, Franny, which occurs not because of Susan's cancer but because their relationship is long distance and troubled. A recurring erotic memory for the bereft Susan involves the sexualization of her scar: "Skinnied on the left side like a girl, I summon my breast and you there where it was with your mouth sucking a phantom flutter from my viny scar" (215). At the end of the play, when Susan has healed from the shock of her cancer and the end of her relationship, she reinvokes her scar, this time as "a mark of experience" to be "cherished":

> It's the history of me, a permanent fix on the impermanence of it all. A line that suggests that I take it seriously. Which I do. A line that suggests my beginning and my end. I have no other like it. I have no visible reminder of the baby I lost. Or the friend. No constant monument to the passing of my relationship. There is no other sign on my body that repeats the incongruity and dislocation, the alarm. A scar is a challenge to see ourselves as survivors, after all. Here is the evidence. The body repairs. And the human heart, even after it has broken into a million pieces, will make itself large again. (236)

Such capacity for regeneration provides hope for all women with cancer, to whom Susan refers metonymically as "the women in the changing booths." Her message to them is simple but profound: "we are still beautiful, we are still powerful, we are still sexy, we are still here" (236). To document her/their resistant, stubborn subjectivity, Susan opens her shirt and reveals to the audience her mastectomy scar.

The Waiting Room interweaves the cancer motifs of leakiness and prosthesis with feminist themes of sexuality and agency. As the play opens, three women meet in a doctor's clinic: Forgiveness from Heaven, an eighteenth-century Chinese woman whose bound feet have become infected; Victoria, a nineteenth-century Englishwoman seeking treatment for "shrunken" ovaries; and Wanda, a modern American woman whose breast implants are malfunctioning. None of these women initially claims bodily autonomy. Forgiveness and Victoria are bound by the judgments of their husbands: the apologetic Forgiveness would like to wash her stinking feet, "but my husband, he's crazy for the smell"; the corseted Victoria enjoys romantic novels but has been forbidden to read them, since her husband thinks that reading causes ovarian atrophy (14). Wanda at first appears to be independent; she is single, flamboyant, mouthy. As she confesses to her nurse, Brenda, in the examining room, however, Wanda received silicone breast implants for her thirtieth birthday as a gift from her father—"no one ever called me 'Pancake' again"—and has since had plastic surgery on everything else: nose, chin, cheekbones, stomach, thighs. Thus Loomer conflates history in *The Waiting Room* to satirize patriarchal control of women's bodies across time and cultures as well as women's complicity in the multibillion-dollar beauty industry.

With Brenda's support and encouragement, however, Wanda approaches first her biopsy and then her cancer on her own terms. In scene 9 of act 1, as the women converge in Central Park, Brenda uses humor to calm Wanda's fears: "We don't even know you got cancer. Where you goin' get cancer? You don't have a single body part that's real" (40). Those silicone body parts, of course, are the *cause* of Wanda's cancer, diagnosed in act 2, scene 4, as a malignant tumor so large that lumpectomy is not an option: only mastectomy will suffice. In the recovery room after surgery, Wanda appears to have accepted the recommended treatment passively. When Victoria asks how she's doing, she replies, "I don't know. I guess that's for the doctor to say. They took a— they took my breast. . . . And my tits, of course. . . . And they took some lymph nodes to see if they're . . . 'clear'" (60). The repetition of "they took" illustrates Wanda's lack of agency, intensified by the fact that the pronoun *they* has no clear antecedent and *took* bears the connotation of theft. But when her doctor later reports on Wanda's "bad" lymph nodes and recommends aggressive chemotherapy, she refuses both his condolences and his treatment: "Don't be sorry, doc. 'Cause you're not shooting me up with a goddamn thing" (64). From telephone calls to her insurance agent and her boss at work, she has learned that her surgery isn't covered and her job is no longer hers; from Brenda she has learned about alternative cancer treatments available in Mexico. What she *can* control, Wanda finally determines, is the body that her cancer inhabits: "This cancer is . . . mine. For better or worse, till death do us part, it's about the one thing I got left that's all—mine. And if I want to take it to Tijuana or Guadafuckinglajara—I've never been out of the tri-state area!" Although Wanda's defiance diminishes as she realizes the enormity of her plight, she continues to assert that "for once in my lousy screwed-up life, it's MY BODY! MY BODY! MINE!" (70)

Even feminist theater, however, rarely escapes entirely the cultural edict that cancer is the female patient's fault—that she ate too much or too little, worked too hard or not hard enough, neglected to seek medical care or sought the wrong kind. In each of these plays the protagonists blame themselves, at least momentarily, for their cancer. *Wit* is especially culpable in this regard. Vivian blanches when she admits to Jason, her intern, that she drinks "two . . . to six" cups of coffee daily: "But I don't really think that's immoderate." She responds more defensively when he inquires how often she has had "routine medical checkups":

Vivian: Well, not as often as I should, probably, but I've felt fine, I really have.
Jason: So the answer is?
Vivian: Every three to . . . five years. (26)

Edson's language and Jason's censorious gaze imply that Vivian could be partially responsible for her own cancer because she did not observe medical protocol. This play's conservatism in this area can best be illuminated if we recall Sontag's challenge to the benighted views of late-nineteenth- and early-twentieth-century physicians, psychoanalysts, and philosophers regarding cancer's origins: Herbert Snow, who claimed that "of 140 cases of breast cancer, 103 gave an account of previous mental trouble . . . or other debilitating agency"; Wilhelm Reich, who described cancer as "a disease following emotional resignation—a bioenergetic shrinking, a giving up of hope"; and Karl Menninger, who saw illness as a result of "what the victim has done with his world and himself" (Sontag, *Illness* 3, 23, 46). Edson's stereotyping of Vivian as so work-obsessed that she fails to have regular pap smears and thus contracts cancer through carelessness comes all too close to the representations Sontag denounces.

The other plays under consideration also engage an implicit rhetoric of patient denigration, although to a lesser extent. Sandra in *Sistahs* laments the time she spends "cursing myself each day for not being more careful," although she fails to explain in what way she has been careless (56). Wanda in *The Waiting Room* implies that her "lousy screwed-up life" has led her to the operating table (70). Even Susan in *My Left Breast,* arguably the most feminist of these protagonists, infuses her probe of environmental causes with self-interrogation:

> When I was pregnant, I took something called Provera. Later it was shown to cause birth defects. So, when I got breast cancer I wondered, was it the time someone sprayed my apartment for roaches? Or too much fat in my diet? Was it the deodorant with aluminum, or my birth control pills? Or was it genetic? (228)

That such anguished questions abound among women diagnosed with cancer, onstage or in life, is undeniable. As Sontag notes, "punitive notions of disease have a long history, and such notions are particularly active with cancer" (*Illness,* 53). Yet cancer patients, she concludes, are "hardly helped" by being blamed for their illness or hearing their disease named "the epitome of evil" (76). Audre Lorde makes this point more fiercely by asserting that blaming cancer patients for their illness is "a monstrous distortion of the idea that we can use our strengths to help heal ourselves" (*Cancer Journals,* 74–75). Unfortunately, these otherwise feminist playwrights at times perpetuate that distortion, although Miller counters it more effectively than do the others.

Considered together, the dramatic representations of women's cancers by Edson, Bailey and Lewis, Miller, and Loomer successfully foreground five transgressive tropes of embodiment that reveal women's ill bodies as disciplined but not subjugated—as subjected to the "stare" that tracks disabled persons but not undone by it (Garland Thomson, *Extra-*

ordinary 26). The medicalized body, most notably Vivian's in *Wit*, experiences invasive treatments and public violations but ultimately resists
appropriation. The leaky body, best exemplified by Sandra's in *Sistahs*,
spurts bloody fluids at embarrassing moments yet asserts authority
through its flesh. The amputated body, particularly Susan's in *My Left
Breast*, speaks through its scar, the lost breast mourned but lovingly remembered. The prosthetic body, exemplified by Wanda's in *The Waiting Room*, embraces contradiction, "posthuman" in its alienation from
itself but powerful in its hybridity (Herndl, "Reconstructing," 150–51).
And the dying body, Vivian's especially, rages before moving toward
"the light." Ultimately these protagonists insist on self-determination, if
not self-healing. They break silence about their illnesses, assume the
right to embodied authority, live with missing breasts or wombs, and,
when necessary, die with dignity. Embodying illness on stage, they
"take the power of words, of representation, into their own hands"
(Friedman, "Women's Auto-Biographical Selves," 91).

MEDICAL POLITICS: CONTESTED SITES OF MEANING AND AUTHORITY

The authors of these four plays offer a profound indictment of callous
physicians, inconsiderate hospital personnel, inadequate or nonexistent
medical treatments, and pharmaceutical companies that skew research
results. The medical practitioners who appear onstage are typically represented as inept or arrogant—at best, uncomprehending of women cancer patients' fears and needs, at worst, dismissive of them. Nurses (who
are all women in these plays) generally fare better than doctors (who are
almost all men), though occasionally a doctor is presented as empathic.
Not only do nurses give care and comfort to the traumatized women,
they often question the physicians' ethics and defy their orders. Yet even
nurses are sometimes represented as apathetic or abusive. As their primary recourse, the protagonists struggle to comprehend and acquire a
complex, ominous, and closely guarded medical vocabulary. These
playwrights thus represent their ill women characters as working to
bridge the gap between medical discourse and embodied authority.

Potts's theory of the ways in which autobiographical breast cancer
texts represent contested knowledge illuminates as well the strategies of

Bailey and Lewis, Miller, Edson, and Loomer: "The body and the *identity* of the woman with breast cancer become contested sites of meaning between the hegemony of the discourse of medical practice and her own sense of the disease and her relationship to it, the meaning she generates through the process" (117). Such contested knowledge is thematically central to the conflicts that protagonists experience in the plays under consideration. In the doctor's office and in the hospital room, they suffer physical, verbal, and psychological indignities. Many of them face invasive treatments whose painful side effects and uncertain outcomes rival the malignancy of the cancer itself. At times the protagonists experience or resist the disposition of their bodies for medical experimentation. Often they claim their own bodily authority and knowledge as equally legitimate to that of physicians, thereby engaging in what medical theorist Kathryn Pauly Morgan, using the metaphor of theatricality, terms a "political drama":

> Women's agency, women's health care practices, and women's political struggles around health care can be seen as a serious political drama involving contesting authoritative knowledge-seekers and providers. It is drama in which medical authorities often believe that they alone are entitled to manage women's bodies, hearts, and minds and to prioritize women's health needs. (84)

As cancer patients, the protagonists in these plays challenge the medical establishment even as they envision little alternative to seeking its assistance.

Both *Sistahs* and *My Left Breast* contain pivotal scenes in which the protagonists question the effectiveness of their prescribed treatment. *Sistahs* explores Sandra's reasons for rejecting further medicalization once chemotherapy and radiation have failed to prevent metastasis. This exploration occurs primarily through the tension that exists between Sandra and her frightened daughter, Assata, who desperately wants her mother to resume treatment. When Sandra complains to her partner that Assata does not do her share of the housework and is told that her daughter really "wants to help," she reveals the source of this tension: "She wants to help?! I'm the one mopping. NO, all she wanna do is stand up and ask me question, why I don't take treatment, why I don't see this and that doctor?" (5). When the weary mother asks her daughter to do more around the house, Assata rages, "Well maybe you wouldn't be so tired if you would go back to the doctor and get that stupid cis-carb-playtane"

(7). Sandra's only response is to implore Assata to "make peace" with her. Later in the play, when daughter accuses mother of a defeatist attitude, Sandra's sister echoes her niece's criticism: "The last time we talked, Sandy, I thought you were trying alternative methods; now it seems you're not trying anything. One of James' clients is an oncologist. I can get the number so you can call" (44). Impervious to such attempts at intervention, however, Sandra stands her ground. When Assata again inquires why her mother is "giving up," Sandra claims her right to protect her body from further invasion:

> I'm not, Assata. I'm fighting with everything I have left. Cutting and more cutting until there is nothing left of my womb. Three years of cutting and slicing, and pricking and burning. . . . It didn't feel like *my* body anymore. So many things in my life have been beyond my control. *I'm* doing the . . . cutting, chopping, and slicing. With help from my daughter. (56)

Ultimately Assata comes to accept, if not understand, her mother's reasons for facing her death unimpeded by additional medical intervention.

In *My Left Breast* the condemnation of inadequate medical personnel is overt. Early in the play Susan recounts implacably one doctor's misdiagnosis of benign fibroadenoma and her initial acceptance of that diagnosis. Months later and in pain, she seeks an opinion from a second physician, who biopsies her breast and confirms that she has cancer. Mistakes she can tolerate, but Susan is moved to resist when the errors of medical practitioners give way to what she perceives as malice:

> There were two positive nodes. I went through eleven months of chemotherapy and I had only one more month to go. But at my next to the last treatment, after they removed the IV, the oncologist and his nurse looked at me with what I distinctly recognized as menace. I thought, they're trying to kill me. If I come back again, they'll kill me. I never went back. (219)

Although some might describe Susan's reaction as paranoid, her act of resistance has worked to her benefit, since she has survived for twelve years without a recurrence of her cancer. Susan's survival, however, occurs at the cost of her bones. Thrown into early menopause by estrogen-depriving chemotherapy, she develops osteoporosis in her thirties and is driven to consult a bone specialist whom she detests.

The subsequent consultation scene reveals Miller's frustration at the imperiousness of some physicians, the imprecision of their treatments, and the economic injustices of the breast cancer industry:

> "Here are your choices," the bone specialist in L.A. said. "Pick one. A shot every day of Calcitonin, which costs a fortune. I wouldn't do it. Etidronate, which can cause softening of the bones. Or Tamoxifen, an antiestrogen that acts like an estrogen."
>
> I really hate this arrogant, out of touch, son of a bitch specialist, you know? But my internist concurs, and him I love. So, I take the Tamoxifen.
>
> Side effects: Increase in blood clots, endometrial cancer, liver changes.
>
> (229)

While Susan's worst side effect from the Tamoxifen is aching ovaries, her ribs continue to fracture when she maintains the prescribed exercise regimen. Hence she consults a gerontologist and experiences yet again the sense that this "gracious woman" is impatient and incompetent. "Tired of hearing me whine," Susan explains, the doctor asks her patient to experiment: "All right, look, I know this sounds like I'm waffling, but I think I want to put you on Etidronate. . . . We'll follow you closely for a year" (229–30). Although Susan takes the prescription, she decides not to fill it, having maintained little confidence in medical authority.

As might be expected since they take place in hospital settings, *Wit* and *The Waiting Room* provide especially ferocious interrogations of medical politics and women's cancers. Unlike *Sistahs* and *My Left Breast*, these two plays feature male doctors and researchers whose own words and actions call their motives into question. Jason, the self-absorbed resident who treats Vivian at the teaching hospital where she is a patient, has a laughable bedside manner. "Why don't you, um, sort of lie back, and—oh—relax," he urges Vivian, as if women whose feet are in stirrups can ever relax. Their doctor-patient relationship is further complicated by the fact that he was her student in a metaphysical poetry course just a few years ago. "Yes," Vivian assures the audience, "having a former student give me a pelvic exam was thoroughly degrading—and I use the term deliberately" (32). No longer in awe of his teacher, Jason uses her body as a text, pointing to various parts and speaking to medical students about and over her still form. Vivian recognizes fully the irony of her situation. "They read me like a book," she tells the audience during one all-too-public medical exam. "Once I did the teaching, now I am taught" (37).[5]

In his lectures, moreover, Jason employs medical jargon designed to exclude the layperson and intimidate students. The medication Vinplatin becomes Vin, tumors are "de-bulked," patient charts are "I & O sheets" (36–37, 47). Vivian, however, refuses to be excluded: "My only defense is the acquisition of vocabulary" (44). As illustration, she riffs on the medical term *neuropenia,* likening it to a series of philosophical words on which *she* is the expert—"ratiocination, concatenation, coruscation, and tergiversation"—terms that connote a movement from logical reasoning to glittering insight to strategic evasion. Surely words in "Cancerland" are often used to obfuscate rather than to clarify, as Vivian is fully aware.

Edson uses the technique of simultaneous discourse to give Vivian's voice equal weight to the voices of her doctors. On stage, Vivian often muses aloud as Jason and her other physician, Dr. Kelekian, instruct their students. Stage directions reveal that the men's words are "barely audible," though their gestures are clear; Vivian's words provide an authoritative voice over:

> *Vivian:* "Grand Rounds." The term is theirs. Not "Grand" in the traditional sense of sweeping or magnificent. Not "Rounds" as in a musical canon, or a round of applause (though either would be refreshing at this point). Here, "Rounds" seems to signify darting around the main issue . . . which I suppose would be the struggle for life . . . *my* life . . . with heated discussions of side effects, other complaints, additional treatments.

> *Jason:* Very late detection. Staged as a four upon admission. Hexam-etho-phosphacil with Vinplatin to potentiate. Hex at 300 mg. per meter squared. Vin at 100. Today is cycle two, day three. Both cycles at the *full dose.* (The FELLOWS are impressed.)
> The primary site is—Here *(He puts his finger on the spot on her abdomen),* behind the left ovary. Metastases are suspected in the peritoneal cavity—here. And—here. *(He touches those spots.)*

Vivian does not lie in silence as she is displayed and probed, nor does she fail to note the competitive atmosphere that Jason's classroom manner fosters—partly because she recognizes it as a style she once employed with her own students. "Full of subservience, hierarchy, gratuitous displays, sublimated rivalries," she observes of her physician's performance; "I feel right at home. It is just like a graduate seminar" (37).

Although Vivian identifies to some degree with Jason's pedagogical pretensions, Edson ultimately presents this young physician not merely as arrogant but as irresponsible. He consistently privileges his own career goals over Vivian's care and rights, an attitude that costs him dearly when he calls in an emergency team to revive the dying woman, having ignored the fact that she has signed a "Do Not Resuscitate" (DNR) order. Jason's character as chief resident contrasts dramatically with that of Vivian's nurse, Susie Monahan, who offers her the option of signing the DNR order in the first place (a job that should have been the doctor's) and then insists that the protocol Vivian has chosen be followed. When Jason brings in the team and begins pumping Vivian's chest, Susie shouts, "She's DNR!" and tries to push the doctor away when he fails to heed her exhortations; Jason shoves Susie in turn, claiming Vivian's body as his object of inquiry: "She's Research!" (81–82). Thus Edson dramatizes the extent to which the cancer patient risks becoming dehumanized in the modern teaching hospital. The Code Team that Jason erroneously summons, however, holds him responsible for his mistake: "It's a doctor fuckup.—What is he, a resident?" (85) As the dying Vivian leaves her bed, "naked, and beautiful," Jason laments "Oh, God," bemoaning not her death but the blemish on his record (85).

The objectifying characters in *The Waiting Room* include Douglas, a surgeon who, the stage directions inform us, is "excellent with bodies, and befuddled by the people who inhabit them"; Larry, the vice president of a drug company and board member of the cancer center where Douglas works; and Ken, a Food and Drug Administration (FDA) official described as "a scientist turned bureaucrat" (7). Loomer uses ironic dialogue to reveal these men's condescension toward cancer patients. "You know how vulnerable these people are—they're like children," claims Larry to Ken (47). She also exposes the men's unwillingness to acknowledge flaws in their treatment methods, their dismissal of alternative treatments, and their complicity in a multibillion-dollar cancer industry. Of the four playwrights under discussion, only Loomer takes on the FDA and the pharmaceuticals, and she does so with a vengeance. In act 1, scene 2, for example, Wanda explains to Douglas that her breast implants have malfunctioned: "The foam broke down. The casing hardened. It's funny, I can keep a couch six years, I can't keep a pair of tits six months" (17). Unmoved by her attempts to use self-deprecating humor as a relaxation tool, the doctor replies by spouting the party line: "Well, the FDA believes there is not enough evidence to justify having silicone implants removed if the woman is not having symptoms." When Wanda expresses relief that her implants are not harming her, however, Douglas acknowledges that "unfortunately, there is no sure way to monitor for bleed, leakage, rupture—" (18). Women and their physicians must obey FDA guidelines, he insists, even if those guidelines are potentially harmful.

Another political topic on which Loomer focuses is the FDA's refusal to make a successful Jamaican-based cancer treatment, Carson's serum, available to patients in the United States. Although Douglas's nurse, Brenda, who is from Jamaica, attests to the viability of this serum, the male researchers dismiss her as an unreliable source. Several scenes in the play take place in the steam room of a local health club, where Douglas, Larry, and Ken are pampered by Asian women they call "hon" and where they discuss the latest clinical trials. To his credit, Douglas hopes that his hospital will test the serum, given its success rates in Jamaica; Larry, however, prefers another drug:

> Larry: Well, I love Jamaica. . . . (Lightly) And you know, from what I've heard, Carson's serum isn't really all that different from INT-2, which Jones Pharmaceuticals is working on at Smith Memorial right now. And doing quite well with actually.
> Douglas: But INT-2 is toxic, isn't it?
> Larry: All drugs have side effects—
> Douglas: Not Carson's serum apparently.
> Larry: (Elbows Douglas) According to your nurse?
> Douglas: The girl's had two years of medical school, Larry.
> Larry: You boning her?
> Douglas: Am I—? No. I just thought it would be interesting for us to give this a try, Larry. And I'd think you'd be interested too, as a member of the board of Smith Memorial . . . if not as a vice president of Jones Pharmaceuticals—which stands to make a killing on INT-2. (32–33)

The playwright uses Douglas' relative open-mindedness to unmask the real reason Larry resists allowing clinical trials of Carson's serum: it is not to his economic advantage. We later learn that the FDA resists it too, on the grounds that the serum is "unproven." Furthermore, this scene exposes the sexist perspective that if Douglas takes his nurse seriously, he must be sleeping with her—or so runs patriarchal logic. Through Douglas's challenge to Larry, Loomer calls this logic into question.

Ultimately nurse Brenda emerges as Loomer's spokesperson on behalf of economic justice and fairness in research of women's cancer. Brenda's case in point regarding the viability of Carson's serum is her own mother in Jamaica, as she later explains to Douglas and his patients: "My mother . . . got cancer. And she couldn't scare it away. Hmmmm-hmmmm. Doctors took a breast, it jumped to the other one. They took that, it jumped to the bones. Like a lizard with little feet. Quick little fucker. Doctors chasing it all over her body" (42). Thanks to Carson's serum, however, she is doing well, "back at work cleaning houses" (42). Such testimonials have little impact on the physician, however, and even less on the FDA and drug company officials. In act 2, scene 4, an enraged Brenda, frustrated by the intransigence of the doctor for whom she works, exposes the motive that despite his goodwill, Douglas refuses to see:

> Brenda: (Quietly.) Maybe you good people just don't want to fix cancer. Maybe there's a cancer industry out there and it does not want to die. After all, no one is in business for their health—
> Douglas: (Voice rising.) Oh fine. Now we are getting hysterical—
> Brenda: I am a hysterical woman, Douglas—I'm *stressed!*—forty-six thousand women died last year—we don't even put their names on a quilt!
> (58)

Traditionally considered a sickness of the womb and used through the ages to denigrate the bodies and minds of women, hysteria emerges as a condition Brenda wants to claim—on her own behalf and that of other outraged women. What does it mean to live in a society in which women's cancers receive too little in research money, where alternative treatments proven effective in other countries are denied to women, where women who call attention to these inequities are denigrated? The playwright ultimately indicts Douglas for his sexism and the U.S. cancer industry for its arrogance and greed. In this indictment Loomer echoes the viewpoint of feminist activists who expose the hypocrisy of "the multinational corporate enterprise that with the one hand doles out carcinogens and disease and, with the other, offers expensive, semi-toxic pharmaceutical treatment" (Ehrenreich 52).

A RECIPROCAL "RICOCHET OF GAZES"

In "Frame-Up: Feminism, Psychoanalysis, Theatre" Barbara Freedman comments on the appropriative dimensions of the "spectatorial gaze" on which much conventional theater depends:

> Theatre calls the spectatorial gaze into play by exhibiting a purloined
> gaze, a gaze that announces it has always been presented to our eyes; is
> designed only to be taken up by them. The spectatorial gaze takes the bait
> and stakes its claim to a resting place in the field of vision which beckons
> it—only to have its gaze fractured, its look stared down by a series of
> gazes which challenge the place of its look and expose it as in turn defined
> by the other. (74)

Although women's bodies onstage have been especially subjected to this
fetishizing and sexualizing gaze, a goal of feminist theater has been to
undermine this gaze without denying its tyranny. If traditional theater
has been, in Freedman's words, "the place where a male ruling class has
been able to play at being the excluded other . . . to identify with the place
of a mother's look . . . and to control the woman's looking back," then
feminist theater offers "the opportunity to reframe that moment from a
point of view alien to it" (74).

While Freedman views such reframing in terms of fracture and alienation, Rebecca Schneider advocates the building of reciprocity among
playwrights, actors, directors, and audiences. "What can reciprocity
look like?" she muses. "How can we *do* it? How do we access reciprocity in our approach to alterity, our approach to "objects" of study as well
as our approach to our "selves"? (7–8). Although such reciprocity is
admittedly difficult to envision, feminist performance narratives that
foreground women's explicit bodies in ways that subvert masculinist
appropriation facilitate a "complicit, satiable reciprocity between viewer
and viewed rather than the traditional perspectival one-way-street relationship" (Schneider 8). As I have argued, women's cancer plays fracture the spectatorial gaze by presenting women's ill bodies without sexualization; they promote reciprocity by inviting audiences to witness
bodily suffering and female agency with both empathy and a heightened
awareness of the plays' political implications.

To be sure, some audience members feel alienated by representations
of women's cancers. Despite rave reviews, for example, *Wit* evoked
ambivalence from viewers unprepared to confront such agony. As one
reviewer noted, this play "was considered so much of a downer that it
was originally rejected by almost every theater that read it" (Martini 23).
Similarly, for many there occurs a tension between witness and spectacle
when, in *Sistahs*, Sandra wipes her vagina, strips off her bloody skirt,
and hides it behind the sofa. *Must* we witness this private ritual in a pub-

lic space? Yet audiences in New York came in droves to see *Wit,* and theatergoers responded positively to *Sistahs, My Left Breast,* and *The Waiting Room* as well. To understand why, we must consider the questions that theorist Jackie Stacey poses regarding audience engagement with cancer texts: "What is the particular appeal of these cancer narratives in contemporary culture? How do the different medical knowledges and practices which people with cancer may come across offer the patient particular ways of constructing stories about themselves and their illnesses?" (21)

Certainly it is the actors' job as well as the playwright's to convince spectators of the empathic power of ill women's onstage embodiment. Indeed, actors are the primary agents of embodied consciousness, as Susan Bassnett has argued:

> For the playwright, the actor's body is, of course, the channel through which the play comes to life, but at a time when physicality is of such significance in theatre and cinema, it is not surprising that there should be a strong emphasis on the body in the work of many playwrights. No longer merely a vehicle for speaking the words written in the script, the body becomes the site of another theatrical language. (79)

In women's performance narratives of cancer, women's ruptured bodies "speak" in ways that many theatergoers have not previously experienced. Graphic depictions of suffering move many members of an audience, reminding them that everyone has lost some beloved woman or child to cancer or fears doing so and that all women and children—and, for that matter, all men—are at risk.

Moreover, the protagonists' outrage and the plays' in-your-face humor call spectators to awareness and action. As Jo Anna Isaak notes in her study of women artists' representations of cancer, the shock of what Freud called "primary narcissism" presented boldly evokes empathic laughter in audiences and mitigates against the attribution of victim status to the artists and their texts. In Freud's words, humor

> has something liberating about it; but it also has something of grandeur and elevation. . . . The grandeur in it clearly lies in the triumph of narcissism, the victorious assertion of the ego's invulnerability. The ego refuses to be distressed by the provocations of reality, to let itself be compelled to suffer. It insists that it cannot be affected by the traumas of the external world; it shows, in fact, that such traumas are no more than the occasions for it to gain pleasure. (quoted in Isaak 50)

Isaak's point in evoking Freudian theory is that many women artists "use narcissism as a performative 'act'" in their depictions of cancer in ways that "open the possibility of women's strategic occupation of narcissism as a site of pleasure and a form of resistance to assigned sexual and social roles" (54).

The fresh "theatrical language" that Bassnett attributes to women's performance narratives of cancer and the "primary narcissism" that Isaak views as transgressive arguably contribute to a collaborative knowledge and ethos that evoke reciprocity among playwright, performers, and viewers. Schneider describes this collaboration as "a project of recognizing the ricochet of gazes, the histories of who-gets-to-see-what-where" (184). Theatrical representations of women's cancers offer reciprocity in part because historically the one-dimensional perspectival gaze has been predictable and overcirculated, thus fostering a distorted audience-actor dynamic by which "masculinized producers are delineated from feminized consumers, just as the masculinized viewer is dislocated from the feminized view" (Schneider 8). Women's cancer plays enrich viewers by presenting them with new forms of embodied knowledge via illness testimonies rarely before recounted in public but available to be witnessed now in unconventional theatrical productions. These plays further enrich viewers by investing in them the power of a reciprocal gaze that richochets daringly rather than targeting them through a linear gaze that narrows and delimits.

Another possible reason for the popularity of these plays, at least among feminist viewers, is that the theatrical foregrounding of women's cancer-affected bodies refuses to reinscribe patriarchy. This is not easy to do. Indeed, one risk that feminist playwrights take in producing cancer narratives for the stage in the age of Oprah is that some audience members will respond as voyeurs rather than as compassionate witnesses to the protagonists' testimonies. Certainly feminist scholars have been aware since the 1970s that a problem with women's onstage reclamation of their bodies, especially their unclothed bodies, was that there could be

no guarantee that the naked body in this "woman-identified model" would subvert the sign of the "feminine" in dominant systems of gender representation. As art historian Griselda Pollock explained, the "attempt to decolonise the female body [is] a tendency which walks a tightrope between subversion and reappropriation, and often serves rather to consolidate the potency of signification rather than actually to rupture it." (Aston 9)

I argue, nonetheless, that patriarchal signification *is* ruptured when the naked body displayed is bald and shriveled yet luminous, as is Vivian's in *Wit*—or when the breast displayed is missing, marked by a puckered horizontal scar, yet eerily present, as is Susan's in *My Left Breast*. Signification is ruptured because the onstage presentation of such forbidden images as a wrinkled female corpse or a flat, scarred breast disrupts the all-too-familiar spectacle of women's sexualized bodies on prurient display, vulnerable to masculinist appropriation. As Rosemarie Garland Thomson has argued, feminist counterrepresentations "produce a powerful visceral violation by exchanging the spectacle of the eroticized breast, which has been desensationalized by its endless circulation, with the medicalized image of the scarred breast, which has been concealed from public view," thereby challenging "oppressive representational practices" ("Integrating" 12). Ultimately, therefore, women's performance narratives of cancer participate in feminist decolonization by offering, in Elin Diamond's words, "a female body in representation that resists fetishization and a viable position for the female spectator" (44)—and, I would argue, a viable position for the empathic male spectator as well.

Thus envisioned, the plays of Edson, Miller, Loomer, and Bailey and Lewis contribute significantly to a feminist theatrical praxis that Schneider has termed "inspecting the cracks": countering patriarchal representations of women's bodies as "always already different, aberrant, cracked," yet "courting aberrance" by featuring explicit bodies, ill or dying, "stretched across this paradox like canvases across the framework of the Symbolic Order" (184). Elaine Aston has described feminist theatrical praxis similarly, claiming that it operates "formally and ideologically as a 'sphere of disturbance'" (17), a sphere in which audience ambivalence can, for many viewers, be transformed into a desire to participate in cancer-related activism. Such activism may be mainstream— racing for the cure, wearing a pink ribbon—or it may be radical: tattooing one's scar, acting up, boycotting certain pharmaceutical companies, engaging in guerrilla warfare. Such is the power of feminist theater, a "live art form in which political change can be effected directly" (Goodman 221). As audience members, potential activists, and intimate *Others*, we bear witness to the fractured borders that women who represent cancer onstage negotiate.

3. ENTERING "THE HOUSE/ OF LIGHTNING"

Resistance & Transformation in U.S. Women's Breast Cancer Poetry

The topic of breast cancer raises urgently the question of how women's discourse can be voiced, and especially in culturally sanctioned forms like poetry.
—Melissa F. Zeiger, *Beyond Consolation: Death, Sexuality, and the Changing Shapes of Elegy*

*I*N HER CHAPTER ON breast cancer poetry in *Beyond Consolation*, literary critic Melissa F. Zeiger laments the fact that thirty years after the advent of the second wave of the women's movement, relatively few U.S. women poets had explored this topic in depth—that breast cancer suffered from a troubling cultural and aesthetic "inaudibility." To be sure, by the early 1990s, when Zeiger began writing, feminist poets from Anne Sexton to Adrienne Rich to Marge Piercy had mourned the passing of mothers or friends from this disease; African American poet Audre Lorde had documented her struggles in poems and in a memoir, *The Cancer Journals;* and Leatrice H. Lifshitz's *Her Soul beneath the Bone,* a collection of breast cancer poems written largely by lesser-known women, had received minor critical attention. Nonetheless, Zeiger argues, the fact that cancer poems remained scattered and encoded suggested a "profound censorship" at work, whether societally or individually mandated. "The peculiarity of breast cancer elegies," she concludes, "is that of an elegiac discourse that disappears even as it forms—a discourse that becomes almost impossible to speak or hear" (138–39).

As the 1990s progressed, however, numerous American women published sustained, dynamic poetic sequences that feature breast cancer as their dominant theme. These clusters of poems range from brief sequential meditations to book-length volumes; they focus on such embodied images as the breast itself, the damaged tissue that surrounds it, the nipple (whether present or excised), and the surgical scar. Interwoven themes recur in these cancer sequences, some of them familiar poetic motifs—the epic journey, the acceptance of mortality, the process of healing; other themes distinctive to women's representations of cancer—the effects of mastectomy on body image and sexual desire, for example, and the ambivalence many women feel toward prostheses. Breast cancer sequences comprise an important new category of long poems by women, a "form of expansion" that can best be characterized, in Lynn Keller's words, as a "generic hybrid" (1–3). Since 1960, Keller observes, there has been a burgeoning of women's long poems whose formal varieties include sonnet and meditative sequences, irregular lyric cycles, collage poems, extended dramatic monologues, and heroic epics (3). These long poems often draw upon such lyrical conventions, in critic Marjorie Perloff's words, as "the solitary 'I' in the timeless moment, the emotive response to the landscape, the reliance on the consort of images to create meaning, and the ecstatic present-tense mode" (425). However, women's long poems privilege as well elements of narrative that may be linear or circular in form, autobiographical or detached in tone, and fragmented, dislocated, or postmodern in style. As part of this oeuvre, breast cancer sequences blend lyric and narrative techniques to resist the marginalization of ill women and inaugurate new poetic representations of cancer.

Breast cancer poetry thus participates in what Susan Stanford Friedman has called "a project to assert female identity and agency in a world that would confine subjectivity in forms of alterity" ("Craving" 23). The alterity of women's cancerous bodies emerges as a theme in many women's cancer poems but nowhere as overtly as in Hilda Raz's "Day-Old Bargain," in which a male interlocutor implores a woman poet, "don't write about that / surgery." Indeed, he is appalled at the prospect of a poetics of breast cancer:

> When you give over your breast
> to cancer, for God's sake don't
> write about it.
>
> (*Divine* 23)

Raz and other women poets resist such prohibitions, however, choosing instead to document both the desperation that many women feel when cancer invades and the sense of redemption that can occur when healing begins. "Next day I opted for surgery," Raz explains, confronting her male colleague wryly, "cut that mama off and saved my life." Now, she continues, "I hang on for dear life." Hanging on to life, as an infant hangs on to its mother's breast, requires that the speaker move on as well, having embraced the possibility of a healthy future. After surgery she finds sustenance in gardening: "filled pockets with seedpods, got bulbs / I shoehorned into clay pots for life's sake" (23). Poems such as Raz's resist efforts to deem women's cancer an inappropriate literary topic; they reclaim women's ailing bodies as sites of personal, political, and aesthetic power.

Moreover, as Zeiger notes, contemporary women increasingly write "against elegy," revising traditional conventions of lamentation in their breast cancer poems. "These poets proceed by exploring the multiplicities of their own subject positions and discourses," Zeiger explains, speaking in particular of Audre Lorde and Marilyn Hacker, the two poets on whose work she focuses. "When doing so within existing frameworks and conventions of elegy—the teleological movement of which has traditionally been toward resolution, female silencing, and detachment from the dead—they almost necessarily mobilize a critique of elegy and a resistance to its norms" (140). For many chroniclers of breast cancer, the melancholia of mourning has given way to other modes of creative expression. Indeed, I argue that cancer poets of the 1990s compose long sequences that are transformational rather than elegiac. They do not deny grief or shock but refuse to dwell there. Instead, these women document the suffering and the healing they have experienced as well as the societal crisis that the breast cancer epidemic represents.

In addition, women who inscribe cancer poetically resist and transform their cultural/psychoanalytic designation as "abject." As Judith Butler points out, "abjection . . . literally means to cast off, away, or out and, hence, presupposes and produces a domain of agency from which it is differentiated. . . . The notion of abjection designates a degraded or cast out status within the terms of sociality; indeed, what is foreclosed or repudiated . . . is precisely what may not reenter the field of the social without threatening psychosis, the dissolution of the subject itself" (*Bodies* 243). Other theorists, from Julia Kristeva to Allison Kimmich, have argued that women with life-threatening illnesses are often viewed pejoratively as abject Others, banished from "the field of the social" by virtue of their pain and medicalization. Yet abjection implies the occupation of a space both inside and outside the body (and the body politic); thus it can also be reconstituted as a powerful locus of transgression. As Kristeva explains, abjection "disturbs identity, system, order"; it is that which "does not respect boundaries, systems, rules. The in-between, the ambiguous, the composite" (4). By moving "from abject to subject," then, women poets destigmatize cancer and delineate alternative definitions of female subjectivity (Kimmich 225).

A number of distinguished U.S. women composed poetic sequences about breast cancer from the mid-1980s through the 1990s, including Linda Pastan, Marilyn Hacker, Judith Hall, and Sandra Steingraber.[1] This chapter focuses, however, on four poets whose representations of the shock of breast cancer diagnosis, the surgical process, and its complicated aftermath are especially distinctive: Audre Lorde, Lucille Clifton, Alicia Suskin Ostriker, and Hilda Raz. All four poets employ as recurring tropes *silence, scars, borders,* and *light(ning);* three of them use the trope of *winter* as well (Lorde is the exception, perhaps because she lived her final years in the Caribbean). Each of these poets writes either an extended lyric sequence (Clifton and Ostriker) or an entire volume of poems dedicated to this theme (Lorde and Raz). Two poets are African American (Lorde and Clifton), and two are Jewish American (Ostriker and Raz); three of the four bring their ethnicity directly into their poetic representations of cancer.[2] In *The Marvelous Arithmetics of Distance* (1993) Lorde draws upon African goddesses and feminist community to document her own process of dying from metastasized breast cancer and to delineate the creative legacy she wishes to leave her readers. In *The Terrible Stories* (1996) Clifton identifies as an African griot who probes the consuming fear she encounters after her diagnosis of breast cancer, her transformation of that fear, and the humility she attains by facing her mortality. In *The Mastectomy Poems* (from *The Crack in Everything,* 1996) Ostriker explores complex issues of family relationships, body image, and erotic desire that arise when she confronts cancer. And in *Divine Honors* (1997) Raz "tells us cancer" in postmodern collage poems that reveal the anger and resilience that breast surgery evokes. As Lorde rightly claims, "each woman responds to the crisis that breast cancer brings to her life out of a whole pattern, which is the design of who she is and how her life has been lived. The weave of everyday existence is the training ground for how she handles crisis" (*Cancer* 9). Certainly these four poets chronicle their experiences of breast cancer without denying either the crisis that cancer instigates or the sustaining power of human connections to help them heal. By paying homage, with Clifton, to "the splendor of one breast / on one woman" (*Terrible* 23), these poets transform cultural narratives of women's illnesses, subjectivities, and embodiment.

"THE SWEET WORK DONE": AUDRE LORDE'S *THE MARVELOUS ARITHMETICS OF DISTANCE*

Death
folds the corners of my mouth
into a heart-shaped star

—Lorde, "Speechless"

In November 1992, after a fifteen-year struggle, the self-described "black lesbian feminist warrior poet" Audre Lorde died of breast cancer that had metastasized to her liver and other internal organs. The journey of her dying, which she chronicled poetically during her last three years in particular, appeared posthumously in a 1993 volume whose enigmatic title she elucidates in the final lines of her opening poem, "Smelling the Wind"

No reckoning allowed
save the marvelous arithmetics
of distance.

(3)

The mathematical images are telling. A person reckons when calculating figures, and s/he solves computational problems via arithmetic, an area of study in which integers, or whole numbers, feature prominently. Certainly the issue of how a woman remains whole after losing a breast, especially once she knows her cancer has spread elsewhere, lies at the core of cancer literature. As a feminist Lorde chose to confront this question directly, to break silence and thereby document her struggle in a manner useful to other women. Since Lorde expressed a lifelong commitment to wholeness, to integrity of voice, her philosophical vision emerges in the title lines as well. What counts, she implies—what, in the face of death, can and must be counted—is the bittersweet task of reflecting back upon an artistic and activist life well lived. She marvels at the awe of witnessing death on the horizon, her "sweet work done" (53).

Lorde analyzed her experience of breast cancer in prose as well as poetry, and her view of the politics of women's cancer, as articulated in *The Cancer Journals* (1980) and *A Burst of Light* (1988), illuminates her final poems in myriad ways. In *The Cancer Journals* she rejects silence on behalf of many women, especially African Americans and lesbians, whose "anger and pain and fear about cancer" had been ignored or disrespected by a white-dominated and patriarchal culture. She employs recurring images of Amazons, those legendary, one-breasted warriors who inspire her to approach her cancer with ferocity. Moreover, she questions the tactics and hegemony of what she refers to as "Cancer, Inc."—the American Medical Association, the American Cancer Society, the Society's Reach for Recovery program: organizations that lack sufficient awareness of racial, sexual, and cultural differences among women. In particular, she resists misogynistic discourses that label women with cancer as victims and then blame them for their disease, medical advice books that prescribe mastectomy for any woman with breast cancer and then present it as a source of "disfigurement" and "mutilation," unexamined assumptions that prosthetic use and reconstructive surgery are vital to all women's self-esteem, and the imperialistic economic agenda to which she believes Cancer, Inc. contributes. As a strategy for resistance and transformation she recommends feminist solidarity; indeed, she writes *The Cancer Journals*

> for other women of all ages, colors, and sexual identities who recognize that imposed silence about any area of our lives is a tool for separation and powerlessness, and for myself, having tried to voice some of my feelings and thoughts about the travesty of prosthesis, the pain of amputation, the function of cancer in a profit economy, my confrontation with mortality, the strength of women loving, and the power and rewards of self-conscious living. (*Cancer* 9)

In *A Burst of Light*, her cancer having metastasized, Lorde approached her illness more urgently. In a journal format she reveals her initial shock at this recurrence, her decision to undergo chemotherapy as well as explore homeopathic alternatives, and the anguish that she finds difficult to subdue. Writing from the politically vexed location of West Berlin, where neo-Nazi groups proliferate and African Americans are welcomed by some citizens but viewed suspiciously by others, she struggles with feelings of alienation. She reveals as well her agonizing suspicion that racial and gender oppression have contributed to a wounded internal landscape that has made her unduly susceptible to the ravages of cancer:

> In this loneliest of places, I examine every decision I make within the light of what I've learned about myself and that self-destructiveness implanted inside of me by racism and sexism and the circumstances of my life as a Black woman.

> *Mother, why were we armed to fight*
> *with cloud wreathed swords and javelins of dust?* (7)

As in much of Lorde's writing, prose and poetry converge here to create a map of the painful cultural and self-scrutiny that breast cancer demands. Her anguished resistance is evident in the italicized question she poses to her Amazonian "Mother," the combative muse who inspires her in struggle. This resistance ultimately facilitates a transformation that celebrates the value of "living fully—how long is not the point. How and why take total precedence" (15).

The strength that Lorde garners through her experience of cancer sustains the poetic landscape of *A Marvelous Arithmetics of Distance*. In this volume she embraces the paradox of living, in wonder and in grace, even as she detaches from this world and sails toward the unknown. The verb *sail* has special resonance, given the epic allusions that occur throughout the book. In its opening lines the poet imagines herself "rushing headlong / into new silence."[3] She anticipates "riding my anchor / one sweet season" before "cast[ing] off on another voyage," heading for "the end of the jetty" (3, 59). With her lover, Gloria, Lorde has lived on a Caribbean island where the surf is omnipresent, the tropical flowers lush. Despite the ravages of cancer and Hurricane Hugo, which destroyed parts of her house, the poet has determined to reconstruct her damaged places and journey whole. In a sequence of lyric poems that reckon with metastasized cancer and imminent death, poems clustered in the volume's final quarter, Lorde travels backward to inspect the interstices of her life; in place, to commemorate the now; and forward toward her next incarnation as "a vessel of light."

"Restoration: A Memorial—9–18–91" situates the poet in "Berlin again after chemotherapy," poised at the edge of what will be her final year of life. Having prescient knowledge of her death, Lorde honors the fluidity of time and the power of her own truth:

I reach behind me once more
for days to come
sweeping around the edges of authenticity.

As in many of Lorde's cancer poems, border imagery is evident here; the
boundaries that the poet negotiates seem especially salient in the context
of Berlin, whose walls between East and West have only recently fallen.
As the chemo works to destroy her cancer, she muses upon another
agent of destruction, Hugo, which "blew one life away" on her distant
island home and ravaged countless other lives. She reflects as well upon
the hovering presence of "Death, like a burnt star, / perched on the rim
of my teacup" and thereby traces yet another shifting boundary. Despite
these ominous allusions, the poet speaks paradoxically of security. After
all, Berlin provides "the safety of exile," even though it offers only an
"alien and temporary haven" as she recovers from invasive cancer treatment. Back home, it would be hard to get the rest she needs, since Hugo
has wreaked havoc. Still,

quite a bit of the house is left
our bedroom spared
except for the ankle-deep water
and terrible stench.

What she longs for most is the sound of laughter. Hope of returning
buoys her, yet this desire is tempered with reality:

a few trees still stand
in a brand-new landscape
but the searoad is impassable.

Penetrating closed roads, however, crossing borders, is this poet's spe-
cialty. "No escape. No return" is a mantra she cannot accept, for she sees
"no other life / half so sane." Reading her lover's letter, then, as her
"poisoned fingers / slowly return to normal," she envisions herself at
home, "learning to laugh again" (*Marvelous* 40–41).
   "Construction" presents a dying woman's *ars poetica*. This brief
poem's controlling images are astrological, its theme a confident prediction of immortality through her art:

*Timber seasons better
if it is cut in the fourth quarter
of a barren sign.*

Followers of astrology know that barren signs occur in autumn, not in the watery Aquarius of January or the vibrant Cancer of June. Ironically, the disease of cancer often causes humans to waste away, but the ailment itself feeds voraciously—a characteristic upon which the resilient poet seizes. A body nourished by cancer has endless potential for growth:

> In Cancer
> the most fertile of skysigns
> I shall build a house
> that will stand forever.

(47)

The poet speaks subversively of the art she has created out of her engagement with cancer and of her own poetic legacy (a word she uses often in this collection to describe gifts left by her parents as well as the gifts she will leave). Writing through and about her cancer, perversely fertile, Lorde bequeaths to her readers the shelter of her poems, the rooms of which comprise a permanent dwelling.

In "Speechless" the themes of silence and awe reappear, as the poet imagines herself a lost child in a fairy tale, seduced like Hansel and Gretel into following a bread-crumb trail toward an unnamed destination, her fingers "sticky with loss." This child-self, "like a goose bound for the oven," travels in partial oblivion through a forest where "giddy trees wait shaken." Clearly Lorde evokes an old adage; her goose indeed is cooked. In previous poems darkness has been a comfort to the poet, who identifies with its blackness, but here the night looms ominously; its primary source of light, the moon, "hangs like a spotlit breast." The drooping moon-breast takes the spotlight as the source of her travails: once diseased, it can no longer nurture. In the final stanza death emerges as the grieving poet's nemesis:

> Death
> folds the corners of my mouth
> into a heart-shaped star
> sits on my tongue like a stone
> around which your name blossoms
> distorted.

(48)

This is the most elegiac poem in Lorde's sequence, for she suffers from anticipating her own demise as well as from the inability to speak her lover's name distinctly. The prospect of separation from the beloved leaves her grasping for words.

Although the "blossom" of her lover's name, distorted, is agonizing, Lorde presents flowers elsewhere in this sequence as metaphors of rejuvenation. Her use of star imagery also shifts: in "Speechless" the "heart-shaped star" defines the contours of a mouth that cannot open, but in "The Night-blooming Jasmine" stars breathe inspiration. Here the jasmine plant, personified, serves as the poet's muse, a source of song even in the face of death:

> Lady of the Night   star-breathed
> blooms along the searoad
> between my house and the tasks before me
> calls down a flute
> carved from the legbone of a gull.

However sweet the music of the flute the muse calls down, the poet recognizes that the searoad beckons; soon she must cross it into alien land. Lorde portrays the surgical scar that traverses her upper body as a militarized zone, herself a hand grenade:

> Through the core of me
> a fine rigged wire
> upon which pain will not falter
> nor predict

Who knows when this wire will be tripped, when debilitating pain or death itself will occur? Neither moment is predictable. Still, the poet has entered this dangerous territory before and has refused to view death as inimical:

> I was no stranger to this arena
> at high noon
> beyond was not an enemy
> to be avoided
> but a challenge
> against which my neck grew strong
> against which my metal struck
> and I rang like fire in the sun.

Lorde alludes here to the classic Western film *High Noon*, with its famous standoff between warring gunslingers—an allusion she employs only to reject, since she views death not an inimical but as challenging. Images of resistance give way to transformation, as the poet recalls having once used the midday sun to forge herself anew. Indeed, her metal/mettle still glows; her fiery voice eschews silence.

In the last half of the poem border imagery recurs but appears less threatening. In stanza 3 Lorde joins the border patrol, charged with protecting her scar and finding insight there:

> I still patrol that line
> sword drawn
> lighting red-glazed candles of petition
> along the scar
> the surest way of knowing
> death is a fractured border
> through the center of my days.
>
> (52)

A poet can cross that "fractured border" more readily, she continues, once her "sweet work" is done. As bees full of nectar "drop where they fly / pollen baskets laden," so the writer whose tasks are finished can be sated. Lorde wants to wait a little while, though—to witness again the miracle of the jasmine, whose heady blooms the drunken bees have missed:

> They do not know the Lady of the Night
> blossoms
> between my house and the searoad
> calling down a flute
> carved from the legbone of a gull
> your rich voice
> riding the shadows of conquering air.
>
> (53)

This stanza's partial repetition of the first has an incantatory effect; the Lady, the searoad, and the flute carved from bone recur as sacred iconography. The "rich voice" of the final lines remains ambiguous: is it the muse's voice, the lover's, or the poet's own that refuses to hide in the shadows but insists upon riding them, triumphant?

Lorde completes *The Marvelous Arithmetics of Distance* with two poems that make peace with death and pay homage to the present moment. "Today Is Not the Day" reveals the poet's double bind: how can she confront death directly, seeking solace even in her anguish—and how can she *not?*

> *I can't just sit here*
> *staring death in her face*
> *blinking and asking for a new name*
> *by which to greet her*
>
> *I am not afraid to say*
> *unembellished*
> *I am dying*
> *but I do not want to do it*
> *looking the other way.*
>
> (57)

Wishing to be vigilant but not obsessive, the poet determines to approach this journey actively, to choose speech, not silence. She takes pleasure in her temporary reprieve: this *could* be the day she dies, "but it is not." Instead, the sun shines on her internal landscape,

> the farmhouse in my belly,
> lighting the wellswept alleys
> of the town growing in my liver.
>
> (57)

Rather than imagining her organs as besieged by cancer, Lorde envisions a vibrant village whose streets and buildings are inhabited by the Yoruba goddess Mawu or perhaps her trickster daughter, Afrekete. These deities appear as muses in many of Lorde's earlier writings; now they reside in her body. Tasks await the ailing poet on the day she has been granted, as they await African women everywhere, and Lorde conjures Afrekete to sustain her in this labor:

> Afrekete   my beloved
> feel the sun of my days surround you
> binding our pathways
> we have water to carry
> honey to harvest
> bright seed to plant for the next fair.
>
> (57–58)[4]

Dying is hard work, the poet knows, but human loved ones too have come to help: her daughter, Beth, a medical student who "dangles her stethoscope over the rearview mirror"; her son, Jonathan, a young astronomer who "fine-tunes his fix on Orion / working through another equation"; and her lover, Gloria, "whose difference I learn / with the love of a sister" (58–59).

Ultimately Lorde offers an eloquent vision of the hereafter—not an afterlife, but rather the life that will continue to be vibrant after she exists no longer. "Today could be the day," she asserts once more;

> I could slip anchor and wander
> to the end of the jetty
> uncoil into the waters
> a vessel of light.

Although that day is yet to come, the poet imagines beyond it, watching her lover in the arms of someone else—a "stranger," she tells Gloria, who

> will find you
> coiled on the warm sand
> beached treasure   and love you
> for the different stories
> your seas tell.

(59)

Many dying people would find agonizing the thought of their beloved with another, but in this poem Lorde takes comfort in the continuity of life's intimate rhythms.

These rhythms also permeate the volume's final poem, "The Electric Slide Boogie," which is set on New Year's Eve 1992, at 1:16 A.M. As the sleepless poet hears the sounds of revelry that echo from nearby rooms, she takes pleasure in the celebration of her family and friends. Indeed, their noisy dancing and Gloria's "rich dark laughter" bind her to this world, even as she rests in bed, poised on the edge of worlds to come. "How hard it is," she muses wryly, "to sleep / in the middle of life" (60).

This Lorde consistently refused to do: life would not catch her sleeping. Instead, she determined to write openly of metastasized cancer in a poetic sequence on which she worked until virtually the moment of her death. Having passed through trauma, she found serenity in the rituals of the now.

"ONE NIPPLE LIFTED":
LUCILLE CLIFTON'S *THE TERRIBLE STORIES*

you know how dangerous it is

to be born with breasts
you know how dangerous it is
to wear dark skin
                                             —Clifton, "1994"

Poetry emerges from a heightened state of consciousness, according to
Lucille Clifton, an awareness that she identifies simply as "paying attention." "I think I have always had a mind that connected things" she told
Akasha Hull in a 1998 interview. "No poetry is consciously done. It
comes out of all of what we are" (115). What Clifton identifies as the core
of her poetry, what she *knows,* is the lived experience of female embodiment, "a woman's certainties" of flesh and blood and bone. This experience contains racial as well as gendered dimensions, for the bodies of
African American women are especially marked by danger: subjected to
racist as well as misogynistic violence, often denied prenatal and preventative health care, and more vulnerable to death from breast cancer than
white women's bodies are (Kolata, "Deadliness"). Attributing her
knowledge of these realities to intellect, intuition, and "a family of very
strong women," Clifton draws upon these sources for the strength to
resist racism and sexism and for creative inspiration (Kallet 83). In doing
so she pays homage to what theorist Patricia Hill Collins terms a "black
women's epistemology," drawn from feminist, womanist, and Afrocentric standpoints—an epistemology characterized by an emphasis on personal accountability, the belief that concrete experience is a source of
wisdom and knowledge, a commitment to dialogue as a tool for exploring commonality and difference, and an ethic of empathy (221–25).

Like Lorde, who marvels at "the arithmetics of distance," Clifton
views both her writing and her experience of cancer as full of mystery.
"My family tends to be a spiritual and even perhaps mystical one," she
wrote in 1983. "That certainly influences my life and my work" (138).
For Clifton, mystery reveals itself in light, an image that pervades her
poetry. She entitled a 1992 volume of poetry *The Book of Light;* claimed
in its title poem "I am / lucille, which stands for light"; and acknowledged, in "the light that came to lucille clifton," "the peril of an / unex-

amined life" (209). Although the light she associates with cancer treatment in *The Terrible Stories* glows more ominously, it offers no less knowledge than the mystery of creativity. After all, "radiance" and "radiation" evolve from the same etymological roots, and entering the "house/ of lightning"—Lorde's name for the hospital wing in which she received radiation therapy—initiates a healing process as well as a procedure that temporarily wounds. Cancer is not the only serious disease that Clifton has inscribed in poetry; she has also written of kidney failure and dialysis, and of her subsequent kidney transplant, successful in part because the organ she received came from her eldest daughter (Kallet 83). In the cancer sequence from *The Terrible Stories*, however, she honors the breast as a site of nurture worthy of intense mourning and praise. She thus becomes a village griot seated around the proverbial campfire, naming the mortal fears and abject states that breast cancer evokes in order, finally, to move through them.[5]

The decision to call these poems stories raises immediately the issue of generic boundaries: why does Clifton choose a narrative rather than a poetic trope? She presents one possible answer in the epigrammatic poem with which this volume opens, "telling our stories." The plural pronoun matters here, for these tales belong not only to the teller but also to the women who surround her, daughters and granddaughters and friends from the community. The poet imagines her cancer in this volume as a fox, that stealthiest of predators, that roams near her house in the night:

> the fox came every evening to my door
> asking for nothing.   my fear
> trapped me inside, hoping to dismiss her
> but she sat till morning, waiting.
>
> (9)

This fox emerges as the poet's dark double, a mirror image into whose eyes she must stare and stare through the glass door. Before each turns away, she will come to know the other. How to interpret this shared knowledge lies at the heart of the third stanza's question, which attempts to penetrate the fox's consciousness of the human on whom she gazed:

> did she gather her village around her
> and sing of the hairless moon face,
> the trembling snout, the ignorant eyes?
>
> (9)

The self-portrait here is ruthless; a woman moon-faced, trembling, ignorant would seem no match for a wily fox. In the final stanza, however, the
poet acknowledges the fox not as an adversary but as a shadow self:

> child, I tell you now it was not
> the animal blood i was hiding from,
> it was the poet in her, the poet and
> the terrible stories she could tell.

> (9)

The adjective *terrible* contains a dual meaning: the poet-fox's tales both
frighten and evoke awe in the listener. Indeed, the power of stories is
archetypal, and surely storytelling lies in the domain of poets as well
novelists. As Friedman notes in "Craving Stories," many African American women poets embrace the strategies of narrative in order to "resist
and subvert the stories told by the dominant culture" (17). Clifton's "terrible stories" participate in such resistance.

This fox poem presages an initial sequence, "A Dream of Foxes," in
which Clifton strives to overcome a paralyzing sense of loss—caused
perhaps by cancer's onset, perhaps by the recent death of her husband. In
"dear fox," for instance, the poet fingers stones in the desert, petitioning
them "to heal, not me but the dry mornings / and bitter nights." As she
prays for strength, she is guarded by the fox, in whose company she
imagines abandoning a life that no longer seems her own. In "leaving
fox" she complains of "so many fuckless days and nights," joined in her
loneliness only by a fox that watches constantly and "barks her compassion." Although the poet finally confronts her demons, she wonders in
"one year later" what would have transpired had she run away with her
"sister fox":

> what if,
> then,
> I had reared up baying,
> and followed her off
> into vixen country?
> what then of the moon,
> the room, the bed, the poetry
> of regret?

> (15–17)

The unknown looms, unknowable.

In the volume's second poetic sequence, grimly entitled "From the

Cadaver," Clifton struggles vigorously to wrest meaning from her experience of breast cancer. To chronicle a woman's journey through cancer is to write from beyond the grave, Clifton's title implies; after this illness one feels life's pulse as if reborn. This nine-part sequence ascribes to what the theorist Laura Potts has called the proairetic code: it moves from diagnosis to surgery to confrontation with mortality, from the trauma of postoperative treatment to the ultimate relief of healing (114). The sequence's narrative trajectory is strengthened by several recurring image clusters, most notably of nipples, scars, lightning, wintry landscapes, and tempestuous journeys. The repetition of these tropes unifies the poems and enhances their emotional resonance.

In the first poem of the sequence, "amazons," Clifton joins Lorde in paying tribute to these one-breasted women as her foremothers and guides,

> warriors all
> each cupping one hand around
> her remaining breast
>
> daughters of dahomey
> their name fierce on the planet

According to African legend, the Amazons amputated their breasts voluntarily in order to become better markswomen. Now they welcome the poet to their ranks, for she too is a daughter of Dahomey, her ancestors having hailed from that ancient empire, and she too may need a breast removed. As

> each
> with one nipple lifted
> beckoned to me
> five generations removed,

the poet answers her phone to hear the diagnosis she awaits. The prognosis is mixed: "cancer early detection no / mastectomy not yet." Although one might expect the fierce amazons to begrudge the poet her reprieve, instead they join ranks to celebrate the preservation of her breast:

> my sisters swooped in a circle dance
> audre was with them and i
> had already written this poem

Here Clifton affirms her affiliation with Lorde, whose passing she has mourned and whose imagined presence among the Amazons sustains her. Like Lorde, she celebrates her Dahomeyan strength and her identity as a warrior poet.

"lumpectomy eve" finds the poet dreaming of the lips of her five children, "lips / that nursed and nursed," and of "the lonely nipple / lost in loss" that no longer serves this vital purpose. The nipple's neediness assumes an ominous tone as Clifton muses upon the cancer coursing through her breast, governed perversely by

> the need
> to feed that turns at last
> on itself   that will kill
>
> its body for its hunger's sake

The phrase "all night" appears twice in this short lyric to emphasize the poet's restless dreams; the whisper that she hears recurs as well: "love calls you to this knife / for love for love." A terrible irony lies at this poem's center: the breast with which she has fed and loved her children has now produced a hungry tumor that must be sated; surgery alone will relieve it. The technique of mirroring recurs as well, not through the symbiosis of fox and woman or poet and Amazons, as in prior poems, but through the care the healthy breast provides its ailing double: "all night it is the one breast / comforting the other" (22).

Few poets describe their cancer surgery, since the anesthesia that most procedures require and the trauma that many women experience tend to disqualify the operating room as a site of poetry. As Lorde did in *The Cancer Journals* and as we shall see in the work of Ostriker and Raz, however, writers do sometimes chronicle their immediate pre- and post-operative memories, viewing them as vital to their emotional recovery. Clifton chooses, though, to move from the restless night before her surgery to several weeks later, when she anticipates another difficult transition. In "consulting the book of changes: radiation" she turns again to the trope of doubling. No longer do the Amazons cup their single breast, preparing to leave the rookery for the hunt, as in the first poem of this sequence. Instead, the cancer patient—here a slightly distanced "you"—must do the cupping:

> each morning you will cup
> your breast in your hand

then cover it and ride
into the federal city

> if there are no cherry blossoms
> can there be a cherry tree?

(23)

Following each of the three initial quatrains, in which the poet offers a blueprint of the steps the patient must follow to receive radiation, an indented couplet appears, framed as a metaphysical riddle. Clifton's reference in this first quatrain to Washington, D.C., as the "federal city" both politicizes the poem and lends it an ominous tone, since the U.S. president forges from the White House national health policies that often are inadequate even as the city welcomes tourists to its annual cherry blossom festival. Clifton is no tourist, and her own "blossoms" are at risk, but *why* remains a mystery. Whether cherry trees require blossoms, or whether breasts must always feature nipples (a question posed in stanza 2), is an insoluble riddle.

"The house / of lightning," the site of radiation, exudes in stanza 3 a troubling aura, for "even the children there / will glow in the arms of their kin." As the patient waits alone, she will long for childhood innocence and the protection of parents and lovers:

you will wait to hear your name,
wish you were a child with kin,
wish some of the men you loved
had loved you

> what is the splendor of one breast
> on one woman?

(23)

Clifton's plaintive question pays tribute to the beauty of one-breasted women yet acknowledges subtly a sense of sexual loss. "If someone should touch you now / his hand would flower," the poet assures her wounded self; such is the power of her glowing breast. What happens once the treatment ends provides the subject matter of the poem's final stanza: "after, you will stop to feed yourself. / you have always had to feed yourself." This declaration of independence, however, offers scant comfort to the anxious patient. Indeed, the poem ends not with the philosophical musings that followed earlier quatrains but with a question that reveals the woman's vulnerability: "will I begin to cry?" This elegiac query has a haunting answer: "if you do, you will cry forever" (23).

"1994" offers a retrospective account of the fear that breast cancer evokes in Clifton and her resistance to that terror. Directed to an audience of African American women, the poem meditates in part upon a shared racial vulnerability, on "how dangerous it is / to wear dark skin." The poem employs as well the icy winter landscape that dominates the cancer sequences of many other poets, including Ostriker and Raz. The opening stanzas establish a dialectic between writer and reader:

> I was leaving my fifty-eighth year
> when a thumb of ice
> stamped itself hard near my heart
>
> you have your own story
> you know about the fear the tears
> the scar of disbelief
>
> you know that the saddest lies
> are the ones we tell ourselves
>
>   (24)

Most prominent of such lies, the poet implies, is the belief that "it won't happen to me." Having breasts makes every woman vulnerable to cancer, and mortality, like racism, rears its fearful head everywhere.

The poet goes on to describe the anguish of the year in which she

> woke into the winter
> of a cold and mortal body
>
> thin icicles hanging off
> the one mad nipple weeping

The emotional resonance of these lines is enhanced by the ambiguity of the present participle "weeping": do the icicles or the nipple mourn? Despair can make the cancer victim question God, and Clifton, whose poetry contains many biblical allusions, is no exception. Why must women bear this burden, the poet wonders; "have we not been good children / did we not inherit the earth"? (24) In its numb despair this elegy is reminiscent of Emily Dickinson's "After great pain a formal feeling comes," which compares human anguish to the experience of "freezing persons" who "recollect the snow": "first chill—then stupor— / then the letting go" (#341). Despite the hopelessness that this cold imagery initially evokes, the poem's retrospection hints that victims might miraculously survive by "letting go"—not to death itself, but to a wintry void. "If outlived," Dickinson warns, trauma can be contained, its survivors haunted but alive. Likewise, the cancer patients of whom Clifton speaks might live on; they are freezing but still breathing. Yet as Cathy Caruth has noted in her work on trauma theory, "survival itself . . . can be a crisis," especially if the traumatized person cannot both bear witness to her suffering and find others to witness it (9). Ultimately Clifton identifies other traumatized women, the "you" of the poem, as witnesses, although she ponders whether her poetic musings can offer these witnesses any new insights. "You must know all about this," she admits, "from your own shivering life" (24).

The breast cancer sequences of many women poets examine the scar that results from surgery.[6] For Lorde this ragged line marks a border to be patrolled; for Clifton, a "ribbon of hunger / and desire." In "scar" she addresses this insignia directly, assuring it that "we will learn / to live together" and creating for it endearing names: "empty pocket flap / edge of before and after." Since reciprocity is essential, the poet wonders what her scar will choose to call her. The scar's answer initiates a series of horse-and-rider metaphors that appears in several poems from the sequence:

> woman I ride
> who cannot throw me
> and I will not fall off.
>
> (25)

Determination underscores the scar's designation: the mare and her unshakable jockey, bound together, will prevail. Yet this poem contains an ominous undercurrent, since her imaginary horse, a "night-mare," seems at time nightmarish. This theme continues in "hag riding," but in this poem the poet mounts the "night-mare" horse—to ride not *on* a hag, ironically, but *as* a hag. In the feminist tradition of theologian Mary Daly (Daly and Caputi 1–5), Clifton embraces the hag as a defiant wordsmith, a potent spinster of woman-centered sagas. Heading not toward death but toward the life she feared might abandon her, the poet wonders whether her ferocity might signify

> the afrikan in me
> still trying to get home
> after all these years

Whatever the cause of her obsessive ride—the poem's title suggests a kind of witchcraft—she is amazed to find herself waking "to the heat of morning / galloping down the highway of my life." Even more incredible, given her prior agony, it seems that as she journeys,

> something hopeful rises in me
> rises and runs me out into the road
> and I lob my fierce thigh high
> over the rump of the day and honey
> i ride   i ride.

(26)

Clifton has claimed that poems begin for her with sound, and here her exuberant assonance jolts the reader from distress; the *I*s in *rises, thigh, high,* and *ride* reverberate as *ayes*. Amidst such jubilation, however, the poet does not deny her immortality; the "rump of the day" describes, after all, life's backside. Still, the rider seizes the reins as she flies inexorably toward the night.

The final three poems in the sequence veer away from cancer per se to explore the sacred spaces of mortality. Although these lyrics feature metaphors of descent and decay, their tone suggests reconciliation rather than despair. In "down the tram" the poet hurtles through layers of the ground, only to find beauty in the subway's netherworld:

> hell is like this   first stone
> then rock so wonderful
> you forget you have no faith
> some pine   some scrub brush
> just enough to clench green
> in the air

This underground environment reminds the poet of hell but hardly seems hellish, for "it is always evening / there are stars   there is sky." Silence looms here, not ominous but comforting. On the approach to the station one gradually grows calm, "watching as caverns / tense into buildings," awestruck at the transformation. The miracle of lives inevitably transformed by death is moving to the poet, who travels forward

> wondering who could live here
> knowing whatever they have done
> they must be beautiful

(27)

For Clifton, glory triumphs down below as well as up above.

Finding redemption in unexpected places emerges also as a theme in "rust," which is prefaced by an epigraph from Brett Singer: *"we don't like rust, it reminds us that we are dying."* What does Singer mean, the poet wonders, addressing him directly:

> are you saying that iron understands
> time is another name for God?
>
> that the rain-licked pot is holy?

Recognizing the sacred in the everyday empowers us as humans, Clifton implies. For women in particular, she wonders, might ordinary items to be cherished reside in the domestic realm?

>   are you saying that they
> are sanctified now, our girlhood skillets
>
> tarnishing in the kitchen?

For women who are black, she queries further, did the dark mothers scour their pans so well that daughters now ignore the grime that lay beneath the surface?

> are you saying that we only want to remember
>
> the heft of our mothers' handles,
> their ebony patience, their shine?

(28)

As this poem reveals, countermemory works selectively to enable humans to idealize their tarnished pasts and deny the frightening future, which holds the specter of mortality.

From the kitchen to the morgue constitutes a bold leap indeed, but Clifton does not hesitate to make it. In this amphitheater of death a human must confront decay head-on, as the final poem in this sequence, "from the cadaver," wryly demonstrates. This confrontation gains momentum when the corpse proceeds to speak. Kristeva has claimed that a human corpse represents "the utmost of abjection" (3); as Kimmich elaborates, this is so because a corpse "signals a break in the border that separates life and death, and those who remain to witness the lifeless body are also at risk of losing their 'selves' to their inevitable physical decline" (225). As poet and cancer survivor, Clifton both accepts the risk of such an ambiguous position and presents it for her reader's consideration. Moreover, she invests this autopsied body with uncanny voice and posthuman dignity. "The arm you hold up / held a son," the cadaver explains to the mortician and the poet-reader-witness; "he became / taller than his father." If this son is watching, he too must confront the haunting specter of mortality:

> let him see
> what a man comes to
> doctor or patient
> criminal or king
> pieces of baggage
> cold in a stranger's hand

(29)

In death we all are equal, the poet reminds her readers; each of the body's once beloved parts will inevitably fall prey to the mortician's scalpel. Such comprehension provides a vital context from which to ruminate upon the deepest meanings of an amputated breast.

"THE JERUSALEM OF THE BREAST": ALICIA OSTRIKER'S *THE MASTECTOMY POEMS*

To love myself courageously I must say mastectomy plainly.
—Ostriker, "Scenes from a Mastectomy"

In *The Mastectomy Poems,* a twelve-part lyric sequence, Alicia Ostriker takes readers on a seasonal journey from the dead of winter, when she is diagnosed with breast cancer, to a spring day on which she recognizes that life after mastectomy can be as vibrant as before. Although her sequence follows Potts's proairetic code in its linear movement from diagnosis to treatment to recovery, Ostriker offers searing details of her biopsy, hospitalization, and pre- and postoperative trauma that push the boundaries of this code. Moreover, she daringly explores a woman's erotic longings before and after the removal of her breast. As Zillah Eisenstein has noted, "the breast has visibility in a way the uterus does not. The breast speaks sexual desire, maternal feeding and mammies, and the objectification of females, reducing them to their bodies" (135). Ostriker confronts this visibility head-on, resisting objectification by celebrating her breast as a site of heterosexual pleasure and maternal nurture even as she mourns its loss.

The poet reveals such intimate details not to evoke the reader's pruri-
ence but as a feminist gesture to speak truth to power and as a personal
commitment to "love myself courageously" ("Scenes" 188). Ostriker's
willingness to break silence about breast cancer's effects on her sexuality
links her to Lorde, who in "Uses of the Erotic" claims that "the erotic
offers a wellspring of replenishing and provocative force to the woman
who does not fear its revelation, nor succumb to the belief that sensation
is enough" (*Sister* 10). Furthermore, both Lorde and Ostriker view as
vital the support and honesty that cancer-stricken women give to one
another. "I say the love of women healed me," Lorde claimed after her
mastectomy, when it appeared that her cancer had been eradicated. "It is
the sweet smell of breath and laughter and voices calling my name that
gives me volition, helps me remember I want to turn away from looking
down" (*Cancer* 39). In "Scenes from a Mastectomy" Ostriker likewise
recognizes the subversive impact of women who share their illness narratives in frank bodily detail:

> On the phone to a dozen people, I am told a dozen stories, heroic, pathetic,
> infuriating. One woman's survival for years beyond what the doctors told
> her she would have. Another woman's experience of waking up without a
> breast when she thought she was merely receiving a biopsy. Stories of
> lumps the size of golf balls materializing overnight. Stories involving pus,
> blood, vomit. Stories about women organizing to demand more research
> into the causes of breast cancer. Women on chemo, women covering or
> refusing to cover their baldness. These are the invisible webs women weave
> together. (188–89)

Exchanging such stories makes the "invisible webs" among ill women
visible. When women publish their cancer sagas, moreover, their discourse becomes public. These writers take the risk of arousing repulsion
in readers by representing women's embodied suffering and abjection,
aware that it is time for the taboos on such representations to be broken.

The first of *The Mastectomy Poems*, "The Bridge," opens with what
are perhaps the truest lines in all of breast cancer poetry: "You never
think it will happen to you / what happens every day to other women."
Despite the prevalence of solidarity among many who are already ill,
most women who have not had cancer deny their vulnerability, especially if they are young or middle aged. But enter the mammography
technician, who approaches you in the waiting room to request that the
procedure be redone,

And you have already become a statistic,
Citizen of a country where the air,
Water, your estrogen, have just saluted
Their target cells, planted their Judas kiss
Inside the Jerusalem of the breast.

(*Crack* 85)

As Christ's disciple betrayed him in the garden of Gethsemane, so has
the poet's divided city been betrayed by those whom she considered
loyal: the cells of her own body. Her environment or her hormones
could be the culprits who have given healthy breast tissue the kiss of
death. Whatever the cause, the shock of this betrayal leaves her numb.
To move at all, she must address herself in the imperative:

Go put your clothes on in a shabby booth
Whose curtain reaches halfway to the floor.
Try saying *fear*. Now feel
Your tongue as it cleaves to the roof of your mouth.

(85)

When a mammogram reveals a tumor, speech will not emerge; the
tongue refuses to do its owner's bidding.

In stanzas 3 and 4 the poet employs a bridge as a spanning metaphor
to connote the compression of time and the need for hope. "Technical-
ities over, medical articles read, / Decisions made," the poet shifts to
her moment of reckoning, as she rides across New Jersey toward the
Manhattan hospital where her surgery will take place. The landscape is
dangerous, and crossing the border from home to hospital presages
trauma:

Elizabeth
Exhales her poisons, Newark Airport spreads
Her wings—the planes take off over the marsh—
A husband's hand plays with a ring.

(85)

The toxicity evoked in this stanza extends Ostriker's association of
breast cancer with environmental pollution and reinforces the sense of
numbness she describes in the preceding poem. A willed detachment is
evident in her use of articles rather than possessive pronouns: she speaks
of "a" husband, "a" ring instead of claiming them as hers. Still, the couple decide together to take the bridge rather than the tunnel, preferring

"elevation to depth, vista to crawling" (85). They need to gain perspective on the surgical procedure to come.

"The Gurney" depicts the lack of agency that an adult experiences on her way to surgery, no longer able to transport herself but wheeled along instead, infantilized. Trauma renders the poet capable of only mundane questions:

> What's this long corridor above the street
> What are these glazed beige tiles
> Why in my horizontal state
> Am I so like an undemanding child
>
> After they wheel me in my bassinet
> Into the operating room
> Who made the muslin sheets so dry and white
> Over my humid body's doom
>
> (86)

These questions are not followed by end punctuation; they dangle in the hallway with the patient and leave the reader, too, in nervous limbo. Irony pervades the speaker's vain attempts at reassurance; if she can only convince herself of her uniqueness, perhaps her fear will dissipate:

> How radiant the ceiling lights, of course
> They buzz appealingly for me alone
> I'm special, special to my Haitian nurse

This gloating tone masks the terror that undoubtedly attacks thousands of patients daily as they watch a surgeon don gloves and hear an anesthesiologist's instructions. As the anesthesia takes effect, the drowsy patient imagines herself "a red moon . . . stripping to her waist"; she finds relief in an overwhelming sense of annihilation: "*How good it is, not to be anywhere*" (86).

In "Riddle: Post-Op" Ostriker extends the theme of childlike frustration by beginning with a grim nursery rhyme: "a-tisket a-tasket / I'm out of my casket." Raised like Lazarus from the dead, the poet cannot quite take in the scenic view from her hospital window, snow falling like a "feathery shawl," her children "plump as chestnuts by the fire." This cozy winter landscape *could* bring comfort but does not, for unbeknownst to loyal mate or caring friends, the patient now has something to conceal: "Underneath my squares of gauze / I've a secret, I've a riddle." To underscore a sense of loss she emphasizes what this secret is *not:*

"a chestful of medals," "a jeweled lapel pin," a suit pocket or a zipper or a worm. Neither drawn nor painted on her, the "it" whose identity we are to guess

> makes a skinny stripe
> That won't come off with soap
> A scarlet letter lacking a meaning

The speaker knows she has been branded, not as an adulteress, like Hawthorne's Hester Prynne, but as a postmastectomy statistic, designated as such by her newly forming scar. Once her breast is gone, there is no there there. "Guess what it is," concludes the speaker grimly. "It's nothing" (87). Although Ostriker here configures her scar in terms of lack, later in the sequence she claims it as a source of power, as we shall see.

Of the four poets considered here, only Ostriker dedicates a poem to her surgeon, whom she addresses directly in "Mastectomy." In presenting the doctor-patient dynamic as reciprocal, the poet breaks new ground, for when oncologists and surgeons appear in women's cancer literature, they are usually either excoriated for their arrogance or presented as distant figures to be consulted, then forgotten. Ostriker, in contrast, addresses her surgeon directly; she admires not only her doctor's professional manner but also her comforting embodiment and dress: "your boyish freckles, / Your soft green cotton gown with the oval neck." Such details underscore the bodily intimacy of cancer patients and the doctors who remove their breasts. Trust is crucial to this dynamic, as the poet indicates in stanza 2:

> I liked your freckled face, your honesty
> That first visit, when I said
> *What's my odds on this biopsy*
> And you didn't mince words,
> *One out of four it's cancer.*

> (88)

Rather than frightening the patient, this forthright assessment reassures her. "A breast surgeon minces something other / Than language," the poet explains. "That's why I picked you to cut me" (88).

Having established her surgeon's competence and frankness, Ostriker probes the boundaries of their mutual journey. She wants to comprehend her breast's internal landscape, a terrain the physician knows in ways that she cannot. "Was I succulent? Was I juicy?" she wonders, drawing upon the age-old comparison of a woman's breast with fruit:

> Flesh is grass, yet I dreamed you displayed me
> In pleated paper like a candied fruit,
> I thought you sliced me like green honeydew
> Or like a pomegranate full of seeds
> Tart as Persephone's, those electric dots
> That kept that girl in hell,
> Those jelly pips that made her queen of death.

(89)

The fruit imagery assumes a mythical dimension here, for the poet likens her breast not only to candied fruit and honeydew but also to the pomegranate eaten by Demeter's young daughter, Persephone, in an act that sealed her fate. Having eaten the forbidden fruit, as legend has it, she was forced to remain in the underworld for half of every year, to become the bride of Hades. Ostriker clearly identifies with Persephone's vulnerability and her citizenry in the land of death.

Once reassured that her own "jelly pip" has been eradicated, the poet shifts her concern from the mythic back to the medical. In the poem's final lines Ostriker describes her operation as she has often imagined it; this time *she* will mince no words. Instead, she employs active verbs that emphasize both the violence of the surgical process and the precision of the surgeon:

> Doctor, you knifed, chopped, and divided it
> Like a watermelon's ruby flesh . . .
> Scooped up the risk in the ducts
> Scooped up the ducts
> Dug out the blubber,
> Spooned it off and away, nipple and all.

(89)

In other contexts these violent verbs would be troubling, but here the speaker's relief is palpable. This doctor made short work of her patient's diseased breast—a realization that may unsettle the poet even as it relieves her. Ultimately, however, she feels grateful to her surgeon for having

> Eliminated the odds, nipped out
> Those almost insignificant cells that might
> Or might not have lain dormant forever.

(89)

In the last half of *The Mastectomy Poems* Ostriker refuses to censor the sexual desire of a postmastectomy woman. Instead, she writes about the pleasure she finds in orgasm and in her husband's caressing of her breast. Such bodily explicit poetry has historically been labeled *confessional,* a word that critics have often applied derogatorily to modern women's verse, especially that of Sylvia Plath and Anne Sexton—women who "told all" about menstruation, intercourse, pregnancy, abortion, adultery, the forbidden topics of the 1950s and 1960s. This designation Ostriker would, I think, embrace, for more than Plath and Sexton she revels in women's cackles and whispers about sex and illness. Indeed, she recognizes that any poetic exploration of a breast cancer patient's erotic life is as revolutionary a gesture today as Plath's and Sexton's different frankness seemed forty years ago.

"What Was Lost" pays tribute to the poet's breast—its maternal sensuality, its erotic force. The poem's title marks it as an elegy, and in stanza 1 Ostriker laments the fact that when cancer struck, she could not protect her breast. What she lost after mastectomy was a sense of family history, a link between maternity and eroticism:

> What fed my daughters, my son
> Trickles of bliss,
> My right guess, my true information,
> What my husband sucked on
> For decades, so that I thought
> Myself safe. I thought love
> Protected the breast.

(90)

She lost as well a source of autoeroticism:

> What I admired myself, liking
> To leave it naked, what I could
> Soap and fondle in its bath.

As the poem continues, elegy gives way to eulogy, as the poet recalls the pride she felt in her breast. "Lifting my chin," she explains, "I'd stretch my arms to point it at people, / Show it off when I danced." She felt the breast's authority in private moments as well:

> I believed this pride
> Would protect it, it was a kind of joke
> Between me and my husband
> When he licked off some colostrum

Even a drop or two of bitter milk
He'd say *You're saving for your grandchildren.*

(90–91)

Ostriker is perhaps the first poet in history to record the image of a lover sucking colostrum from the nipple of his beloved and is certainly among the first to acknowledge that mothers of grown children sometimes produce breast milk when they are sexually aroused. This image not only moves the erotic lives of aging women from the margins to the center of poetic discourse, it also moves the reader to consider how richly symbolic a sexual organ the breast is (Yalom 49–90).

In the poem's final stanza Ostriker invests her breast with an ethical dimension, as she explores its inherent goodness. She also discounts the illusion that any woman's breast is safe from harm. Acknowledging that she had been saving "the goodness of it for some crucial need," Ostriker likens the nourishing potential of her breast to that of Rose of Sharon in *The Grapes of Wrath*, who nurses a dying stranger. The poet recalls this scene at the novel's end as something read aloud to her years before her own breast formed, when she was sick with measles and nurtured by her own mother. "How funny I thought goodness would protect it," the anguished poet muses. As the poem ends she eulogizes her breast in all its vulnerability, calling it "jar of star fluid, breakable cup" and mourning its grainy tissue, shoveled after surgery into plastic "like wet sand at the beach." Like a slowly ripening orange, her sacrificial breast gleams by lamplight in its citrus grove, "ready to be harvested and eaten" (90–91).

Several poems in Ostriker's sequence address the theme of returning to life as usual after breast cancer surgery. In "December 31" this poet celebrates New Year's Eve, as Lorde did in her sequence, despite the fact that Ostriker had left the hospital only shortly before. "I say this year's no different / From any other," she insists, protesting perhaps too much as she repeats her mantra: "No different, no / Different." Surely "survival itself . . . can be a crisis," even when the speaker denies that crisis by claiming that nothing has changed (Caruth 9). Unlike Lorde, who in "Electric Slide Boogie" listened to her loved ones usher in the year, herself too ill to participate, Ostriker embraces wellness by partying with her family. Rock and roll inspires her to dance provocatively: one-breasted, she still can be "that rolling stone, that / Natural woman" that Bob Dylan and Carole King sang of in the 1960s, when the poet was young. She acknowledges, however, that come 3:00 A.M., when her children finally settle down, she will long have been asleep, too weary to continue past midnight. Instead, she will bless her children in mutters from her slumber (92).

This theme of the "natural" woman continues in "Wintering," whose epigraph comes from a poem by Lucille Clifton and therefore further confirms the intertextual dimensions of these poets' cancer sequences:

> *I had expected more than this.*
> *I had not expected to be*
> *an ordinary woman.*

What Ostriker had envisioned after mastectomy, stanza one reveals, was monumental change, and in some respects she got it. She is "half a boy" now, "flat as something innocent, a clean / Plate, just needing a story." The stories she deserves to tell, the poet realizes, are awe inspiring:

> A woman should be able to say
> *I've become an Amazon,*
> *Warrior woman minus a breast,*
> *The better to shoot arrow*
> *After fierce arrow,*
> Or else *I am that dancing Shiva*
> *Carved in the living rock at Elephanta,*
> *One-breasted male deity . . .*
>
> (93)

Unlike Lorde and Clifton, who embrace their new identities as one-breasted Amazons, Ostriker questions such legendary status for herself: although she "should be able" to claim an Amazonian strength, she finds it hard to do so. Nor can she, finally, be like Shiva, for she feels neither "holy enough or mythic enough." Come January, the drama of surgery behind her, she prefers to envision herself as an ordinary woman recovering from cancer.

Although others sometimes make it difficult for her to feel whole again, Ostriker claims autonomy in this matter. In stanza 2 of "Wintering" the outraged poet rejects the condescension of a man who will not meet her gaze when she tells him she feels sexy with one breast:

> Spare me your pity,
> Your terror, your condolence.
> I'm not your wasting heroine,

Your dying swan. Friend, tragedy
Is a sort of surrender.

(94)

The poet resists the prevailing cultural theory that postmastectomy
women are either victims or newly enlightened survivors. Like Barbara
Ehrenreich (44–45), who decries the popular rhetoric that urges breast
cancer patients to embrace pink teddy bears and gush about their new
identities, Ostriker refuses to be feminized or sentimentalized. Instead
of pitying me, the speaker insists, "tell me again I'm a model / Of
toughness. I eat that up." She embraces as well the intimate rituals of
daily life:

I grade papers. I listen to wind.
My husband helps me come, it thaws
A week before semester starts.

The interwoven landscape of her professional, sexual, and domestic life
pleases the speaker, as does a phone call from an acquaintance who has
lived for fifteen years without a recurrence of her cancer. "*Do you know
what?*" this woman tells the speaker reassuringly.

> *You're the same person*
> *After a mastectomy as before.* An idea
> That had never occurred to me.
> *You have a job you like? You have poems to write?*
> *Your marriage is okay? It will stay that way.*
> *The wrinkles are worse. I hate looking in the mirror.*
> *But a missing breast, well, you get used to it.*

(93–94)

The speaker clearly gains confidence from her friend's reassurance. Still,
exactly *how* a woman learns to live with one breast "as before" continues
to perplex her.

This perplexity is evident in "Normal," where she addresses the
vexed topics of scar and breast prosthesis. In "December 31" the phrase
"no different" recurs three times; in "Normal" the title word echoes similarly in a manner that questions its viability. When the poet returns to
work after the holiday break, her colleagues

tell me I look normal. I am normal.
The falsie on my left makes me
In a certain sense more perfectly normal.

Indeed, the prosthesis in her bra matches its counterpart so perfectly that who can tell one from the other? After all, "crafted of latex, it repairs the real." Perhaps the breast cancer survivor is more "normal" now than before; perhaps her refurbished body will last longer than its predecessor; how clever indeed she has become! The poet clearly recognizes *normal* as a word used, however unwittingly, by others who would impose a traditionally feminine normativity upon her postmastectomy body.[7]

> Like one of those trees with a major limb lopped,
> I'm a shade more sublime today than yesterday.
> Stormed at with shot and shell,
> A symbol of rich experience,
> A scheme to outlive you all.
>
> (95)

With wry humor the poet probes the concepts of normality and mortality in all their hegemonic arbitrariness.

What emerges as "abnormal," Ostriker explains in stanza 2, is the "short piece of cosmic string" that has somehow attached itself to her chest. By turns threatening and seductive, this string, her scar, belies the notion that nothing of significance has changed:

> Ominous asp, it burns and stings.
> Grimaces to show it has no idea
> How it arrived here.
> Would prefer to creep off.
> Yet it is pink and smooth as gelatin.
> It will not bite and can perhaps be tamed.
>
> (95)

Nowhere in her sequence does this poet struggle harder to confront the physical transformations her cancer has produced, and nowhere is her ambivalence more in evidence than in this veiled allusion to Eve in the Garden of Eden and to Shakespeare's Cleopatra, felled by a stinging asp. Although her resident snake lacks poison, it still has the ability to paralyze its anxious owner. It might or might not harm anyone else: indeed, the process of accepting the viper involves proposing to expose it to others. "Want to pet it?" the poet asks her friends and colleagues, grim yet playful. "It cannot hurt you. / Care to fingertip my silky scar?" Ultimately she resists the view that cancer does not change a woman; this falsehood is designed to silence her. "Now I am better, charming," she insists sarcastically in stanza 3; "I am well." Well and well behaved:

> I never say
> The thing that is forbidden to say,
> Piece of meat, piece of shit.

Writing about surgery or sex or even scars adheres at least minimally to late-twentieth-century standards of female propriety, it seems; expressing bitterness and rage about one's butchered breast does not:

> Cooled, cropped, I'm simple and pure.
> Never invite my colleagues
> To view it pickled in a Mason jar.

>   (95)

Like Dickinson, from whose poem she quotes as an epigraph to "Normal," Ostriker realizes that "much madness is divinest sense / to a discerning eye" (Dickinson 435). Conforming to society's expectations may bring social approbation, but it may also distort the truth. Assent does *not* signify sanity, these two poets agree; often only a fierce demurral rings true. Yet by inviting inquisitive others to "fingertip my silky scar," Ostriker paradoxically claims it as a source of agency—as her own potent bodily insignia, capable of turning words like *normal* inside out.

While mastectomy initially traumatizes many women who experience it, many of them do ultimately move toward reconciliation. As Ostriker notes in "Healing," however, this process requires more than exercising their arm regularly to avoid lymphedema or plying their scars with cream. For poets, she suggests, writing about cancer can be therapeutic, but it is also emotionally and aesthetically demanding. She uses the image of a broken icicle,

> A brandished javelin
> Made of sheer
> Stolen light

to stand in metonymically for the poetic discourse she must generate to do justice to her cancer experience. Like the icicle's brittle cold, which "instantly shoots through the arm / To the heart," her words must serve as weapons. "I need a language like that," she insists, speaking of the shocking pain such cold evokes, "a recognizable enemy, a clarity" (96). Such language often eludes her, the poet acknowledges, for healing involves silence as well as animal rage. To represent her experience with accuracy, Ostriker concludes, she must apply

White udder cream
To the howl
I make vow after vow.

(96)

The assonance of *howl* and *vow* heightens the impact of these final lines by creating a wounded echo. To heal, the writer must vow to howl when necessary, seeking the primal clarity of an infant's preverbal cry—purer, perhaps, than written language can ever be.

Although Ostriker finds the healing process difficult, she ultimately creates a postmastectomy identity as a "subject-in-process." In discussing contemporary women's long poems, Keller has analyzed the poetic formation of such a subject and has noted women poets' tendencies to privilege narrative strategies—dialogue, collage, and generic interrelation in particular—as useful techniques for composing it. "The elusive subject-in-process (to adopt Julia Kristeva's term) may be best rendered in forms other than lyric," Keller explains—"that is, in capacious forms which stretch to accommodate multiple voices and discourses, forms which may even defer closure indefinitely" (3). These multiple discourses are evident throughout Ostriker's breast cancer sequence, and the deferral of closure can be readily seen in its final poem, "Epilogue: Nevertheless." This adverb connotes a determination to persevere—as in "nevertheless, I must go on"—yet it finally remains enigmatic. The poem presents the poet strolling across the campus where she teaches, enjoying spring weather and momentarily unaware of what the friends she encounters mean when they ask her, anxious, *"How are you feeling?"* As she responds by recounting

> the latest
> About my love life or my kids' love lives,
> Or my vacation or my writer's block,

she realizes suddenly the nature of the query; they want to know the status of her cancer. *"I'm fine,* I say, *I'm great, I'm clean,"* she insists, and means it. Yet she cannot stay to scrutinize her claim more closely, for life, as ever, beckons unpredictably: "The bookbag on my back, I have to run" (99).

What Ostriker runs toward for solace, finally, is her poems, for writing illuminates her transformed world. Still, closure is disrupted as her sequence ends, since she may or may not remain free of cancer. As a metaphor, running connotes either evasive or purposeful movement; Ostriker, it seems, chooses momentum, but her destination remains ambiguous.

"THE SPACE / WHERE MY BREAST HAS BEEN": HILDA RAZ'S *DIVINE HONORS*

Open is the mouth of the metal tunnel.
Tomorrow, mmmmu, the knife.

—Raz, "Mu"

Of the hundreds of women who have written poems about breast cancer, only Hilda Raz has published a volume of poetry in which virtually all of the poems contained therein—sixty, to be precise—address this topic. Clearly she writes "as a strategy for survival" ("Writing" 121). The title of her collection comes from a whimsical yet thought-provoking line from W. H. Auden that serves as the collection's epigraph: "Divine honours will be paid to shallow depressions in the ground, domestic pets, ruined windmills, or malignant tumours." Raz's poems, too, combine whimsy and intellectual provocation as they probe both "the space / where my breast has been" and the spaces that surround that emptiness. Formally and linguistically experimental, her poems disrupt linearity and foreground fragmentation in their frequent use of slashed titles ("Breast / fever"), preverbal sounds ("I'm afraid mmmmmo"), and excerpts from journal entries ("Waiting for oncologist with you, v. scared"). Raz finds lyricism in unexpected places—the rubble of a kitchen under construction, a "six foot stalk of brusselsprout"—as well as in more orthodox sources of beauty: the copper petals of an amaryllis, an ocean stone "the color of moss." Like many contemporary poets, however, she refuses to privilege the lyric moment. Instead, she creates narratives that are quintessentially postmodern, poems that, in Susan Friedman's words, "expose the equation of poetry with the lyric as an ideological construct and deconstruct the modernist separation between the poetic and the everyday, between the timeless lyrical moment and the historical" ("Craving" 17).

In *Divine Honors* Raz employs tropes familiar from the cancer poems of Lorde, Clifton, and Ostriker: silence, scars, borders, winter, journeys.

Another cluster of images that Raz returns to often, however, is gardens, soil, and planting, whether in the yard at home or in nearby prairie fields. As she notes in the introduction to *Living on the Margins,* her edited collection of breast cancer literature, women, gardens, cancer, and art intersect in richly metaphoric ways:

> It's summer. In the garden two women are cutting up fruit for lunch. One takes a golden peach, twists free the pit. She hands half to her friend, points to a spot of mold attached to the stem. "No problem," the other grins, twirling her knife. She hands back the half. "Clean margins," she whispers. They both laugh. Clean margins around a compromised site may indicate successful treatment for cancer. (vii)

Raz points out that women have long been associated with gardens: as victims of temptation, like Eve, and as the human gender identified with nature more than culture. Yet the women who inhabit her imaginary garden "might be seen as nature run riot":

> Each has given up a breast to treatment for cancer. Both understand their loss is hidden. Each knows this amputation is different from others, the breast an erotic, sexual, and maternal emblem in a culture that reveres breasts if not women. . . . Each has searched the work of women writers for records of direct experience. Neither can find them. (vii)

If the women in this garden represent "nature run riot," the task of the poet who has survived the chaos of cancer might be to bring order to the scene. This impulse Raz resists. Although she insists upon the importance of women's recording their breast cancer experiences, she provides no blueprint as to the form this record should take. Instead, she recognizes that each woman who confronts this disease must convey in her own way "the fracture of her expectations" (x). For Raz, such engagement requires the fracturing of words themselves and the transgression of generic margins in order to examine "where I am now" ("Writing" 105).

Divine Honors begins with a prologue that consists of four poems, each of which conveys what this poet resists and what she seeks to transform. The title of the first poem, "Repair," underscores her methodology: like the workers tearing out her kitchen floor, she must "wear safety glasses for this work" of rebuilding after cancer. Her emotions run the gamut here: delight appears, but as "a paste bubble in my throat" that threatens to choke her; so do anger and a sense of risk. As

the men "who let fly plaster" inadvertently release "the smell of something very old, letting go," so the poet delineates her reconstructive
project as one of letting fly and letting go. The workers in the kitchen,
like the writer at her desk, "unmake what I made / with my life, or
where I made it" (3). Subsequent poems feature variations on the theme
of unmaking and remaking. In "Narrative without People" the speaker
roams through moldy rooms, watching as "soaked books lip open in
piles," listening as "the sounds on air / wail, a nail in the thumb." She
encounters ghostly presences—"something here enters the trees"—
and ominous rubbish in the rafters, "burnt rubber / hooks for skeleton
elbows" (4). Only ash remains. In "Let's Consider the Consequences"
she surveys an old, damaged house, wondering how to repair its
cracked bricks, what to do about

> doors swollen
> by water-rot, frames to pare down,
> mildew to scour, how much
> to seal up, or seal out.

The advice she receives from experts, whether construction workers or
other cancer patients, is to read the damage report but put it quickly
aside, to

> Move ahead and not refer, never refer to
> anything other than the sweet taste in your mouth of breath,
> the steady blood beat, the road hot and loud under your feet,
>   infinite.

(5–6)

Denial—sealing fear up and sealing it out—represents a seductive
option, and in the poems to follow the poet does indeed "move on, move
along." But in affirming the breath and blood of life, she refuses to "burn
the notebook," her cancer journal, as others advise (5). Instead, she will
write against forgetting.

This refusal to be silent or silenced—and its obverse, an insistence on
speaking—lies at the heart of the prologue's fourth poem, "Isaac Stern's
Performance." At home alone, the poet finds solace in the classical music
that "roils in the room / where I wait, my chest holding even at the scar's
edge." This first, oblique reference to the aftermath of breast cancer
surgery disrupts the proairetic code by beginning not with diagnosis and
treatment but with the disease's ultimate insignia, the scar on Raz's chest.

What remains for the poet to consider, and what Stern's stunning performance of a Beethoven concerto conjures, is the question of how to live from this point forward:

> Whatever chances I took
> paid off and now I have only
> the rest of my life to consider.
> Once it was a globe, an ocean
> to cross, or at least a desert—
> now a rivulet, or a blowhole.

(7)

This stanza reveals the poet's psychological state via spatial images that contrast then and now. Before cancer, her life spread out before her, vast as earth or sea or certainly, she wittily insists, as a desert. Now the future merely trickles; like an underwater whale, she can breathe only through her blowhole, and with effort. Surely she will eventually move on, but for now she feels reduced.

As the poet listens further to her classical station, however, she is moved by a comment of Jean-Pierre Rampal on the power of Stern's performance the night Rampal heard it live: "I remember it was like a story: / He told you the Beethoven concerto." The poet views her own task as equally definitive: "I am telling you cancer" (7). How does a poet *tell* cancer, the reader invariably wonders; how can she make art of it, foreground the interpretation rather than the score? Has she not already *performed* cancer, after all, with every fiber of her being? In these poems Raz aspires to make cancer into an art form that is potentially as moving as was Stern's magnificent treatment of the Beethoven. *How* a poet tells cancer demands as full consideration for Raz as *what* she tells; the telling must be careful, delicate, fierce. The poem's final stanza offers as an analogy to the creative process the late-winter transformation of an amaryllis from bulb to fragile bloom:

> I am telling you like moisture
> at soil's edge after winter, or
> the bulb of the amaryllis you brought
> raising stem after stem from cork dirt,
> one hybrid flower after another unfurling
> for hours, each copper petal opening its throat so
> slowly, each shudder of tone—mahogany, coral, blood—
> an ache, orgasm, agony, life.

(7)

The excruciating risk of dying that a tropical plant raised indoors faces requires that it have meticulous care from any gardener who takes on this task. The terrible, blood-red beauty of each petal that unfurls; the plant's complex hybridity; the agony and bliss the process of tending evokes—these elements combine when cancer is the story to be told.

Once Raz has introduced her themes and strategies in these epigraphs, she assesses her emotional landscape. Although each of the five sections of *Divine Honors* deals with cancer's traumas, part 1 records her experience of diagnosis, surgery, recovery, and prosthesis with particular intensity. The poet's movement in this sequence eschews linearity, however, as she shifts abruptly from the pleasure she takes in family to anxiety over an upcoming biopsy report, from relief at healing to reawakened trauma from remembering her ordeal. "Weathering / boundaries / what is good," for example, offers myriad angles on Raz's time at home just before her cancer diagnosis is confirmed. One perspective emerges in the joy of a morning in which she gazes upon her beloved, sleeping, and talks with her adult children. In stanza 1 she addresses her partner from the privacy of their bedroom, for the body's beauty deserves to be apostrophized; thus she praises "your sweet silence, your hands, skin, your mouth." As her lover sleeps, the poet speaks on the phone to "the son of my body" and simultaneously celebrates, with delight in the pun, "the sun on my body." She talks by phone as well with the "daughter / of my body, Persephone and I Demeter," aware of her child's need to process her mother's possible cancer by researching the subject in the library (12). Interestingly, when Ostriker alludes to the Greek myth of Demeter and Persephone in her cancer poetry, she imagines herself the doomed daughter, forced to winter in Hades; Raz, in contrast, identifies with Demeter, wishing she could protect her daughter from fear about her mother's health, and perhaps from the fear that she might be vulnerable to inheriting her mother's breast cancer.

The poet also finds pleasure in sharing with her spouse the domestic tasks of planting, cooking, and rebuilding:

> You with your $125 worth
> of spring bulbs divided three ways, three friends, three graces.
> We plant them together, warm earth in the garden where your
> mother watches, who has cancer too. I make stew—you bring
> veggies I cook with meat—and rice custard. You build onto our
> patio garden. The patio is rich and crunchy with acorns. . . .

(12)

A woman weathers cancer in the same way a midwestern family hunkers down for winter, it seems: by planting bulbs that hold the promise of spring, by eating hearty food, by remodeling outdoors as long as the sunshine holds. Moreover, the travails of one woman with cancer recede when the poet reminds herself that her mother-in-law has confronted this disease as well. One can only pray for protection and find comfort in "what is good":

> Dear God, keep us all safe. My
> breast is healing well. I am supple of body. My spirit what? Still at
> home in my body.
>
> (12)

This loosely structured prose poem ranges rather than rambles, recording the day's events and the poet's inner thoughts impressionistically. The terse second stanza contrasts vividly with the expansive first, as Raz reminds herself that winter does end, that cancer's boundaries are fluid:

> Cancer is one of the few internal diseases that can be cured. I am a
> person who has cancer
> now.
>
> (12)

In stanza 3 this reassuring mantra is bolstered by a rejuvenating walk on which the speaker and her spouse view

> fronds of prairie grasses, beige
> lavender in sun in your garden—sun, sun all day—in high 70s—on your
> garden. On
> ours.
>
> (12)

Beauty can counter fear and pessimism, these lines suggest, as can the sublimity of a sunny autumn day and the shared aesthetic project of a garden still miraculously in bloom.

Although the tone shifts in the poem's final stanza, as the poet learns the results of a breast biopsy, the sense of wonder she acquired earlier in the day reassures her. By incorporating into her narrative fragments from her journal, terse abbreviations devoid of articles, starkly medical diction, and thoughtless comments from others, Raz vividly conveys her vulnerability:

> Waiting for oncologist with you, v. scared. I'm still me, same me no matter
> what he says. Biopsy report shocks me. You say, "So you know more than

the doctor?"—you with me all afternoon, read report with me. Necrotic tissue. Adjacent cells abnormal. We go shopping, for a walk. His nurse says, "Recovery is partially dependent . . ." on my attitude. (12)

Clearly the poet walks multiple boundaries here, from the edgy conversations with her spouse to the borders of her vibrant garden to the transgressive margins of her cancer. She enters as well the dreamscape of the oncologist's nurse, herself a cancer survivor, who shares with this worried patient her own sustaining "dream of ribbons and banners, floating upward / into light." Raz listens as the nurse recounts her dream, uncertain whether to find its visions comforting or alarming: "I am fascinated / and afraid" (13).

Subsequent poems document the poet's trauma as she faces surgery. In "To Explain," gardening continues to sustain her, in part because it provides her solitude in which to mourn. In her garden she can release preverbal sounds too agonizing for other human ears:

> . . . all week
> I have been grieving, pouring deep gutturals
> into the stone edgings of the back garden,
> down on my knees, seeming to dig the impatiens.
>
> (14)

Like Ostriker, Raz adopts a stance of supplication as she lets loose gutturals of grief. This position on her knees behooves a mourner as well as a gardener, and the garden's location behind the house protects her privacy: "nobody heard me but the shade and rain in air." Grief renders this wordsmith inept with words, causing her to wonder "how to say / why I couldn't say." As language drifted away, only her body held firm:

> words had gone
> in their ashy fans,
> and only the wrap of my body
> around loss, stayed.
>
> (14)

What remains, it seems, and what is finally inexplicable, is the complex intersection of embodiment and loss.

This musing on inexpressibility continues in "Mu," identified in an epigraph from Lewis Thomas as *the old root giving rise to mystery . . . with cognates* MYSTICAL *and* MUTE. MYSTERY *came from the Greek* muein *with the meaning of closing the lips, closing the eyes*" (15). Exploring the mute root of mystery—the silence of unyielding lips, the blankness of unseeing eyes—lies at the core of Raz's confrontation with cancer. In an attempt to calm the grim fears that the prospect of a second surgery unleashes, the poet transforms trauma into testimony. Still, the "mmmm" sound at the poem's center evokes the shuddering cadences of a frightened child:

> Misery a block in the head
> a block I hum mmmm through, the way mother
> mmmm helps me move to. Umber attaches to shadows
> in hedge-ribbons. Feet mmmmmmmm, hit-sounds like murder
> stitched to lips, the miles, hummm, eyes shut shuttered, cement walk
> studded with dark I'm afraid mmmmmo
> and now I am come alone at midnight onto the pineneedles of the park.
>
> (15)

As vulnerable as a solitary toddler stumbling through an urban park, Raz finds herself speechless with terror as she anticipates the loss of a vital body part. "I am come to say good-bye in the dark," she admits, "but my mouth won't open." This childlike aspect of the suffering self is jolted into preverbal speech, however, by the sight of a nearby sliding board, its shiny surface both alien and familiar, like the landscape of her nightmare. Undone by the awesome rite of passage that sliding down a slick surface requires, the poet, infantilized, identifies her plight with that of children fearful of the monstrous slide. Who will save them, she wonders, save her?

> Who
> bashes into my arms so we open our mouths to this cadence no no
> no no mmm mommy up again to ride the big slide they and I falling
> into the dark air. Open is the mouth of the metal tunnel.
> Tomorrow, mmmmu, the knife.
>
> (15)

This passage evokes the simultaneous joy and fright a child experiences when coming down the scary slide; here the terror is so great that it transports the speaker from competent adult to dependent child. As adults we know our mothers cannot save us from harm, yet still we long for them to have that power: "no no mmm mommy up again." What Raz wishes to repress, the source of her verbal regression, is the next day's cutting that her precious flesh must endure. The poem's rhythms replicate the process of anesthetization: the center of consciousness cannot

hold if trauma takes over. Inscribing her trauma represents an only partially successful strategy for moving through it.

One of the most powerful poems in *Divine Honors* pays homage to the
poet's "fallen" breast and the scar that marks it. As Stephanie Hartman
has demonstrated in "Reading the Scar in Breast Cancer Poetry" and as
works by Lorde, Clifton, and Ostriker discussed here have revealed, scar
poems frequently appear in women's cancer poems as signs of mutilation, loss, and reclamation. Raz's representation is unique, however, in
depicting her amputated breast as a fallen warrior and in addressing her
scar, the "you" of the poem, as a fierce guardian. In addition, the title
epigraph evokes Old Testament war rhetoric ironically, given its male
gender emphasis through the pronouns: "Two Are Better Than One . . .
For If They Fall, the One Will Lift Up His Fellow; But Woe to Him
That Is Alone When He Falleth, For He Hath Not Another to Help Him
Up." The poem begins in medias res:

> . . . opened my chest
> . . . opened my belly
> You stayed close
> your food bowl empty
> your feet unclean. The steppes in your head
> filled with wind, static, a glow of sand and grit.
> Or were you only sleeping those days
> you sat by my bed, our hands touching,
> the concave round of your skull
> a focus mirror, your eyes radiant?

(18)

Like a hungry cat that refuses to leave its owner's lap, the scar shadows
its host; the patient must confront its presence even as she sleeps. Eerily,
the scar assumes voice and stands in for family, answering the ringing
bedside phone and whispering "later, sick." "I knew whom you spoke
to," the waking poet insists, identifying the caller as her once healthy but
now amputated breast: "God! Your handmaiden, her fruit cheek / rosy
with health, not bloat." Envisioning her former breast as a hospital visitor who brings her a camellia, she claims it as

> the only flower in that
> floral room I could see, night or day,
> follow with my bare shoulders, shiny,

intact above the bandage wrapped like skin
in moonlight, in midnight shadow.

(18)

The breast's marauder, this waxy scar, has now become the poet's con-
stant companion: "You never left me. / Now I call you scar" (18). Naming the guardian serves to unite signifier and signified.

In "Writing the Impossible" Raz pays further tribute to the act of
composition itself as well as to the friends and family members around
her as a source of strength during her recovery. "Getting Well"
addresses this confluence of art and loving-kindness, as the poet
expresses gratitude to a friend who leaves in her mailbox a book about
recovering, along with "four fair hairs / from your head, locked in the
pages"—accidental physical remains in which she takes comfort. The
epigraph from the book, Anne Truitt's *Turn*, promises the ill reader an
eventual return to the quotidian: "*If I get well . . . I can take a walk in the
snow and eat a red apple.*" Raz knows that the giver of this book "would
have me know how to write / an essay, commissioned, on the stuff of my
life"; for this confidence in her healing and her art the poet expresses
thanks. Surely the dual gift of book and hairs conveys an empowering
message, yet she struggles to capture it in words:

> Work
> can keep us alive to the world?
> Writing down some truth will help?

She determines, finally, that her friend's fair hair and loyalty herald the
possibility of healing and that writing alongside her companion will
indeed inspire her:

> . . . Fair, you sit down
> in the sun to read, your head
> bent down to eat an apple. Here,
> you draw in the breath of the air
> and breathe it out so we can write.

(19)

The emphasis on writing that permeates this sequence reminds readers
that little more than two decades ago, women were expected to be silent
about breast cancer. Raz confronts this prohibition directly in "Day-Old
Bargain," in which she challenges an unidentified man who urges her to

inscribe traditionally feminine losses, not the amputation of female body parts. The tacit pact between women and men—that women should suffer in silence, not protest in rage—deserves to be broken:

> Bargain tarts, raspberry, goose,
> he said, don't write about that
> surgery, women who have hacked off write
> all parts and natures of women
> who lose food in the bottom parts
> of refrigerators, onions, scallions,
> sour tomatoes, tiny cocktail weenies
> lost in the airless dark write . . .

(22)

This stanza's fragmented syntax connotes the irate man's irrationality; he cannot quite articulate why this topic makes him sputter. The poet knows, however, as do her readers: he cannot bear the thought of his own castration, for "hacked off" women surely endanger "tiny cocktail weenies." Nor has this man ever valued the "parts and natures of women" other than in a sexual way. Only trivial subjects will do for women's writing, he believes:

> Write about silliness, holding hands
> in sandboxes, small girls playing fudge-
> and-find-me-alley-tag at dusk, Rochester,
> state of pubescent, New Yorka roonie.

(22)

For this man, girls' experiences, not women's, deserve to be portrayed literarily, perhaps because girls seem to him both safe and perversely sexy.

The angry poet resists male objectification of women by revealing its voyeuristic excesses. Determined to beat this man at his own game, she critiques his sexual indiscretions and imagines him stroking a postmastectomy breast:

> He's got a girlfriend works at his office, don't you know,
> she thinks he's licorice stick swinger. I caught them
> hugging in the mimeo room. Ain't nothing to it, he said,
> rolling his cup of a palm over the scar. Mmmmmm-mmmmm,
> this hillock is a sweet raisin, roll over baby, pour me out.
> Okeydokey.

(22–23)

Imagining this sexist man toying with women's scarred breasts behind closed office doors, Raz empowers herself by ridiculing his juvenile behavior and discourse. Having neither time nor patience for his censorious admonitions, she determines to write what she pleases.

In "Breast / fever," the final poem in this sequence, Raz introduces readers to her prosthesis, acknowledges its sterility, eroticizes it, and seeks reassurance from it. Such ambivalence characterizes the process of recovery and reconstruction, she suggests. Her edginess is evident from her repetition of the phrase "my new breast" and from her clinical presentation of it:

> My new breast is two months old,
> gel used in bicycle saddles
> for riders on long-distance runs
> stays cold under my skin
> when the old breast is warm;
> catalogue price, $276. My serial number,
> #B-1754, means some sisters under the skin.
> My new breast
> my new breast is sterile,
> will never have cancer.
>
> (24)

Matter-of-fact on the surface, the poet implies a disturbing sense of alienation from this commercial breast and its artificial properties. She also wonders what her prosthesis will feel like during sex. Writing during the Chinese year of the golden horse, an anniversary that recurs only once each sixty years, the poet imagines the horse as a lover unperturbed by the blankness of her breast. "Over me your skin is warm," she tells this suitor, whom she showers with endearments—"sweetgel, ribbontongue, goldhorse. / You suck the blank to goosebumps." As the golden horse mounts her (in a wry reversal of the usual horse and rider positioning), she cries out lustily and bemoans the moment that this dream image will disappear, leaving her unfulfilled: "HowmIgonnaget there when you're gone / back to your youngthing, sweetcurl?" She appreciates in particular the golden horse's attention to her artificial breast:

> My scar
> means nothing to him, a mapletwirl
> a whirligig, your center and maypole.
>
> (24)

Exuberant wordplay and pleasure in assonance, alliteration, and ono-matopoeia characterize all of Raz's poems but this one in particular; *twirl* and *whirl* perform verbal tricks, while *mapletwirl* and *maypole* resonate playfully. Yet the poem's tone is ominous as well as erotic. As in Clifton's "hag riding," when the speaker mounts her night-mare with both terror and excitement, Raz's feverish persona often finds the golden horse's power overwhelming.

This element of nightmarish fantasy distinguishes Raz's delineation of a breast cancer erotics from that of Ostriker, whose lovemaking is located securely in the "real" world. Raz, in contrast, traces the surreal landscape of a patient with fever—both illness and erotic longing. In the fourth stanza she imagines the golden horse and her breast prosthesis making love sixty years hence, herself long dead and forgotten. She addresses her prosthesis directly, complaining about this sterile appendage's longevity:

> You'll curl red over him when I'm under
> the ash, gone, all mind or nothing.
> Who the hell loves a tree?

Dust to dust, ashes to ashes provides no consolation to the desiring poet; she prefers living and lovemaking to lying under the ground, pushing up trees. As her fever peaks, the poet shifts focus in the final stanza to a bizarre mother-daughter fantasy of rage and reconciliation, apparently triggered by a phone call from her daughter, whether real or imaginary:

> Don't tell me on the phone your voice
> a fine ringing replica of mine that you've
> got sickies, fever, ticks from the job
> you won't worry about don't I either
> you nut, you bitch dog mother I bred you
> out of leaves and mash my blood on the floor
> my liver colored placenta curled in a cold bowl.
> Who do you think you are with my sick breasts
> on your chest. Oh God let me live to touch her
> working out the next generation of women.

(24–25)

As a "dog mother" the poet is appalled at the possibility that her daughter, the "bitch" whom she bred and bore and who wears her mother's "sick breasts," might someday inherit the cancer gene. Raz fears as well that she will not live to nurture this daughter into adulthood, to launch "the next generation of women" on their life's journey.

The poems discussed here comprise only one of five sequences contained in *Divine Honors*, all of which explore breast cancer's vexed terrain. Section 2 departs from the final stanza of "Breast / fever" to focus on the response of Raz's daughter, Sarah, to her mother's cancer. Nipple imagery dominates this sequence. In "Balance," for example, Sarah brings the poet a gift of Indonesian goddess earrings "with a golden nipple on each domed center, ear breasts / we joked, touching and touching: Live!" In "Order," this daughter, a jeweler, creates another present, "a fabulous pin," a "tiny silver moon / with dark brass nipple." She thus has fashioned for her mother a new breast, as her mother many years earlier had birthed a female infant who would grow a bosom: "She pins it fast to heal my loss: / a breast she made, as I made her" (50). Section 3 of the volume celebrates cancer survivors who continue to live and work—women clustered in a "crowded place . . . grieving and armed"—and returns to the eroticized scar as a major motif. In "Petting the Scar," for instance (which is dedicated to and inspired by Ostriker), Raz describes touching the "cold blank" of her prosthetic breast and feeling nothing. But when she learns to stroke her scar, she succumbs to an autoeroticism that both shocks and delights her:

> But the scar!
> Riverroad, meandering root, stretched coil, wire chord, embroidery
> > in its hoop, mine, my body.
> > Oh, love!
>
> > > (52–53)

Section 4 of *Divine Honors* explores bodily fetishes, from swollen, fiery feet (in "Chigger Socks") to tongues (in "Zen: the one I love most holds my tongue") to breasts that ache yet yearn: "My breast hurts, shoulder hurts—hurt body— / as I lift my arm to pour, in ecstasy. Alive!" (in "Service"). And section 5 returns to the theme of mortality, as the poet reflects upon death ("Someone is dying; someone wants to die") and is stalked by the terror that cancer evokes ("Like air you seep into my body cavities / and take up residence, open charge accounts") (61, 68, 77–79, 84–85).

In the epilogue to this collection of poetry, however, Raz seeks solace in the prospect of survival. She exults, in "Recovery," that "the fingers of

the rain are tapping again"; in response, "I send out my heart's drum"
(99). She reflects, in "My Award / The Jews of Lukow," on her good
fortune in healing from cancer surgery, winning a prestigious writer's
prize, and being alive to celebrate it, especially when so many other Jews
through the ages have fallen, when "so many of us [are] in the ground"
(100–103). Finally, in "Ecstasies," she finds joy once more in sex, "my
body opening / lilacs entering your wide mouth." She revels in the present moment:

> Where I am now,
> every ecstasy dissolves
> back into the pool,
> the lap of waves,
> the filled basin.
>
> (104–5)

Where she is *now* sustains the poet, for it seems to her miraculous that she
is still alive.

WRITING AS A HEALING ART

Warm in the late afternoon sun, I fondle my remaining breast, my flat half-
chest, my armpit, my forearm. I let the flat of my hand rest against my scar.
From a distance it would look as if I were making a vow. Then I pick up my
notebook and begin to write.
                              —Ostriker, "Scenes from a Mastectomy"

Breast cancer poems move from elegiac to transformational when the
poet releases any lingering sense of "contagion" at having fallen ill,
interrogates her cancer experience unflinchingly, and explores new discursive modes of gendered subjectivity and feminist affiliation. All four
poets considered here have reflected at length, in prose as well as poetry,
upon the role of writing in helping them affirm their bodies, selves, and
communities after the diagnosis of cancer. For Raz, writing, more than
anything else, brings a reconciled peace. What has often *kept* her from
her art, she admits in her essay "Writing the Impossible," is "fear, cancer, his suicide, their departure." Sometimes writing feels impossible,
she further acknowledges, but not writing feels worse: "I'd rather be
swimming in the ocean, waving not drowning, than writing when I'm
afraid, sick, or grieving. But what else can you do?" (124). What else

indeed? For the cancer survivor every word counts, as does every instant.

Writing for Ostriker serves as a locus from which to pay homage to the lives of ill women, to love her changed body fully, and to see and speak afresh. Near the end of her essay "Scenes from a Mastectomy" she pauses to reflect on her postmastectomy identity:

> The pond sparkles, the trees at the wood's edge stir slightly, I sit and let my breath slow down, I try to let my mind decelerate. No longer do I need to be tense and in control, speeding through my vigilant days and weeks as if a moment's relaxation would bring some nameless disaster. I can let go. . . . Remember the joy and power I felt as an adolescent when my breasts finally began to grow. How I had always enjoyed them, been proud of them, wanted them admired under my sweaters. How I liked them being fondled and appreciated by men. What pleasure I had nursing my three children, rocking and being suckled by their small mouths, while their small hands patted my breast. . . . And all of that is in the past. (199)

Yet Ostriker chooses to honor instead of mourn her amputated breast. She caresses its scar as lovingly as she does her remaining breast, then "pick[s] up [her] notebook and begins to write" (200). Both of her breasts, then, function as sites of joyful recollection, maternal as well as sexual. Through memories of her youthful breasts and honest representation of her aging ones, the poet inscribes a postmastectomy sublime that empowers her and inspires other women whose lives have been touched by cancer.

By exploring human strength and vulnerability and by affirming the wholeness of one-breasted women, Clifton's poems also move beyond elegy toward a state of grace. In an article on Clifton's ancestral muses, Gloria (Akasha) Hull argues convincingly that much of the poet's worldview comes from African spiritual traditions. In contrast to conventional Christian doctrine, which forbids ancestor worship and privileges a single holy spirit as a manifestation of God himself, Clifton's Afrocentric vision reveres dead ancestors (especially women) and accepts the presence of a vibrant, varied spirit world. Hull describes six features that characterize Clifton's poetry, all of which appear in her cancer poems from *The Terrible Stories:* the presentation of mystical experiences as everyday occurrences; the deconstruction of a corrupt social order in favor of humane alternatives; a revision of traditional Christianity in a manner that foregrounds its "racialized, feminized, and mysticized" dimensions; a view of all living beings as connected; a belief in "hope, higher values, and joy in the midst of destruction and despair"; and the recognition that any self is ever changing. Indeed, Clifton has spoken often of writing as a gateway to the mystical, there for the opening: "If you allow room in your life for mystery, mystery will come" (Hull 112).

A question that Lorde posed in *The Cancer Journals* reflects beautifully the intentionality with which she approached the intersection of cancer, writing, and gender/ethnic identity: "How do my experiences with cancer fit into the larger tapestry of my work as a Black woman, into the history of all women?" (16–17) For the last twelve years of her life she wrestled with this question, publishing poems about apartheid in South Africa, poverty in U.S. cities, sexism, racism, homophobia, but also about love and solidarity between women, challenges to the political status quo, and the effects of metastasized breast cancer on one woman—herself—knowing she was one of many. As a final offering, Lorde summarized her vision of *A Marvelous Arithmetics of Distance* on the jacket of the book. In its emphasis on resistance, transformation, and dialectic, her commentary reminds us that cancer never has the last word. That prerogative remains the poet's.

> Beyond the penchant for easy definitions, false exactitudes, we share a hunger for enduring value, relationship beyond hierarchy and outside reproach, a hunger for life measures, complex, direct, and flexible. . . . I want this book to be filled with shards of light thrown off from the shifting tensions between the dissimilar, for that is the real stuff of creation and growth.

Emotionally, Lorde refuses objectification and abjection, embracing instead a vibrant subjectivity and a communal dialogue with her imagined audience. Aesthetically, she eschews elegy in favor of a hopeful discourse whose key metaphors—"shards of light," the "real stuff of creation and growth"—will serve as redemptive touchstones for generations of future readers.

4. DYING INTO THE LITE

Popular Fiction, Cancer, & the Romance

of Women's Relationships

Although we may imagine ourselves to be well past the era of patriarchal medicine, obedience is the message behind the infantilizing theme in breast-cancer
culture, as represented by the teddy bears, crayons, and the prevailing pink-
ness.

    —Barbara Ehrenreich, "Welcome to Cancerland"

At its most extreme, this nineteenth-century ideal of the frail, even sickly
female ultimately led to a glorification of the dead or dying woman. . . . An
extraordinary imperative . . . underlay much of the nineteenth-century ideology of femininity: in one way or another, woman must be "killed" into passivity in order for her to acquiesce in what Rousseau and others considered her
duty of self-abnegation.

    —Sandra M. Gilbert and Susan Gubar,
    The Norton Anthology of Literature by Women

The dominant language that eroticizes women's suffering and their submission
to male dominance has itself frequently been an important means of exploring
and expressing desire.

  —Marianne Noble, *The Masochistic Pleasures of Sentimental Literature*

IN A PROVOCATIVE 2001 ESSAY in *Harper's Magazine*, journalist Barbara Ehrenreich chronicles her experience of being diagnosed with
breast cancer and thereby entering "a cult of pink kitsch." From
classified ads for breast cancer teddy bears, festooned with ribbons, to
the Bosom Buds and other Web sites, where survivors embrace their illness as a source of life renewal, Ehrenreich finds an active "breast cancer
marketplace" whose simplistic, highly commercialized approach to this
disease she eschews. "Let me die of anything but suffocation by the pink
sticky sentiment embodied in that teddy bear," she begs the gods, her
rampaging cells, anything that a feminist agnostic can invoke. Ehrenreich analyzes astutely the "ultrafeminine themes" and "infantilizing

tropes" of the American cancer industry as a seductive strategy for focusing women's energies on treatment rather than prevention—and on corporate-sponsored activities like the Komen Foundation's Race for the Cure rather than more radical forms of activism.[1] Although public attention to women's cancers does matter, their commercialization domesticates women already frightened by the diagnosis of a potentially fatal disease. " 'Awareness' beats secrecy and stigma of course," Ehren-reich concludes, "but I can't help noticing that the existential space in which a friend has earnestly advised me to 'confront [my] mortality' bears a striking resemblance to the mall" (44–46).

The phrase "pink sticky sentiment" recalls the popularity in nine-teenth-century England and America of the literary domestics, best-sell-ing novels by, for, and about women that romanticized home and hearth. Many novels followed the guidelines established in the eighteenth cen-tury by the philosopher Jean-Jacques Rousseau, who claimed that women's duty was to serve men: "to please them, to be useful to them, to make themselves loved and honored by them" (Gilbert and Gubar 168). Yet sentimental novels valorized as well a private, feminine language of the heart and venerated motherhood and female bonding as important sources of moral power. Textual portrayals of the sentimental developed differently across the Atlantic. In the United States, popular novels such as Susan Warner's *The Wide, Wide World* and Maria Cummins's *The Lamplighter* celebrated the shared sympathies of women and caused male novelists such as Nathaniel Hawthorne to bemoan the "d–d mob of scribbling women" whose works outsold his own. In England, works such as Susanna Rowson's *Charlotte Temple* altered the seduction and betrayal plots that had dominated eighteenth-century sensational novels to appeal to middle-class women's domestic situations. George Eliot's 1855 condemnation of "the frothy, the prosy, the pious, [and] the pedan-tic" in "Silly Novels by Lady Novelists" set the tone for a debate that pit-ted the "masculine" literary values of reason, realism, and emotional restraint against the dangers of emotional excess, the "feminine," and commodity culture (Eliot 248).

As Jane Tompkins and Marianne Noble have pointed out, these debates flourish even in the present day, since the audience for sentimen-tal novels has continued despite the critical disparagement. Tompkins argues persuasively that "the popular domestic novel of the nineteenth century represented a monumental effort to reorganize culture from the woman's point of view" and that this body of work "is remarkable for its intellectual complexity, ambition, and resourcefulness" (21). She further posits that women's popular novels of both the nineteenth and twentieth centuries have received too little serious attention, even from feminist critics, partly because generations of readers have learned "to equate popularity with debasement, emotionality with ineffectiveness, religiosity with fakery, domesticity with triviality, and all of these, implicitly, with womanly inferiority" (21). Noble, who focuses on the prevalence of masochism and suffering in women's sentimental texts, agrees with Tompkins that sentimentality can be an empowering "means of exploring and expressing desire," though unlike Tompkins, Noble acknowledges as well its "impulse toward female erasure" (8, 21). As we shall see, the question of what constitutes "pink sticky sentiment" and what constitutes an effective exploration of female desire asserts itself vigorously into any consideration of women's recent cancer fiction.

The "ultrafeminine themes" and "infantilizing tropes" to which Ehrenreich refers also populate the landscape of contemporary women's romance fiction. As Janice Radway noted in *Reading the Romance,* her landmark study of this genre, typical readers of romance novels in 1980 were middle-class, suburban, married white women, young adult to middle aged; as mothers of children under eighteen, they most often were unemployed or were part-time workers who sought the leisure of reading as a means of coping with the exhaustion of caring for husband, children, and, often, aging parents. While today's romance readers are more diversified—they include college students and older adult women of all races, single as well as married—these readers continue to interpret the novels they cherish as "chronicles of female triumph" in which an intelligent, attractive heroine overcomes adversity to find a loving man, usually to become her husband. Such romantic narratives, as Radway argues, fill readers' entertainment needs by serving as a "tranquilizer or restorative agent" that offers uninterrupted time for relaxation or escape, provides emotional release, and reinforces the idealistic view that perfect love is possible ("Readers" 582).[2] Although some have argued that the romance novel's dominion has waned, a glance at any recent *New York Times* best-seller list confirms the genre's continuing popularity. On the January 5, 2003, fiction list, for example, three of the top ten novels were written by Nora Roberts, who combines romance and suspense to explore such topics as "chefs and their love lives" and creates protagonists who "fall in love with someone who might be involved in murder." Reading these romances can entertain, distract, and temporarily revive women who find their daily lives or primary relationships depleting. However, as Radway concludes, "more often than not, those relationships remain unchanged and in returning to them a woman is once again expected and willing to employ her emotional resources for the care of others" ("Readers" 582–83). Pleasurable as they can be, romance novels rarely serve as agents for feminist transformation.

This chapter probes the links among the cancer marketplace that Ehrenreich critiques, the sentimental novel that Eliot satirizes and Tompkins and Noble defend, the romance fiction that Radway scrutinizes, and an increasing body of women's popular fiction about cancer. Specifically, I claim that mainstream cancer fiction of the past ten years employs ultrafeminine and, at times, infantilizing themes to forge an updated version of the nineteenth-century domestic novel. This new version draws heavily upon the doctrine of separate spheres for women and men and revises in intriguing ways the Victorian "cult of true womanhood," with its emphasis on domesticity, purity, piety, and submission (Welter 1). Like domestic fiction of the nineteenth century, today's popular fiction glorifies its dying heroine, who becomes of necessity increasingly passive. Indeed, the claims that critic Michelle A. Masse makes for eighteenth- and nineteenth-century gothic fiction hold true as well for much sentimental cancer fiction today: "What characters in these novels represent, whether through repudiation, doubt, or celebration, is the cultural, psychoanalytic, and fictional expectation that they *should* be masochistic if they are 'normal' women" (2). In certain contemporary cancer novels, moreover, authors rewrite the romance plot as well as the domestic one. Instead of a conventional love story that develops between a woman and the male beloved she has long been seeking, popular cancer fiction privileges idealized love between a dying woman and the female supporters who surround her bedside. These caregivers put their own lives on hold to nurse the cancer patient they love, thus reifying the domestic sphere and positioning women at the center of sickbed, hearth, and home. The dying woman becomes either their surrogate lover or their wounded child—sometimes both.

I will focus on two categories of women's relationships that popular cancer fiction inscribes: *best friends* and *dutiful daughters*. Rarely in these novels do husbands, fathers, brothers, sons, or male friends provide primary care for women dying of cancer, although they sometimes appear as a final rescuer; for the most part, however, in fiction as in life, women nurse and nurture the gravely ill.[3] My study emphasizes four novels that represent most compellingly the difficult task of close friends and obedient daughters who serve as caregivers. In Patricia Gaffney's *The Saving Graces* (1999) a women's group supports its eldest member and spiritual center, Isabel, when her breast cancer metastasizes two years after her initial mastectomy. Her closest friend, Lee, is particularly critical to this process, but the two other "Graces," Emma and Rudy, also care for Isabel as she prepares to die. These friendships are passionate, romantic, and primary, and the dying woman acts as moral teacher as well as a passive but dignified victim. In Elizabeth Berg's *Talk before Sleep* (1994) Ruth, a divorced artist dying of breast cancer in her forties, receives comfort from her best friend, Ann, a former nurse who temporarily abandons the home she shares with her husband and young daughter to spend Ruth's last days in an intimate womanspace. What Berg has termed "the strength and salvation of women's friendships" sustains these protagonists "through trials, tears, and laughter," as one reader of sentimental fiction proclaims (Crowley; Armstrong). These novels suggest as well that women friends can attain a deathbed intimacy that may elude husbands and wives.

A variation on these themes holds true for contemporary cancer fiction that features mothers and daughters, whose strong connection can become a psychic symbiosis through gender-role imprinting. As Nancy Chodorow has argued in *The Reproduction of Mothering*, intense mother-daughter bonds are both socially and psychologically constructed: "Women are prepared psychologically for mothering through the developmental situation in which they grew up, and in which women have mothered them" (158). In cancer novels that foreground mother-daughter relationships, the "female world of love and ritual" (to borrow historian Carroll Smith-Rosenberg's phrase) replaces the romance theme as the primary source of sentiment, although the mother-daughter bond can have romantic elements (1). As Tompkins points out, the "ethic of sacrifice," the "story of salvation through motherly love," and "the power of the dead or the dying to redeem the unregenerate" recur as themes in early sentimental fiction (22–24). These motifs appear as well in recent mother-daughter novels about cancer. In Anna Quindlen's *One True Thing* (1994) Ellen Gulden, a New York writer in her twenties, foregoes career and lover when she returns home to care for her mother, Kate, a homemaker whose cancer has invaded her liver and ovaries. Through the process of caring for her mother, Ellen in effect *becomes* her mother as she focuses on cleaning, cooking, and nursing; Kate, in turn, regresses to a childlike dependency. Yet before she does, she instructs her daughter about maternal devotion and true womanhood. In Jayne Anne Phillips's *MotherKind* (2000) a thirty-year-old poet, Kate Tateman, nurses her dying mother, Katherine, alongside her newborn son in a stressful blended household that consists as well of the baby's father and his two sons from a first marriage. As Kate feeds, launders, and nurtures, she reflects on words but no longer writes; instead, she idealizes Katherine and embraces "motherkind" as a bond among generations of women. Although this caretaking exhausts both Quindlen's Ellen and Phillips's Kate, they view it as their duty and, much of the time, their privilege. Both novels thus foreground the private sphere in a way that recalls the literary domestics, and they "essentialize" women as "naturally" compassionate and nurturing (Fuss 1–5). In addition, Quindlen's and Phillips's novels highlight the bond between mothers and daughters, a connection that may involve anger and ambivalence but ends in affirmation. Taken together, these four novels expand Ehrenreich's critique of the ultrafeminine cancer marketplace, but they also support Tompkins's claims that domesticity need not be equated with triviality, nor popularity with cultural insignificance.

"SISTERS OF THE HEART AND SOUL": CANCER AND WOMEN'S ROMANTIC FRIENDSHIPS

Sentimental domestic novels of the nineteenth century "elaborated a myth that gave women the central position of power and authority in the culture," a myth defined by the virtues of traditional femininity, the heroism of individual sacrifice, and the spiritual resonance of dying women and/or children (Tompkins 22). Sentimental cancer novels of the late twentieth century inscribe a similar myth, although their heroines have stronger voices, less religious piety, and more sexual autonomy than their Victorian counterparts. Romance novels emphasize the development of love and arousal of desire over time; as one of Radway's readers explains, "generally there are two people who come together for one reason or another, grow to love each other and work together solving problems along the way—united for a purpose" ("Readers" 566). Recent romantic cancer novels follow this formula, with the significant differences that love between women is as valorized as love between women and men and that the women unite for the purpose of helping one of them to die. In *The Saving Graces* and *Talk before Sleep*, domesticity and romance intersect to produce new representations of cancer and women's bonds.

The support group of nearly ten years' duration that lies at the center of *The Saving Graces* offers itself, in the book's opening lines, as a web of connection stronger than the typical marriage. "If half of all marriages end in divorce, how long does the average marriage last?" wonders Emma, the first of four revolving narrators. "This isn't a math problem; I'd really like to know. I bet it's less than nine and a half years. That's how long the Saving Graces have been going strong, and we're not even getting restless. We still talk, still notice things about each other, weight loss, haircuts, new boots. As far as I know, nobody's looking around for a younger, firmer member" (1). The wry musings of Emma establish the novel's tone, which uses irony to offset the seriousness of its themes: cancer, infertility, adultery, psychological abuse. Ultimately, however, it dramatizes death and enduring love among women. Emma's introductory comments further reveal the diary technique that allows Gaffney to feature as alternating narrators four engaging women—white, professional, and upwardly mobile—whose lives have mingled irrevocably. A disenchanted journalist in her thirties who secretly desires to write a novel, Emma is best friends with Rudy, an emotionally abused woman in a troubled marriage from which the group must help her escape. These two founded the Saving Graces with Lee, a businesswoman and self-described "Jewish American princess" who is trying to become pregnant at forty-one, and with Isabel, a divorced artist, the mother of an adult son, and a breast cancer survivor.

Depicted, at forty-six, as the oldest and most mature member of the group, Isabel views her initial bout with cancer retrospectively as "a blessing in disguise." Although clichés abound in her self-analysis, she evinces an attractive blend of strength and stoicism. "It was *good* that it happened to me," she insists, despite having formerly been infuriated by cancer testimonies she read that adopted this placid tone; "it's turned my

life around" (37). Isabel credits the Graces, who meet monthly to eat,
talk, laugh, and cry, as the primary source of her postmastectomy transformation:

> I wonder if I could have survived my cancer without their loving-kindness.
> Survived— yes, probably. But only that: barest survival. Nothing, no other
> experience has ever leveled me to such an extent. I believed I would never
> recover, that I was forever changed. And I was, but not in the way I'd
> expected. (36)

Like Emma, who describes the group as "like grace in its benevolence
and generosity," Isabel views its longevity as a miraculous gift, achieved
in part as compensation for its members' having been lonely children.
"Occasionally we four play the intriguing 'What keeps us together?'
game, and the fact that we all survived our childhoods is mentioned early
and often" (36). In addition to gravitating toward popular psychology,
Isabel fully embraces a new-age worldview as an alternative to conventional religious piety. Among the totemic devices and belief systems on
which she relies are "crystals and rocks, the Tarot, reincarnation, past
lives, astrology, numerology, meditation, and hypnotherapy." Having
rejected her father's strict Lutheran philosophy, she acknowledges "how
purely delighted I am to see God in so many new places" (37).

   Gaffney explicitly ascribes to the Saving Graces a feminine rather
than a feminist ideology. Indeed, these women take pride in being a
social club, not an intellectual or activist circle. When the four protagonists meet monthly they talk about their unloving parents, their changing appearance, their relationships with men (though some intimate
experiences remain secret). When a prospective new member wants to
explore sociopolitical concerns, the group ridicules her, oddly, as male-
identified. "She did say she thought we'd discuss issues more. Topics,"
explains Lee when an acquaintance named Sharon phones to say that
after one visit she has decided not to join the group. "Topics? Please,"
snorts Emma, the narrator of this chapter.

> "Women in the workplace. Postfeminism in a preliberation era. Authenti-
> cating your life. Juggling work and family in a—"
>   "Didn't you tell her," Isabel interrupted mildly, "that we quit having
> topics quite a few years ago?" (137)

Although Lee indicates an interest in having the group discuss certain
women's issues—"mothers and daughters, ambition, trust, sex, that sort

of thing"—her sister members eschew this practice, and Gaffney presents Lee as uptight and slightly authoritarian in her aims. "From time to time I'll suggest to the group that we reinstate it," reflects Lee, "but I'll never get any support. 'We've already talked about everything under the sun,' Emma argues, 'there's nothing left'" (8).

The friendship of the Saving Graces intensifies midway through the novel, when Isabel is diagnosed with cancer that has metastasized, endures invasive treatments that fail, and prepares to die. Gaffney portrays this heightened female intimacy in three settings in which the group convenes. The first intimate space is the office of Isabel's arrogant oncologist, which the Saving Graces invade in a show of solidarity for their beloved patient. Here they act as avenging furies, asking the doctor probing questions about Isabel's prognosis, heckling him when he refers to her as "the patient," and eventually condemning him as an "flaming asshole" and convincing her to choose a different physician. Although the three friends mount a resistance to patriarchal medical authority that can be seen from a feminist perspective as admirable, their outrage silences Isabel, who sits passively, "chalk white but calm" (165–67). This tendency to infantilize Isabel because she is ill continues, as Emma's subsequent narrative acknowledges: "I monitor her these days like a mother with a sick child. We all do. She hates it" (213).

The second intimate space, Isabel's apartment, becomes her refuge after chemotherapy, to which she is regularly accompanied by Lee. After her first treatment, Isabel undresses and gets into bed at eight o'clock, not yet nauseated but in need of rest. In the scene that follows, Isabel basks in Lee's maternal care.

> "How do you feel now?" Lee asked, leaning over me, smoothing the sheet over the top of the blanket. Tucking me in.
>
> "Hard to describe. Warm, and my skin feels a little tight. I just feel odd. A sort of humming."
>
> She sat on the edge of the bed. "No fever," she noted, resting her hand on my forehead. "Don't worry, Isabel, I'll stay with you. We'll get through this."
>
> "Of course we will." I wanted to tell her what a wonderful mother she'd have been—would be—but I was afraid we'd both cry." (233–34)

When Isabel does begin to vomit, Lee holds and comforts her, leads her back to bed, and cleans up the mess. Her devotion continues to manifest itself in a heightened form of domesticity.

The third space of female intimacy is Lee's family beach house, Neap Tide, where the group convenes as Isabel declines and they can no longer deny that she is dying. Here the Graces extol Isabel's virtues in terms strikingly similar to the Victorian cult of true womanhood, with emphasis on her purity. Lee, who narrates this section, describes a conversation in which Isabel worries that she has caused her cancer to recur "with my own negative energy" and then acknowledges that a self-help book has confirmed her fears. To their credit, the Graces react angrily to the book's thesis and try to dissuade Isabel from self-blame. Although Emma reacts most vehemently—"That *Isabel* would make herself sick. . . . It's bullshit"—Lee defends her friend's purity: "I think sometimes we make ourselves sick, and sometimes it just happens. But Isabel isn't toxic to herself. There's nobody . . . purer. I mean it. No one gentler" (261).

Gaffney also describes the Graces' time together at Neap Tide in romantic terms. In response to Lee's praise, Isabel extends her hand to Lee lovingly. "I took it and she pulled me close," Lee recounts. "Instead of weeping, we four looked at one another with sharp, intense stares. I felt a thrill of fear and excitement" (261). Later, when Isabel strolls alone on the beach, her friends discuss her plight in obsessive ways. "It's what we do when we're together now, we three," Lee explains (262). In revealing the group's single-minded concern for its love object, this scene parallels those in romance novels in which the protagonist scrutinizes every detail of her beloved's behavior, searching for signs of commitment or withdrawal. As the week at Neap Tide draws to a close, the Graces commit themselves to Isabel in a manner that recalls the traditional wedding vows: "to love and to cherish, in sickness and in health, till death us do part." Having completed a healing circle whose actions include a laying on of hands in an effort to reduce the pain in Isabel's hip, the group assures her, in Rudy's stumbling words, "that no matter what happens, we're here. I mean—we're here for the long haul. You won't be alone. Ever" (275). To be sure, this novel presents women's friendships in romantic terms from its beginning: Emma and Rudy, for example, delight in asking each other repeatedly, as lovers might, "What did you first see in me?" (47) At Lee's cabin, however, the friendships assume an erotic urgency. Lee puts Isabel to bed in her cabin; Isabel speaks in a voice that is "higher, lighter, a little breathy" as she "runs her index finger back and forth across the top of Emma's hand" (412). Such acts depict what the poet Adrienne Rich has described as "a primary presence of women to ourselves and each other," a presence intensely manifested in romantic friendship (*On Lies*, 166).

To keep this female intimacy from succumbing to lesbian overtones, Gaffney takes pains to develop heterosexual romance in her novel. Men matter a lot to these women, and their lovers tend to be idealized (or demonized, in the case of Rudy's manipulative husband, Curtis, who jealously pretends he has leukemia so that his wife's attention will focus on him). Lee's Henry, a "blue-collar gentile," is sexy, attentive, long-suffering; Emma's Mick, a married man who wants to start a sexual affair with her but resists, is presented as nobly loyal to a wife he no longer loves. Most idealized is Isabel's relationship with her upstairs neighbor, Kirby, which begins after her incurable cancer has been diagnosed. Having told Isabel that he has been secretly in love with her for months, Kirby joins Lee in the intimate act of shaving Isabel's head in a preemptive strike against the Adriamycin that she must take. When, days later, the two become lovers, it is against Isabel's better judgment: "I'm sick, Kirby, and I'm bald, I'm not the real Isabel in my body. I don't know how you could want that, but if . . . if you do . . ." Kirby responds with loving touch, and, as Isabel explains, "I was so easily seduced. 'Don't think,' he said, pressing hard inside, giving me his fierce, romantic kisses. Easier said than done, and yet I did forget. He made me forget the strangeness, my clumsiness, the freakishness—some would say—of our joining" (334). The language of seduction, the description of his kisses as "fierce, romantic," and the euphemism "joining" are reminiscent of the classic romance novel, which sensationalizes foreplay but presents sex shyly if at all. From this point on Kirby joins the Graces in caring for Isabel; in fact, in the last diary entry before her death, Isabel lists Kirby as her primary caregiver, despite the ongoing care of the Graces.

In addition to this emphasis on heterosexual romance, Gaffney invests the group with a subtle form of homophobia, which has the effect of reassuring straight readers that these women are not, heaven forbid, gay. The most telling scene, narrated by Emma, recounts a conversation between Lee and her mother-in-law, a lesbian named Jenny who recalls the early days of consciousness-raising groups and praises the Graces for the longevity of their connection. Lee is quick to demur: "'But you know,' Lee pointed out amid the laughter, 'we're—ha ha!—not that kind of group.' She lifted her hand to Henry, the one here with the penis, as if to say, Look: living proof I'm heterosexual" (211). When Jenny continues to reminisce about bare-breasted 1960s protests, Lee issues another disclaimer: "'We're not very political. . . . We just have dinner." This time Jenny responds, "But you're still *together*, that's what I envy. Ten years, and you're still a group. Y'all still love each other" (211). In the scene that follows, as Emma tweaks Lee's paranoia, Gaffney reinforces the point that "that" kind of love between women does not describe the Saving Graces' bond:

> "Oh, we do," I agreed, sliding my arm around Lee's waist. "We still love each other *so much*." At the last second Lee figured out what I was going to do—kiss her on the mouth—and jerked her head away in panic. All I got was cheek.
> "Well, I'd better pass these," she muttered, sidling out of my affectionate grasp.
> "Before they get cold. Excuse me?" Always polite. But the look she threw me on her way out glittered with homicidal longing. (212)

This scene could be read as a humorous challenge to Lee's homophobia were it not for Gaffney's inflated rhetoric: the italicizing of *so much*, the noun *panic*, the phrase *homicidal longing*. This discursive extremity reflects the author's desire to deny any homoerotic dimension to the Graces' friendship.

The advice that Isabel offers each friend in a letter they read after she has died reinforces the novel's emphasis on female intimacy and extends the heterosexual plot. In the section addressed to Rudy, Isabel extols her "strength and valor" and urges her, in sentimental language, to "never forget your true friends, who will always be there and will always love you" (487). Isabel further encourages Rudy to try again with a man, despite Curtis's hurtful manipulation, "because you have so much to give" (488). In the section written to Emma, Isabel employs "smug-sounding little epigrams" such as "Fear kills" and "Failure isn't failure, it's a step" to encourage her friend to attempt a novel. Its subject? "Us, my darling," Isabel insists. "Don't you think? Write a book about us." She further implores Emma to take a chance on Mick, for life is "so short. You can take what you want now" (489–90). Finally, to her "Sweetest Lee," Isabel offers sisterly and maternal love: "You are strong—but also tender in the center. I can't imagine the last dozen years of my life without you. You've been my friend and my daughter. My delight" (487–88). Isabel encourages Lee to adopt the child "somewhere right now who's looking for you," a child whom "you'll have to love with your whole heart" (493). As the group's romantic object and spiritual anchor, Isabel speaks an inflated language of the heart from beyond the grave to orient each woman toward "new beginnings" (506).

Should the argument that Gaffney's novel rewrites the romance plot seem tenuous, consider the fact that *The Saving Graces* receives high marks from reviewers and readers who respond on such Web sites as "All About Romance," "Romantic Times," and "The Romance Reader" (Sova; Wachsmith). These reviews appear there in part because Gaffney has also written popular romance novels with more conventional heterosexual themes, but the reviews also reveal the fine line between the love plot and its "death from cancer" counterpart. Reviewer Nora Armstrong rejects the notion that *The Saving Graces* could be considered romance fiction even as she revels in its exquisite tenderness: "This book is emphatically not a romance. Don't let that stop you, though, because Gaffney's written a beautiful story of four women and their friendship . . . as a series of crises puts their friendship to the test. Yes, I'm in mourning for romance, but I couldn't be happier." Other Web testimonials claim that "readers will rapidly be turning pages," praise the novel for "pack[ing] an emotional wallop," and assert that this is "women's contemporary fiction at its absolute best" (Klausner; Sova; Wachsmith). Nora Roberts herself, the current queen of romance fiction, pronounces this "a jewel of a book, and every facet sparkles" (book jacket). In agreement with the romance aficionados that Radway surveyed twenty years ago, current readers seem to value "a slowly but consistently developing love" between protagonists, "some detail about the [two] after they have gotten together," and, indispensably, a happy ending (Radway, "Readers" 567). Certainly the first two traits well describe Gaffney's novel. The final requirement, however, might give us pause in labeling *The Saving Graces* romantic, since Gaffney's representation of Isabel's death wrenches readers. Still, the peace of mind that each Grace gains from her spiritual adviser's posthumous letter ultimately provides readers with the requisite upbeat ending.

In Berg's *Talk before Sleep* the friendship dyad replaces the women's support group as the narrative focus. As in *The Saving Graces*, domesticity, romantic attraction, and death from cancer converge to create a late-twentieth-century revision of the sentimental novel. When Ann Stanley and Ruth Thomas meet at a party, their differences initially mitigate against the possibility of shared sympathy. Conventional, plain, and competitive with other women, Ann initially resents Ruth's flamboyance and beauty; the result is "hate at first sight," at least on the part of Ann, who narrates the novel. When Ruth boisterously invades the bathroom where Ann has gone to seek refuge, however, the two women end up sharing martinis and exchanging confidences; from this point on they are inseparable. Early on in the novel Berg foregrounds the romantic ideal of the soul mate. "She was capable of a scary kind of honesty I was ready for," Ann proclaims, "although until that moment, I hadn't realized how much I'd been needing to meet someone I might be able to say anything to" (14). Several chapters later Ann describes the two friends' bond as mystical: "she hears my unspoken sentences" (61).

These scenes and observations are presented retrospectively, however; much of the novel's sense of urgency exists because readers know from the beginning that Ruth is dying of metastasized breast cancer and that Ann is her primary caregiver:

> There is a stack of magazines piled high on the floor, and a collection of crystals on the bedside table: rose quartz, amethyst, and a clear white one with a delicate fractured pattern running through it. They are not working. She is dying, though we don't know when. We are waiting. She is only forty-three and I am only forty-two and all this will not stop being surprising. (6–7)

Unlike *The Saving Graces*, which at times offers stilted and one-dimensional dramatic monologues, *Talk before Sleep* (as the title suggests) is enlivened by dialogue that conveys both pathos and redemptive humor. No subject is too intimate for Ann and Ruth to discuss, and as Ruth declines, their conversations increase in both frequency and intensity. "I was wondering what happens when I die," Ruth muses; "I was thinking, how are they sure? Are they really sure? I mean, what if I get buried alive?" A nurse who has put her career on hold to stay home with her young daughter, Ann responds candidly. " 'They're sure,' I tell her. 'You sort of . . . shut down. Your heart stops, and your breathing. Certain reflexes disappear, you know, like the pupils in your eyes don't react.' She watches me, holding absolutely still, looking like a colorized sculpture of herself. . . . 'Oh,' she says. 'Okay. Just checking.' She is relieved; you can see it in the uncreasing of her forehead, in the loosening to normal of the area around her mouth" (7–8). Other friends of Ruth visit often: her boss, Sarah; her elementary school classmate,

Helen; and the fiercely maternal L. D., a lesbian who denies that Ruth is dying. But the primary intimacy belongs to Ruth and Ann, who share secrets, baths, kisses, and sometimes the same bed. Ann accompanies Ruth to the oncologist's office, chemotherapy, and the wig shop; it is Ann to whom Ruth voices her final instructions: "If my brain goes and I can't do anything and they bring those fucking bedpans into my house, shoot me" (15–16).

Assertive and ebullient, Berg's Ruth represents a different breed of dying heroine from Gaffney's modest Isabel in her sexual transgressions and her exuberant ruminations on life and death. Although she has divorced her philandering husband by the time cancer strikes, Ruth had lived with him for many years as "slightly hostile roommates" for the sake of their teenaged son, Michael, when she and Ann met. Ruth does not hesitate to inform Ann of her extramarital affairs; indeed, she blithely urges the unhappily married Ann to seek the same fulfillment. "You won't get caught," Ruth insists; "I can promise you that. I've been doing this for six years, Ann. It doesn't take much intelligence to not get caught. Although, at first, you really wish you would" (48). This coda reveals the performative dimension to Ruth's rebelliousness and the emotional vulnerability that Ann gradually recognizes; at one point Ruth confesses that she wishes she could return to her marriage, so depressed is she at being alone. Although she never adheres precisely to the cult of true womanhood, Ruth, like Isabel, values domesticity, evinces a new-age piety, and ultimately submits to a male caregiver—her brother, Andrew—despite the fact that she knows Ann will feel abandoned.

That Berg valorizes the domestic arts and the doctrine of separate spheres is evident in the novel's opening paragraphs, which portray Ann's guilt at spending time away from family:

> This morning, before I came to Ruth's house, I made yet another casserole for my husband and my daughter. Meggie likes casseroles while Joe only endures them, but they are all I can manage right now. I put the dish in the refrigerator, with a note taped on it telling how long to cook it, and at what temperature, and that they should have a salad, too.
>
> Next I did a little laundry—washed Meggie's favorite skirt, then laid it on top of the dryer and pressed the pleats in with the flat of my hand. I love doing this because I love the smell of laundry soap and the memory it brings of lying outside on warm days, watching my mother peg huge white bedsheets onto the clothesline. (3)

As these passages reveal, Ann uses domesticity as a compensatory gesture but also revels in tedious chores, finding in them instead maternal
satisfaction and matrilineage. Indeed, self-sacrifice is vital to Ann's identity: "I have learned so much lately about the salvation to be found in
caretaking, whatever form that caring takes" (4–5).

Both Ann and Ruth become increasingly pious as the novel progresses and do so in a manner that recalls and revises the kind of piety
that dominates many nineteenth-century literary domestics, whose heroines bend to God's miraculous will. Ann's piety manifests itself not in
Christian rituals but in her healing crystals, yet she too believes in miracles: "I always think incipient miracles surround us, waiting only to see
if our faith is strong enough. We won't have to understand it; it will just
work, like a beating heart, like love" (58). Ann shares this new-age spirituality with Ruth, who demands that "a grown-up woman angel" be
placed on her tombstone, "with huge wings that look really powerful.
Like she works out. I've been dreaming about angels. I think they're
real" (133). This discourse of salvation, faith, miracles, and angels lends
a religious tone to an otherwise secular novel and emphasizes the spiritual power that Berg invests in femininity, women's friendships, and the
dying woman.

A fascinating mixture of feminine and feminist ideologies permeates
Talk before Sleep. In addition to helping Ruth bathe and dress, tucking
her in, and lullabying her to sleep, Ann preoccupies herself with food
and feeding, despite the fact that the patient often does not feel like eating. Indeed, the entire circle of friends who care for Ruth treat food
obsessively, in part as a source of escape from grim reality but also as a
source of group camaraderie. When Ruth laments that her refrigerator is
filled with healthy food like banana bread and fruit salad, her women
friends treat her with lobster, McDonald's french fries, and beer, which
they all devour. After Ruth acknowledges, "I'm not going to make it,
Ann. I know that now," the two indulge a craving for cinnamon toast
(133). Food imagery serves as a synecdoche for nurture, of course, and
compulsive eating assists in both momentary denial and life affirmation.
Still, the scenes around the dinner table reinforce the author's emphasis
on the conventionally feminine and facilitate talk about that most enduring of female topics, body image. "After I die, you guys have really got
to go on a diet," insists Ruth. There follows a tense exchange between
enormous L. D. and petite Sarah, "the only one of us who hasn't gained

a lot," over whether skinny women are attractive or, in L. D.'s words, "look like assholes" (167); this debate reveals tensions among the women, all of whom vie to be Ruth's most important friend, but it is one of many scenes in which they focus on appearance. At times these scenes feature feminist rebellion, as when Ann accompanies a balding Ruth to buy a wig and the two challenge a rude saleswoman, who asks Ruth, "Have you been walking around like that?" While Ruth responds defiantly—"Jesus Christ. What else? If I had a wig, I wouldn't be here now, would I?"—the usually reticent Ann confronts the clerk directly: "Why do you have to be such a bitch? Why do you have to make a hard thing harder?" (56). Ann also displays feminist consciousness in critiquing American culture's view of bald women: "I wish we could get over our horror of baldness and appreciate instead the tender revelations it provides" (53). Ruth does buy a "feminine" wig, however, and purchases prostheses "three times the size she was—she went from a 34A to a 38C"—a decision Ann admires (54).

As in *The Saving Graces,* intimate spaces where the women gather further reveal the romantic nature of their bond. Readers first meet Ruth in the bath, when she invites Ann into the room to talk. Ann's narration of this scene reveals its sensuality:

> I sit on the floor beside her, rest my arms along the edge of the tub to lean in close, though what I am thinking is that I ought to get in with her. . . . I can see the outline of her body in the water. She is half-swimming, turning slightly side to side, hips rising languidly up and down. Her breasts are gone. (7)

The intimacy of their talk mirrors their physical closeness, as Ruth reflects upon dying. "Maybe when we die we go back incrementally," she muses. "You know, a little to the sea, then on to the heavens. . . . I was just lying in here . . . and then I thought, wait—is this it? I mean, how will I know?" Ann's reply both soothes her friend and idealizes her: "You will know, though. You won't be the same person you are now when it happens. You'll be, I don't know . . . wiser" (7–8). Later we learn that Ann and Ruth first met in another bathroom, where Ann was hiding from a stressful party, and that Ruth in effect rescued her. Moreover, one of their last scenes of intimacy before Ruth dies takes place in the bathroom, as Ann shaves her friend's legs and urges her to relax. Here Ruth breaks the news that she will spend her final days with her brother, a revelation that causes Ann anguish: "What for? What do you mean? . . . We're fine here. I'm fine here. I'll stay with you." Ruth's explanation that "he was there when I was born, Ann," does little to relieve Ann's distress. "I say nothing. I feel a tightening in my chest that is a terrible fear" (175–76). Instead of trying to dissuade her companion, however, Ann resorts again to domesticity: she shaves Ruth's other leg, puts talc on, dresses her.

The second space in which Ann and Ruth explore their intimacy, Ruth's artist studio, is particularly eroticized as the site of their first kiss. Yet ironically, the space in which Ruth paints and encourages Ann to sculpt with clay resembles a child's playroom. When Ann, assured that her sculpture will be acceptable, shows it proudly to Ruth (as a child would to her mother), Ann recounts that Ruth "put her hands on my shoulders and kissed me full on the mouth" (60). As Ann reflects back upon this moment, she revels in its perfection and its purity: "There is a pure place in all of us that makes no judgments about anything, ever. That place recognizes what Ruth did as being absolutely right. The rest of me was nervous. I stepped back, blushing, and she laughed" (60–61). Berg's choice of an art studio/playroom as the site of the women's kiss is clearly designed to underscore the innocent playfulness of this gesture, yet the gesture itself is sexualized, as Ann's blushes indicate.

The third romantic space, a tent under the stars, provides the setting for Ann to kiss Ruth in an even more sexualized way: "I leaped up, lay on top of her, and kissed her passionately. Then I got back into my sleeping bag" (138). Ann's uncharacteristic gesture is in part a response to Ruth's seductive entreaties:

> "Have you every thought about loving me?"
> "I do, I do love you, that's what I meant."
> "No, I mean physically loving me."
> "No!"
> "No?"
> "Well, I'm sorry, Ruth, but no, I haven't."
> She put her face close to mine. I didn't move. She put her hand along the side of my face, pushed my hair back, raised her eyebrows slightly. I didn't move. The stars surrounded her, they and her face were all that I saw. (138)

Ruth is idealized as well as sexualized by the starry-eyed Ann. An impassioned exchange, a romantic interlude under the night sky—the stuff of romance novels, revised to depict erotically charged love between women.

A final intimate space, Ruth's bedroom, takes center stage as her cancer progresses; although this room serves initially as a romantic setting, it gradually becomes a site of sentimental exchanges. As Ann recalls, she and Ruth slept together in Ruth's bed on the evening of her initial cancer diagnosis: "I stayed with her that night. Both of us crowded onto her little bed, like sisters. 'Aren't you at all scared?' I asked, just before we fell asleep" (76). Once Ruth's response that she will be fine reassures her, Ann is free to smell the scent of her friend's shampoo, feel her body nearby, and relax into sleep "because I believed her" (76). Another indication of the bedroom's sexualized atmosphere is the homoerotic print on its wall of several women "sleeping outside in a field, some of them with the tops of their dresses loosened to reveal their cleanly white breasts, their soft stomachs"; when Ann wonders wryly how the women in the print avoid grocery shopping, Ruth replies that "they feed each other. They don't need a thing" (104). Such exchanges foreground the bedroom as a woman-centered environment. Once Ruth weakens physically the women no longer sleep together, but Ann often climbs in her bed to talk. In the bedroom Ruth confesses that she knows she will die soon: "I can't breathe, my back hurts so bad, especially at night. And I feel like . . . I feel so . . . sort of . . . vague, you know? It's not just weakness, it's vagueness. . . . I think it's just my time now." Distraught, Ann caresses the top of her head, feeling "the heat of her life," and implores her, "Don't go" (129–30). These scenes reinforce the romantic aspects of same-sex allegiance and suggest that Berg lacks Gaffney's ambivalence toward this topic—a fact that arguably contributes to the feminist dimensions of *Talk before Sleep*.

This novel, like *The Saving Graces*, contains elements of heterosexual romance as well. Shortly after Ruth begins chemotherapy, she begins to date an old college boyfriend, Joel, who calls after many years apart "because he's never stopped being crazy about her, and he wanted to see if the old stuff was still there" (118). Although Ruth tells her friends of Joel's nurturing and sexual capacities, she sends him away after a few weeks, confessing to Ann that it is too late for her to develop a lasting bond with a man. Joel's appearance serves to reaffirm the women's heterosexuality, however, as do the rare scenes in which Ann talks or sleeps with her husband, Joe, whose similarity in name to Ruth's lover bears its own symbolic weight. Yet there exists no romance between Ann and Joe; not only does Ann fail to describe any sexual activity with him, but when she returns home shortly before Ruth dies, she asserts that "if he tries to get laid I will kill him with a butcher knife" (197). Alternately impatient and gentle, Joe tries to comfort Ann by touching her hair, an intimacy that she appreciates because "it is whitely innocent" (197). Although Joel and Joe play minor roles and are somewhat caricatured, their existence disrupts readers' views of the intimacy between Ruth and Ann as potentially lesbian.

Throughout the novel Ann refers to women in an essentialist manner that recalls the nineteenth-century literary domestics: she views women as emotionally stronger than men, exalts matriarchy over patriarchy, and, with Ruth, believes their bond is fated to continue after death (Fuss 1–5). Imagining how Ruth's mother might feel were she alive to watch her daughter die, Ann posits that she would "draw from the reservoir of sacred strength that women are born with" (141). She further claims that "the souls of women flatten and anchor themselves in times of adversity, lay in for the stay," like elephants who run toward each other, not away, when attacked. "Perhaps it is because they are a matriarchal society," she muses (142). As the two women lie in bed together shortly before Ruth leaves for Andrew's house, she reminds the sobbing Ann that "I will come back to you as a little breeze. You will feel me on your face, and you will know that I am listening. . . . I want you to always talk to me. I think I'll hear" (183). To be sure, Berg offers narrative gestures of humor and irony that undermine sentimentality. For instance, after Ann agrees to converse with Ruth after she dies, Ruth insists that her friend agree to inherit not only her plants and seashells but also her vibrator. When Andrew phones to tell Ann that Ruth has died, she picks up the phone and, ironically, gets "halfway through dialing before I realize who I am calling: Ruth, to tell her she died" (204). After Ruth's death, Ann acknowledges that her friend has not visited as promised, an acknowledgment that further undercuts the novel's sentimentality. Although Ann senses Ruth's presence, "she does not appear"; the weeping Ann then calms herself by imagining Ruth's exhortation to "knock it off" (205). Typically, however, Ann's rejection of sentimentality provokes reflection that reinvigorates it. This is evident in her insistence that she communes with her own "life force" despite Ruth's failure to appear: "I believe I am effectively unconscious at that moment, in a holy place between me and the Mystery" (210).

When this novel appeared in 1994, it received rave reviews from many popular sources and Web site readers. Reviewer Leslie Crowley claimed that "as a reader, I felt that this novel elevated all of my relationships to something sacred, but also reminded me with a profane clarity just how tenuous and fragile these relationships are." Other readers applied the book's lessons to their family experiences with cancer: Beth, writing in an online chat room, admitted that Berg's novel "stirred all of my emotions" and explained that when her mother-in-law was diagnosed with cancer, "it made it a little easier for me to face the reality of it all"; in the same chat room Sandra, an English teacher, responded that "anyone who has lost someone to cancer will be able to relate to it. Everybody should read this book" (barnesandnoble.com). A few reviewers, however, did find Berg's novel formulaic. Reviewing for the Literature, Arts, and Medicine Database, Richard M. Ratzan claimed that "unfortunately, like many books with much pathos, *Talk before Sleep* missteps into the territory of bathos." Most critical of the novel's tendency to idealize Ruth was Lauren Belfer of the *New York Times:* "One danger in fiction about mortal illness is that a writer may, albeit unwittingly, so glorify a dying character that the reader loses sympathy for her. This happens in Elizabeth Berg's otherwise haunting and sensitive second novel." Ratzan's and Belfer's critiques recall George Eliot's indictment of the nineteenth-century sentimental heroine as "the ideal woman in feelings, faculties, and flounces," though the contemporary critics' analyses are less scathing than Eliot's (249). Of all the criticisms heaped upon the literary domestics during the nineteenth century, the most enduring one challenged the movement from pathos to bathos—a movement that Ehrenreich decries in the "sticky pink sentiment" of breast cancer culture as well (44).

"BREATHING IN TANDEM": DYING MOTHERS & DUTIFUL DAUGHTERS

Women writers have written with anger, ambivalence, and affirmation about the mother-daughter relationship, one of the most complex of any human dynamics. Many have questioned whether mothers are powerful or powerless in their roles as the primary caregivers of children and whether daughters should respect, revise, or challenge maternal authority. In her feminist treatise on motherhood, *Of Woman Born*, Adrienne Rich distinguishes between two definitions: *motherhood as experience*, which encompasses the potentially powerful relationship of any woman to her reproductive capacities and her children; and *motherhood as institution*, which in a patriarchal society tries to keep women and children under male control. The institution of motherhood is underwritten by a series of unexamined assumptions that valorize the conventionally feminine: that motherhood is woman's destiny, her sacred calling; that mothers lack further identities and are selfless; that mothers feel only tenderness for their children, never resentment. Motherhood is not preordained for women, Rich argues; it has a history, an ideology; it is "more fundamental than tribalism or nationalism." The experience of motherhood, varied according to race and class and geographic location, acknowledges that maternity is one part of life for many (not all) women rather than an identity for all time; it bears witness to anger at one's children as well as joy at their growth. As contemporary women writers rethink the maternal, Rich claims, its landscape shifts: "the words are being spoken, are being written down; the taboos are being broken, the masks of motherhood are cracking through" (24–25).

Women's sentimental fiction of the nineteenth century extolled the virtues of "motherhood as institution" by idealizing mothers, especially on their deathbeds, reifying the sanctity of home, and embracing the tenets of "true womanhood"—praising mothers and daughters who were pure, pious, domestic, and submissive. Contemporary popular novels that feature dying mothers as protagonists often reinforce this ideology, even as they foreground daughters with emerging feminist consciousness. A cultural feminism underlies these texts, an essentialism about which feminist theorists who study mother-daughter bonds offer cautionary words. In writing about mothers and daughters, Marianne Hirsch notes, "I am aware of the dangers of idealizing and mystifying a certain biological female experience and of reviving an identification between femininity and maternity which certainly has not served the interests of women" (163). Linda Rennie Forcey echoes Hirsch's concern about essentializing women as fundamentally different from men and thereby assuming that nurturing mothers will challenge male aggression, yet Forcey is sympathetic to writers who reify mothers as peace loving—after all, "who among us would want to imply that there could ever be too much caring in this violent world?" (365). To write thoughtfully about motherhood, she concludes, women must "acknowledge the tension between needing to act as women who value mothering/caring labor, and needing an identity not overdetermined by our gender" (375).

The struggle to value the maternal care they have received, to nurture their dying mothers in turn, yet to maintain an identity apart from that of caregiver dogs the daughters in Quindlen's *One True Thing* and Phillips's *MotherKind*. While Quindlen focuses initially on what Rich terms "the most painful estrangement" that can occur between conventional mothers and their daughters, Phillips emphasizes "the deepest mutuality" that mothers and daughters can attain, especially when the daughter gives birth to children of her own (*Of Woman* 226). When the mother is diagnosed with cancer, of course, both estrangement and mutuality are disrupted, as each member of the dyad realizes that ultimately the roles of nurturer and nurtured must be reversed. For Quindlen's Ellen, who feels ambivalent about her mother, this realization evokes resentment, whereas for Phillips's Kate it represents a welcome opportunity to give back to a mother she admires. In each novel, however, the mother-daughter cathexis motivates the daughter figure to idealize her dying mother; in Quindlen's text, the daughter also emulates her mother's submissive behavior. The resulting narratives replicate certain aspects of the nineteenth-century literary domestics even as they applaud a feminist sensibility in the younger generation.

That domesticity defines Kate Gulden, the maternal protagonist in *One True Thing*, at least through her daughter's eyes, is evident early in the novel when Ellen, a journalist, travels from Manhattan to the small town where she was raised to visit her ailing mother. To the rather smug Ellen, Kate exemplifies the quintessential housewife: "Our mother was in the hospital that day, and as it always did, the house seemed like a stage set without her. It was her house, really. Whenever anyone is called a homemaker now—and they rarely are—I think of my mother. She made a home painstakingly well. She made balanced meals, took cooking classes, cleaned the rooms of our home with a scarf tying back her bright hair, just like in the movies" (23). The daughter's discourse highlights a performative dimension to her mother's behavior that Ellen resents;

while she appreciates the clean house and healthy meals, she acknowledges having felt "vaguely contemptuous" that "things like this were my mother's whole life" (23). Throughout the novel Ellen demonstrates what Rich calls "matrophobia," or fear of becoming one's mother: "Matrophobia can be seen as a womanly splitting of the self, in the desire to become purged once and for all of our mothers' bondage, to become individuated and free. The mother stands for the victim in ourselves, the unfree woman, the martyr. Our personalities seem dangerously to blur and overlap with our mothers'; and, in a desperate attempt to know where the mother ends and daughter begins, we perform radical surgery" (*Of Woman* 235). This matrophobic resistance and fear of symbiosis clearly underlie Ellen's view of her mother, especially when Kate is diagnosed at forty-eight with metastatic cancer and Ellen returns home to care for her. "All my life I had known one thing for sure about myself," Ellen asserts, "and that was that my life would never be her life. I had moved as far and as fast as I could; now I was back at my beginning" (31).

A primary source of both her matrophobia and the pressure to return home is Ellen's overbearing father, George Gulden, a womanizing college English professor with whom both daughter and mother have an unhealthy relationship. Influenced by him as a child to patronize her mother, Ellen has followed the path he chose for her, having graduated magna cum laude from Harvard (the same as her dad, who nonetheless berated her for not achieving summa) and begun a successful career as a writer. His condescension toward his wife appears even when he tells Ellen and her two brothers about Kate's cancer: "'Your mother procrastinated,' he said, as though she was somehow to blame. 'First she thought she had the flu. Then she imagined she was expecting. She didn't want to make a fuss. You know how she is" (24). His authoritarian manner and Ellen's passive-aggressive tendencies are evident as he presents further details.

> "Chemotherapy," my father said. There were verbs in his sentences but I didn't hear them. "Liver. Ovaries. Oncologist." I picked up a glass and walked out of the room.
> "I'm still speaking, Ellen," my father called after me.
> "I can't listen anymore," I said. (24–25)

Concerned for his wife but motivated also by self-interest, George guilttrips his daughter into resigning her job and moving home to care for her mother.

By placing the doctrine of true womanhood in the words of an unappealing patriarch, Quindlen seems initially to critique this ideology, and indeed she sometimes does. However, Ellen's best friend, Jules, and eventually Ellen herself ascribe to this traditional perspective as well. At first Ellen resists her father's manipulations, mounting a spirited defense of her autonomy. "Ellen, your mother needs you," he insists. "She is coming home Tuesday and she won't be well for long. The disease is apparently advanced. Soon she may not be able to bathe herself. In a month or two she will not be able to cook or clean" (29). When Ellen suggests that they hire a nurse, her father evokes the power of motherhood as institution: "Your mother didn't hire a nurse when you had your tonsils out. She didn't hire a nurse when you had chicken pox or broke your arm" (30). To Ellen's protest that her life in New York matters, George screams that although she has a Harvard education, she has "no heart." When Ellen confronts him once more, asking why he does not curtail or quit his job: her father, predictably, employs the rhetoric of separate spheres, citing the necessity of both masculine earning power and feminine duty: "It seems to me another woman is what's wanted here" (32–33). Although Ellen criticizes her father, she indicts him for his selfishness rather than his stereotypical thinking about domesticity, largely because part of her shares this view. "Kate Gulden and a hired nurse did not parse," she realizes upon reflection; "I felt I had no choice. I felt I had to be what my father wanted me to be, even if it was something so unlike the other Ellen he'd cultivated and tutored for all those years" (34). Once Ellen is buried beneath the weight of duty, she feels "a burgeoning sense of claustrophobia worse than if I'd been caught in an elevator between floors" (35). In several phone conversations, however, Jules replaces George as the ideologue for separate spheres. "You have to do this," she urges Ellen; "You would want your daughter to do it for you. . . . Your brothers can learn how to run a microwave. Your father can learn where the Goddamn dry cleaner is. But no one . . . can help your mother with the shit she'll be going through but you" (38–39).

Ironically, the only person who resists this essentialist rhetoric of daughterly duty is Ellen's mother, who does so, however, not out of conviction but out of martyrdom. "No no no no no," she protests upon learning that Ellen has moved home. "Not a nursemaid to me, to take care of this house, to take care of my house. You'll hate me" (45). To be sure, as mother and daughter spend time together over the months, Kate emerges as a more complex woman than her dismissive daughter had realized even as she continues to valorize domesticity. For example, Kate cleverly requests that they form the "Gulden Girls Book Group" to read the nineteenth-century classics so that Ellen will not be bored; between cleaning and shopping, they discuss *Pride and Prejudice* and *Anna Karenina*, and Ellen learns that her mother had studied these novels at Columbia years before. Although recognizing her mother as an educated woman enhances Ellen's esteem for her, she is swayed by her mother's sentimental responses to these novels—her conviction, for instance, that the domestic sister, Jane, rather than the autonomous Elizabeth Bennet was the true heroine of *Pride and Prejudice*. "It didn't seem fair to me, that Jane was so good and yet Elizabeth is the one who is admired," Kate explains. When Ellen protests that Austen was "fighting back" on behalf of outspoken women like herself, her mother insists that "Jane Austen should have known better than to make women into that kind of either-or thing . . . the smart one, the sweet one" (54–55). In a later conversation with her father, Ellen defends her mother's preference for Jane's domesticity over Elizabeth's rebellion and learns to her astonishment that her father shares it: "Jane Bennet is as satisfied with her lot as any young woman in nineteenth-century fiction, as you well know" (64). Clearly her parents are united in their reification of separate spheres for women and men. Although the beleaguered Ellen responds with sarcasm that appears to denigrate the domestic sphere—"I'm not sure I remember. Now that I'm a housewife I've got other things to think about. Floor wax. Ironing"—she is attempting to make her father feel guilty rather than criticizing his ideology of femininity. "You and I have different roles to play here," George concludes, as Ellen again backs down (64).

Women do the emotional work in *One True Thing*, and although Ellen remains ambivalent about that reality, she increasingly admires her mother's perceptiveness about male-female relationships. On one occasion, for instance, Kate indirectly challenges her daughter to resist her father's domination:

> "It's a mistake to base your entire life on one man's approval," my mother added quietly.
> "It was the way women lived when you got married," I said.
> "I was talking about you, Ellie," she said.

"Jonathan and I don't have that kind of relationship."
"I wasn't talking about Jonathan," she said. (59)

However, Kate's confessions to Ellen about her own courtship and marriage reveal conventional views on gender dynamics that undermine this rhetoric of independence. She describes with pride having wooed George by pretending to read in the university library until she attracted his attention, and on their first date she informed him that "I would be the ideal faculty wife" (57). When she nears death and urges Ellen to reconcile with her philandering father, Kate insists that

> There is nothing you know about your father that I don't know, too. . . .
> And understand better. . . . You make concessions when you're married a
> long time that you don't believe you will ever make when you're beginning. . . . He's your life. The house and the children and so much of what
> you do is built around him and your life, too, your history. If you take him
> out it's like cutting his face out of all the pictures, there's a big hole and it's
> ugly. It would ruin everything. (223–24)

"Everything" refers, of course, to the storybook illusion of a happy family that her mother has resolutely embraced, but Ellen applauds her mother's resilience rather than questioning her lack of agency. Ultimately Kate valorizes conventional femininity and implores her daughter to as well; deathbed advice about recipes and recommendations about the wedding Ellen may never have are central to her matrilineal legacy.

Because Ellen loves her mother and is anguished by her decline, she shifts in the novel's second half from trivializing to emulating Kate, burying her matrophobia beneath a manic routine of holiday cooking and unobtrusive caregiving. When Ellen's family and her lover, Jonathan, convene for Thanksgiving, she greets them in an apron of her mother's, speaks of "my turkey, my yams" as Kate always did, and colludes in the "elaborate fiction" that her mother's health is improving (114). By Christmas, with Kate having obviously worsened, Ellen again decorates and prepares an elaborate dinner, for which her unappreciative brother ridicules her (195–96). To be sure, Ellen recounts her kitchen feats with a desperate irony, and her matrophobia does not dissipate entirely even after her mother's death. As a retrospective narrator reflecting back upon the five months she spent with Kate, she continues to resent her mother's wish to remake her even as she acquiesces: "She and her daughter finally had the relationship she had always imagined would accompany the canopy she had made for the four-poster bed in the attic bedroom"—a relationship immersed in domesticity (82). Ellen further claims to have detested playing the role of her mother's "girl-friend" and domestic surrogate: "The truth is that while it was happening I tolerated it, and when I thought about it I hated it all" (83). This protestation reveals Ellen's pent-up rage at an illness and a death she could not control, however, rather than a renunciation of her perhaps unwitting decision not only to care for her dying mother but also to *become* her—perhaps as a means of hanging onto her.

When the household expands as Kate nears death to include an oncologist and a visiting nurse, Ellen initially treats them as intruders who wish to disrupt the mother-daughter dyad. Although caregiving has worn her down, Ellen staunchly refuses Dr. Cohn's advice that she consider putting her mother in hospice or at least see a psychologist: "No hospice, no hospital. I had a good job in the city and a nice apartment and friends and places to go and people to see and I junked it all to take care of my mother. And I am going to take care of my mother. I will do what is required" (103). Her language, of course, reveals her obsessive sense of duty and echoes the passive-voice syntax used earlier by her father, who insisted that "another woman is what's wanted here," a fact that signifies Ellen's continuing thralldom to him. She dismisses as well the doctor's advice that she should obtain counseling for her mother: "I talk to my mother. . . . My mother can talk to me" (103–4). Although she eventually comes to rely on the support of these two health professionals, Ellen increasingly identifies with her dying mother and disintegrates emotionally, as is evident in the scene in which Kate experiences her death throes with Ellen at her bedside, "breathing in tandem . . . dying in tandem." As the parallelism of this line reveals, Ellen experiences a disabling symbiosis with her dying mother.

A strength of *One True Thing* is Quindlen's convincing portrayal of the dying process—both its emotional landscape and the daily struggles of patient and caregivers. Neither *The Saving Graces* nor *Talk before Sleep* presents suffering with such gritty precision; to do so would diminish the romantic aspects of their narratives. Yet Quindlen rarely shrinks from presenting painful confrontations with bodily vulnerability. The first time that Kate experiences uncontrollable back pain and calls shrilly from her bedroom for a heating pad, for instance, Ellen is shocked to encounter her mother's bruised and wrinkled body: "I could see how much she had hidden from me until now" (99). In retrospect, Ellen understands that Kate's concealment allowed her to embrace maternity as long as possible: "She was not yet ready to let her child be the grown-up in the house. She had had one great calling, as a mother, and she would not be forced from the field" (99). When Ellen becomes speech-less in her suffering mother's presence, she reflects eloquently upon her mute regression to infancy: "My throat had closed around the knot of my fear and grief and no matter how I worked I could not make it open and let my words out. Although what I could possibly say, except 'Mama,' like a baby, a good child, I did not know" (102). As Kate worsens, her uncharacteristic bouts of rage terrify her daughter: "The outbursts seemed so different from her usual self that I sometimes felt as though the cancer itself had a voice, and I was hearing it. Or it was the voice of the morphine. . . . I was frightened of this other Kate, this enraged and desiccated imposter" (110). Most agonizingly, her mother accuses Ellen of wishing her dead, an accusation the daughter deems partially accurate: "She was right about that; I did want that angry stranger gone" (111). Near the end, when the nurse gives Kate a copy of "The Dying Person's Bill of Rights," Ellen breaks down upon reading the final item: "I have the right to be cared for by caring, sensitive, knowledgeable people who will attempt to understand my needs and will be able to gain some satis-faction in helping me to face my death." "'What satisfaction?' I sobbed, and the tears ran hot down my face and I cried into a pillow until my face was as swollen as I imagined my mother's stomach was beneath my father's shirts" (160). Quindlen also portrays realistically Kate's sense of humiliation as her body decays. "I would have died before I would have let you see me like this," she cries to Ellen, who must help her from the bathtub. "Just . . . rotten. That's what I look like now, like a peach when it's all rotten. Like bad fruit. Why can't I die and be done with it? It's a crime for a human being to have to live like this. Rotten like this." Her anguished daughter can only agree: "It was an apt description" (215).

Another of this novel's strengths, and again a feature that distin-guishes it from previously discussed works, lies in its serious treatment of the controversial topic of euthanasia. When Kate, relegated to diapers and in and out of consciousness, determines that she has suffered enough, she implores her daughter to help her die: "You're so smart. You'll know what to do. Please" (229). Although Ellen cannot bring herself to inject her mother with a fatal quantity of morphine, she longs for her mother to have a dignified death and tacitly affirms her right to take her own life. Unfortunately, Quindlen's progressive position on this important social issue gets lost in the implausible framing device that begins and ends the novel: charged with her mother's murder when an autopsy reveals that she died of an overdose, Ellen recounts her weeks in an upscale jail, her betrayal by Jonathan, who testifies that she had wished her mother dead, her father's abandonment, and her subsequent trial and acquittal. Little of this rings true, and the shift from an often moving representation of a mother's death from cancer to a daughter's murder trial weakens the novel's realism and heightens its identification with a particularly vexing aspect of nineteenth-century sentimental literature, its penchant for melodrama. "Sometimes people have wondered why I'm not more bitter about what happened to me," Ellen muses near the novel's conclusion.

> And I was bitter for a long time, but at base I understand. Death is so strange, so mysterious, so sad, that we want to blame someone for it. And it was easy to blame me. Besides, when people wonder how I survived being accused of killing my mother, none of them realizes that watching her die was many, many times worse. And knowing I could have killed her was nothing compared to knowing I could not save her. (370)

Death's mystery not withstanding, Ellen's pious sentiments reinforce her immersion in a feminine ideology that demands that daughters sacrifice their lives for their dying mothers and then feel guilty about not having done enough.

The most commercially successful of the four novels under consideration, and the only one to have been made into "a major motion picture," as Hollywood rhetoric goes, *One True Thing* is more widely known today as a film than as fiction. The movie's critical reception has been mixed, with some reviewers praising its feminist insights and others critiquing its artifice. Both types of reviews err. Susan Granger claims, for example, that

> with all that has been written about the feminist movement, it took Pulitzer Prize–winning Anna Quindlen to write an engrossing story that dramatizes the complex difference between our mother's generation and us, a confrontation between a woman whose expectations never extended beyond her home and her children and her husband's career, who viewed her life as an adjunct to those things, and her daughter, whom she raised not only to work but to expect the world.

While Granger describes correctly the film's emphasis on generational differences between mothers and daughters, she errs in attributing Ellen's focus on career as her mother's (rather than her father's) doing; moreover, she fails to clarify the link between the "feminist movement" and the mother-daughter tensions that the novel and the film address. Granger assumes that Quindlen challenges the ideologies of traditional femininity and motherhood as institution, but as we have seen, Quindlen often reifies them. In the epiphany that occurs just before her mother's death, which both novel and film foreground, Ellen idealizes Kate and misrepresents her own understanding of her mother's character: "Everything you know, I know, she'd said, and it was true. I was the ignorant one. I'd taken a laundry list of all the things she'd done and, more important to me, all the things she'd never done, and turned them into my mother, when they were no more my mother than his lectures on the women of Dickens were my father" (228). Yet Ellen *has* read her parents well rather than constructing them as she wishes them to be; her father has consistently defined himself through his professional life, her mother through her domesticity. The daughter's newly furbished view of her conventional mother emerges, finally, as sentimental and guilt-ridden, not objective.

Conversely, reviewers such as Harvey Karten, who wishes for a "wittier, edgier family drama," miss the strengths of Quindlen's novel-turned-film. By focusing on Kate's monologue on marriage and arguing that "for all of its histrionics, the manifesto is lifted above the banal only by Meryl Streep's remarkable abilities as a performer," Karten ignores grim deathbed exchanges between mother and daughter that reveal well the emotional ravages of cancer. Finally, binary logic fails to decipher *One True Thing*, which should not be typecast as either feminist treatise or sentimental melodrama; clearly it features elements of both.

Jayne Anne Phillips's *MotherKind* meditates on the mysteries of death and the power of the mother-child bond in sentimental language that once again recalls that of the nineteenth-century literary domestics. The novel's title refers to an agency that provides in-house infant care for new mothers, a gift from the terminally ill Katherine to her daughter after Kate's son is born. As Phillips has acknowledged, however, "in a larger sense, of course, 'motherkind' . . . refers to the human family women enter when they become mothers—a term that should be com-

mon usage" (quoted in McLeese). Although the omniscient narrator
chronicles the daily tasks that Kate must undertake, poised between a
growing baby and a dying mother, the book's emotional landscape
explores not only the quotidian but the metaphysical. In Phillips's
words, the novel "occurs on two planes at once: the year within the novel
is inter-cut with an ongoing past that becomes a kind of eternal present.
Memory sometimes offers up the past as living, dimensional, sensory
presence. In that world, there is no death" (quoted in McLeese).

In contrast to Ellen in *One True Thing*, Kate experiences no matrophobia; rather, she views her mother idealistically as her best friend and
mentor. Phillips foregrounds this shared sympathy, perhaps too predictably, by giving her protagonists a name in common. To be sure, the
two women have different interests and values: Kate is a poet, her
mother a former reading specialist; Kate lives with her partner, a physician who is going through a divorce, and she becomes pregnant outside
of wedlock, whereas her divorced mother opposes live-in arrangements
and takes conservative stands on many social issues. Nonetheless, their
relationship is defined by mutual love and trust, and when Katherine's
breast cancer metastasizes, Kate encourages her mother to move to her
daughter's chaotic home and convinces her mother to undergo
chemotherapy so that she will live to greet her grandchild. In the first
two months that mother and daughter spend together, Phillips presents
their domestic lives as interwoven. As Katherine endures invasive cancer
treatment and Kate experiences her own prenatal medicalization, the two
women anticipate the imminent arrival of Kate's baby by sorting
through mementoes of Kate's own infancy—a christening dress, a "tiny
hand-knit sweater"—calm relics of infancy that serve as an antidote to
the aggression of the invading toxins (8). The relief Kate feels as her
delivery date approaches and the chemo extends Katherine's life is palpable: "this much was certain—the time drew near. Her mother would
see the baby; she would hold Kate's baby" (17).

Such passages celebrate the sustaining power of matrilineage, the
legacy passed down from mother to child through generations. Indeed,
Kate's advanced pregnancy evokes in her mother memories of her own
childbirths and her initial realization of her children's biological sex:
"There were no amnios, just that moment of truth. And so exhilarating!"
(43). Kate's pregnancy also prompts Katherine's recollection of nursing
her endlessly thirsty daughter: "You were so fat your boobs hung to

your waist" (43). The novel's emphasis on matrilineal heritage is also evident in one of the novel's many italicized retrospective passages, when Kate, visiting her mother in Pennsylvania just after her cancer diagnosis, reflects upon "*'the Grandmother Dodd bed, where her mother and grandmother slept. . . . Katherine likes to say she 'didn't know and wasn't told' where her grandmother died, 'but Mother died in that bed, where her babies were born.' There was the implicit assumption Katherine would die in it too, one day*" (105). Although this part of the chain will be broken, Katherine does die in the presence of her daughter, with her grandson nearby, and in her confusion imagines herself as a child at home with her own mother. "Mother's windows are above the tree by the road," she mutters to Kate shortly before her final agony begins. When Kate asks, "What road is that, Mom?" her mother remains silent (288–89).

Despite the pull of matrilineage, Kate maintains her own identity when she combines households with her mother. Unlike Ellen in *One True Thing*, Kate never tries to *become* her mother; instead, she honors Katherine's traditional views even as she disagrees:

> She realized she often knew in advance her mother's response to a given topic, but she elicited the responses anyway, sometimes to her annoyance, more often for pleasure. She so valued her mother's sheer dependability, the slight cynicism of the old wives' tales she favored, her bedrock common sense, even the rigid provincial innocence with which she approached discussions of what Kate referred to as "modern life." There were so many topics on which Katherine held strong opinions based on scant experience. (32)

Instead of emulating her mother, Kate respects Katherine for her *difference*. In addition, she values her mother as a bridge between present and past, between the home that she and Katherine inhabit now and the murky landscape of Kate's childhood:

> Kate gazed at her mother's face and felt her wholly familiar presence. In this place, this house where they'd all lived less than four months, her mother was so real, so connected to all they'd come from, to everything Kate had taken with her, the burden and the weight, and the furious beauty. She kept trying to turn around and see. She wondered if she would see anything of that first world, the world she'd come from, when her mother was gone. (42)

While mother helps daughter to feel grounded, Phillips represents this daughter figure as having inherited her mother's resilience. Thus Kate is

ultimately able to meditate philosophically on time and loss rather than
to become despondent. As the narrator explains, "Kate viewed time in a
controlled panic, yet a part of her stood back from her anger and the various shades of her despair. Why be disturbed, she thought in a still version of her own voice, a voice far from alarm. Countless lives came and
went. Wind passed over the grass" (118). Through listening to her inner
voice, Kate gathers the resources to face her mother's death as an aspect
of the spiritual legacy that Grandmother Dodd's bed epitomizes.

Phillips clearly values the domestic world that mother and daughter
inhabit, and she valorizes their shared sympathy even as she sentimental-
izes it. Both Kate and Katherine display patience toward the inevitable
complications of family life, from squalling infant to rambunctious stepsons to late dinners. Although Katherine becomes increasingly bedrid-
den, she assists her daughter with household management and infant
care as long as she can; indeed, the women display a poignant reciprocity in their nurture of one another. Two scenes in which one woman
offers to read to the other, the first early in the novel just after Kate
returns home with her baby, the second near its end as her mother lies
dying, demonstrate this mutuality of care. In the first scene the act of
reading is completed, while in the second it is disrupted, but the desire to
provide unconditional love governs both women's impulses. In the initial scene Katherine reads a passage from Dickens to her resting daughter, and the two reflect together upon the emotional resonance of its final
line: "*I tried to lay my mind before her, truly and entirely.*" In Dickens's
words they find a reflection of their mutual devotion:

> There was a hush in the room. Kate's mother had looked back at the lines
> once. Then she leaned forward and touched her open palm to Kate's face.
> Kate touched her own hand to her mother's wrist and inclined her head as
> her mother stood to embrace her. Listening, she heard the beating of her
> mother's heart as snow brushed the windows in sweeps of wind. (46)

This passage recalls Rich's assertion that the "mother-daughter
cathexis" remains "the great unwritten story" (*Of Woman* 270) of modern literature, a story that Phillips recounts. As the author explains, she
believes that when women nurture their own infants, "they reassess their
mothers' lives and are 'reborn' themselves" (quoted in McLeese). In
MotherKind Kate's rebirth occurs, ironically, as her mother's health disintegrates.

In another scene of mother-daughter intimacy, Kate proposes to read to Katherine because her mother, confined to bed and dependent on a morphine pump, can no longer read herself. "'I'll stay, Mom,' Kate reassures her mother. 'Shall I read to you?' Incapable of responding fully, Katherine "didn't answer, but the force of her gaze changed, became softer, almost beseeching." Sensitive to her mother's anxiety, Kate listens to her mother's fragmented complaint instead of reading and discerns that "something had happened" and that "whatever it was, Katherine was afraid" (277–79). When Kate determines that her mother is uncomfortable with one of her nurses, she dismisses the problematic caregiver and insists on helping the new one to bathe her mother and change her soiled sheets. Such scenes reveal the novel's dominant ideology: no one can care for a dying mother as well as a daughter can.

This daughter undertakes the task of nursing her dying mother without the single-minded absorption of Ellen in *One True Thing*, however, because Phillips represents Kate's domestic life as having balance. As she cares for Katherine, Kate also nurses her new baby, plays with her stepsons, and contends with her lover's worry about their increasingly complicated relationship, about "what we'll have left when this is over" (285). Phillips's Kate also relies on an entire team of nurses and infant care providers, whereas Quindlen's Ellen's desire to "do what is required" for her mother keeps her from hiring more than one nurse to assist her. Even on the last days of Katherine's life, the narrator describes Kate as balancing the care of mother and baby: "Afternoons, alone, timed to Alexander's nap, Kate sat by the bed. . . . When Katherine spoke, she was increasingly confused, indefinite. Kate always responded, talked to her, tried to explain or acknowledge" (279). Eventually unable to care fully for her increasingly disoriented mother, however, Kate acknowledges that her mother needs a full-time nurse:

> She checked on her mother at midnight, again at two or three, when she nursed the baby, and again at five. It wasn't enough. They needed one more person. Katherine shouldn't be alone anymore, not for half an hour, not at all. She was not *with herself;* she was not there. She was like a babe adrift on the ocean in a basin the size of a bedpan, or a beating heart exposed in the palm of a hand. Someone must stay by her. (282)

Kate honors both her mother's needs and her own, and in Katherine's final weeks, "she was never alone" (283).

Like Quindlen, Phillips refuses to spare readers the grim details of death from cancer; Katherine, helpless, must be spoon-fed liquids, bathed in bed, given quantities of morphine unimaginable weeks before. Yet dying has a solemn dignity in *MotherKind* that is lacking in *One True Thing*. Moreover, as the work of dying becomes the mother's final task, the daughter faces death with equanimity despite her grief: "Katherine was unconscious. . . . The rasping agonal power of her breath was heard in every room. All else hushed, and Kate found she was not afraid" (286). On the night of her mother's death, Kate dreams that she helps Katherine cross death's borders: "arm in arm, they turned their backs and proceeded higher still, into the mountains of a strange country" (289). Readers do not witness Katherine's death throes, however; Phillips instead ends her novel with Kate's memory of a celebration at which Katherine's friend Rip and Kate herself toast her mother just before her scheduled move to Boston. As Kate's mother lifts her champagne flute to her pregnant daughter's water glass, Katherine "*wets her finger in the bubbling fizz of her glass, then leans forward to touch Kate's lips with a moistened fingertip. 'For luck,' she whispers*" (292). By ending her novel with this nostalgic scene rather than elaborating on Katherine's dying moments, Phillips evinces the sentimental but affirming philosophy that death cannot undo the mother-daughter bond.

POPULAR CANCER FICTION
& FEMINISM LITE

Like domestic and romance novels, much popular cancer fiction exudes sentimentality. Impassioned kisses, secret or communal tears, and the ideal of the soul mate—realized here as another woman or a group of women—characterize what one irritated critic calls the "terminal disease cum moving woman's melodrama genre" (G. King). As Tompkins has pointed out, however, such fiction serves not solely as melodrama but also as a resourceful means of "reorganiz[ing] culture from a woman's point of view" (21). Women's popular literature represents the cancer experience realistically by offering the "sandwich generation" a gripping rendition of a domestic crisis familiar in many contemporary women's lives. This cancer fiction is romantic in its use of pathos to evoke in readers an emotional catharsis that emerges from the perspective that love conquers all, outliving even death. Building on the traditions of domestic and romance fiction, popular novels that chronicle women's cancer posit that "an ideal love is possible, even in the worst of circumstances" (Radway, "Readers" 567).

The Saving Graces, Talk before Sleep, One True Thing, and *MotherKind* are best-selling novels that have continued since their initial publication to enjoy a strong popular following. Yet each novel arguably contributes to the sentimentality of the breast cancer marketplace that Ehrenreich critiques by emphasizing ultrafeminine representations of women's subjectivity and by domesticating and sometimes infantilizing the dying protagonists. As we have seen, these novels also revise conventions of the heterosexual romance novel to valorize women's friendships in romantic terms. Despite their sentimentality, however, fictional representations of cancer, love, and romance can be read as feminist because they validate women's nurturing capacities instead of trivializing them.

Often, however, this fiction undermines its feminist potential by promoting an essentialist vision that conflates motherhood with womanhood. Such essentialism occurs in the following passage from *MotherKind,* where through her protagonist's ecstatic musing Phillips exalts the act of childbirth as the pinnacle of any woman's life:

> Ravenous, Kate knew, this need to birth babies, to hold one's own child. The fact was, birth dwarfed sex, swept sex before it. . . . For years, she'd avoided babies, which was easy, because most women she knew didn't have them. Most women thought they were looking for men, not babies. Kate thought now that they were wrong: they were all looking for babies, even those who said they didn't want children. (117)

Disturbing for its sexist and heterosexist assumptions as well as its essentialism, the narrator's assertion brings to mind Marianne Hirsch's admonition that contemporary women writers strive to recognize the risks of "idealizing and mystifying" female reproductive capacities and thereby "reviving an identification between femininity and maternity that has not served the interests of women" (163). By representing the pregnant Kate as "magical and fierce," as "girded for battle" (117), and by strongly implying that all women should partake of this magic, Phillips endorses an ideology of true womanhood that mirrors the underlying message of many didactic novels from the nineteenth century—an ideology that contemporary feminist ideologies have challenged.

While it would be easy to label women's popular cancer novels as retrogressive, it is important to consider reasons for their appeal to many readers and look without condescension at their cultural value. First, they are engrossing reads. *The Saving Graces, Talk before Sleep,* and *One True Thing* rely on first-person narratives and retrospective reflection to instill in readers a sense of immediacy; *MotherKind,* in contrast, employs an omniscient point of view that creates a less urgent but more philosophical tone. The authors of these novels use these narrative techniques to honor the feminized world of women cancer patients and their caregivers—a world in which sisterhood, motherhood, and daughterhood emerge as critical sources of support. Second, this fiction celebrates themes of female empowerment, although it does so in a "feminine" way. These novels represent bonds between women as equally important to those between women and men, and they acknowledge female solidarity as a gift from which both healthy and ill women can benefit. As one reader claimed after reading *The Saving Graces,* such fiction reveals that "together, this group can conquer anything; separately any one of them can fail" (Klausner). Ultimately, popular cancer fiction promotes a form of cultural feminism—a "feminism lite" that positions women as, by nature, the kinder, nobler sex—rather than a multicultural or materialist feminism that scrutinizes hierarchies of gender, race, and class in America and worldwide. For many readers, however, a feminine angle of vision makes feminist themes palatable.

5. "FLOATING OUT ON A YACHT CALLED EROS"

Memory, Desire, & Death in
Women's Experimental Cancer Fiction

Ava is a living text. One that trembles and shudders. One that yearns.
                                    —Carole Maso, *Break Every Rule*

Memory, along with desire and death, are the themes that won't leave me.
                                    —Susan Minot, Interview

What would happen if we could imagine in ourselves authentic desire?
                                    —Jeanette Winterson, *Art Objects*

Almost everything is yet to be written by women about their infinite and complex sexuality, their eroticism.
                                    —Hélène Cixous, *The Laugh of the Medusa*

*A*s DISTINCT FROM POPULAR fiction, with its linear narratives and sentimental sensibility toward illness, dying, and women's relationships, experimental cancer fiction typically features characteristics of modernist and postmodern fragmentation: textual lacunae, stream-of-consciousness technique, fluid and/or multiple narrative voices, poetic lyricism, and an emphasis on the transgressive power of language and memory. The experimental novelists considered here use these techniques to illuminate the embodied and erotic worlds of women dying from cancer. Although what these writers do in their narratives varies widely, all of them thematize bodily disintegration, trauma, and loss via the dismemberment of traditional narrative structures. At the same time they employ innovative strategies of rememberment to represent the desiring cancer patient as a powerful speaking subject.

At the heart of this chapter lie several questions about the intersection of experimental fiction, memory, death, and desire. Why explore the erotic power and expressions of desire by dying women when so much remains to be articulated by and about the still-living? Is this impulse a revisionist gesture toward Freud's ineluctable linking of sex and death? A voyeuristic fantasy designed to obscure the suffering most cancer patients confront during their final weeks? An act of feminist solidarity between healthy women survivors, whose sexuality remains intact, and their cancer-ridden sisters, whose erotic life threatens to disappear entirely? What happens when avant-garde women writers address what Hélène Cixous terms a woman's "infinite and complex sexuality" through the disruptive lens of terminal cancer?

Carole Maso's *Ava* (1993), Susan Minot's *Evening* (1998), and Jeanette Winterson's *Written on the Body* (1993) exemplify the extraordinary range and quality of contemporary women's inscriptions of cancerous bodies and the consciousnesses that inhabit them. Among the themes these writers explore are the sensual dimensions of dying, when bodily sensations intensify and one's flesh is caressed by a caregiver as it once was stroked by a lover; the complex parallels between passivity and aggression in acts of human intimacy; and the transformative power of erotic memories that may drift or coalesce near the moment of death. Taken together, their novels reveal the power of experimental fiction to represent cancer and women's desire in new and daring ways. Maso, Minot, and Winterson claim with narrative authority and as lived possibility the knowledge that never does a woman's erotic longing find such complex expression as when she approaches death, free to experience and represent her sexuality on her own terms. In this chapter, therefore, I argue that these writers' penetrating, compassionate representations portray women's medicalized bodies not merely as potential sites of betrayal, pain, and abjection, although their characters do confront these issues. These novelists instead create protagonists for whom fatal illness engenders a fluid subjectivity, an intense eroticism, and a postmodern sensibility that help them cope with dying.

Maso's *Ava* takes place on the last day of the life of thirty-nine-year-old Ava Klein, a thrice-married, childless professor of comparative literature, Jewish, a lover of men, women, music, and words. Ava's illness is a "rare blood disease," apparently some form of leukemia; having undergone unsuccessful chemotherapy and bone marrow transplant, she is dying at home, attended by nurses but otherwise alone. The novel is comprised of three sections, overtly linear in their temporal sequence— "Morning," "Afternoon," and "Evening"—but Maso dismantles linearity through a strategy that one critic calls "chaotic fluency" (Kuebler 1). In a collection of her essays on writing, *Break Every Rule,* Maso has described her narrative technique in *Ava* as "my most spacious form thus far" and has claimed that this novel "allows in the most joy, the most desire, the most regret. Embraces the most uncertainty" (64).

Minot's *Evening* chronicles the final days of Ann Lord, sixty-five, also married three times and the mother of four adult children who surround her bedside, as do a devoted nurse and assorted family friends. Most compelling to Ann, however, is the ghostly presence of Harris Arden, the lost lover who continues to rouse Ann's passion. Like Ava, Ann is dying of cancer, shrinking daily and in extraordinary pain, but despite shadowy bouts with morphine, her mind and memory remain remarkably clear. This novel consists of five sections, each dominated by a controlling image cluster featuring the sensual sea, as a lyrical poem might do: a canopy, a sail closet, the fog, a swim, the night. In precise, spare language Minot probes what she terms the "treasures" stored in every human's lifetime fund of memories—those "mysteries and secrets" that contribute to "the unfathomability of another person" (interview).

Winterson's *Written on the Body* diverges from the "last rites" theme in that its unnamed first-person narrator does not have cancer but rather becomes intimately involved with a married woman, Louise Rosenthal, who suffers from leukemia. Not identified by gender, the narrator hints that her relationship with Louise is lesbian, but since Winterson never states this definitively, gender ambiguity abounds.[1] This novel shares with *Ava* and *Evening* both linguistic experimentation and a fluid reverie on how most effectively to "imagine in ourselves authentic desire" (Winterson, *Art* 117). Such desire would evoke neither the shocking vistas of pornography nor the staid landscape of being in love. In the creative lexicon that Winterson develops in a volume titled *Art Objects,* authentic desire evokes an "untamed" landscape in which a highly visceral eroticism might flourish. Readers come to experimental fiction, and perhaps to representations of cancer and desire, to transform what Winterson terms our "aesthetic environment" from the manicured to the wild: "We have already tamed our physical environment. Are we happy with all this tameness? Are you?" (15).[2]

Maso's emphasis on the uncertain, Minot's on the unfathomable, and Winterson's on the untamed reveal important aspects of their narrative strategies and feminist visions—aspects that feminist theory can help

readers more fully to appreciate. Specifically, these novelists find inspiration in the feminist modernism of Virginia Woolf and the sexual/textual
experimentation of contemporary French feminisms.[3] Maso and Winterson identify Woolf as a major influence and acknowledge using her writing as a lens through which to theorize traumatized women's heightened
longings, while Minot draws on Woolf implicitly. In an essay from *Break
Every Rule* Maso pays homage to Woolf as a literary mentor and to *The
Waves* as *Ava*'s closest precursor in its lyricism and open-endedness (23,
34–37, 46). As critic Carolyn Kuebler notes, Maso "strives for a fiction of
what Woolf calls life's 'uncircumscribed spirit,' its 'semi-transparent
envelope'" (1–2). Winterson's artistic theory is equally indebted to
Woolf, whom Winterson considers the modernist writer most interested
in the "effort of exactness," in holding "the world in her arms" and
returning it "to itself again; coherent, whole" (*Art* 93). Like Maso, Winterson views *The Waves* as a key forerunner of her own novel; *Written on
the Body*, she claims, resembles Woolf's writing in its attention to a "language of rapture" (93). Moreover, Winterson seeks to emulate Woolf's
freedom from "a falsity in fiction that has now reached epidemic propor-
tions" (87). This concern Maso shares, although she views the falsity as
the pretense of offering truths: "Mainstream fiction has become death
with its complacent, unequivocal truths . . . its predictability and stasis"
(*Break* 67). Additionally, Maso and Winterson find in Woolf an attention to the luminous that they strive to replicate; in Winterson's words,
"lifting the pavements, [Woolf] did not lie, she found a language for
shells, bones and silence" (*Art* 87). Minot, in turn, evinces a more indirect indebtedness to Woolf in her narrative commitment to a luminous,
poetic transparency. As she explains regarding *Evening*, "I wanted to
write a book that was dreamlike, with the rhythms of dreams mixed with
waking life, for that is often how life seems to be. As I was writing I
thought of the book as a kind of poem" (Welch).

These three novelists are also connected to French feminist theories of
l'écriture féminine, or writing the body, in their approaches to representing
ill women's subjectivity. In the 1970s and 1980s French feminists offered
women many reasons to write: to disrupt and subvert patriarchal
definitions of "the feminine," to reconstruct a fluid yet forceful female
identity, to locate women's agency and voices centrally in the realm of the
body and its pains and pleasures. In her now-famous manifesto "The
Laugh of the Medusa," for example, Cixous implores women to "Write

yourself. Your body must be heard. Only then will the immense resources of the unconscious spring forth" (395). The cancer novels under consideration here draw most visibly upon French feminisms by inscribing what Luce Irigaray calls *jouissance,* a blend of sexual and creative pleasure that emerges from a secure woman's erotic depths (101). Maso, in particular, relies extensively on the theory of Cixous, whom Maso cites often in *Ava,* and on Irigaray's concept of *jouissance;* indeed, Maso claims that her own writing is driven by the body and its desires: "I cannot keep the body out of my writing; it enters the language, transforms the page, imposes its own intelligence. If I have succeeded at all, you will hear me breathing. You will hear the sound my longing makes" (*Break* 70). As Leigh Gilmore has noted, Winterson's narrative recalls Monique Wittig's experimental novel *The Lesbian Body* in its reliance on the trope of book as body and its imaginary dissection of the lesbian lover's organs and viscera (123–24, 137–38). The influence of French feminism on Minot is less direct, but she shares a belief that both Maso and Cixous espouse: that desire is gendered. In Minot's words, "it seems to me a woman has, in general, a different mode of desire from a man" (Welch). French feminist theory can thus be useful in interrogating how the protagonists' identities in these texts are transformed by illness and violation, on the one hand, and by pleasure and sexual reverie, on the other.[4]

"THE SOUND MY LONGING MAKES": CAROLE MASO'S *AVA*

The opening lines of *Ava* present at once the orgasmic intensity of a living body suffused with desire and the visceral suffering of a dying body suffused with pain. In this novel Maso invites readers to cohabit the lush psychological environs of a protagonist who has lived richly and wishes to die that way as well:

> A throbbing. A certain pulsing.
>
> The villagers grew violets.
>
> We ran through genet and wild sage. (3)

Ava Klein has been exuberant as part of a family for whom "each holiday [was] celebrated with real extravagance . . . with verve" and as an individual who has responded to life as "a perpetual pageant" (3). Her emo-

tional landscape is erotically charged, her shifting consciousness heightened by sensual rhythms:

> A throbbing.
>
> Come quickly.
>
> The light in your eyes.
>
> Precious. Unexpected Things. (3)

It takes several pages for readers to recognize that Ava no longer lan-
guishes in an olive garden in Crete or frolics with a lover in fields of wild
sage but merely recalls having done so; she lies instead on her deathbed,
her body tended by caregivers whose ministrations evoke memories of
former touches. Frequently a lover's remembered gestures and a nurse's
converge:

> Tell me everything you want.
>
> Wake up, Ava Klein. Turn over on your side. Your right arm, please.
>
> Tell me everything you'd like me to—your hand there, slowly. (4)

In perusing such lines readers confront a startling juxtaposition of sexuality and medicalization that leads to questions about narrative experimentation, female sexuality, and cancer literature. Is *Ava* an erotic saga
or a cancer novel? An example of *l'écriture féminine* and, as such, an innovative inscription of women's endlessly circulating desire, or a postmodern illness narrative filled with textual machinations and unsettling lacunae? In fact, by disrupting such binaries *Ava* is and does all of these
things.

In an article on *Ava* entitled "Textual Bodies," feminist critic Nicole
Cooley argues compellingly that Maso develops strategies of narrative
disintegration that focus readers' attention on the invasion of Ava's medicalized body and on her subsequent loss of autonomy. In Cooley's
words, "Maso creates a tension between medicine's desire to make Ava
an object and Ava's own desire to return to her status as a speaking subject by continually positioning the language of pleasure and the language
of pain side by side" (2). A second feminist critic, Monica Berlin, likewise considers Ava's bodily appropriation a kind of textual breakdown
and, in support of her argument, foregrounds Maso's claim that "the
world falls apart as you read. Language enacts the speed and degree and
manner of the breakdown" (1–2; Maso, *Break* 30). Much of the novel's

language supports these critical views, most notably Ava's reference to "the daily betrayals of my body that are taking place. This perfect traitor that has afforded me so much pleasure, which has served me so well" (54). Nonetheless, I see Maso as celebrating the dying Ava's embodied subjectivity rather than eradicating it and the apparent breakdown of narrative in the text as belying its actual reconstruction. Ava's position as subject and the erotic pleasures she remembers are enhanced by her medicalization, not merely violated by it; her dying body finds ecstasy in both the memory of intimate touch and its current hourly *reality* through palliative care. Such touch emerges paradoxically, then, as at once invasive and inviting.

In the preceding passage, for instance, which begins, "Tell me everything you want," Cooley views Ava's sexualized recollections as being "interrupted by the voice of a clinician giving the patient different directions" (2). However, a closer reading suggests that the clinician's voice facilitates rather than disturbs Ava's erotic reverie, in part because Ava takes pleasure in recalling sex acts that were both mutual and aggressive. "Turn over" thus serves simultaneously as medical instruction and as the arousing memory of a lover's command. Whereas Cooley claims that "with each order, Ava seems to further relinquish her position as subject and to become the object on which medicine can inscribe its interventions," I view Ava's willingness to turn over on her side and extend her arm as an impassioned gesture toward a recollected partner—a sexual response to this lover's insistence that Ava "tell me everything you'd like me to [do]" and an affirmation of her ecstatic reply: "[Put] your hand there, slowly" (2; Maso, *Ava* 4). For Cooley, moreover, the fact that Ava's attendants typically address her by both her first and last name suggests their appropriation of her identity, but arguably such address reveals respect and maintains Ava's dignity. This designation also echoes the way that past lovers have used her name as a sign of endearment: "You are a wild one, Ava Klein"; "'Ava Klein,' Francesco says, helping me on with my feather headdress"; "Ava Klein, you are a rare bird"; "Tell me what you want, Ava Klein" (4, 6, 11).

Maso does reject the idea of pleasure and pain as dichotomous, viewing them instead as merged in language as in eroticism, but Ava's desiring body in pain, while medicalized, is not violated. Indeed, the novel's rapturous (and closely connected) opening and closing lines, with their recurring imagery of orgasmic pulsations, reveal that Ava maintains her erotic autonomy until her moment of death. Her sexually charged body is never overtaken by her medicalized one; rather, her medicalization facilitates ecstatic memory and an autoerotic sensibility. As a feminist writer Maso suggests that enormous psychosexual capacities exist in dying women and that representing their desire constitutes a neglected part of "bring[ing] women to writing," to borrow Cixous's famous phrase (391). Indeed, Maso's narrator—Ava herself, via free indirect discourse—cites approvingly Cixous's edict that "female sexual pleasure constitutes a disturbance to the masculine order" just before she recollects a romantic evening with Carlos, a former husband, "swimming in the tropical sea" (178). As an experimental novelist Maso recognizes the postmodern dimensions of such representations: "I see experimentation as redemption. . . . Form is content, of that I am sure. The way one tells the story is the story" (*Break* 6).

Three thematic concepts, often realized through recurring tropes, dominate the textual landscape of *Ava*. The first of these is the protagonist's *fluid subjectivity*, which occurs through a narrative emphasis on the multiple landscapes of the dying woman's body and psyche as a sign of her porous identity (re)constructions. The second is her *heady eroticism*, which can be seen in Ava's repeated claim that she and her lovers "were writing an erotic song cycle," the titles of which vary, interweave, and accumulate; and in Ava's embracing of "the Zodiac Killer," not as betrayer but as ultimate lover. The third is her *postmodern perspective on cancer*, a perspective that embraces irony without becoming cynical, that recognizes the violence that lies at the heart of late-twentieth-century culture, that acknowledges gaps without trying to fill them and holds contradictions in productive tension. This sensibility is most evident in Maso's connection of the medicalized female body and the world's body in pain, a linkage that makes *Ava* a profoundly political novel. A close analysis of these three concepts, which appear in different formulations in *Evening* and *Written on the Body* as well, will clarify how the writer interrogates memory, death, and desire.

A recurring query throughout *Ava* is the protagonist's meditative question, "What is this fluidity I move through?" (117) The novel's many references to the sea enhance the representation of Ava as metaphoric swimmer, amazed at water's buoyancy and the vibrancy of underwater landscape. Her consciousness blends memories as through a sieve, separating but also merging various facets of her gendered and sexual identities. As Kuebler notes, Maso's form enacts this fluidity, particularly in her use of double spacing between syntactical units of dialogue, literal textual gaps: "the white spaces between the lines are not line breaks per se, but places where thoughts can rest, places where the words reverberate or sink and fall" (2). Kuebler rightly claims that this technique allows Maso to "avoid discursive explanation, leaving desire to grow in the silences" (2). However, while it is true that desire can lie static in *Ava*, it often becomes restive, exploding the boundaries of the interstitial spaces of the text. From the beginning of this narrative to its end, Ava's claims for desire loom large; indeed, she feels "determined to shape the world according to the dictates of desire" (6).

Not all of the novel's fluidity resides in Ava's body; memory shares this feature with somatic experience. A passage from early in *Ava* illustrates how transformations in memory and in embodiment flow concurrently. This passage addresses both the bodily suffering caused by cancer and its overwhelming mundanity; it also depicts the imagination's role in transporting the sufferer to other vistas:

> Let me describe my life here.
>
> You can't believe the fruit!
>
> I'd like to imagine there was music.
>
> Pain in the joints. Dizziness. Some pain.
>
> A certain pulsing.
>
> She's very pregnant.
>
> I'd like to imagine there was music in the background.
>
> And that you sang.
>
> What is offhand, overheard. Bits of remembered things.
>
> Morning. And the nurses, now. Good morning, Ava Klein. (6)

The ambiguity of "here" reminds readers that through memory Ava "resides" in various European locales with her former lovers as well as in the confined bedroom space where she will soon die. The fragmented, jerky movement of this passage mirrors the ways a dying woman's thoughts might accumulate and synchronize from experiences remembered. There clearly is a gap, however, between what Ava would like to remember and what she actually does: she longs for the swell of music but instead dredges up "offhand, overheard" remarks. The last line reveals Ava's desire to focus not only on her past but also on the now— to acknowledge the nurses who wish her good morning, to submit her dying body to their care.

The diagnostic moment bears enormous weight in many women's cancer narratives, and *Ava* is no exception. However, Maso represents diagnosis as a process, not a single event, a representation that signals Ava's relative freedom from trauma. To be sure, her effort to face her cancer with courage is not initially successful; clearly she feels frightened and disoriented:

> Often there is nowhere to go but forward or back. It is hard to stay here in one place and especially at moments like these.
>
> I'm afraid the news is bad, Ava Klein. (15)

Yet Ava demonstrates resilience, for as Berlin notes, she remains "deeply secure" about her life (4). In Ava's universe, bad news pales beside the ineluctable draw of inchoate murmurs and impassioned words. Such words, in turn, are life-affirming:

> After sex, after coffee, after everything there is to be said—
>
> The hovering and beautiful alphabet as we form our first words after making love.
>
> And somehow I'm still alive. (17–18)

Another trauma to which Ava brings her fluid subjectivity is her memory of confronting the hair loss that inevitably results from chemotherapy, an experience that causes many women to mourn a loss of femininity. For Ava, the falling locks of hair emerge as an intimate Other, paradoxically both attached to and detached from any notion of self: "Shiny hair on the pillow next to me: it was mine and not mine" (61). Cooley rightly observes that "Maso captures here the simultaneous sense of ownership and estrangement experienced by the very ill" (3), but we see in addition Ava's confident embodiment, which allows her to welcome the profligate hairs rather than find them repulsive. Ava also finds baldness a painful source of solidarity with the Holocaust survivors who populate her family:

Undeniably, the chemotherapy makes me most resemble them then.

What about wigs? So as not to be ghoulish. Rachel and Philip. Sophie. Sol. So many bad memories. (34)

Despite her suffering at the memories of her family's violation, Ava refuses the stigmatization that often accompanies women's experience of fatal cancer. Specifically, she determines her own medicalized environment by spending her last days at home, not in a hospital, and by rejecting her physicians' intrusive questions that implicitly blame the patient for contracting this disease. As inspiration for this self-affirming stance Ava cites Cixous:

Cixous: we've been turned away from our bodies, shamefully taught to ignore them, to strike them with that stupid sexual modesty.

I make no apologies.

Jesse Helms, health insurance, the NEA, no family leave, all perfectly good reasons to get out of here *as soon as possible*. . . .

I can go then. (56)

No longer will Ava be driven away from her body or her home; she does not require conservative American senators or corporate spokespersons to mediate her experience with cancer. She can instead create spaces of her own in which to remember, desire, and die.

Such psychic autonomy near the moment of her death liberates Ava, who becomes increasingly exhilarated:

What is this curious lack of depression? This lack of fear? This buoyancy? This free sailing, all of a sudden?

A certain restlessness.

What is this improbably, this unlikely lightness? This fluency? I am unburdened, dying, free.

I think of those dancers and how hard they listened to hear the music that is silence. (78)

The image of dancers listening to silent music is a trope for Ava's reliance on her own strength to guide her toward the unknown. This image recurs at the end of the Morning section, when Ava's fear of death momentarily returns. Listening to silent music—her own internal rhythms—helps Ava to overcome this terror.

Ava's fluid subjectivity can ultimately be seen in her openness to death's vicissitudes and to the bodily transformations she experiences. Indeed, Ava's words in describing this openness resemble strikingly Maso's description of her writing technique as a "spacious form":

I'm feeling the form—finally.

A more spacious form. After all this time.

Breathe. (212)

Cooley notes perceptively that "the body of the text and the text of the body move closer to one another as Ava draws nearer to death" (3). Yet this critic underestimates, I believe, the power of Ava's epiphany in the preceding passage. "While Ava wants to claim agency, to make her body a site of resistance," Cooley observes, "she weakens, her health fails, and, ultimately, her body betrays her. But as her death approaches, the narrative acknowledges its own structural transformations, as body and narrative 'form' increasingly enact one another" (3). Although narrative and bodily fragmentation do intersect, there is no indication that Ava feels betrayal or lacks agency; quite the contrary: she revels in her new-found "spaciousness" and remains fully conscious of her own life force, her breath. She feels liberated at last from death's terrors and any sense of bodily treason.

The erotic intensity that dominates the dying Ava's consciousness is nowhere more evident than in the frequent recurrence of the line, "We were writing an erotic song cycle." This image of the erotic song cycle is the most oft-repeated metaphor in *Ava*, occurring nearly fifty times. Its repetition and variations demonstrate how illness, memory, and desire intersect in Ava's imagination. Indeed, her recollections of having undertaken this artistic composition reveal a link between sexual and creative life, for the project begins because its rhythms stir her blood:

We had made a plan to work on an erotic song cycle because 'you are a poet in your blood, Ava Klein,' the young composer said.

Songs the blood sings. (59)

Ava's many references to writing the song cycle reveal the delight she finds in the collaborative nature of this project and in its playful renaming. A letter to Ava from her fellow composer indicates the success of the piece: "Do you remember our erotic song cycle? It was performed here again just a few months ago. It strikes me still as an extraordinary collaboration" (92). For Ava, however, the composition remains unfinished; like Penelope, she ravels and unravels her handiwork. During the Morning section of the novel, remembering what she named the composition at any particular moment brings her pleasure: "It was called *A Place We Can Still Go*" (46); "It was called *Pavane for a Dead Princess*" (49); "It was called *Flirting in the Life Café*" (58); "It was called *The Alignment of the Planets*" (95). However, the prospective titles darken as cancer takes hold: "It was called *She Finds Herself on a Foreign Coast*"; "It was called *Long Life*"; "It was called *Not Yet*"; "It was called *Just Before Dark in the Forbidden City*"; "It was called *Try Not to Be So Afraid*" (197). In the Evening section all prospective titles refer to death, though often with grim comedy, for example *"Preparations for Nuptials on the Other Side of the Abyss"* (225). These catalogs reveal a penchant for narrative excess that Maso shares with Cixous, who indulges in similar stylistic extravagances.

One purpose of such excess is the revelation of Ava's *jouissance,* her heightened narrative and sexual pleasure despite the illness she encounters. On one occasion, for instance, Ava protests her cancer's interruption of the songwriting process due to a necessary journey for emergency treatment. Yet this trip evokes her *jouissance* in new ways, as she now views even mundane air travel through an eroticized lens:

I was composing an utterly beautiful line of the erotic song cycle when—

All crafts are equipped with flotation-aid devices. In some cases it will be your seat.

It feels tilted even before it goes up.

The effects of flying on sexual response.

People are going everywhere. Caracas, Brussels, Chicago. I am going to the Dana Farber Cancer Institute. (181)

The standard airline security message reveals how desperate Ava's medical situation is: she clings metaphorically to her flotation device in the hope that some new protocol at the Farber Institute will save her. But Ava's eroticization of the security message also displays the transgressive imaginary of someone who revels in sexual memories even while traveling alone to a cancer center. Maso continues this linkage of the airborn, the orgasmic, and the cancerous in a related passage in which Ava's explicit memories reveal all she fears losing:

> No touching, no fantastic explorations with fellow passengers under blankets or winter coats on international night flights.
>
> Blood in a cylinder.
>
> A throbbing. A certain pulsing.
>
> I'd like to fuck you right here. (187)

For Ava, the memory of actual airplane sex that she once experienced is both titillating and painful. She knows that she must revise her erotic song cycle in the face of a daunting new project: facing death, "writing on a foreign coast" (251).

The erotic intensity of *Ava* is also manifested in her specific sexual memories of three husbands and numerous lovers. Foremost among them is an ominous and symbolic lover whom she refers to as the "Zodiac Killer," so called because "before he shoots he asks your sign" (25). Embracing this final lover, an eerie anthropomorphic manifestation of her cancer, is essential to Ava because without the agency of desire she would feel raped, and she wishes to resist envisioning her illness as a bodily territorialization. Yet a woman's embracing of a serial murderer remains a problematic image, even as Maso insists upon its necessity to mark the convergence of violence, death, and eroticism in the text. The Zodiac Killer is cruel to seek young women, as Ava recognizes: "I am only thirty-nine. But I am only thirty-nine, Dr. Oppenheim. As if the Zodiac Killer, or the body, can be reasoned with" (55). Maso's metaphoric use of the Zodiac Killer implies that a woman's premature death from cancer must be conceptualized as an act of violence, despite any reconciliation to it that the woman musters.

The juxtaposition of tenderness and aggression in Ava's sexuality heightens the novel's erotic intensity. Hence Ava's recurring claim that she is composing "a hundred love letters, written by hand" (122) lies in sexual/textual tension with her graphic representations of lust:

> But you are married, I thought, I said to the stranger. You have a woman and child.
>
> Keep the light on.
>
> Take me from behind this time. (51)

For Ava, adulterous sex is satisfying in its anonymity and transgressive-ness. Moreover, erotic and linguistic transgression intersect for Ava. As support for her views regarding the need for a "liberated discourse," Ava again cites Cixous:

> Language for women is closely linked with sexuality for Cixous. She believes that because women are endowed with a more passive and con-sequently more receptive sexuality, not centered on the penis, they are more open than men to create liberated forms of discourse.

> Overheard, bit of remembered things,

> In letters, or on the beach

> How I can be walking that path again if I concentrate. Holding your hand. The perfect leaves on the French oak. Rue de Marché. Rue de Beaujolais.

> Take me from behind this time.

> Or at the moment of desire. (51)

This passage reveals the erotic methodology of Maso's text. Since Ava's dying memory is imbued with "bits of remembered things," she must concentrate fully to unleash her sexual recollections, from "holding your hand" to being "taken from behind."

The touches of the Zodiac Killer evoke those of the other lovers who comprise facets of Ava's erotic history: "Unaccountable lovers. All forgotten. All cherished" (171). These ex-lovers are not idealized, however: as Berlin notes, "the role of the sexual in the text allows Ava Klein constantly to reinvent herself through its fragmented form, thus enabling a complete abandonment of the ideal sexual relationship" (4). Often Ava addresses her sexual partners directly as she recalls a definitive experience: "I was your Cunning Little Vixen. You were my Forester, longing for animals. One look was enough. It took one touch" (36). At other times she describes her encounters from a first-person plural point of view: "We took the overnight train. He kissed me everywhere. Shapely trees passing in the windows" (13). In still other passages she relates her memories in third person via the lan-guage of omniscience: "She finds herself on her thirty-third birthday on a foreign coast with a man named Carlos" (10). Anatole, Danilo, Franz, Jean-Luc, Carlos—"I have so many things I would like to tell you," Ava sighs shortly before her death (260). Ultimately, however,

she listens to each lover's disembodied voice and often finds sustenance there:

> Trust your body now, he says, the way you did then,
>
> Under the pomegranate tree. (260)

Ava does decide to trust her body; aided by her nurse's ministrations,
she rebirths herself on her deathbed. Like a woman in labor she focuses
on the sensual rhythms of breath, both regular and ragged, to combat the
bursts of pain that come with increasing frequency. Alternately soothed
and tormented by the zodiac lover's ghostly presence, Ava begins the
arduous journey of "losing the vague dread" that humans have been
socialized to connect with dying (31, 236). Aroused by probing hands—
her caregivers', her former husbands', her final lover's—Ava pulses in
the realm of eschatology, "pulled toward the irresistible music of the
end" (195, 258).

The postmodern feminist sensibility that *Ava* manifests can best be seen
in Maso's juxtaposition of the individual female body in pain and the suffering of the world's body.[5] The politicization of illness is an important
topic in this novel, as Maso subtly connects the women's cancer epidemic
to the global AIDS pandemic, invasive cancer treatments to colonial and
genocidal invasions, and the violence of illness to the violence of military
actions from World War II to the 1990 Persian Gulf War.

The AIDS connection occurs primarily through Ava's recollections
of her dead friend Aldo, whose early symptoms—"forgetfulness, night
sweats"—ironically plague Ava as well (99). Memories of Aldo's admission that he has HIV flit through Ava's consciousness: "Yes, I am positive, he said, that day in the snow. Holding Italian magazines in the
street" (44). Alongside these are memories of Aldo's musical talent
("Aldo, building cathedrals with his voice") and of his caring:

> I was burned from too much sun. I remember, Aldo, the bottles of pastes
> and lotions you lined up for me in the kitchen. Aloe, other things, a sort of
> white goo, a tonic. We were feeling desperate and middle-aged. Even
> though we were still young, quite young. I had almost forgotten that night
> completely until just now, Aldo— (21, 50)

The extremity of Ava's grief for Aldo is evident in her recollection of his
deathbed vision: "Aldo's last hallucination: there's a floor high up in the

hospital filled with pyramids and on the outside of each pyramid a list of things the dead might have done that day had they lived . . ." (139). What those dead from AIDS might have accomplished haunts Ava. Indeed, she often refers to the AIDS pandemic as well as to the particular experience of Aldo. Early in the novel she quotes an insight by Arthur Danto, author of a book on AIDS and contemporary art: "With AIDS a form of life went dead, a way of thought, a form of imagination and hope. Any death is tragic and the death of children especially so. . . . But this other death carries away a whole possible world " (22). Connecting the tragedy of her own imminent demise to the greater tragedy of an entire generation's death from AIDS helps Ava confront her cancer with grace.

The colonial-genocidal link occurs through concurrent representations of Ava's parents' trauma during their internment at Treblinka and her own unsuccessful treatment regimen for cancer. This juxtaposition, Cooley argues, "suggests a connection between collective, mass destruction and individual suffering" as well as that "between war's destruction and Western medicine's cures that poison the body to make it well" (3). A key passage that illustrates these interweavings occurs early in the narrative, when Ava feels most distressed by her realization that this day will probably be her last, her parents will again suffer (this time from a beloved daughter's death), she leaves no heirs, and medical science has failed her:

> What is wrong with you, Ava Klein?
>
> The effects of chemotherapy in the childbearing years.
>
> My uncle wore a pink triangle through the gray of Treblinka—a rather musical word.
>
> How have I ended up back here, again?
>
> The only industrialized country in the world, beside South Africa, without health care. (35)

Countless twentieth-century bodies have been devastated by atrocities that an ethical world body, Maso implies, might have prevented: Jews, gays, and lesbians killed at concentration camps; premenopausal women given cancer drugs that destroy their childbearing capacities; poor citizens of wealthy countries denied access to medical care. These atrocities require both testimony and witness: "For the testimonial process to take place, there needs to be a bonding, the intimate and total presence of an *other*—in the position of one who hears" (Laub 70). For Maso, readers must bear witness to one woman's senseless death and to the century's atrocities.

Maso's representations of Ava's invasive illness often parallel the bellicose actions of President George H. W. Bush during the 1990 Gulf War. "The President draws a line in the sand" is a recurring line, often juxtaposed with images of Ava's ill body making its final, futile stand (88, 244). That Maso opposes the Gulf War can be seen in the language of mourning she uses in referring to it through a requiem and in comments she made in her essays that the war was important to her writing of this novel (*Break* 66). In the novel, as Ava's collaborator on the erotic song cycle creates a movie about war, Ava is ironically called upon to make a soldier's sacrifice:

> He is making a film now called *The War Requiem*. He sends me a helmet.
>
> We could go for a song.
>
> He drags pails of sand
>
> It was called *The Darkest Evening of the Year*.
>
> It was called *In the Land of Sand and Ashes*.
>
> Her life for a song. (225)

The disturbing image cluster of war, sand, and ashes reminds readers that *Ava* is set during a conflict glibly entitled "Desert Storm" by the U.S. military. The slaughter that occurs recalls the arbitrary nature of Ava's cancer. Her collaborator's understanding of this link between battles and cancer is evident in his writing of a requiem—for the war's dead and for the dying Ava—and in his gift to her of protective head wear. As Ava begins to release her tenuous hold on life, death becomes her final composition. Yet she knows that her own cruel death is one of many, and in this realization she evinces a postmodern sensibility. For Maso "the twentieth-century body is always socially inscribed, marked by violence" (Cooley 1).

Dying can be violent, but it can also be erotic, Maso implies. Rather than sinking into death at thirty-nine from cancer, Ava "floats out on a yacht called Eros"—an allusion to an experience recounted by French feminist writer Colette, who owned a boat with this name and who emphasized in her own fiction "the resilient determination, the will to live, the prodi-

gious and female aptitude for happiness" (*Ava* 132, 209). Certainly Ava
grieves: for the child she never had ("We lost the baby, Anatole"), the
daughters for whom she longs ("one feels the need . . . for hundreds of
daughters"), the illness she cannot control ("Strange blood counts. Mysterious fevers"), the body she fears losing ("Not another transfusion"),
the life she must leave ("Tell me if you are going") (237, 143, 78, 242).
She mourns most fiercely the words she hates to relinquish:

> A, and she repeats it: A. Letters of the alphabet. The most lovely
> configurations.
>
> This is probably the last time. (126)

Finally, however, Maso succeeds in the goal she shares with Cixous:
"creat[ing] a language that heals as much as it separates" (*Ava* 258; *Break*
68). Indeed, Maso offers her protagonist a reprieve, not from death—for
Ava must and does die in this text—but from the trauma of abjection.
Her body dissolves, but her status as a subject remains intact. Ava dies
with her own name on her lips, a palindrome that launches her forward
as well as backward. She is strengthened for her journey by the power of
memory and desire; by the "ravishing" caress of death, the final lover;
and by her strong and stable female subjectivity:

> The girl draws an A. She spells her name:
>
> AVA.
>
> Today is of course a holiday—
>
> Snow falls like music. . . .
>
> Come quickly—
>
> You can't believe,
>
> A throbbing. A certain pulsing.
>
> You are ravishing. (265)

LOVE "THROWN ACROSS THE GAP": SUSAN MINOT'S *EVENING*

In *Evening* Minot offers an elegiac exploration of desire and death
through the shifting consciousness of Ann Lord, who lies dying of an
unidentified type of cancer. Ann's dominant awareness is of a violent

upheaval, faintly ominous in nature but also exciting: she observes the movement of shadowy forms through a "new lens," feels her body "flung back" and "split open," experiences nothing short of "a revolution" (5). Ann's deathbed transfiguration brings to readers' minds the poet Muriel Rukeyser's famous lines, "What would happen if one woman told the truth about her life? / The world would split open" (131). Although Ann is not presented via a first-person narrative— Minot's omniscient narrator instead controls the discourse—readers do bear witness to Ann's transformation. Like Ava, whose lovers called her a "wild one," a "rare bird," Ann is initially envisioned as a "wild bird"— not one that soars jubilantly, as Ava does, but one longing to be set free. Whereas Maso emphasizes her protagonist's deathbed agency, Minot explores the effects of confinement and disorientation on female subjectivity, erotic desire, and memory. As she explained in an interview with randomhouse.com, "If you have ever watched someone on his or her deathbed it is hard to get the vision of suffering out of your mind. And worst of all is the great divide between the sick and the healthy, no matter how much love is being thrown across the gap."

To interrogate the visions that jolt Ann as she nears death, Minot employs the twin lenses of obsession and delirium. The subject of Ann's repeated reflections, Harris Arden, a man with whom she had become sexually involved forty years earlier, crashed into her life during a friend's wedding and left her that same weekend, unwilling to abandon his fiancée. The dying Ann's single-minded focus on Harris is evident in her inability to communicate with the four adult children who visit her daily, the scant attention she pays to recollections of her former husbands, and the fact that not only does she remember each detail of her sexual encounters with Harris, she also conjures an older, wiser Harris to her bedside for disembodied conversation. Although Minot never uses the word *obsession* to describe Ann's attachment, her narrative does acknowledge thralldom: "If there had been a part of her not in thrall with him that part was gone" (64). Moreover, in the randomhouse.com interview Minot admits her interest in the psychology of delirium: "Hearing the delirium of someone drugged with painkillers and dying can be a glimpse into the person beyond the social masks." The delirious rambling that transports Ann beyond these masks is induced partly by the morphine she takes to ease her suffering, partly by the heady mixture of pleasure and pain that her memories of Harris evoke. In *Evening* the intersection of cryptic and excessive language, of memories alternately tender and lurid, provides the tension between the static nature of obsession and the wildness of delirium.

Obsession and delirium converge in Ann's first hallucinatory dialogue with the imaginary Harris, a dialogue that reveals her grief at his abandonment, her despondency over her illness, and her fragmented awareness that an actual reconciliation between them is impossible. This passage also supports the insight of reviewer Cristina Del Sesto, who claims that Harris "remains the fixed point" for Ann not so much for himself but "because of the untapped possibilities he represents":

> Where were you all this time? she said. Where have you been?
>> I guess far away.
>> Yes you were. Too far away.
>> They sat in silence. . . .
>> You looked as if you didn't need anyone, she said.
>> But those are the ones who need the most, he said. Don't you know that?
>> I do now, she said. Too late.
>> Never too late to know something, he said.
>> Maybe not, she said. But too late to do any good. (7)

The arbitrariness of memory, with its exasperating lacunae and sudden revelations, leads Ann toward an epistemology that initially appears pessimistic; new knowledge comes "too late." However, as she comes to terms with dying, Ann gradually moves beyond both obsession and delirium: "She woke before dawn coughing. . . . She lay still as the room grew light. . . . It seemed to be the beginning of something more than just day. For a few long moments she lay and felt—what was it? The dawn light put her in mind of creation. It must have been this way on the actual first day of the world" (37).

Harris serves as a catalyst for Ann's movement from despair to hope, even though, as Minot notes in an interview with Dave Welch, it is "by chance" that Ann remembers him:

> Ann did actually forget this guy and did go on. It wasn't a *Bridges of Madison County* thing where every year she lit the candle on their day. She forgot the guy. But in a self-defensive way she wasn't aware of, a psychological way, she turned her heart in a different direction. She decided, *I'm not going to love that way,* or *I'm not going to risk like that again.* . . .

It was only by chance that she happened upon the memory of Harris again and realized how much it meant to her. Which I think happens in memory. (Welch)

What her deathbed conversations with the elusive Harris and the memory of their mutual passion rejuvenate in Ann, finally, is her long-dormant capacity to take emotional risks.

Like *Ava, Evening* features a protagonist whose fluid subjectivity, erotic intensity, and struggle for a postmodern sensibility provide the dominant narrative momentum. Ann Lord differs significantly from Ava Klein, however. For one thing, Ann is less fully present on her deathbed ("Everyone's here but me," she tells her daughters regretfully). Moreover, her sexual memories bring her momentary rapture but more frequent regret than Ava's do, as she looks to Harris to fill emotional gaps that she has not acknowledged having (94). Ultimately, however, Ann's sensibility, like Ava's, is postmodern in its emphasis on the contingency of human consciousness.

Ann's fluid subjectivity can be seen in her effort to maintain lucidity, her circular patterns of thoughts, her frustrated responses to her medicalized status, and her paradoxical security in and estrangement from her body. Attended by inquisitive daughters, her former husband's sister (Aunt Grace), and a vigilant nurse, Ann often feels her privacy invaded; the morphine on which she relies further reduces her autonomy. With her shifting consciousness she finds it difficult to distinguish past from present, and her solitary mental wanderings are frequently disrupted in the communal environment of her sickroom:

> Have you moved her?
>> She was sitting up this morning. Mrs. Lord?
>> The smell of rose water.
>> I'm sorry I'm late, said Ann Lord. We stopped for a long time in
>> Providence.
>> Mrs. Lord, you have a visitor.
>> Ann Lord opened her eyes. No he's not, she said. It wasn't a
>> visitor, it was Dr. Baker. (11)

The movement to which Ann's children and her nurse refer has strictly to do with her positions in bed, which they monitor so that she might avoid sores. In Ann's consciousness, however, she is journeying to Cape Cod by car with Buddy Winterborn, brother of Lila, the friend whose wedding she will attend, and with Harris Arden, whom she has just met.

Her apology makes sense when delivered to Lila upon Ann's late arrival at the wedding site forty years ago, but to her caregivers in the present it smacks of irrationality. Likewise confusing to them is Ann's insistence that Dr. Baker is not a visitor: she is correct, since readers learn elsewhere in the narrative that he is an old family friend, but her apparent denial that someone is visiting convinces her attendants of her disorientation. "Let's hope Ann is lucid," remarks Aunt Grace to Ann's daughter, Constance. "What do you mean? She's been lucid," Constance replies. "So far, said Aunt Grace mysteriously" (13). Aunt Grace hints at what Constance would deny: that the mother she has known is gradually disappearing. However, Constance and Aunt Grace share a conventional definition of lucidity, while Ann's (and Minot's) postmodern vision demands that any definition of lucidity be contingent.

Minot represents Ann's swirl of memories as disorienting, although less so to her than to her family members, yet while these spinning recollections confuse Ann momentarily, they also provide an opportunity for life review. By foregrounding the arbitrary nature of remembering and forgetting, her floating thoughts facilitate an essential detachment:

> She lay on her back staring up at the trees the way she used to when she was young. She could not focus or stop or hold onto a thought for very long. . . . It all floated by, random and nearly transparent. They were the props of her life but she had no more sense of them than one does for the stage scenery of a play one saw ages ago then forgot. No doubt at the time they affected her, stirred some reaction, irritated or pleased her, but now most of them gave off neither heat nor cold and she watched them drop into the gaping dark hole of meaningless things she had not forgotten, things one level up from the vaster place where lay all the unremembered things. (15)

The metaphor of life as theater and past events as props recalls Shakespeare's claim that "all the world's a stage"; it reminds readers as well that Ann's body is performing in the theater of her sickroom, that cancer is diagnosed in stages, and that Ann's cancer has reached its final level. Suffering from stage 4 metastasized cancer typically robs the patient of emotional intensity, and Ann is no exception; most memories have little meaning for her now, and she watches without interest as they "drop into the gaping dark hole" backstage that houses scenery no longer valued. The memory of meeting Harris, in contrast, galvanizes the dying Ann: "Only when she was near did the back turn around and the long leg come off the running board and she saw the man's face. . . . She felt as if she'd been struck on the forehead with a brick" (8). Ann scrutinizes this memory in cinematic detail, foregrounding Harris's sexy body and her visceral response to it, in part because it offers philosophical illumination: "The person's face seemed lit from within" (9). Forty years later she continues to seek—and at moments to find—illumination in Harris. Such insights are complicated, however, by the fact that as her erotic memory gains momentum, her body fails.

The erosion of bodily autonomy is a vexing aspect of terminal cancer, and Minot represents well both the frustration of a patient confronting invasive medicalization and the dignity she strives to maintain. Ann finds annoying the unconscious condescension that many medical attendants manifest toward their patients:

> *Let's turn ourselves a bit let's try lunch let's have a little sip let's sit a little up*
>   I'm not hungry.
>   Keep up our strength, said the nurse.
>   A wave of nausea swept through her. This is not what she'd planned, she'd always planned to go quickly. (23–24)

The nurse's use of first-person plural pronouns attempts to mask the solitary nature of dying from cancer, but Ann is not fooled; she finds nauseating her medications, the smell of food, the nurse's infantilization, her slow-moving illness. As distressing as her lack of agency is the sense that her decaying body, almost devoid of flesh, no longer resembles its former self:

> Her legs and arms were being moved and she watched the sheet fold back then rolled on her side then felt the sheet being pulled under her and rolled back. The nurse tucked it in. This was not her body she looked at, the leg with the long bone, the hip jutting out. She recognized it but it belonged to someone else. My God, it belonged to her mother. (102)

Ann's horror as she imagines staring at her mother's emaciated body can best be explained by the feminist theory of matrophobia, the "fear of becoming one's mother" when that mother represents passivity, martyrdom, repression, or decay (Adrienne Rich, *Of Woman* 235).

The fluidity between her mother's body and her own initially shocks Ann, but it leads her to meditate on both the vulnerability and liberation that nakedness can bring. Being bathed by a nurse engenders in Ann a countermemory of the erotics of undressing:

Let's slip this off, this arm first. That's it. A warm sponge moved over her shoulders. Strange how little people were naked. . . . *Would you mind if I undid this what are you doing just one button I can't reach the hook would you mind I can't seem to manage what would you do without me here let me take this off I like to undo it may I will you let me I want to see you I think I better leave this on.* (103)

This passage reveals the sexual courtesies of a bygone era (*"Would you mind if I undid this"*) as well as the caution with which Ann approached erotic experience with all men except Harris (*"I think I better leave this on"*). The dying Ann recognizes, however, the freedom that nudity offers, as she recalls a solitary moment years ago on a balcony in Europe:

> She stood at tall French doors in bright noon light with a shower running behind and when she opened the latch the loud revving of *motorinos* and cars going round and round, the black and white statue of horses and pointed wings, the balcony shallow in this foreign place thinking what to put on and wear and standing naked at the window thinking this might be the nearest thing to showing herself truly. (103)

Having chosen a life of self-concealment after Harris's defection, Ann recalls on her deathbed the pleasure of self-revelation.

Ann's fluid subjectivity cannot protect her, however, from the knowledge that her cancer has metastasized. The cryptic conversation she has with Dr. Baker produces traumatic images of the blood tests that led to her diagnosis:

> The line between her dreams and waking life disappeared. She had no idea what day it was. They said it was July. A month had gone by since the last of the tests. A chilling phrase: run some tests. They made her drink poison, poked and prodded, pulled blood out in purple threads, then came Dick Baker's casual voice could she come into the office. She felt like hell, silence on the line. Why don't I stop by on my way home? He said, in this way telling her. (33)

The word *chilling* underscores the anguish that occurs when a cancer patient realizes that hope for recovery is gone as well as the recurrence of that anguish when memory forces her to relive this scene. As theorist Cathy Caruth has noted, trauma typically results from a victim's "inability fully to witness the event as it occurs, or the ability to witness the event fully only at the cost of witnessing oneself. . . . The force of this experience would appear to arise precisely . . . in the collapse of this understanding" ("Trauma," 7). Such a collapse in understanding characterizes Ann's recurring memories of her final diagnosis. Nonetheless, Ann maintains a certain agency by resisting hospitalization, much as Ava does. Every recollection of her hospital experience reinforces Ann's determination not to return:

> Then the days in the hospital, which is no place for sick people. There you blurred into something else in rooms with brown stripes down the halls and plastic under the sheets and curving aluminum bars and windows that didn't open. People wore crumpled masks and the furniture rolled. She lay under the machine shaped like a bull's head and needles were taped into place and needles pulled out. Visiting hours were over. In the middle of the night buzzers went off and in the morning when you rolled your I.V. by the next room saw the empty bed with the blank clipboard and no more bald woman named Gwenivere.
>   . . . No there was no question of her going back to the hospital. (33)[6]

This passage represents the cancer wing as a virtual prison, the hospital garb as humiliating, and a neighbor's death as a jolting reminder of what the future holds in store. By insisting on palliative care, Ann demands the right to die with dignity at home, where she can maintain the fluidity between dreams and waking life. Yet when the factory that her body becomes produces pain as its only product, both agency and fluidity become elusive: "The engine chugging quietly beneath her manufactured pain ceaselessly. It was not going fast enough. She wanted it to speed up but whenever she urged it forward the effort only bound her faster to life" (15). She holds in complex tension her desire to embrace life and the contradictory wish to sever ties.

Ultimately Ann realizes that she can compose her life script until the moment of her death. The following dialogue with her daughter, Margie, best illustrates this maintenance of creative agency, even as it reveals Ann's recognition that she has failed at motherhood:

> She should not have had children. She didn't know how to answer their eyes. She tried to think of something to say. The ceiling was there with its uneven plaster.
>   I'm a writer now, she said.
>   Margie leaned forward, her expression changed. What?
>   She pointed up. My blank page. (61)

This passage's imagery recalls Cixous's claim that women and especially mothers write with "white ink," inscribing their own insignia on the

blank page on which female sexuality and embodiment have traditionally been seen to exist ("Laugh," 396).

Ann's fluid subjectivity is also apparent in the imaginative voyages
she takes, a psychic mobility that characterizes Ava's response to dying
as well. While Ava imagines returning to French beaches where she
danced till dawn, Ann finds pleasure in solitary travels. Yet Ann, like
Ava, finds escape from grief in recalling the rhythms of the ocean and
imagining herself there:

> Someone was sobbing down the hall in one of the guest rooms then it
> turned into waves. The sea, she thought, the sea, she'd not seen the sea in
> the longest time. God she'd love to swim.
>
> She shot herself out of a cannon and flew from the house. The lawn
> below grew small and the rooftops of the Cambridge houses turned flat and
> square. She followed the grey snake of the Charles River . . . to where in
> the morning the water was still and green and waiting. (103)

Ann thus shares with Ava a certain resilience. Both women face debilitating illness by refusing hospitalization, recomposing their own life stories,
and traveling via memory to locations where their desires can be met.

The erotic intensity in *Evening* emerges from Ann's deathbed memories
of the transformative weekend in 1954 that she spent with Harris. That
weekend ends in two tragedies: the alcohol-related death of Buddy Winterborn, which occurs late on the night of the wedding when he and
other guests go for a midnight swim; and Ann's loss of Harris, whose
passion for Ann gives way to duty when his fiancée arrives late for the
weekend and informs him she is pregnant. Minot represents Ann's erotic
memories of Harris in the gendered terms of the era: she is innocent, he
experienced; she is passive, he aggressive; she questions the speed of
their involvement, he argues that it is inevitable:

> Ann, he said. He was running his finger under the gathered elastic of her
> shirt at the neck. . . . She pulled back slightly, wasn't it too fast? But do I
> know you? Yes, he murmured. He pulled her up to him. . . . What were
> these arms. Who did he know and what other girls did he kiss and where
> did he go. . . . She felt an overpowering urge to lie down. (70)

The memory of this "overpowering urge" becomes ironic, however, as
Minot juxtaposes Ann's recollection of youthful pleasure with a present-
day sensation of pain: "She removed the sharp black teeth imbedded in

her side. It's where the cancer was" (73). To escape this pain Ann returns to memories of sex with Harris, when her body responded in ways she did not realize were possible: "They stood and each time he touched a new place she sort of fell off an edge and each time he said something she dropped deeper into herself and further into the night around them. She would have fallen over if he'd not held her up" (77).

Despite the sexual repression to which she had been socialized as a 1950s woman, the young Ann finds delight in giving and receiving pleasure, as her deathbed reveries make clear. Initially she performs acts that Harris initiates and maintains modesty by not undressing. As their encounter progresses, however, Ann experiences for the first time the raw pleasure of orgasm, a pleasure she relives through her deathbed memories:

> She gasped when his mouth found her nipple and he stayed there, flooding her. He worked down the other strap without moving his mouth. Please don't stop, she thought *stay like that always* and she felt exposed to the night till his other hand came over her. He was steering her, she rose to it, she could not get enough of what he was doing to her. (197)

Ann's sexual epiphany and her almost simultaneous revelation that Harris will leave her results in her realization that the memory of their passion will remain: "This flying would go on forever. His mouth vibrated over her breast, nibbling at her, and when she was gone it would still be there in history, she would be forever unraveling and peeling back for him" (199). Despite the sentimentality of such passages, Minot also represents Ann as pragmatic: "Later her life would be full of things, full of houses and children and trips to the sea and husbands and hats with brims and dogs catching sticks and tables to set and lists to cross off and she would have left singing behind and the stars would never look this way again " (199). Minot thus explores how the human struggle to confront death and loss is mitigated by the elusive power of memory.

Ann Lord's worldview appears narcissistic, largely because she lacks political awareness; even as an older woman, she fails to grapple with late-twentieth-century atrocities. Still, Minot's Ann shares with Maso's Ava a postmodern recognition that while every human existence has meaning, that meaning defies full comprehension: "She scanned the shelves of her life. . . . Bits of things swam up to her, but what made them come? . . . After she was gone there would be no one who knew the whole of her life. She did not even know the whole of it" (16). To foreground her novel's emphasis on unknowability, Minot includes an epigraph from Faulkner's *The Sound and the Fury* in which the alcoholic Jason Compson gives his suicidal son a new watch as Quentin leaves for university: "I give it to you not that you may remember time, but that you might forget it now and then for a moment and not spend all your breath trying to conquer it." When applied to Ann Lord's experience of terminal cancer, Faulkner's words suggest that "forgetting time" can facilitate an acceptance of death's incomprehensibility rather than a resistance to it. In her random-house.com interview Minot commented on her understanding of the passage from Faulkner:

> The sense that I get from his quotation is that the attempt to conquer the past is just another battle one has with time, and a losing one. . . . Memory, that activity of the mind and heart which both gives meaning to life and pulls us back from it, which has a dim basis in history but is far more tenuous than we can admit, determines the way we narrate our lives—our experience is stored there—but is never stored in one mind like another. Memory is another example of the isolation of individuals.

A sense of isolation embitters Ann at moments, but as the following imaginary deathbed dialogue with a penitent Harris reveals, memory also helps her confront loss:

> Ann, he said and took her hand.
>   Forgetting, remembering . . . why should I care?
>   I couldn't forget you, he said.
>   What difference does it make anyway? she said.
>   It makes a difference.
>   I don't know.
>   You made a difference, he said. You changed my life.
>   And I never got to see it, she said. (18)

Despite Minot's irritating use of cliché, this passage illuminates Ann's awareness of the irreducible gaps in human knowledge. The word *difference* occurs three times in this dialogue, as Minot stresses the contingency of every human narrative.

This contingent vision reappears in the final paragraphs of *Evening*, as Minot offers three disparate accounts of Ann's moment of death: her children's, her nurse's, and her own. The children's conversation about when Ann's death will occur reinforces Minot's epistemology of unknowability:

> Would it make a difference if we knew?
>> We could . . . I don't know . . . plan. We could . . . we'd just know.
>> It wouldn't make a difference. We'd still be waiting. That's all we can do. Be here and wait. (262)

While anticipating death strips mourners of agency, nurses maintain it by recording, in clinical jargon, the patient's visceral responses:

> 12 Noon Turned o void Still moaning Morphine sulfate 15 mg IM for pain Congestion noted o pulse Resp very labored 1 pm Turned over Resp 10–13 1:10 o response o pulse Body convulsions Vomitus expelled from oral cavity Dr. Baker notified Daughters present Son present in room 1:30 Dr. Baker in to verify expiration. (263)

In contrast to the unsettling death that Ann's family witnesses and the nurse records, Ann's final dialogue with Harris seems almost mundane. Since their shared history positions Harris as the leave-taker, Ann envisions him as departing and her dying self, ironically, as remaining:

> I'm going to have to go.
>> Yes, I know.
>> Her mouth was parted and her breath rattled in her throat. After a silence she said, Will you come back.
>> Of course!
>> Tomorrow? You'll come back tomorrow?
>> I'll do my best. But it may have to be the day after. . . . I won't say good-bye.
>> No, she said. Don't.
>> He did not come the next day, he did not come the day after. He did not come again. (263–64)

The final lines of *Evening* diverge significantly from those of *Ava*, whose protagonist dies with her own name on her lips and with orgasmic intensity: "A throbbing. A certain pulsing. You are ravishing" (265). Ann Lord's last words—"No . . . Don't"—raise the question of how much deathbed agency she maintains. Does Harris Arden fail to come again because Ann cannot conjure him or because she has released him? For Minot such questions remain unanswerable, serving only to demonstrate "how dense our interior life is" (interview).

"A SECRET CODE ONLY VISIBLE IN CERTAIN LIGHTS": JEANETTE WINTERSON'S *WRITTEN ON THE BODY*

Winterson's *Written on the Body* explores its unnamed narrator's obsessive desire to mine the depths of a lost lover's body, not only to pay tribute to its beauty but also to probe its cancerous cells and tissue and sinews. According to the lens of French feminist theory, any desire by women to "write" the female body, historically misrepresented by masculinist recorders, represents an attempt to restore to women their subjectivity. Yet arguably the narrative dismembering that Winterson's protagonist undertakes is appropriative. After all, Louise Rosenthal, the beloved of Winterson's narrator, does not control her own narrativized body; rather, the narrator dissects the organs and inspects the orifices of her lover without permission. To be sure, this narrator dismembers Louise in order to re-member her—to recall her and to reconstruct her cancerous body—yet by her own admission the narrator does so out of selfishness rather than generosity. Variously representing herself as paramour, surgeon, mortician, and raconteur, Winterson's narrator assumes strategic guises to justify an objectification of Louise that finally emerges as emotional treason as well as a paradoxical form of erotic loyalty.

Boundary crossing is a distinguishing feature of sexual desire, however, and even as Louise is written, she too inscribes the narrator's body, or so the narrator believes. "Written on the body is a secret code only visible in certain lights," she explains, "the accumulations of a lifetime gather there" (89). For Winterson's narrator, Louise serves as decoder and translator:

> In places the palimpsest is so heavily worked that the letters feel like Braille. I like to keep my body rolled up away from prying eyes, never unfold too much, or tell the whole story. I didn't know that Louise would have reading hands. She has translated me into her own book. (89)

By reading the Braille of the narrator's body Louise pulls back the layers of a palimpsest and reveals her lover's underbelly. Indeed, *Written on the Body* examines acts of composition, code breaking, and translation by both the narrator and her lover, each of whom recognizes erotic knowledge as a form of violation as well as homage. There exists between the two apparent mutuality until the narrator learns that Louise has cancer, at which time she infantilizes her lover: "My child. My baby. The tender thing I wanted to protect" (159). She cannot face the specter of her lover's perfect body falling prey to a ravaging illness: "Eventually chemotherapy would contribute to the failure of her bone marrow. She would be thin, my beautiful girl, thin and weary and lost. There is no cure for chronic lymphocytic leukaemia" (102). Hence the narrator decodes Louise in a way that distances her and defies reciprocity.

"Why is the measure of love loss?" The novel's opening line fore-shadows a key theme: the complexity of distinguishing between obsessive passion and abiding love. Just as cancer can be defined as the body betraying itself, so can one lover betray another arbitrarily—not by sexual infidelity but by desertion at a time of need. Having promised Louise that she will "be true" to her, the narrator finds her lover's illness unbearable. Thus when Louise's conniving physician-husband convinces the narrator that no one but he possesses the skills to keep Louise alive—skills Elgin will use only if his wife's lover goes away—the narrator abandons Louise. Alone in a Yorkshire cottage, she fixates on the memory of her lover's body: "If I could not put Louise out of my mind I would drown in her" (111). Since she cannot save Louise, she cries out in self-absorption for Louise to save her: "Do you see me in my blood-soaked world? Green-eyed girl, eyes wide apart like almonds, come in tongues of flame and restore my sight" (139).

As do *Ava* and *Evening*, *Written on the Body* examines the fluid subjectivity, erotic intensity, and postmodern sensibility of a woman confronting terminal cancer. It departs from the other two novels, however, by interrogating the subjectivity and eroticism of the physically healthy but psychically damaged narrator as well. The narrator justifies her narcissistic interrogation of self and Other/self as Other by emphasizing the two women's similarity:

> I thought difference was rated to be the largest part of sexual attraction but there are so many things about us that are the same.
> Bone of my bone. Flesh of my flesh. To remember you it's my own body I touch. Thus she was, here and here. (129)

However, the narrator's unreliability is evident in her inability to articulate difference between herself and Louise, a woman stricken with leukemia but not without her own agency and desires. Although the narrator ultimately does distinguish Louise's difference, she does so only after many months of obsession.

That Winterson emphasizes the fluidity of female subjectivity can be seen in the merger of the narrator's body with that of Louise—initially through sex and eventually through a blending of identities. Early on the narrator describes their sexual merger as a mutual colonization: "Louise, in this single bed, between these garish sheets, I will find a map as likely as any treasure hunt. I will explore you and mine you and you will redraw me according to your will. We shall cross one another's boundaries and make ourselves one nation" (20). Louise exhibits possessive tendencies as well; after lovemaking she draws a heart on each lens of her lover's foggy glasses, "so you won't see anybody but me" (146). Winterson's fluid narrative resembles Woolf's in its rapturous language, although Woolf never wrote in such a sexually explicit way:

"You're shaking," she said.
"I must be cold."
"Let me warm you."
We lay down on the floor, our backs to the day. I needed no more light than was in her touch, her fingers brushing my skin, bringing up the nerve ends. Eyes closed I began a voyage down her spine, the cobbled roads of hers that brought me to a cleft and a damp valley then a deep pit to drown in. What other places are there in the world than those discovered on a lover's body? (82)

Clearly the lovers share a sense of mutuality and fluidity that the narrator's final question encourages readers initially to idealize.

During the novel's first half the narrator depicts Louise's fluidity by associating her body with water, with a pulsing electrical current, and with the changing contours of a newfound continent. The two women first meet in the park on a rainy day the narrator loves to recall: "Her hair was shining with bright drops of rain, the rain ran down her breasts, their outline clear through her wet muslin dress" (85). She remembers swimming with Louise, viewing her as not just in the river but somehow part of it: "You turned on your back and your nipples graced the surface of the river and the river decorated your hair with beads. You are creamy but for your hair your red hair that flanks you on either side" (11). Louise's fluidity makes her sometimes seem alarming: "There was a dangerously electrical quality about Louise. I worried that the steady flame she offered might be fed by a current far more volatile" (49). The power her lover recognizes in Louise calls into question the lovers' fusion and threatens the narrator's fantasy of merging identities. Although she denies any desire to possess Louise, she fears her lover's confident nudity: "Louise, your nakedness was too complete for me, who had not learned the extent of your fingers. How could I cover this land? Did Columbus feel like this on sighting the Americas? I had no dream to possess you but I wanted you to possess me" (52). Here the narrator protests too much: if she does not want to colonize her lover's body, why does she compare herself to Columbus, who approached new territories with possession as his goal?

The specter of Louise's leukemic body throws into disarray the narrator's assumptions regarding their merger, since she can neither prevent nor identify with the bodily deterioration that she assumes her lover will undergo. During the novel's second half, when the narrator learns from Elgin that Louise has cancer, she responds with grief and shock. She imagines herself floating in space, then imagines herself and/or Louise coming apart: "Two hundred miles from the surface of the earth there is no gravity. The laws of motion are suspended. You could turn somersaults slowly slowly, weight into weightlessness, nowhere to fall. . . . You will break up bone by bone, fractured from who you are, you are drifting away now, the centre cannot hold" (100–101). In addition to describing her own disintegration, the narrator envisions her lover's ominous transformation: "When her spleen started to enlarge she might have splenic irridation or even a splenectomy. By then she would be badly anaemic, suffering from deep bruising and bleeding, tired and in pain most of the time" (102). Abdicating responsibility to the woman she once identified as integral to her self, the narrator bequeaths Louise to the husband she does not love—a bequest that Louise rejects. The reader realizes quickly what the narrator slowly comes to comprehend: that Louise's subjectivity remains intact, its boundaries traversed only at her will.

The erotic intensity in *Written on the Body* is most evident in Winterson's emphasis on three forms of transgressive desire: fetishism, sadomasochism, and necrophilia. That these desires have been controversial among psychoanalysts and feminists makes their narrative representation appealing to Winterson due to her aesthetic affiliation with wildness (*Art* 15). Winterson represents transgressive sexual practices as healthy, violent only when the narrator's narcissistic desire becomes invasive—

when she imagines colonizing the body of the lover she has abandoned in order to "save" her.

As Lynda Hart notes in her study of lesbian sadomasochism, *Between the Body and the Flesh*, "women are not supposed to be capable of fetishism according to psychoanalysis; perhaps it is time to think of women as more adept fetishists than Freud ever dreamed" (55). Winterson's narrator is definitely adept; her fetishism is evident in her imagined dissection of her lover's body, facilitated by her incessant reading of anatomy texts. She fixates not merely on Louise's face and skin, which as a lover she knew intimately, but on the very muscles of her being: "I didn't only want Louise's flesh, I wanted her bones, her blood, her tissues, the sinews that bound her together" (51). Voyeurism is apparent here, along with a self-absorption that masks itself as devotion: "I could have held her for a thousand years until the skeleton itself rubbed away to dust. What are you that makes me feel thus? Who are you for whom time has no meaning?" (51). The aggressive nature of the narrator's questions reveals her outrage at the depth of her thralldom. She later performs a narrative autopsy on the absent Louise, imagining the removal of her organs and bodily fluids:

> I became obsessed with anatomy. . . . Within the clinical language, through the dispassionate view of the sucking, sweating, greedy, defecating self, I found a love poem to Louise. I would go on knowing her, more intimately than the skin, hair and voice that I craved. I would have her plasma, her spleen, her synovial fluid. I would recognize her even when her body had long since fallen away. (111)

In an ironic mirroring of Louise's manipulative husband, the narrator thus begins her own "obsessional study of carcinoma," in large part because studying female anatomy and cancer constitutes "sexy medicine" for her as well as for him (66).

Not all of the narrator's fetishistic impulses are narcissistic, however; they are sometimes born of erotic longing for her partner's sexual organs. She fetishizes in particular Louise's genitalia, thus engaging in what we might call cunt worship and clit worship. Recalling with pleasure an afternoon of oral sex, she memorializes the smell, taste, and appearance of her lover's vagina:

> She arches her body like a cat on a stretch. She nuzzles her cunt into my face like a filly at the gate. She smells of the sea. She smells of rockpools

when I was a child. She keeps a starfish in there. I crouch down to taste the salt, to run my fingers around the rim. She opens and shuts like a sea anemone. She's refilled each day with fresh tides and longing. (73)

To re-member Louise more intimately still, the narrator zeroes in on the taste of her lover's clitoris, which she likens to the rich flavor of an olive pit once its flesh has been devoured: "My lover is an olive tree whose roots grow by the sea. Her fruit is pungent and green. It is my joy to get at the stone of her. The little stone of her hard by the tongue. Her thick-fleshed salt-veined swaddle stone" (137). Cunt worship and clit worship, provocative aspects of Winterson's erotic narrative, serve as an antidote to the aesthetic tameness that she claims in *Art Objects* is antithetical to "true art" (15).

Louise's cancer disrupts the narrator's ability to fetishize her lover's body, which she wishes to remain the perfect specimen that she remembers. Since cancer produces radical physical changes, the narrator perceives it as dangerous to herself as well as to Louise:

> You were milk-white and fresh to drink. Will your skin discolour, its brightness blurring? Will your neck and spleen distend? Will the rigorous contours of your stomach swell under an infertile load? It may be so and the private drawing I keep of you will be a poor reproduction then. It may be so but if you are broken then so am I. (125)

The rhetoric of spoilage sounds faintly Victorian, as narrator imagines the fresh Louise soured by leukemia, but Renaissance imagery also occurs, representing Louise as a once valuable work of art now known to be a fraud. Again the narrator conceals her unconscious objectification behind a curtain of mutuality—if her lover is "broken," so will she be. She seems incapable of recognizing that to fetishize Louise without returning to her *is* to break her.

Hart's study of sadomasochism also sheds light on Winterson's treatment of s/m as pleasurable because it is risky and taboo: "If 'the lesbian body' in feminism was the site where a referent could be fixed, lesbian s/m has played a large part in launching lesbian identities out of their safe harbor and into the sea of the arbitrary play of signifiers" (*Between* 60). In *Written on the Body*, as in Wittig's *The Lesbian Body*, the narrator's sadomasochism reveals the erotic pleasure she takes in danger:

> After sex you tiger-tear your food, let your mouth run over with grease. Sometimes it's me you bite, leaving shallow wounds in my shoulders. . . . I

wear the wounds as a badge of honour. The moulds of your teeth are easy
to see under my shirt but the Louise that tattoos me on the inside is not visible to the naked eye. (118)[7]

Pride in the display of tooth marks and in the secrecy of an invisible tattoo are evident here, as the narrator delights in what marks her as
Louise's prey. Moreover, Louise's teeth are not her only weapon; her
flank contains nails, but the narrator would ride her anyway: "Nail me to
you. I will ride you like a nightmare. You are the winged horse Pegasus
who would not be saddled" (131). The sadomasochistic elements of the
narrator's desire can be seen in the thin line she perceives between pain
and pleasure, a perspective that recalls the frequent erosion of this
boundary in *Ava*. Finding pain exciting, the speaker revels in the memory of Louise's sharp shoulder blades: "I fear you in our bed when I put
out my hand to touch you and feel the twin razors turned towards me.
You sleep with your back toward me so that I will know the full extent of
you. It is sufficient" (131). Ultimately the narrator mourns the fact that
Louise's cancer will make s/m love play impossible: "The leukaemic
body hurts easily. I could not be rough with you now, making you cry
out with pleasure close to pain. We've bruised each other, broken the
capillaries shot with blood. Tubes hair-thin intervening between arteries
and veins, those ramified blood vessels that write the body's longing"
(124). Claiming bruises and broken capillaries as insignia of her desire,
the narrator defines "the body's longing" as fervently sadomasochistic.

Images of necrophilia recur as well in *Written on the Body*, especially
in the section in which the narrator obsesses on her dying lover's
anatomy. Winterson's necrophiliac imaginary is evident when the narrator labels herself a tomb raider and Louise's body a mausoleum: "Let me
penetrate you. I am the archeologist of tombs. I would devote my life to
marking your passageways, the entrances and exits of that impressive
mausoleum, your body" (119). Grotesque imagery dominates this section, though the narrator envisions her ghoulishness as an homage to
love. Once she has invaded the tomb, she imagines herself a mortician
taking charge of the corpse she has unearthed: "As I embalm you in my
memory, the first thing I shall do is to hook out your brain through your
accommodating orifices. Now that I have lost you I cannot allow you to
develop, you must be a photograph not a poem. You must be rid of life
as I am rid of life. We shall sink together you and I, down, down into the
dark voids where once the vital organs were" (119). To be sure, this

grotesquery contains a comic element, as Winterson's protagonist assumes the posture of a mad scientist of 1950s B movies, determined to drain the corpse of life. Yet a vengeful tone permeates this passage, though again the narcissistic language of merger conceals the revenge motif. Blaming Louise for her suffering, the narrator would punish her by removing the brain that makes her who she is, for obsessive devotion precludes autonomous identity.

In the section of the novel titled "Skin" the narrator shifts her blaming tone to a meditative one. She acknowledges her "necrophiliac obsession" but posits it as a virtue:

> Odd that the piece of you I know best is already dead. The cells on the surface of your skin are thin and flat without blood vessels or nerve endings. Dead cells, thickest on the palms of your hands and the soles of your feet. Your sepulchral body, offered to me in the past tense, protects your soft center from the intrusions of the outside world. I am one such intrusion, stroking you with necrophiliac obsession, loving the shell laid out before me. (123)

Her necrophilia finally takes a grim turn, however, as she walks among the catacombs in an actual graveyard, witnesses a funeral, and meditates on what it means to "return to the hole, as we all will": "For the bereaved, the hole is a frightful place. A dizzy chasm of loss. This is the last time you'll be by the side of the one you love and you must leave her, must leave him, in a dark pit where the worms shall begin their duty" (177). This nihilistic meditation serves as a turning point for Winterson's narrator, jolting her into recognizing that Louise may actually die—that no amount of fetishizing or s/m fantasizing or necrophiliac imagining can save her. Ultimately the narrator comes to realize that if her beloved must "go down to a foreign land," she must accompany her (178).

Slowly, then, the narrator perceives her error in judgment in abandoning Louise: "Why didn't I hear you when you told me you wouldn't go back to Elgin? Why didn't I see your serious face?" (187) And with this realization comes a renewed attention to Louise's identity as a speaking subject, not as an extension of the narrator's desiring ego. In Jessica Benjamin's terms, the narrator begins to love Louise intersubjectively: "Understanding desire as the desire for recognition changes our view of the erotic experience. It enables us to describe a mode of representing desire unique to intersubjectivity which, in turn, offers a new perspective on women's desire" (Benjamin 24). The narrator's friend, Gail Right, helps her understand Louise's autonomy in new ways; when the narrator asks "Did I invent her?" Gail responds, "No, but you tried to. . . . She wasn't yours for the making" (189). This insight marks what Benjamin views as a healthy intersubjectivity between lovers, as the narrator sees Louise for who she is, not as the narrator's own erotic construction.

Winterson's postmodern and feminist sensibilities are evident in her narrator's scathing critique of the medical establishment, of masculine heroics, and of the traditional happy ending of romantic narratives. The author's angry scrutiny of the violence of cancer and the barbarism of contemporary treatments can be seen in the narrator's condemnation of the "brutal and toxic" regimen she imagines Louise undergoing: "Louise would normally be treated with steroids, massive doses to induce remission. . . . She would be constipated. She would be vomiting and nauseous" (102). The medical personnel who are qualified to treat Louise's cancer share the narrator's frustration; one surgeon acknowledges, for instance, "how little we know. It's the late twentieth century and what are the tools of our trade? Knives, saws, needles, and chemicals. I've no time for alternative medicine but I can see why it's attractive" (150). Medical professionals' inability to cure leukemia is obvious from the title of the book the narrator takes home from a hospital she visits in her quest for information about Louise's disease: "The Modern Management of Cancer" (150). Via this title Winterson ironizes the prevailing medical perspective that cancer cannot be effectively treated, merely "managed."

Winterson also challenges masculinist medical posturing, especially that of Elgin, whose hubris leads him to tell the heartsick narrator that only he can save Louise:

Will she die?
  That depends.
  On what?
  On you.
  You mean I can look after her?
  I mean I can. (102)

Although Elgin acknowledges that "cancer is an unpredictable condition . . . the body turning upon itself," he exaggerates his own power to arrest it. When the narrator replies "then you have nothing to offer Louise," Elgin responds "Except her life" (105). As she critiques Elgin's pseudo-heroics, however, the narrator fails to examine her own patriarchal objectification of Louise. Although Louise tells her that she does not trust Elgin's diagnosis and will seek a second opinion, the panicky narrator leaves her lover with merely a hyperbolic note: "You are safe in my home but not in my arms. If I stay it will be you who goes, in pain, without help. Our love was not meant to cost you your life" (105). Instructing Louise to "go with Elgin," the narrator mourns for months before she realizes that she has been "a hero without a cause" and determines to search for Louise and ask her forgiveness (160).

Although critics are divided as to whether Winterson "intends" to represent her narrator as finding her lover or as fantasizing about doing so, I view the conclusion of *Written on the Body* not as a validation of conventional fiction's romantic endings but as a postmodern challenge to them.[8] "I'd like to be able to tell her the truth," the narrator insists shortly before she finds (or imagines finding) Louise, but what truth would she tell? Truth is partial, multiple, contingent, as is Louise's identity. "I can't find her," the narrator mourns after weeks of searching. "It's as if Louise never existed, like a character in a book" (189)—precisely and ironically what she is. At this textual moment, however, Louise appears, though Winterson is playfully vague about how "real" this apparition is: "From the kitchen door Louise's face. Paler, thinner, but her hair still mane-wide and the colour of blood. I put out my hand and felt her fingers, she took my fingers and put them to her mouth. The scar under the lip burned me. Am I stark mad? She's warm" (190). In her closing scene Winterson invites readers to conjure not the "actual" Louise reunited with her lover but the explosive power of narrative, subject to endless readerly interpretations and interventions:

> This is where the story starts, in this threadbare room. The walls are exploding. We can take the world with us when we go and sling the sun in your arm. Hurry now, it's getting late. I don't know if this is a happy ending but here we are let loose in open fields. (190)

FEMINIST NARRATIVES OF *JOUISSANCE* & HOPE

The fluid revelations that occur in *Ava*, *Evening*, and *Written on the Body* open spaces for readers to reimagine our own erotic lives, up to and at the point of our deaths. These texts also help us examine how experimental cancer fiction might shape gendered subjectivities anew—as women envision our futures, face our mortality, renew our hope. For Maso, Minot, and Winterson, one way of renewing hope is to celebrate the sexually discursive potential of women's creative imaginaries. In Maso's words, "Language is a rose, and the future is still a rose, opening. . . . The future is women, for real, this time" (*Break* 172).

What Maso means by this generalization becomes clear through her frequent textual references, in *Ava* and in *Break Every Rule,* to French feminist theories of *jouissance*. This concept is integral to Maso's efforts to employ "healing language" in her fiction and to her claims regarding the erotic dimensions of her narratives: "I want to get closer to sexual abandon in language, erotic wonder, spiritual awe" (*Break* 135). Moreover, she insists on revaluing the feminine in her narratives: "Without apology, I have tried to create something of a feminine space. New kinds of intimacies. I do not believe in the myth of ungendered writing. . . . It is essential, I believe, for women to make their own shapes and sounds, to enact . . . their own desire, and not just mimic the dominant forms" (130). As a novelist committed to gendered writing, to inscribing the feminine anew, Maso envisions her prose as open-ended:

> I want there to be space enough for all sorts of accidents of beauty, revelations, kindnesses, small surprises. A space that encourages new identity constructions for the reader as well as the writer. New patterns of thought and ways of perceiving. New visions of the world, renewed hope. (132)

Ideally, she explains, this revelatory prose will facilitate moments of self-interrogation, healing, and hope for readers as well as for Maso herself.

Although Minot has written little about her feminist strategies, she has described her writing variously as minimalist, stream of consciousness, and experimental. In addition, her fiction, like Maso's, is known for its sexual explicitness, for "rais[ing] the erotic ante" (Welch). Minot has acknowledged this focus in interviews by noting that her two most critically acclaimed novels feature female protagonists lying in bed—Ann in *Evening,* who recalls her erotic life from a morphine haze, and Kay in *Rapture,* who performs a lengthy act of fellatio on a man with whom she shares a complex sexual history. Minot has also claimed that desire differs by gender: "I think desire is one of the main forces during a person's life—and it seems to me a woman has, in general, a different mode of desire from a man" (Welch). While she does not specify what form this difference takes, in life or in fiction, she refuses to identify heterosexual women's desire as centered on husbands and children. As reviewer Martha Stoddard Holmes points out, part of the "valuable iconoclasm" of *Evening* lies in Minot's luminous representation of a dying woman's erotic life, a life defined separately from her roles as wife and mother (2).

Winterson has acknowledged dismantling traditional narrative in an effort to create postmodern structures:

> What have I said in *Written on the Body?*
> That it is possible to have done with the bricks and mortar of conventional narrative, not as monkey-business or magic, but by building a structure that is bonded by language. (*Art* 189–90).

She has decried the realist form of nineteenth- and many twentieth-century novels, claiming instead that "What I am seeking to do in my work is to make a form that answers to twenty-first century needs" (191). Unlike Maso and Minot, however, Winterson refuses to identify desire in gendered terms, preferring instead to engage in gender-bending or to eschew definitive representations of gender altogether in her fiction. She has also criticized incisively the essentializing of literature by sexual orientation: "I am a writer who happens to love women. I am not a lesbian who happens to write. . . . The Queer world has colluded in the misreading of art as sexuality. Art is difference, but not necessarily sexual difference" (104).

The grouping of these particular writers reveals intriguing links regarding their literary-historical influences and narrative techniques. Maso and Minot reveal a similar elegiac quality in their narrative emphasis on what Maso refers to as "a farewell to the body" (*Ava* 208) and what Minot describes in the epigraph to *Evening* as a "body . . . flung back over a thousand beds in a thousand other rooms." They likewise share a life-affirming vision, realized through their representation of dying protagonists whose clarity of purpose jolts readers, juxtaposed as it is with images of raw suffering:

> The pain rose in her and she remembered. That's right, this is what she was now. . . .
> Life would not hold any more surprises for her, she thought, all that was left was for her to get through this last thing. But her eyes were as sharp as ever and she saw everything that went by. (Minot, *Evening* 15)

Hold me, I've got to say I'm a little afraid.
   Pain. Some pain.
   After everything there is to be said
   Our lives still counted for something. (Maso, *Ava* 122)

Both writers have commented on why they scrutinize the dying process. "For the sick person [dying] can be an opportunity to look at his or her life from a different perspective," Minot explains. "I was interested in what it must feel like to have a fatal illness" (interview). Maso emphasizes the stripping away that terminal cancer demands as well as the difficulty of understanding life's meaning. "No other book eludes me like *Ava*," she claims in *Break Every Rule*. "It reaches for things just outside the grasp of my mind, my body, the grasp of my imagination. It brings me up close to the limits of my own comprehension, pointing out, as Kafka says, the incompleteness of any life—not because it is too short, but because it is a human life" (64).

Minot and Winterson share a focus on sexual obsession. As we have seen, each of their protagonists probes her love relationship, erotic encounters, and lover's body in an all-consuming manner. These writers also explore the potentially trite and always controversial phenomenon of love at first sight. Minot's Ann fantasizes about what Harris Arden's arms "could do with a girl" before she knows his full name, while Winterson's narrator longs to hold Louise Rosenthal upon first meeting her, even with Louise's husband present. These motifs assume original, wry, and often radiant dimensions in each writer's hands as she recounts the ways in which her protagonist processes her obsessive desire for an elusive Other through the eroticized lens of memory. For Minot and Winterson, obsession serves as a point of intersection between fatal illness and fetishistic love.

These writers have in common certain artistic goals for their experimental fiction, goals they outline eloquently in interviews and essays. For instance, all three women acknowledge transgressing the boundaries of genre. Such transgression Maso calls "the desire of the novel to be a poem"—a shared perspective with Minot and Winterson that explains in part the luminosity and compression of their language. Minot sees her novelistic task in *Evening* as capturing the numinous in the way that poetry does (Welch). Winterson rejects both poem and novel as delimiting labels; she strives instead for generic hybridity, for "a form that is not 'a poem' as we usually understand the term, and not 'a novel' as the term is defined by its own genesis" (*Art* 191). Moreover, each writer claims that experimental writing contains an element of desire. When Maso discusses her fiction's wish to be a poem, she celebrates "the obvious erotics" of this fluidity (*Break* 23). Minot, too, connects writing and desire in describing her artistic aims: "How a person expresses desires, follows them, ignores them, reacts to their satisfaction or lack of fulfillment is a measure of a person's character, and therefore an inviting avenue of fiction if you want to explore human behavior and try to get at what it is like to be alive—two of my interests" (interview). Winterson likewise insists, in *Art Objects,* that "all my books are about boundaries and desire" and that "reading is sexy," especially for the new generation that comprises her primary audience (192). In addition, these three writers expect active readers. In Winterson's words, "All my work is experimental in that it plays with form, refuses a traditional narrative line, and includes the reader as a player. By that I mean the reader has to work with the book" (home page). Maso echoes this emphasis on reader involvement: "In *Ava* I have tried to write lines the reader (and the writer) might meditate on, recombine, rewrite as he or she pleases" (*Break* 67–68). Minot, in turn, describes the relationship between writer and reader as "an intimacy between strangers" (interview).

By writing the eroticized bodies of women with cancer, Winterson, Maso, and Minot ultimately construct new cultural narratives about the effects of memory, desire, and death on women's subjectivity. They do this, in Winterson's words, by interweaving and interrogating "the metaphors of desire and disease":

> Disease, especially a disease like cancer or AIDS, breaks down the boundaries of the immune system and forces a new self on us that we often don't recognise. Our territory is eaten away. We are parceled out into healthy areas and metastasised areas. . . .
>   Against this, I wanted to look . . . at love's ability to shatter and heal simultaneously. (home page)

Both cancer and patriarchy have colonized women's bodies; literary representations of dying women's desire, when redefined in feminist terms, can undermine such colonization. By redrawing the boundaries of what constitutes erotic and deathbed agency, these writers create feminist fiction that can help us to confront—and possibly to heal—the foreign bodies within ourselves.

6. "ENTERING CANCERLAND"

Self-Representation, Commonality, &
Culpability in Women's
Autobiographical Narratives

What is the self that it can be represented in writing? Who am I and how did I become who I am? What does skin have to do with autobiography? What is the relationship between self and others? What sort of muse, guide, or judge is memory?

—Leigh Gilmore, *The Limits of Autobiography*

[A] modification of the traditional masculine lifestory genre, with its emphasis on the accounting of/for an individual and frequently idealized life story, objectively constructed, yields a double stranding in these narratives. There is both the discrete and individualized experience of breast cancer, and the sense of it as a common and shared story.

—Laura K. Potts, "Publishing the Personal:
Autobiographical Narratives of Breast Cancer and the Self"

AUTOBIOGRAPHERS IN THE Western male-dominated tradition, from St. Augustine to Jean-Jacques Rousseau to Henry Adams, have long presented the self as both universal and representative, the mirror of its era; they have assumed an inviolable authority from which to speak. Many women writers, in contrast, have inscribed marginalized, mediated, or relational selves rather than highly individualistic or culturally representative ones.[1] To be sure, certain aspects of the autobiographical project transcend gender. The questions that Leigh Gilmore raises in the epigraph to this chapter from *The Limits of Autobiography,* for example, reflect "persistent and constitutive issues in autobiography" for writers of both sexes—questions of subjectivity, identity, embodiment ("skin"), community, and memory.[2] Yet as Gilmore notes, "women, people of color, gay men and lesbians, the disabled, and survivors of violence have contributed to the expansion of self-representation by illuminating suppressed histories and creating new emphases" in their autobiographies

(16). When women's life writings illuminate a submerged history of sexual oppression, they emphasize both the difficult forging of a self-representational *I* and the importance of connection to a politicized group of Others.

Contemporary autopathography, or life writing about illness, sheds further light on this merger of subjectivity and commonality.[3] Since medicalization thrusts formerly healthy individuals out of the comfortable illusion of bodily autonomy into a disruptive maze of hospitals and invasive procedures, narratives that recount this experience frequently represent a self in crisis, reliant on a network of supportive caregivers and bound to fellow patients likewise struggling for agency. Moreover, the arbitrariness of life-threatening disease may confound the nascent autopathographer: if, as Patricia Duncker claims, autobiography is "often a search for coherence and explanation," then autopathography illustrates this quest with special intensity (56). Thomas Couser has rightly asserted that although serious illness "threatens to obliterate the self," autopathography serves ultimately as "a sign of cultural health— an acknowledgment and an exploration of our condition as *embodied* selves" ("Autopathography" 71). Women's illness narratives, in particular, reject the "doubly marginalized" status that patriarchal culture ascribes and "demonstrate that 'ill' women may be well-equipped to reconceptualize the relation between psyche and soma, to write the life of the body as well as the life of the mind" (73).

The illness narratives published most often today by women in the United States and the United Kingdom chronicle the experience of cancer—primarily breast cancer, but also uterine, ovarian, colon, and bladder cancers. As Potts explains in "Publishing the Personal," these narratives frequently approach self-representation via a "double stranding" by foregrounding both the writer's subjectivity and her sense of cancer as a "common and shared story" (102). Certainly autobiographical representations of both self and community are discursively constructed; as Sidonie Smith notes in *The Poetics of Women's Autobiography*, they comprise "a cultural and linguistic 'fiction' constituted through historical ideologies of selfhood and the processes of our storytelling" (45). Yet when the story under construction involves breast cancer—a shared epidemic, a communal experience—its "fictiveness" is often dismantled by an urgency that reveals the writer's compulsion to generate her own "truth" and intensifies the reader's connection to the narrator and the recounted trauma.

Women's cancer autobiographies first appeared during the mid-1970s, on the heels of the second wave of the women's movement.[4] Rose Kushner's *Breast Cancer: A Personal History and an Investigative Report* (1975) was among the earliest narratives to chronicle the experience of radical mastectomy; Kushner also criticized the common practice of "one-step" surgery that allowed doctors to amputate women's cancerous breasts during the process of biopsy. A year later journalist Betty Rollin's account of her modified radical mastectomy, *First, You Cry*, became a best-seller and spawned a made-for-TV movie starring Mary Tyler Moore. In 1980 Audre Lorde brought an African American and a lesbian critique to the experience of breast cancer in *The Cancer Journals* by challenging the assumption that the typical postmastectomy woman was white, straight, and eager for reconstructive surgery. Yet Lorde recognized that breast cancer patients of all races and sexualities shared "a commonality of isolation and painful reassessment" that offered them a potentially strong bond (10). Women's cancer narratives reached their zenith in the 1990s, as women's health activists in the United States and the United Kingdom lobbied for government-funded research and increasing numbers of women learned of their one-in-eight chance of developing breast cancer. These written accounts found ready publishers and audiences due in part to the burgeoning of women's autobiography as a genre and the trend toward a culture of confession, as exhibited by the popularity of self-help books, the Oprah Winfrey and Larry King Live talk shows, and reality television. As cancer gained media attention and more women were diagnosed with this disease, increasing numbers were drawn to write or read first-person testimonies.

Although great diversity exists, women's cancer autobiographies can be conceptualized according to three general categories. *Personal narratives* focus on the individual writer/patient's diagnosis, treatment, and recovery or, more rarely, her decline. Friends and family provide crucial support but rarely develop as central figures; although these writers often value their participation in cancer support groups, involvement in identity-based movements does not figure prominently in their narratives. In addition, while medical personnel often evoke criticism, the health care system itself does not. *Multicultural narratives*, in contrast, emphasize identity politics and community as integral to the individual cancer patient's experience. These narratives establish links to the women's cancer movement and question the judgment of both practitioners and policies that rob women of agency during the process of medicalization. Finally, *environmental narratives* scrutinize connections between rising incidences of cancer in the industrialized world and degradation of the environment; they emphasize the need to eliminate the causes of cancer as well as find cures. The writer's own cancer saga is typically subordinated to an analysis of how hazardous chemicals might contribute to the contemporary cancer epidemic.

These narrative categories correspond to the paradigm that sociologist Maren Klawiter has outlined in her study of San Francisco's three most prominent breast cancer fund-raising events during the 1990s. The first "culture of action" that Klawiter describes, Race for the Cure, was established in 1982 by the Susan G. Komen Breast Cancer Foundation. As one of the best-known and best-funded sources of U.S. cancer activism, the Komen Foundation draws hundreds of thousands of women and men annually to its Web site, marches, and other events in many cities.[5] As Klawiter points out, this organization "emphasizes individual agency, honour, and survival. It connects breast cancer to the display of normative femininity, mobilizes hope and faith in science and medicine, and promotes biomedical research and early detection" (65). Like Race for the Cure literature, women's personal narratives about cancer focus on tales of often remarkable survival in prose that ranges from hopeful to triumphant; for the minority of narrators for whom death is imminent, the tone varies from spirited to elegiac. Popular 1970s and 1980s autobiographies of this type include Rollin's *First, You Cry* and Gilda Radner's *It's Always Something*. Noteworthy examples from the 1990s and early twenty-first century are Christina Middlebrook's *Seeing the Crab*, Kim Davies's *Me, Amazon Woman*, Katherine Russell Rich's *The Red Devil*, Andrea Gabbard's *No Mountain Too High*, Suzanne Strempek Shea's *Songs from a Lead-Lined Room*, Jerri Nielsen's *Ice Bound*, Barbara Pate Glacel's *Hitting the Wall*, and Joni Rodgers's *Bald in the Land of Big Hair* from the United States; Jenny Cole's *Journey (with a Cancer)*, Joyce Wadler's *My Breast*, Elisa Segrave's *The Diary of a Breast*, Marion Woodman's *Bone*, and Ruth Picardie's *Before I Say Goodbye* from Great Britain; and anthologies such as *Speak the Language of Healing* (edited by Susan Kuner et al.), *Uplift* (edited by Barbara

Delinsky), and *Celebrating Life: African American Women Speak Out about Breast Cancer* (edited by Sylvia Dunnivant).

Proponents of the second "culture of action" that Klawiter analyzes, Women and Cancer Walk, place more confidence in cancer activism than in the medical and scientific establishment.[6] In Klawiter's terms, this organization "connects breast cancer to other women's cancers, challenges the emphasis on survival and the hegemonic display of heteronormative femininities, emphasizes the effects of institutionalized inequalities, mobilizes anger against the institutions of biomedicine, and promotes social services and treatment activism" (65). Like Women and Cancer Walk, multicultural cancer autobiographies are overtly feminist; they typically question the nomenclature of "survivor," preferring the more activist identity of "living with cancer" or "not dead yet." In addition, they critique systemic problems that complicate cancer patients' access to and experience of treatment. Prominent examples of multicultural autobiographies from the 1970s and 1980s are Kushner's *Breast Cancer*, Deena Metzger's "Tree," and Lorde's *The Cancer Journals*. Examples from the 1990s include Sandra Butler and Barbara Rosenblum's *Cancer in Two Voices*, Eve Kosofsky Sedgwick's "White Glasses" (from *Tendencies*), Joan Nestle's "My Cancer Travels" (from *A Fragile Union*), Marilyn French's *A Season in Hell*, and Jane Lazarre's *Wet Earth and Dreams* from the United States; Kathy Acker's *The Gift of Disease*, Jo Spence's *Cultural Sniping*, and Felly Nkweto Simmonds's "A Remembering" (from *Cancer: Through the Eyes of Ten Women*) in Great Britain; and the anthologies *Living on the Margins* (edited by Hilda Raz) and *Coming Out of Cancer* (edited by Victoria A. Brownworth).

The final "culture of action" that Klawiter identifies, Toxic Tours of the Cancer Industry, conducts a rhetorical form of guerrilla warfare against chemical, pharmaceutical, nuclear, and other corporate polluters, especially those that sponsor events for cancer activists in one breath and spew carcinogens into the environment in another.[7] In Klawiter's words, Toxic Tours "represents breast cancer as both the product and the source of profits of a global cancer industry, mobilizes outrage against corporate malfeasance and environmental racism, and replaces the emphasis on biomedical research and early detection with demands for corporate regulations and cancer prevention" (65). Women's environmental cancer narratives offer similar scrutiny of possible ties between environmental toxicity and rising incidences of cancer; they probe cor-

porate culpability, argue for governmental accountability, and emphasize the need for more research on cancer and the environment. The prototype for the environmental narrative is Rachel Carson's *Silent Spring*
(1962); examples from the past fifteen years include Sandra Steingraber's
Living Downstream, Terry Tempest Williams's *Refuge*, and Zillah
Eisenstein's *Manmade Breast Cancers* in the United States and Jackie
Stacey's *Teratologies* in the United Kingdom.[8]

As Sidonie Smith points out, it is important to consider "how the
woman autobiographer establishes the discursive authority to interpret
herself publicly in a patriarchal culture and androcentric genre that have
written stories of woman for her" ("Introduction" 45). In the analyses
that follow I first explore the themes and discursive strategies of two representative personal narratives of cancer, Rich's *The Red Devil* and
Picardie's *Before I Say Goodbye*, and two multicultural narratives that
foreground issues of sexual orientation, Butler and Rosenblum's *Cancer
in Two Voices* and Sedgwick's "White Glasses." Because environmental
cancer narratives have received less scrutiny from feminist scholars than
have other types, I examine three of these narratives, beginning with
Silent Spring; I read this formative text alongside Carson's letters
describing her own experience of breast cancer.[9] Finally, I analyze how
an ecological investigation of cancer intersects with self-representation
in two narratives from the 1990s, Steingraber's *Living Downstream* and
Williams's *Refuge*. My focal questions will be these: By what means do
women establish the discursive authority to record and interpret their
experience of cancer? What themes dominate their narratives? How do
strategies of self-representation vary in the different types of narratives?
How do tensions between contrasting conceptualizations of the autobiographical self as individual and as communal play out in these texts?
How might memory function as a tool for probing the writers' identities
as women, cancer patients, and (at times) activists? What kinds of formal
experimentation and hybridity occur in these cancer narratives? With
what feminist, political, and/or human rights issues do these narratives
grapple, and how effectively? I argue that while all three types of cancer
autobiographies raise readers' awareness about the personal and communal contours of this disease, multicultural and environmental narratives undertake more radical activist agendas. Multicultural writers do so
by aligning their narratives and themselves with global feminisms
and/or gay rights as well as the women's health movement, while envi-

ronmental writers establish links to ecofeminism and other global movements to sustain our planet and those who inhabit it.

PERSONAL CANCER NARRATIVES

Cancer autobiographies that "publish the personal," to borrow Potts's
phrase, typically detail the trauma of diagnosis and subsequent medical
procedures, the fear or experience of recurrence, the comfort given by
loved ones, and either the miracle of recovery or the need to face death
courageously (Potts 98). These narratives foreground women's medicalized bodies in the context of heterosexual relationships and present
themes associated with hegemonic femininity: appearance, body image,
and consumer culture. Some works also examine the challenge to professional identity that a cancer diagnosis poses. Although these narratives
may represent medical personnel as callous or inept, the doctors, nurses,
and technicians who provide chemotherapy, radiation, and/or bone
marrow transplants evoke either praise or brief complaint; the health
care system per se receives no sustained critique. Prominent strategies of
self-representation include gallows humor, ironic self-deprecation, and
the narrative forging of a defiant or a stoic *I* that values community support but is not overtly activist.

Feminist theorists vary in their assessment of the autobiographical
project and rhetorical strategies of personal narratives. Potts, for example, claims that such autobiographies present women's strength in the
face of adversity and thus function "in opposition to the 'master narratives' of what it is to be a woman and to have breast cancer" (124).
Stacey, in contrast, argues that as idealized tales of triumph over tragedy,
personal narratives by cancer survivors "generate fantasies of heroic
recoveries and miracle cures" that do not oppose master narratives but
rather reverse them, as protagonists "are transformed from *feminised victim* to *masculinised hero*" (10–11). Stacey's critique has merit; as we shall
see, certain narratives develop a rhetoric of triumph that transports the
narrator from dazed victim to glib victor in a manner that strains credibility. As Potts points out, however, by emphasizing ill women's agency,
personal narratives effectively challenge the ubiquitous stereotype of the
passive female cancer patient.

Katherine Russell Rich's *The Red Devil* illustrates both the triumphalist rhetoric that Stacey questions—the book's subtitle is "A Memoir about Beating the Odds"—and the representation of female agency that Potts lauds. A thirty-two-year-old New York magazine editor at the time of her initial diagnosis, Rich chronicles her struggle with metasta-sized breast cancer in a narrative whose immediacy belies its retrospec-tive vantage point. Over a ten-year period Rich survived every cancer treatment then available; she also suffered persistent lymphodema, a pul-monary embolism, collapsed vertebrae, and a nearly severed spinal cord before ultimately recovering the physical stability that allowed her to approach cancer as a chronic disease. Although her experiences are har-rowing, Rich's spirited account of her struggle to cope after "entering Cancerland" makes the narrative inspiring (15).

Central to this autobiography is a litany of medical procedures, from lumpectomy to chemotherapy to radiation to bone marrow transplant. The title itself reinforces the centrality of medical nightmares to Rich's saga by demonizing Adriamycin, the corrosive "champagne" of chemo that she both dreaded ingesting and relied upon to cause remission. Memory provides for Rich not a gentling reprise from cancer's traumas but rather a deeply embodied reliving of them:

> Even now, from a distance of ten years, my memories of the days con-nected to chemo can bring on actual nausea, a horrible druggy stomach burn, insistent and severe as if the Adriamycin has just gone in three hours ago. All my memories of the first time are like that—vitrine, not celluloid, hard and jagged, shards. Whenever I've tried to return to them, to reach down into the container and bring them up, nausea surges through me, nar-rowing my attention, distracting it from thought into sensation. (54)

This passage addresses a problem that many cancer memoirists face: the tension between the desire to recount their saga and the mind/body's insistence upon a protective amnesia. For Rich, memory's reluctant evo-cation of cancer's lived experience reveals the disease's power; indeed, cancer in this text becomes a shadow protagonist, a deceitful adversary that Rich characterizes variously as a killer, a crippler, a panther, a stalker, a parasite, a pig, and a bully: "Cancer still has the power to make me retch. Cancer has a way of swelling on its own threat, for cancer likes to be a bully" (54, 77, 81, 113, 180).

Rich's response to this malevolent force is to become a "kick-ass can-cer patient" like her acquaintance, Lisa, with whom she appeared on a talk show featuring women with breast cancer. As Rich explains, Lisa refuses the approach espoused by cancer guru Dr. Bernie Siegel, whose books urge women to become "ECaPs," Exceptional Cancer Patients who refuse to ask, "Why me, Lord?" but instead proclaim, "Try me, Lord" (52).[10] Rich satirizes such women as "obnoxious can-do paragons" and decides instead to emulate Lisa's "KCaP" attitude: "She didn't say, 'Try me.' She said, "Oh yeah? Try this.' Like a lot of kick-ass patients, she was younger, weaned on feminism, rock and roll, and self-assertion training. She was a tough babe, who'd gotten tougher still since becoming sick" (105). As this passage demonstrates, Rich defines feminist resistance through the "masculinist" trope of toughness. Reflecting back on her ordeal, she recognizes why she emulated Lisa's strategy: cancer bullied her so often that she eventually determined to confront it head-on. "The disease has pummeled me one time too many," she concludes. "It's forced me down, smashed my head, it's nearly killed me. Then what's a little nausea? I think. By the end of my treatment, nausea was the least of it. So let the replay slash and burn, I'm not afraid any more to turn and stare" (54).

Given her kick-ass attitude and her recurring problems with physicians and hospitals, Rich offers surprisingly few complaints against individual practitioners and no in-depth critique of the medical system. This compliant stance is characteristic, however, of personal narratives as a category. Although the behavior of many of her health care providers is shocking, Rich either downplays their seriousness or extricates herself without formal objection. Early in her narrative, for example, she describes a phone call in which her internist not only trivializes her concern about a persistent breast lump but also assures her that "I'll feel your breasts anytime you want me to"; in recounting this sexual objectification, she expresses anger that her doctor "was hustling me off the phone with a joke" but decides "to drop the matter for a while" (17). When an oncology nurse speculates, years later, that "the disease might have spread because [this internist] wouldn't see you" and asks Rich, "Did you ever think of that?" she admits to readers, "I hadn't, not till she said it" (17). Here Rich both acknowledges and reaffirms her self-imposed amnesia as a coping strategy: "And now I try, as much as I can, not to" (17–18). Many recurrences later, when an oncologist fails to return her phone calls, neglects to diagnose a fractured rib, breaks confidentiality by discussing her case with another patient, and refuses to continue as Rich's doctor when confronted with these infractions, Rich responds initially with self-blame:

> "Wait," I said. I was sick, an advanced case, she'd said so. I had to be with a doctor. She couldn't. "The scan . . . I didn't mean . . . Can't we fix this?"
>
> I'm sorry," she said. "I think it's better this way." And when I found no compassion in her voice, just a wall, I was abject with despondence. I was so bad—so hopeless—even a woman paid to care didn't want me. (157)

To be sure, the narrator's abjection shifts to anger when friends convince her that the oncologist withdrew due to fear that Rich would file a malpractice lawsuit, but her anger wanes when she learns that this physician is leaving medicine so she can be at home with her children. Such "bad doctor" accounts portray realistically the difficulties that even assertive patients can experience during medicalization but offer readers little sense that such problems might be systemic or that one might hold incompetent physicians accountable.

The importance of heterosexuality to this narrative can be seen in the framing device that governs its structure: the book begins by recounting a painful divorce, chronicles midstream a joyful but brief affair, and concludes with a crush on a research fellow who visits the narrator's bedside. For Rich as for many straight women, the experience of breast cancer evokes a fear of male rejection and abandonment. Early in her memoir Rich recounts how just prior to her cancer diagnosis she mourns her decision to separate from her husband due to incompatibility, even as she knows this decision is right. Yet once her cancer appears, she paradoxically worries that marital stress has caused it and reasons that she should try to reestablish a sexual relationship with her ex-spouse. Writing retrospectively, she acknowledges the inappropriateness of this attempt; indeed, her account of heterosexual insecurity is remarkably forthright (12–15, 75–77). Later in the narrative she probes her tendency to become passive in unhealthy relationships with men that she constructs as happy: "Happiness is my protection, my talisman. If I'm happy I can't die. I can't be this sick—I'm too alive" (176).

In recounting both her sexual relationships and her professional life, Rich frequently calls attention to such key markers of conventional femininity as a sexy appearance, glamorous dress, and mandatory slenderness. Indeed, she acknowledges striving to meet such expectations before determining to critique them: "In Europe Ben hadn't thought twice about telling me to change my clothes before we went out. 'I think you should find something a little more attractive to wear,' he'd suggested before a dinner with friends in Paris, and without hesitation, I did. Now, when he tried this, I thought he was out of line" (190). Once she recognizes as sexist and controlling such directives as "I'm not saying those jeans make your ass look fat, but I think you should put something else on," Rich determines to maintain both her jeans and her agency. Elsewhere in the narrative she demonstrates that the professional risks inherent in having cancer are linked to the requirements of femininity. The New York magazine for which Rich works endorses these requirements by expecting her to deny the painful effects of her cancer treatment, continue to dress elegantly and act energetic at work, and conceal her bald head under stylish hats and scarves. Using the narrative strategy of ironic self-deprecation, Rich both recounts and reevaluates her struggle to comply.

The rhetoric of triumph that pervades *The Red Devil* can ultimately be viewed as either empowering or unconvincing, depending on the reader's point of view. This rhetoric is most empowering when Rich combines it with what she characterizes as cancer humor:

> Cancer humor is like the Zen laugh; it's a way of gathering back forces, a means of breathing in absurdity, darkness, and pain and blowing them out in one great, joyous guffaw. It is, finally, a form of power, laced with machismo. *Fuck you, death. I laugh at you.* (71)

Yet her acknowledgment of machismo as a psychological stance and, implicitly, a textual strategy gives credence to Stacey's claim that autobiographies in which ill women become conquering heroes reverse rather than challenge "master narratives" (11). Rich's triumphalist tone seems least convincing in the narrative's brief epilogue, in which she recounts another recurrence of her bone cancer, three years after her last, but assures readers that this is not a problem. Indeed, she insists that not only do oncologists increasingly view metastasized cancer as a chronic disease, many doctors now consider it curable: "Not that they could get rid of it for good. Yet. But they could often rout it for extended periods, and when it came back, rout it again. Or they could keep it in stasis, impotent and checked" (240). Rich inadvertently colludes in this passage with those physicians who redefine the word *cure* so as to make it meaningless, yet her longing to conceive of metastasized cancer as curable is poignant—a longing to which readers can relate. That Rich's beloved Dr. Antonelli indulges this fantasy is clear: "You have triumphed in every battle in the past. I have no doubt whatsoever that you will triumph again." By concluding her narrative with Antonelli's reassurances, presented with no apparent irony, Rich endorses the medical doublespeak that elsewhere in her narrative she criticizes:

> "The fact that you keep coming back stable is a really encouraging sign," she said.
> "Really," she said. "It's all good news." (240)

Ruth Picardie's *Before I Say Goodbye* employs no comparable rhetoric of triumph, since its primary narrator does not survive her metastasized breast cancer. Yet an exuberant attitude toward life and a jolting humor toward death pervade this narrative. A freelance British journalist, thirty-three years old at the time of her death and the married mother of infant twins, Picardie chronicled her cancer experience in weekly columns for *Observer Life* magazine during her final months of life. These columns drew hundreds of reader responses and were eventually incorporated by her sister, Justine Picardie, and Ruth's husband, Matt Seaton, into a narrative pastiche that also includes readers' letters, Ruth's e-mails to and from friends, letters to her children, and her husband's reflections. In her columns Ruth Picardie often exploits what trauma theorist Kevin Newmark has termed the "shock of laughter" (242) that can momentarily disrupt the terror of the abyss:

> It's official, then. After nine months of talking bravely about 50:50 survival rates . . . of bone disease being a really "good" form of secondary breast cancer . . . of a new, "natural" chemotherapy regime which is showing really promising results . . . I now have a brain tumour. Oh, and by the way, the cancer is advancing rapidly into my liver and lungs, so there's no point in continuing with treatment. So no more false dawns, no more miracle cures, no more *Alien*-style eruptions of disease. I now have a "full house" of secondary breast cancer sites—or "mets," as we professionals like to say. The bottom line is, I'm dying. (38)

Picardie's casual tone ("oh, and by the way"), her reference to the classic horror movie *Alien,* her satiric appropriation of medical jargon ("'mets,' as we professionals like to say") evoke horrified laughter in readers, thereby engaging their empathy. Although many readers might initially resist identification with a narrator who acknowledges that she is dying of cancer, Picardie's ironic persona breaks down such defenses even as it provides a useful mask through which to confront incipient trauma.

While these published articles recount few details of Picardie's experience of medicalization, e-mails to close friends describe the nature of her metastases, her responses to chemotherapy, and her psychological method of confronting stage 4 cancer. To Carrie, she explains that her tumors are hormone receptive, which is atypical in premenopausal women, and expresses a fleeting hope that Tamoxifen might therefore help her; she also reveals both the disorientation of sudden hair loss ("I was a bit freaked out at first—it's really alarming running your hand through your hair and handfuls coming out") and her own resilience ("Anyway, I am now used to hoovering the bed every morning and it's easier to cope with very short hair. Meanwhile, I'm asking everyone I know to buy me a hat") (3). To Jamie, Picardie admits her struggle with nausea and justifies her decision to "chuck in the chemo after 4 cycles (supposed to have 6) because it's not having much (if any) effect and I've been reacting really badly to it eg puked during last session, despite intravenous anti-emetics" (6). After her oncologist diagnoses bone metastasis, Picardie describes her reaction in an e-mail to Carrie with characteristic irony: "Felt very neutral when I made Dr. Death phone me up with results. He had his patronizing, 'Now, Ruth' voice on. Though have had a few weeps since, since I am now accepting the inevitability of death" (20). And in a later e-mail to Carrie, Picardie shares her strategy for staving off terror:

> I feel I can cope best by accepting that I have an 18 per cent chance of lasting five years ie despite all the euphemistic crap about stage four, advanced breast cancer, management, palliative care, that I am going to die sooner rather than later—could be this year, could be five years, might even be 10. That way, the fear and dread of new symptoms disappears. (20–21)

In the letter Picardie slices through the optimistic rhetoric that managers of "Cancerland" produce and embraces her own discursive and emotional reality. Indeed, in all of these letters vulnerability and strength are equally in evidence, along with a gallows humor that deflects sympathy and affirms agency.

Elsewhere in *Before I Say Goodbye* Picardie reveals her wry perspective on how cancer has affected her sexuality, femininity, and appearance. These themes converge in an e-mail that offers her friend, India, a lively account of plans for a weekend retreat with her husband:

> I did an insane thing yesterday. Matt and I are going away for our FIRST NIGHT WITHOUT THE KIDS in a couple of weeks' time—Gravetye Manor in West Sussex, where we spent our wedding night. I'm writing about it for the Observer, so it's a freebie. So instead I just blew 425 pounds on underwear (including stomach hiding silk slip) from Agent Provocateur. Stupid, or what? But I look like such a slob most of the time, and Matt will be so excited and, what the fuck, I'm dying. You can wear it after I've copped it. (24)

Although the portrait of a dying woman buying expensive lingerie for a final romantic getaway could evoke pity in readers, Picardie's profanity and self-deprecation make the passage humorous. In addition, her emphasis on concealing her weight gain and attracting her husband via seductive clothing promotes identification in some heterosexual readers based on shared definitions of femininity. Picardie's proposal of fancy undergarments as a legacy from one female friend to another reveals a sly irreverence to which India replies with her own brand of body humor: "I would love to have your underwear after you've copped it, but I fear you seriously underestimate my stupendous girth. Perhaps I could wear your knickers as remembrance bracelets around my outsize wrists" (24). For many readers this "don't worry, I'm fatter than you" rhetoric between buddies resonates, as does the sexual innuendo implicit in the arch metonymy of "FIRST NIGHT WITHOUT THE KIDS."

Although she rarely alludes to sexuality in her *Observer* columns, Picardie gives humorous attention there to issues of body image as it relates to cancer. "You're 32, a stone-and-a-half overweight, depressed by the stains on the sofa and have never come to terms with having piggy eyes, but, still, life is pretty great," begins her first column on June 22, 1997—until, that is, the pleasure of "a husband who can make squid ink pasta and has all his own hair" and delight that "your one-year-old twins are sleeping through the night" collapse before a diagnosis of stage 3 breast cancer with extensive lymph node involvement (44). An obsession with weight dominates Picardie's published articles, vying at times with cancer for center stage: to readers of that initial column she reports that the cropped hair she sports after chemo would look "fabulously Jean Seberg if you weighed less than 10 stone"; to readers of her July 27, 1997, article she declares that "everybody thinks cancer makes you thin. In fact, I'm getting fatter and fatter. I know this because people keep coming up to me and saying, 'You look so well.'" . . . what they really mean is, 'You look so fat'" (45, 52). Although this emphasis on size might well deserve a feminist critique, Picardie's displacement of narrative emphasis from the jarring reality of cancer to the familiar "feminine" trope of obesity invites reader identification.

Picardie's representation of motherhood in *Before I Say Goodbye* is poignant, even when she uses humor as a shield. In one *Observer* column she reveals the pain she feels at having to leave her infants, then undercuts her suffering through a wry cultural and personal critique:

> I won't be there to clap when my beloved babies learn to write their names; I won't see them learn to swim, or go to school, or play the piano; I won't be able to read them *Pippi Longstocking*, or kiss their innocent knees when they fall off their bikes. (All right, so I won't have to clean pooh out of the bath, or watch *Pingu* for the 207th time, or hose spinach sauce off the floor.) Then there's the really important stuff: I won't be able to watch the fourth series of *ER* (will Ross and Hathaway live happily ever after?); I'll never know if the pregnancy stretch marks on my legs would have disappeared without surgery; I haven't got time to grow my patchy, chemotherapy crop into a halo of life-before-cancer curls. (69)

Picardie avoids sentimentality here by foregrounding the mundanity of motherhood as well as its delights. She also draws upon popular culture and body fetishizing to demonstrate that her own life is as trivial as anyone else's—and as full. When she fully acknowledges her maternal grief, however, the narrative becomes anguished. Indeed, she admits feeling overwhelmed by "the agonizing task of compiling 'memory boxes' for Lola and Joe" and concludes, in characteristic understatement, that "whichever part of my failing anatomy collapses first, I'm pretty upset" (69–70). While cancer survivors can often eject despair from their texts, Picardie has little recourse but to wrestle with it: "What hurts most is losing the future" (69). Ultimately Picardie's blend of joie de vivre and anguish intensifies the tragedy of her death and the power of her writing. As Stacey points out in *Teratologies*, "death confers authority upon the narrative and the narrator" (243), and Picardie's resolute approach to death facilitates this authorization.

Although Picardie's narrative differs from Rich's in temporal perspective and mode of authority, largely because of the writers' different

FRACTURED BORDERS

status regarding survival, both autobiographies employ certain strategies of self-representation characteristic of personal narratives: an ironic
mode of public disclosure, an emphasis on the self in crisis rather than a
communal or politicized self, and a heteronormative foregrounding of
male-female relationships and conventional tropes of femininity.[11]
Rich's retrospective narrative problematizes the role of memory for the
cancer survivor and the selection of detail for the autobiographer, since
she frequently both acknowledges and enacts moments of denial and
selective amnesia. Picardie's posthumous narrative serves as both autobiography and commemoration; it also reveals the complexities of narrative pastiche by foregrounding the composite strategies of textual construction that editors must employ to tell the story of a nonsurvivor.

MULTICULTURAL CANCER NARRATIVES

Autobiographies that chronicle cancer from a multicultural perspective
typically emphasize women's community and lesbian, queer, or interra-
cial households rather than conventional heterosexual or single-race
family structures. These texts offer feminist, gay, and/or left-leaning
readers alternatives to the worries about appearance, weight, or baldness
that plague many cancer patients. In addition, such narratives link AIDS
and cancer activism, probe the limitations of the medical system and
available treatment options, place more trust in *Our Bodies, Ourselves*
than in American Cancer Society literature, and address overtly issues of
race/ethnicity, class, gender, and/or sexual orientation. In terms of discursive strategies, multicultural narratives analyze or theorize cancer's
contested meanings and probe the effects of these meanings on the
writer's experience of medicalization and modes of self-representation.

Sandra Butler and Barbara Rosenblum composed *Cancer in Two
Voices* between 1985 and 1988, when Rosenblum was living with and
dying of cancer. As Butler explains, "Barbara and I started to write
within days after her diagnosis of advanced breast cancer—understanding that 'attention must be paid' to this, as yet, unrecorded experience"
(ii). The only published breast cancer narrative written collaboratively
by a lesbian couple, this hybrid text features four interwoven types of
writing: jointly composed essays about the women's relationship and
worldviews, individual essays about their strategies for coping with the

shock of diagnosis, letters sent to each other and to members of their les-
bian-feminist community, and journal entries that detail the women's
emotional landscape from the time of Rosenblum's biopsy until her
death. The narrative's multicultural dimensions lie not only in its lesbian
feminism, however, but also in its emphasis on systemic problems in the
U.S. health care industry, the class inequalities that contribute to these
problems, and the meaning of Jewish identity in the writers' lives.

A primary focus of this narrative is the sexual, emotional, and creative
bond that exists between Butler and Rosenblum as life partners facing the
trauma of metastasized cancer. As Butler notes in her preface, the women
met in 1979 and connected as Jews, urban dwellers, intellectuals, former
heterosexuals, and lesbians open to a new relationship. They found differences as well: Rosenblum was "contemplative, cerebral," Butler
"extravagant, public"; Rosenblum struggled with anxiety, Butler with
depression. But a month of intimate conversation made them "visible to
each other" (iii). When cancer strikes, their relationship is tested: "We
cannot use words to build bridges between us as we have done in the
past. We are each trapped in our own terror and cannot find our way
towards each other" (25). Ultimately, however, they find sustenance in
one another: "It is so replenishing when we play and dance. Eat new
foods. When I bathe and oil her dry and flaking skin. Lie with her in bed
and watch videotapes. To love in all the ways we love together" (42). As
they travel to Europe together, plan a commitment ceremony, and find
"new ways of being intimate" when Barbara's physical deterioration
makes lovemaking difficult, Butler and Rosenberg remind readers that
joy does not end with a cancer diagnosis. A critical source of affirmation
is the book they jointly compose: "Together we have developed a new
form that can accommodate our individual and unique voices into a dialogue. We write about things that are important to us. We make love at
the typewriter, not in the bedroom" (159).

These women do not confront cancer in a vacuum; the narrative
strongly emphasizes the power of feminist community. When Rosenblum receives her diagnosis, she invites to her home "twenty women
who would be involved in my healing and caretaking," a "conscious and
deliberate choice to mobilize a battalion of friends to help and assist me
in every phase of fighting my disease." Refusing to "stand alone on a
ledge so steep and so scary," she instead creates her own lifeline (12).
The narrative includes letters she composes to these friends at various

stages of her medicalization, instructing caregivers on the fluids she will need during chemo, describing her phobias during the anxious months between treatments, finally telling loved ones good-bye: "It was a wonderful life and each of you who reads this is part of the fabric that made it wonderful, whole, and meaningful. I shall miss you" (200). Butler relies on this community as well, as seen in her journal entry acknowledging the women's support at an anniversary party she and Barbara hosted: "The gathered women were silent after Barbara finished reading and leaned back on the sofa, tired now. First one woman spoke, then another, the sounds of their voices picking up speed until we were laughing, crying, remembering together" (188).

Despite this foregrounding of women's community, *Cancer in Two Voices* shares with personal cancer narratives an emphasis on the suffering and new insights that an individual experiences during prolonged medical treatment. This subjectivity is mediated, however, by the joint venture of the narrative. Rosenblum's journal entry of September 3, 1985, for example, contrasts the effects of radiation with those of chemotherapy: "The side effects of radiation are extremely unpleasant, enervating, creeping in slowly and catching me unaware. I'm exhausted but it's different from the exhaustion of chemotherapy. A different depletion, different sense of lassitude" (50). The anguish of the process of radiation itself provides the focus of her September 9 entry: "Waiting is agony. Waiting for the machine to mechanically scan the body. Turn to the left. Move to the right. Don't move. Hold your breath. Relax. Undergoing the procedure feels like a form of torture. I don't understand. Lying there stiffly, I weep" (51). In such entries Rosenblum captures vividly the lack of agency that cancer treatment can provoke as well as the violence of its methodology. Although Butler's journal accounts similarly describe the traumas of her partner's medicalization, they also pay homage to Rosenblum's resilience. On September 28 Butler writes, "We celebrated the end of radiation last week. The skin across her chest appears sunburned, red, and bubbly, and Barbara creams it every day with aloe. The image of her lying beneath the massive radiation machine, staring up at the ceiling while being zapped with poison, is permanently traced on my brain. Her indefatigable good spirits are as well" (51).

The stresses of conducting a lawsuit for medical malpractice figure prominently in *Cancer in Two Voices,* one of a handful of cancer autobiographies that recount not only anger at the medical establishment but action taken against it. As Rosenblum explains, after her chemotherapy begins, she feels "prepared for a long fight in many, many ways": "One fight I'm waging is a malpractice suit against Kaiser Hospital, which failed to diagnose my tumor as cancer over a year ago. They dismissed it, time after time, as benign fibrocystic disease" (20). Once Rosenblum acknowledges her anger at such incompetence and her grief that she did not receive an early diagnosis, Butler fills the narrative gaps:

> It wasn't until the skin around her nipple began to pucker that she grew frightened and called from New York asking me to arrange for an examination with a doctor outside the Kaiser system. I scheduled an appointment with an older, established, woman physician affiliated with a prestigious hospital. That was the turning point for Barbara, I think. That was the point at which she began gathering information outside the public health system. The shift from public to private was a major one for it took a while for us to understand she had been misdiagnosed. The lump we found in March of 1984 was not diagnosed as cancer until February of 1985. During that time, it grew from two cm to six cm; her breast enlarged to nearly twice its original size. A mammogram that Barbara had demanded be taken was read incorrectly as negative by a radiologist. She saw three doctors and, still, no one was concerned. (25)

Both women probe the disturbing sense of self-blame that can accompany a misdiagnosis. Rosenblum describes these poignantly as "if only" days: "'If only' I had gone to a women's clinic. 'If only' I had better doctors. 'If only' I had described my symptoms to friends more. . . . Today I feel my death sentence painfully" (38). Butler finds painful her partner's "overwhelming sense that she should—somehow—have known," even though Barbara did everything possible, from regular self-exams to insistence upon tests that were not routine (25). Unlike Katherine Russell Rich, however, Rosenblum decides to trade self-blame for action: "I know there is a point, an important point to this fight. It's about women's bodies. It's a struggle to overcome negligence and incompetence. I try to remember" (50).

Yet while Rosenblum and Butler determine that the lawsuit is just, they each admit ambivalence when the hospital unexpectedly offers a hefty settlement. Rosenberg calls the subsequent award "blood money" and struggles to find again her core self: "With all this focus on the medical malpractice suit and financial settlement, I have lost a quiet center. . . . It's time to get back to quiet. To read, write book reviews, work with

students, go to the opera. Time to think" (59). Butler experiences the settlement as troubling because her partner has been objectified: "It's been
just a few weeks since Barbara's settlement and my feelings fill me with
anxiety and confusion. My hand feels heavy as I write. A price tag on
Barbara's life" (57). In recounting the complexities of a successful medical lawsuit, these women analyze as well its emotional aftershock and
political implications.

An important aspect of Butler and Rosenblum's indictment of the
medical system is the emphasis they place on class inequities. Their narrative posits an America divided into unequal forms of health care delivery: public clinics for the poor and private hospitals for the middle and
upper classes. As a Jew from a working-class family, Barbara explains,
she had never had access to private physicians:

> All my life I believed that, if I became ill, I would go on the subway to the
> hospital, wait patiently to see the doctor, and be appreciative of the small
> hurried bits of time they proffered. . . . Mass medicine was for the mass of
> people—I was one of the masses. I never had a private physician, never had
> been to a private hospital. . . . Now I go to the Heads of Departments; the
> Chief of Oncology refers me to the Head of Radiology and the Head of
> Surgery, and they spend time with me. Not like the HMO's quota of one
> patient every twelve minutes. I never deeply understood that class was a
> matter of life and death. (27)

Here Rosenblum gives implicit voice to thousands of U.S. residents for
whom entry via education into the middle class brings recognition of discrimination against the poor. Because she naively misplaced her trust in
a health care system she assumed was democratic, Rosenblum admits,
she "never learned to recognize a good doctor," an inability that tor-
ments her as she reflects upon her misdiagnoses by incompetent physicians (26). Nor does the private medical system fully ease a patient's
way, since different specialists advocate different treatment: "Surgeons
tend to see breast cancer as a local disease, so they want to cut first.
Oncologists see cancer systemically, as an immune system disease, and
they attack with chemotherapy." Having received diverse opinions from
three different oncologists, Rosenblum represents her subsequent struggle as "a crisis of uncertainty" (26).

A final multicultural element of *Cancer in Two Voices* can be seen in
the authors' analysis of their relationship to Jewish religion and culture,
a relationship that affects the narrative representation of their families of

origin and the rituals they devise as Rosenblum's health deteriorates. Early in the narrative each woman describes her Jewish origins through the metaphor of home. For Rosenblum, coming home as a Jew involves a recognition of social injustice and an affirmation of human freedom. She recalls being alienated from Judaism as a youth, rebelling when her parents sent her to Hebrew school and "Jewish cultural school" because they marked her as marginal: "We had to learn Jewish culture and some Yiddish songs. I could not bear the smell. . . . I was dressed like a poor immigrant kid in hand-me-downs. We were still very poor then. I wore funny-colored leggings and other girls pointed and laughed at me. That was to shape my sense of myself as an outsider" (2). Although Butler grew up in a suburb rather than a ghetto, she also experienced conflict over her ethnic identity, as her family sought "to erase all traces of the *shtetl*" and instructed her at "being Jewish but not 'too Jewish'" (2). As part of their journey through cancer both women reassess their ethnicity, a process that figures centrally in their narrative. Butler explains that for her, this reassessment began years earlier in the form of a political and an academic "immersion in the Holocaust," which in turn created "the beginning of my bonding with all Jews"; this bond grows stronger shortly after Rosenblum's cancer diagnosis, when the women attend Temple to commemorate Yom Kippur, the Day of Atonement, and shed their grief by weeping throughout the service (5, 54). A reemphasis on Judaism manifests itself in the rituals the narrators plan for their commitment ceremony, from the chuppah under which they stand to exchange vows to the Torah-shaped scrolls from which friends read to the klezmer music to which the couple dance (117–20). As Rosenblum nears death, a "sacred time," she reaffirms in her journal a commitment to Judaism, manifested in her study of scriptures and commentary with a progressive rabbi and her participation in "a transformative experience known as *mikvah*, which consists of a ritual bath" that signifies "entering holiness or union with God" (196). As readers enter Butler and Rosenblum's narrative, they learn not only how cancer affects the women's relationship but also how working-class and Jewish identity informs their autobiographical project.

If Butler and Rosenblum analyze the cancer experience from a lesbian perspective, Eve Kosofsky Sedgwick, in *Tendencies*, "queers" it. A well-known academic theorist, Sedgwick first conceived of "White Glasses," a pivotal essay in *Tendencies,* as a eulogy in honor of her friend Michael Lynch, who was dying of AIDS. Ironically, during the writing of this essay Lynch's health temporarily improved, even as Sedgwick herself was diagnosed with metastasized breast cancer. Much of the essay pays homage to the unique friendship of a "queer but long-married young woman whose erotic and intellectual life were fiercely transitive" and the gay poet and scholar with whose retro white spectacles she had fallen in love (253). Thus the narrative foregrounds sexual orientation, feminism, and class as they pertain to illness, but it does so through a more theoretical lens than that of *Cancer in Two Voices.* In one passage about the vicissitudes of gender and sexuality, for example, Sedgwick describes her pleasure at receiving a beloved blanket as a gift from Lynch shortly after telling him that she had cancer:

> The first thing Michael did after my diagnosis in February was to bundle into the mail to me a blanket that has often comforted me at his house—a blanket whose meaning to him is its association with the schoolteacher aunt whose bed he used to lie in in childhood, sandwiched in the crack between her and her lifelong companion, wondering whether (after all, he was adopted) it might not be this Boston marriage whose offspring he somehow really, naturally was. (257).

Clearly the blanket functions as a sign of intimacy from one ill friend to another, but Sedgwick probes as well its gendered, sexualized, and philosophical significations. "If what is at work here is an identification that falls across gender," she concludes, "it falls no less across sexualities, across 'perversions.' And across the ontological crack between the living and the dead" (257).

In other parts of "White Glasses" Sedgwick considers how the experience of breast cancer has informed her thinking about shifting cultural representations of gender. A critique of hegemonic femininity underlies this narrative, as Sedgwick acknowledges her chromosomal status as "woman" yet refuses to accept mainstream cancer culture's interpretation of its parameters. "Received wisdom has it that being a breast cancer patient, even while it is supposed to pose unique challenges to one's sense of 'femininity,' nonetheless plunges one into an experience of almost archetypal 'femaleness,'" she explains, and indeed she acknowledges that "one of the first things I felt when I was facing the diagnosis of breast cancer was, 'Shit, now I guess I really must be a woman'" (262). Moreover, she identifies herself as a white woman who interrogates racial constructs and a fat woman who succeeds in forging, "with all a fat *woman's* defiance, my identity?—as a gay man" (256). Although she does not probe the transgendered aspects of her gay male identity, Sedgwick admits having long resisted identification with womanhood for political reasons. As a cancer patient, however, she complains that society has constructed breast cancer in gender-essentialist terms—as "the secret whose sharing defines women as such"—and that mainstream cancer organizations support breast cancer patients only if those patients collude with conventional heterosexist assumptions about femininity (262). She critiques, for instance, the social worker who informed her and her cohorts that "with proper toning exercise, makeup, wigs, and a well-fitting prosthesis, we could feel just as feminine as we ever had and no one (i.e., no man) need ever know that anything had happened. As if our unceasing function is to present, heterosexually, the spectacle of the place where men may disavow their own mortality as well as ours" (262). As Lorde did fifteen years earlier in *The Cancer Journals,* Sedgwick challenges the heteronormative emphasis that many cancer advocacy groups promulgate.

The connection between AIDS and cancer activism and the systemic discrimination ill persons encounter comprise another thematic cluster in "White Glasses." People living with AIDS, Sedgwick contends, have developed a "liberatory identity politics" from which women with breast cancer can learn: "From Michael I also seem always to hear the injunction . . . 'include, include': to entrust as many people as one possibly can with one's actual body and its needs, one's stories about its fate, one's dreams and· one's sources of information or hypothesis about disease, cure, consolation, denial, and the state of institutional violence that are also invested in one's illness" (261). In using the politically volatile trope of "institutional violence," Sedgwick endorses the strategies of Act Up and critiques both the lack of subsidized health care in the United States and the continuing paucity of governmental dollars directed toward AIDS and breast cancer research. From her perspective, these atrocities constitute a basis for further activist protest: "What needs to happen now, and I believe can happen, is the even more radical and shaming realization that under the present regime of systemic exclusion from health care in at least the United States, *every* experience of illness is, among other things, a subjection to state violence, and where possible to be resisted as that" (261–62).

The problem of agency in the face of medicalization is an issue with which Sedgwick, like other cancer autobiographers, grapples. "White Glasses" joins other multicultural narratives in critiquing the high-tech eeriness of the medical system even as the writer by necessity participates in it. After surviving surgery, chemotherapy, and hormone therapy, Sedgwick feels unsure how many breasts she is sporting "(a voice in me keeps whispering, *three*)" and whose bald head she confronts daily in the mirror, her father's or her own. "Indeed, every aspect of a self comes up for grabs under the pressure of modern medicine, with its strange mix of the most delicate and the coarsest of knowledges and imaging capabilities," Sedgwick asserts. Take, for example, the anticancer drug Cytoxan:

> That pretty, speckled, robin's-egg blue pill with the slightly sinister name "Cytoxan"—it was developed during World War II as a chemical warfare agent; when, as per doctor's instructions, I drop four of this "agent" into my bloodstream every morning, the *mildest* way to describe what is happening is via the postmodernist cliché that I am "putting in question the concept of agency"! (263)

What might it mean, she wonders, to serve as agent in a desperate poisoning of one's cancer-inflicted self?

In a more positive vein, Sedgwick acknowledges the essential presence of caring others in the lives of people with breast cancer or AIDS. Part of the "transformative political work" accomplished by AIDS patient-activists has involved "being available to be identified with in the very grain of one's illness"—available not only to loved ones but also to detractors who "nonetheless may be brought consciously, even if haltingly, into the world of people living with this disease" (261). For breast cancer patient-activists, Sedgwick posits, identification with the grain of one's illness requires a rejection of "the mysteries of essential femaleness" in favor of a diverse and inclusive community: "The people to whose exquisite care I can attribute my present, buoyant spirits and health are the same companions, students, friends, of *every* gender and sexuality, who have always been as vital to my self-formation as I think I have been to theirs" (263).

In her introduction to *Tendencies* Sedgwick presents breast cancer as the ultimate sign of postmodern indeterminancy, a sign that insists on breaking down dichotomous thinking. "How could I have arrived at a more efficient demonstration of the instability of the supposed oppositions that structure an experience of the 'self'?" she wonders—

the part and the whole (when cancer so dramatically corrodes this distinction); safety and danger (when fewer than half of the women diagnosed with breast cancer display any statistically defined "risk factors" for the disease); fear and hope (when I feel—I've got a quarterly physical coming up—so much less prepared to deal with the news that a lump or a rash *isn't* a metastasis than that it is); past and future (when a person anticipating the possibility of death, and the people who care for her, occupy temporalities that more and more radically diverge); thought and act (the words in my head are aswirl with fatalism, but at the gym I'm striding treadmills and lifting weights); or the natural and the technological (what with the exoskeleton of the bone-scan machine, the uncanny appendage of the IV drip, the bionic implant of the Port-a-cath, all in the service of imaging and recovering my "natural" healthy body in the face of its spontaneous and endogenous threat against itself). Problematics of undecidability present themselves in a new, unfacile way with a disease whose *best* outcome—since breast cancer doesn't respect the five-year statute of limitations that constitutes cure for some other cancers—will be decades and decades of freefall interpretive panic. (12–13)

This complex passage indicates Sedgwick's theoretical position regarding her unstable identity as "cancer patient," yet it also sheds light on the emotional particulars of her experience. Like many other medicalized women, she feels fear easily, finds hope difficult, becomes accustomed to expecting the worst, and acknowledges both personal and "interpretive" panic. She finds herself simultaneously awed and horrified by the instruments that determine her fate: the alienating bone-scan machine that presents its own exoskeleton even as it evaluates hers, the appalling "bionic implant of the Port-a-cath." Her language of invasion is strikingly similar to that which Sontag unmasks in *Illness as Metaphor:* cancer *corrodes* any sense of bodily autonomy, the IV drip seems *uncanny* in its invasiveness, the unfaithful body has foregone its *natural* healthy state and undertaken instead a "spontaneous and *endogenous threat* against itself" (5–10, my italics)—yet, like Sontag, Sedgwick scrutinizes these metaphors.

Finally instability offers an opportunity for gender bending and other transgressions, and Sedgwick is determined to mine it. "I have never felt less stability in my gender, age, and racial identities," she concludes, "nor, anxious and full of the shreds of dread, shame, and mourning as this process is, have I ever felt more of a mind to explore and exploit every possibility" (263–64). For Sedgwick as for Butler and Rosenblum and many other writers of multicultural narratives, the experience of cancer functions as a source of personal, systemic, and sociopolitical interrogation.

ENVIRONMENTAL CANCER NARRATIVES

The environment, it seems, keeps falling off the cancer screen.
                    —Sandra Steingraber, *Living Downstream*

The remainder of this chapter examines works by three writers who argue for a causal connection between cancer and environmental degradation: Rachel Carson, Sandra Steingraber, and Terry Tempest Williams. Despite their diversity of form and focus, these writings contribute to an innovative autobiographical subgenre—the environmental cancer narrative—that constructs new knowledge about cancer, ecology, activism, and women's subjectivity. While their narratives do not prove that environmental carcinogens cause cancer, these writers, who also are ecologists, speculate compellingly that a link exists between the rise in cancer incidence since 1900 and the increase in toxicity of the environment, especially in the United States and other parts of the industrialized world. By breaking silence about corporate, governmental, and scientific apathy or complicity in allowing these toxins to plague our environment—and doing so at no small risk to their professional lives—these writers practice a "heroics of witness" that constitutes a vital form of discursive activism (Tallmadge 205). Moreover, each writer weaves her own experience with cancer into her narrative, creating an ecological and autobiographical tapestry. Feminist consideration of such texts seems timely given that cancer rates in industrialized nations continue to rise (from 4 percent in 1900 to 20 percent today), that only 5 percent of all cancers have genetic causes and a maximum of only 30 percent can be attributed to technological advances in early detection, and that connections between cancer and chemical exposure have been proposed by researchers for more than half a century.[12]

Rachel Carson's *Silent Spring* (1962) serves as the prototype for the environmental narratives that follow in the 1990s; she argues persuasively that the steady increase in U.S. cancer rates and the steady increase in air, soil, and water contamination are linked. Carson had a personal stake in considering the relationship between cancer and pesticides, although she largely kept this stake a secret: during the early 1960s she contracted breast cancer with lymph node involvement. Subsequently she wrote numerous letters to her chosen oncologist, Dr. George Crile, and her closest friend, Dorothy Freeman, about her experience of cancer; these letters reveal the ways in which her research guided her treatment choices. Taken together, *Silent Spring* and Carson's letters constitute a hybrid and powerful cancer narrative by one of America's foremost ecologists.

Early in *Silent Spring* Carson asserts that human vulnerability to carcinogens, and thus to cancer, has reached unacceptable levels: "For the first time in the history of the world, every human being is now subjected to contact with dangerous chemicals, from the moment of conception until death" (15). In the chapter "One in Every Four" she develops this argument further, offering five lines of reasoning to posit direct or indirect links between carcinogens and cancer. First, she notes that while some cancer-producing substances occur naturally in our environment, the chemical industry in the twentieth century has added countless new carcinogens against which humans lack natural defenses. Second, Carson claims that since the onset of the atomic age, not industrial workers alone but all humans receive exposure to these carcinogens throughout their lifetimes, for these chemical agents have pervaded every aspect of our environment, from soil to water to air. Third, she points out that although incidences of cancer rose remarkably from 1900 to 1960 in children and young adults as well as the elderly, physicians and researchers have had difficulty explaining why. Fallout from the postwar chemical era seems to Carson one possible and troubling explanation. Fourth, since laboratory experiments have increasingly revealed that repeated exposure to pesticides and other environmental contaminants causes cancer in mice, rats, and dogs, while migratory birds exposed to pollution develop large numbers of malignant tumors, Carson deduces that the human population might be similarly at risk. Finally, newly developed DNA research in the early 1960s leads her to speculate that cells themselves are vulnerable to chemically induced forms of cancer: through chromosomal damage and genetic mutations caused by carcinogens; through carcinogens' ability to imitate and disrupt sex hormones, especially estrogen; and through the capacity of chemical pollutants to alter human metabolism (Carson 219–43; Steingraber, *Living,* 27–29). Carson based her argument in part on pioneering research by Dr. Wilhelm C. Heuper, director of the National Cancer Institute's Environmental Cancer Section from 1948 to 1964 and the most vocal critic of cancer-inducing workplace conditions in the United States.[13] Drawing extensively on Heuper's studies of the effects of an arsenic-contaminated environment on animals and humans, she joined him in defining DDT as a menacing carcinogen that causes liver tumors in laboratory animals and may do so in humans. As a result of her claims in *Silent Spring* that DDT had already moved up the food chain, causing genetic mutations in a process similar to the workings of radioactive agents, forty states began to regulate the use of pesticides, loopholes began to close in federal environmental legislation, and the Environmental Protection Agency was founded in 1970 (Proctor 50–53).

Ultimately Carson concurred with Heuper that blame for the rise of cancer lay in part with "biological death bombs" created by industry and allowed by government. She also speculated about what future scientific breakthroughs would prove regarding cancer and the environment, predicting, in Steingraber's words, that "future studies on the mysterious transformation of healthy cells into malignant ones would reveal that the roads leading to the formation of cancer are the same pathways that pesticides and other related chemical contaminants operate along once they enter the interior spaces of the human body" (28–29). Carson concerned herself, however, not only with the dangers carcinogens caused but also with what could be done about them. Addressing "reactions of despair and defeatism" that she often heard—speculations that it might be better to concentrate on finding a cure for cancer rather than trying to "eliminate these cancer-producing agents from our world"—Carson cites Heuper's admonition that even in the unlikely event that a cure could be found, any attack concentrated on "therapeutic measures . . . will fail because it leaves untouched the great reservoirs of carcinogenic agents which would continue to claim new victims faster than the as yet elusive 'cure' could allay the disease" (241). In addition, Carson quotes Heuper on a matter that even today invokes controversy among scientists and cancer researchers: the sexiness of the prospect of a cure as opposed to the mundanity of a focus on prevention. In Heuper's words, "the goal of curing the victims of cancer is more exciting, more tangible, more glamorous and rewarding than prevention," yet he and Carson agreed that prevention was more critical (Carson 241; Proctor 265–67).

In her climax to *Silent Spring* Carson claims that exposure to deadly chemicals need not continue: "It would be unrealistic to suppose that all chemical carcinogens can or will be eliminated from the modern world. But a very large proportion are by no means necessities of life. By their elimination the total load of carcinogens would be enormously lightened, and the threat that one in every four will develop cancer would at least be greatly mitigated" (242). Her subsequent claim stakes the future of humanity on cancer prevention: "For those in whom cancer is already a hidden or a visible presence, efforts to find cures must of course continue. But for those not yet touched by the disease and certainly for the generations as yet unborn, prevention is the imperative need" (243). Her tone is urgent, her appeal for change impassioned.

These quotations assume additional poignancy when we consider that Carson herself was among those for whom "cancer [was] already a hidden or visible presence." Yet she never mentioned her own breast cancer in *Silent Spring* because she eschewed gossip and because she did not want her many detractors to claim that her research lacked objectivity. In two letters to Freeman she explains her desire for privacy. " 'You know she had a cancer operation'. . . 'They say she's down to 85 pounds.' . . . That's the sort of thing I can't bear and the reason I've told so few people," Carson wrote. "Whispers about a private individual wouldn't go far; about an author-in-the-news they would go like wildfire" (quoted in Leopold 121–22). A later letter speaks more succinctly and ironically to this point: "I have no wish to read of my ailments in literary gossip columns. Too much comfort to the chemical companies" (quoted in Leopold 248). Nonetheless, in letters to Freeman and Crile, Carson recorded her cancer journey with a scientist's clarity of vision and an activist-patient's commitment to her right to know.

Social historian Ellen Leopold, to whose publication and assessment of Carson's cancer letters I am indebted, argues convincingly that Carson's secrecy about her cancer reflects the ethos of her time: "Women of this generation simply had no sense of breast cancer as something to be shared with other women, no consciousness or understanding of a common ordeal" (114). After all, as Leopold notes, not until 1965 did the American Cancer Society and the American Medical Association (AMA) begin to classify "cancer of the breast," as it was formerly termed, separately from other types of cancer (113). Leopold also claims accurately that Carson chose self-advocacy rather than compliancy in her approach to medicalization and that she "violated implicitly the confidentiality of the doctor/patient relationship (traditionally binding on the patient but not on the doctor) by reconstructing her own narrative of illness," most specifically by seeking a second medical opinion (118). Less convincing, however, is Leopold's assertion that Carson completely separated her professional and personal lives in dealing with her cancer and Leopold's implication that had Carson not done so, she might never have completed *Silent Spring* (121, 139–40). To the contrary, both the content and the tone of Carson's letters to Crile and Freeman reveal that Carson brought the research she undertook in *Silent Spring* directly to bear on her own cancer experience in at least four respects.

First, Carson's letters record what in 1960 constituted a radical determination not to accept the diagnosis of her initial physician, Dr. Sanderson, who subjected her to the subterfuge that many doctors of the era used on their female cancer patients. Indeed, he lied to Carson by insisting that she had "a condition bordering on malignancy," even though he knew her cancer had metastasized, and he prescribed no follow-up treatment. In seeking a second opinion from Crile, Carson asserted her right to evaluate both her physician and her medical status. As Leopold points out, Carson wrote to Crile because of his status in the field but also because she knew that his wife, Jane, had metastatic breast cancer and that the physician's stake in the matter would be high (117). In her first letter to Crile, her criticism of Sanderson is initially muted; she uses the passive voice to inform Crile that according to her attending physician "the permanent sections did not reveal definite malignancy, though something was said about 'changes.' No follow-up with radiation was deemed necessary." Later in the letter, however, she describes her concern when "a curious, hard swelling appeared on the third or fourth rib on the operated side, at or near the junction with the sternum" and acknowledges her dawning realization that under Sanderson's care, "the whole procedure has been rather slap-dash in an area where that is hardly desirable" (quoted in Leopold 128–30). After reviewing her records, Crile told Carson the truth—her breast cancer had spread to the lymph nodes—and recommended first an oophorectomy, or removal of the ovaries (because she was menopausal and he wished to remove all estrogen stimulation to determine whether her tumor was hormone sensitive), and second extensive radiation therapy (chemotherapy was at this time in trials and unavailable to the public). Carson responded immediately to Crile, indicating her gratitude for "your having enough respect for my mentality and emotional stability to discuss all this frankly with me" (quoted in Leopold 132).

Thereafter Carson participated actively with Crile in making decisions regarding her cancer treatment, and she rejected advice by consulting physicians when it did not make sense to her. For example, she agreed to have an oophorectomy and subsequent radiation only after considerable discussion with Crile because she realized that the risks associated with both procedures might outweigh the benefits. "I know too well that both radiation and chemo-therapy are two-edged swords," she wrote, nor would she accept "an over-zealous surgeon" (quoted in Leopold 129). During this period she refused the advice of a consulting specialist in arthritis, called in because of pain that turned out to be from cancer located in her cervical vertebrae, that she undergo intramuscular gold injections. In a letter to Crile Carson justified her refusal on the grounds that gold injections could have "toxic effects" on the bone marrow; she also reminded him that she was in charge of her own health: "As you know, I'm not an especially tractable patient, and don't just go along with such things without doing some inquiring and thinking on my own." When subsequent research into the effects of gold injections revealed that they were indeed risky for women who had recently undergone radiation, she exulted to Crile, "I guess my hunch was not far off" (quoted in Leopold 136–37). After experiencing bone metastasis in February 1963 she wrote Crile to ask how near to death she was, as she had arrangements to make: "I need your honest appraisal of where I stand" (quoted in Leopold 142). Crile told her the worst and recommended, as a last resort, the removal of her pituitary gland—a recommendation that Carson did not follow until just weeks before she died.

Carson also decided independently to change her diet in an attempt to halt the spread of cancer. Rather than consulting Crile, she sought advice about appropriate dietary changes from a retired nutritionist and toxicologist with whom she had earlier discussed her research on the ways that pesticides harmed humans. Thereafter she eliminated from her diet all chlorinated hydrocarbons, toxins found in meat and animal fat, because they depleted restorative B vitamins and were believed to cause liver damage (Leopold 138). In understanding dietary factors in cancer metastasis and acting upon that knowledge, Carson was decades ahead of her time.

Finally, despite Crile's skepticism and the AMA's dismissal of this technique, Carson chose to undergo an experimental treatment that she considered more hopeful than pituitary surgery: injections of krebiozen, a horse serum laced with deadly fungus that prominent holistic health advocates believed could cause cancer remission. The letter in which she justifies her decision to Crile reaffirms Carson's insistence on following her own scientific judgment: "I am well aware of the controversy over krebiozen and of the AMA's longstanding war against the Foundation and Dr. Ivy—but then I have seldom if ever found myself in agreement with the AMA" (quoted in Leopold 145). Although Carson took krebiozen treatments for three months, she received no relief from her pain or change in her symptoms. Yet having admitted the failure of her chosen treatment, she continued to resist Crile's recommendations when they did not dovetail with her own research findings. For example, Carson records her rejection of androgen treatments out of concern that the medical use of testosterone served as "only a means of determining hormone dependence on the tumor," not "a continuing or final treatment" (quoted in Leopold 146).

The accounts in Carson's letters of these autonomous or collaborative decisions provide an important coda to her arguments in *Silent Spring* regarding connections between cancer and environmental toxins. Indeed, her letters inextricably link the autobiographical and the ecological, revealing much about the world that Carson occupied in the early 1960s as a woman, a cancer patient, and a scientist.[14] Taken together, *Silent Spring* and Carson's letters to Crile and Freeman create a hybrid ecological cancer narrative that should be published in one volume.

In *Living Downstream: An Ecologist Looks at Cancer and the Environment* Sandra Steingraber argues that some cancers may be caused by environmental toxins, from DDT to dioxin to industrial waste. She explores in particular the chemical pollution that has contaminated the central Illinois landscape of her childhood and considers the ways that cancer clusters have ravage numerous rural communities. Interwoven throughout her narrative are accounts of her own experience of bladder cancer in her twenties and the death of a close friend, Jeannie Marshall, from a rare cancer of the spinal cord. Both Carson and Steingraber hold their fellow scientists, governmental regulating agencies, and corporate America accountable for the failure to control environmental pollution. They call

upon these entities to respect the public's right to a clean environment
and to insure the people's "right to know" when their environmental
well-being has been compromised.

Steingraber updates Carson's research by examining recent data
revealing that where high levels of cancer exist, unusually strong traces
of DDT and other pesticides can often be found. Unlike Carson, however, who employs in *Silent Spring* a measured scientific discourse, Steingraber personalizes her attack on DDT, PCBs, and atrazine by linking
their origins to her own:

> I was born in 1959 and so share a birthdate with atrazine, which was first
> registered for market that year. In the same year DDT—dichlorodiphenyl
> trichloroethane—reached its peak usage in the United States. The 1950s
> were also banner years for the manufacture of PCBs—polychlorinated
> biphenyls—the oily fluids used in electric transformers, pesticides, carbon-
> less copy paper, and small electronic parts. DDT was outlawed the year I
> turned thirteen and PCBs a few years later. Both have been linked to can-
> cer.
>   I am compelled to learn what I can about the chemicals that presided
> over the industrial and agricultural transformations into which I was born.
> Certainly, all of these substances have an ongoing biological presence in
> my life. Atrazine remains among the most common contaminants of Mid-
> western drinking water, and all of us in the United States carry detectable
> levels of DDT and PCBs in our tissues. PCBs lace the sediments of the
> river I grew up next to as well as the flesh of the fish that inhabit it. DDT
> can remain in soil for several decades. (*Living* 6)

Although DDT's registration was revoked in the United States more
than thirty years ago, thanks in large part to Carson, Steingraber notes
that as of 1998 DDT persisted not only through trace levels in soil but
also in migratory songbirds, many freshwater fish, and most hazardous
waste sites. Moreover, just four years after the banning of DDT, studies
began to reveal that women with breast cancer had significantly higher
levels of DDE (the form that DDT assumes in the human bloodstream)
in their tumors than in surrounding breast tissue. Although subsequent
studies have offered mixed results, Steingraber finds most convincing a
1993 investigation led by biochemist Mary Wolff of 14,290 New York
City women who had had recent mammograms, fifty-eight of whom
were subsequently diagnosed with breast cancer. Wolff's study revealed
that "the blood of breast cancer patients contained 35% more DDE than
that of healthy women" (Steingraber, *Living* 10–11). Steingraber also

endorses epidemiologist Nancy Krieger's research suggesting that a full-term pregnancy early in life lessens a woman's risk of contracting breast cancer "precisely because it reduces a woman's vulnerability to carcinogens and other cancer promoters, such as estrogen"; she joins with Krieger in calling for "a redirection of breast cancer research toward environmental questions" (264). Throughout her narrative Steingraber combines statistical evidence and personal testimony to argue that environmental factors in the rise of cancer deserve further research.

More explicitly even than Carson, Steingraber criticizes the Food and Drug Administration (FDA) and Environmental Protection Agency (EPA) for having failed adequately to address the prevalence of chemical pesticides in our daily lives. For example, she extends Carson's criticism of the federal government's improper monitoring of "tolerances," the maximum traces of pesticides considered acceptable in food, by claiming that the flawed system that existed in 1960 continued into the 1990s. Despite the fact that "in 1993, the National Research Council concluded that the current regulatory arrangement permits pesticide levels in food that are too high for children and infants," Steingraber argues that the EPA often refuses to reduce these levels and the FDA often fails to enforce the restrictions that exist (*Living* 164). As illustration of the latter claim she cites a 1994 study by the Environmental Working Group (EWG), a research institute:

> In their review of FDA monitoring data, EWG staff discovered that many more violations were detected by FDA chemists than were reported by FDA enforcement personnel. The actual violation rate, according to their reanalysis, is 5.6 percent—nearly double the FDA's official claim—and involves sixty-six different pesticides, including many banned or restricted for use. Green peas showed a violation rate of nearly 25 percent, pears 15.7 percent, apple juice 12.5 percent, blackberries 12.4 percent, and green onions 11.7 percent. In response, the FDA asserted that many of the additional violations uncovered by the group were technical in nature and "of no regulatory significance." (165)

In this example and many others, Steingraber confronts readers with troubling and well-supported statistics about pesticides in the food they eat and the water they drink; she lays these problems in the laps of federal regulatory agencies.

Steingraber weaves seamlessly into her environmental narrative two personal accounts: her own experience of bladder cancer, which she believes resulted at least in part from environmental toxins in her central Illinois childhood community, and the death of her friend, Jeannie Marshall, from spinal cord cancer. In recounting retrospectively the cancer diagnosis she received while in college, Steingraber evinces the vulnerability and shock that informs most writers' accounts of this experience: "I felt flattened down, like an animal wounded by something cruel and meaningless" (*Living* 135). In describing her cancer's virulence she relies on both scientific and artistic metaphors: "Cancer is mitosis run amuck. . . . Cancer cells are dancers deaf to the choreographer" (240). At several points in her narrative she claims the cancer experience as life altering: "Even if cancer never comes back, one's life is ultimately changed" (137). Although Steingraber's cancer story constitutes only a small part of her narrative, it personalizes her scientific argument and explains the passion that informs her mode of scientific inquiry and her narrative voice.[15]

Steingraber's chronicle of Marshall's struggle with cancer assumes a central role in the narrative; it serves to further humanize her scientific and statistical analyses. As Steingraber explains, the two women establish a friendship based on both a shared experience of cancer and a mutual commitment to studying its link to environmental pollution:

> Both of us are writers in our thirties. Both of us became cancer patients in our twenties. Both of us grew up in communities with documented environmental contamination, high cancer rates, and suspicions that these two factors are related to each other. Both of us grew up in families constructed through adoption . . . and we each have a keen curiosity about the interplay of heredity and environment in our lives. (*Living* 18)

When her friend's cancer recurs, Steingraber wryly describes Marshall's process of "getting well in preparation for becoming sick in an attempt to get well" (18). She explains, too, that "what my friend and I do not choose to talk about this afternoon are the dark days that lie ahead for her. Days of lying under the crosshairs of a proton-beam cyclotron. Fatigue, vomiting, blood tests. Continuously handing one's body over to technicians and doctors in a process that we call becoming medicalized" (20).

Despite this momentary silence, Steingraber clarifies that she and Marshall talk honestly about cancer and that these conversations strengthen both their knowledge base and their bond. Recalling their strolls through oak groves and salt meadow grass in the Rachel Carson

National Wildlife Refuge in Maine, a poignant backdrop for such reminiscences, Steingraber pays luminous homage to their intimate discourse, distinguishing it from both repressive silence and evasive bravado:

> The depth and ease of our talking carry us along today. . . . It seems to me in these moments that Jeannie and I have words for everything. We have rejected the cultural taboos of the past that wrapped the topic of cancer in shrouds of silence, but we have also turned away from the happy cancer chatter that regularly arrives in our mailboxes in the form of brochures and magazines dedicated to the concepts of coping, accommodating, and adjusting to this disease. In its place, we have created a language between us that is compassionate, smart, fearless, and open. (*Living* 20)

In this passage Steingraber takes radical aim at sunny cancer-agency discourse in a manner similar to Lorde's critique in *The Cancer Journals* and Barbara Ehrenreich's in "Welcome to Cancerland." Unthinking optimism is highly inappropriate for Marshall's situation, which involves recovering from painful surgery in preparation for radiation to control metastasized cancer. The alternative discourse that the two friends develop sustains them both as Marshall prepares for the next invasive stage in her treatment. "Between us, we have years of experience with cancer," Steingraber concludes. "I have no doubt that when those days arrive we will find a vocabulary for every experience" (20).

Words falter during moments of crisis, however, and Steingraber never wavers from depicting openly her own failures of language and nerve. The prediction that she and her friend "will find a vocabulary for every experience" does not hold when Marshall completes eight weeks of back radiation only to learn that the original tumor has moved to her neck. In her narrative Steingraber critiques both the coldness with which a physician delivers searing news and the numbness that prevents her from comforting her friend. As Marshall's companion and scribe at the oncologist's office, Steingraber listens in horrified silence as "the doctor spoke quickly and relentlessly," describing graphically "the tissues that were being 'destroyed' or 'strangled' by the chordoma's advance. He was clearly upset but seemed unable to blend his despair with a demonstration of compassion or hope" (*Living* 23). Finding it difficult to take notes or to speak, Steingraber struggles to control her shaking hands and even to listen; her angry friend, in contrast, engages the physician in "a battle of narrative," claiming that her symptoms have improved and asking him to conduct a neurological examination, a request he flatly refuses: "What would be the point?" Once the two stunned women arrive at Marshall's apartment, Steingraber confronts with dismay her continuing inability to speak. Indeed, she links it to the fear that has plagued her since the instant when, many years earlier, she had received her own cancer diagnosis:

> *Say something*, I order myself. The words I have just transcribed in the doctor's office are the same ones I have dreaded since my own diagnosis. Now I have heard them spoken—by a doctor who was looking into the eyes of the person sitting next to me. Not mine. Not me.
> *Say something.* (23)

A combination of relief and shame contributes to her survivor guilt, for Steingraber relives the terror of her own diagnosis as she listens to Marshall's. The death of her friend, which Steingraber renders movingly, is equally disorienting: "The whole concept of time was unbearable. I wanted to be back in Illinois in the middle of winter. I wanted to walk across frozen fields. No ocean. No leaves. She was gone" (40). In this part of her narrative Steingraber celebrates the power of women's friendships and explores the trauma of a friend's death from cancer on a cancer survivor.

Ultimately Steingraber advocates a "human rights approach" to the study of links between cancer and environmental contaminants. Indeed, one of her narrative's most valuable contributions is articulating this methodology through a combination of logical and emotional appeal. She defines a human rights approach initially as one that "recognizes that the current system of regulating the use, release, and disposal of known and suspected carcinogens—rather than preventing their generation in the first place—is intolerable" (*Living* 268). Government and industry, she insists, must work together to change this system. Moreover, a human rights approach "would recognize that we do not all bear equal risks when carcinogens are allowed to circulate within our environment"; workers at chemical plants and residents living near chemical graveyards bear disproportionate burden, as do people with genetic predispositions toward cancer and infants, whose immune systems are not fully developed. "When carcinogens are deliberately or accidentally introduced into the environment, some number of vulnerable persons are consigned to death," she further argues. A human rights approach would "make these deaths visible" (268).

Steingraber concludes by offering readers three important guidelines that can help to "reduce the carcinogenic burden" of humans: "the *precautionary principle*, the *principle of reverse onus*, and the *principle of the least toxic alternative*" (*Living* 270–71). The first principle she defines as a duty to enact protective policies when a threat of harm exists rather than when proof of harm becomes available: "Our current methods of regulation, by contrast, appear governed by what some frustrated policymakers have called the dead body approach: wait until damage is proven before action is taken" (270). Steingraber's second principle reasons that safety must be demonstrated, a policy that would shift the burden of proof from the public to the alleged polluters: "The principle of reverse onus requires that those who seek to introduce chemicals into our environment first show that what they propose to do is almost certainly *not* going to hurt anyone. This is already the standard we uphold for pharmaceuticals, and yet for most industrial chemicals, no firm requirement for advance demonstration of safety exists" (270). Her final principle "presumes that toxic substances will not be used as long as there is another way of accomplishing the task"—that farmers, dry cleaners, and hospitals, for instance, should be required to find nontoxic alternatives to dioxin or benzene or vinyl chloride (271). To up the rhetorical ante, she makes a potent analogy between deliberate destruction of the environment and the practice of enslaving human beings. If her three principles can be met, she argues, "the routine release of chemical carcinogens into the environment" will appear "as unthinkable as the practice of slavery" (271).

Steingraber acknowledges that not all of the evidence she uses to link environmental degradation and high U.S. cancer rates is definitive. However, she reminds readers that until the late 1990s little solid evidence existed to support the claim that cigarette smoke caused lung cancer, yet new scientific knowledge has proven this—after decades of unheeded warnings based on hotly contested animal experiments and statistical links. Similar possibilities exist that studies to come will connect atrazine, DDT, and PCBs even more directly to breast, bladder, and other forms of cancer. After all, "from dry-cleaning fluids to DDT, harmful substances have trespassed into the landscape and have also woven themselves, in trace amounts, into the fibers of our bodies. This we know with certainty. It is not only reasonable but essential that we should understand the lifetime effects of these incremental accumulations" (*Living* 13).

Terry Tempest Williams's *Refuge: An Unnatural History of Family and Place* (1991) probes the relationship between the death of many relatives from cancer—in particular, her mother and grandmother—and the environmental disasters that have befallen her home state of Utah. As a naturalist who studies migratory bird patterns in the Great Salt Lake area, Williams draws lyrical parallels between the lake's catastrophic rise in 1982, when flooding destroys her beloved bird sanctuary, and her mother's invasive treatments for and eventual death from ovarian cancer. She further identifies an ominous potential source of that cancer: nuclear fallout from the U.S. government's controversial testing of atomic bomb in the Mohave Desert during the 1950s. Like Carson and Steingraber, Williams calls for governmental accountability to its citizens regarding environmental contamination, and especially to "downwinder" families like her own.

Although Williams connects metaphorically the lake's rise and her mother's untimely death, she represents the first event as a natural disaster and the latter as unnatural. In her retrospective narrative, however, she strives to make peace with both. Early on she notes that her mother's was one of many cancer-related deaths the Tempests had been forced to face: "Most of the women in my family are dead. Cancer. At thirty-four, I became the matriarch of my family. The losses I encountered at the Bear River Migratory Bird Refuge as Great Salt Lake was rising helped me to face the losses within my family" (3). The bird refuge and the lake serve as sources of sustenance for Williams, much as her family does. Like Rachel Carson, Williams loves the grace, fragility, and song of birds; she identifies as well with their vulnerability. Birds serve, therefore, as a controlling image in her narrative. The chapter titles of *Refuge* identify the birds whose habits Williams monitors, from birds of paradise to snowy plovers to great blue herons. Burrowing owls she deems "birds you gauge your life by" because "they alert me to the regularities of the land" (8). As she explains, "the birds and I shared a natural history. It is a matter of rootedness, of living inside a place for so long that the mind and imagination fuse" (21). Throughout her life Williams has retreated to the Migratory Bird Refuge: she remembers happy childhood afternoons there with her beloved grandmother, Mimi, and upon hearing bad news about her mother's test results, she recounts having "fled for Bear River, wishing someone would rescue me" (15, 68). Great Salt Lake also functions as a place of solace: Williams recalls having swum there as a child with her mother and siblings—"for hours we floated on our backs, imprinting on Great Basin skies"—and as an adult in search of solitude: "I go to the lake for a compass reading, to orient myself once again in the midst of change" (33, 75). She also describes the relief she and her mother find there after Diane Tempest's cancer worsens:

> This afternoon, I coaxed Mother into going swimming at Great Salt Lake, something we have not done for years. On our backs, we floated, staring up at the sky—the cool water held us—in spite of the light, harsh and blinding. . . .
> We drifted for hours. Merging with salt water and sky so completely, we were resolved, dissolved, in peace. (78)

Given its peaceful associations, Williams jars readers when she depicts the lake as threatening. As she begins to draw parallels between the Great Salt Lake's tumultuous rise and the cancer that overwhelms her mother, she envisions the once beloved tides as invasive: "The pulse of Great Salt Lake, surging along Antelope Island's shores, becomes the force wearing against my mother's body" (64). Since the lake's rise also threatens the marshes of the bird refuge, Williams becomes ambivalent toward its waters and acknowledges a resulting disorientation.

Yet Williams reserves her fiercest anger not for Great Salt Lake, whose rise is cyclical and therefore "natural," but for the U.S. government, whose nuclear testing policies during the 1950s were deceptive. "I belong to a Clan of One-Breasted Women," she asserts in the epilogue to *Refuge,* where she articulates most fully her belief that cancer and nuclear contamination are linked:

> My mother, my grandmothers, and six aunts have all had mastectomies. Seven are dead. The two who survive have just completed rounds of chemotherapy and radiation.
> I've had my own problems: two biopsies for breast cancer and a small tumor between my ribs diagnosed as a "borderline malignancy." (281)

The Clan of One-Breasted Women serves for Williams as a trope that reflects both her family's "unnatural history" of premature deaths from cancer and her alliance with mythological Amazons who waged war against the forces that stole their breasts and lives. The most likely cause of her family's cancers, she asserts, is not genetic predisposition, fatty diets, or late pregnancies, as government sources often claim, but rather "living in Utah" (281). Williams explains that after her mother's death she told her father of a recurring dream of seeing mysterious flashes of light in the desert, only to learn that the scene was real: on September 7, 1957, she sat on her mother's lap as her parents drove north of Las Vegas and witnessed a mushroom cloud rising in the distance. "I thought you knew that," her father replied when she expressed shock. "It was a common occurrence in the 50s" (282). This realization evokes Williams's rage:

> It was at this moment that I realized the deceit I had been living under. Children growing up in the American Southwest, drinking contaminated milk from contaminated cows, even from the contaminated breasts of their mothers, my mother—members, years later, of the Clan of One-Breasted Women. (283)

Her new knowledge unleashes in Williams a trio of "weapons": research, activism, and writing. Near the end of her narrative she quotes extensively from governmental literature that falsely reassured the public about the safety of its aboveground nuclear testing policies in the 1950s and 1960s. Williams interrogates and subsequently condemns the manipulative rhetoric of these documents: "assuaging public fears was simply a matter of public relations" (284). She also explains her decision to become an antinuclear activist, a decision with personal and gendered as well as political dimensions. Recalling her Mormon mother's admonition to respect authority, Williams views her rejection of this advice as homage to her family's women:

> For many years, I have done just that—listened, observed, and quietly formed my own opinions, in a culture that rarely asks questions because it has all the answers. But one by one, I have watched the women in my family die common, heroic deaths. We sat in the waiting rooms hoping for good news, but always receiving the bad. I cared for them, bathed their scarred bodies, and kept their secrets. I watched beautiful women become bald as Cytoxan, cisplatin, and Adriamycin were injected into their veins. I held their foreheads as they vomited green-black bile, and I shot them with morphine when the pain became inhuman. In the end, I witnessed their last peaceful breaths, becoming a midwife to the rebirth of their souls.
> The price of obedience has become too high. (285–86)

Although Williams admits that she cannot prove that her mother and grandmothers developed cancer because of their exposure to nuclear fallout, neither can she disprove it: "The more I learn about what it means to be a 'downwinder,' the more questions I drown in" (286). What she knows for certain is that the U.S. government misled its citizens: "When the Atomic Energy Commission described the country north of the Nevada Test Site as 'virtually uninhabited desert terrain,' my family and the birds at Great Salt Lake were some of the 'virtual uninhabitants'" (287). Williams ends her narrative with an account of her participation in antinuclear demonstrations at the Nevada Test Site in 1991, an opportunity she embraced even though she knew she would be arrested: "It was more than a gesture of peace. It was a gesture on behalf of the Clan of One-Breasted Women" (290). She also claims as weapons the pencil and paper she carried at the time of her arrest, tools she plans to use for subversive narrative purposes.

Williams has stated that in *Refuge* she sought to embrace not "the scientific mind or the poetic mind" but "the feminine mind," which she defines not in essentialist terms ("yes, women are the caretakers of the earth . . . but no, we cannot solely be seen in that nurturing role") but through tropes of "healthy indignation" and silence breaking: "as women, we need to sit at any table mindful of what it means to be silent" (Bartkevicius and Hussmann 9–12). In a 1997 interview, moreover, Williams posed a provocative question to which the language of *Refuge* offers a possible answer: "What would it mean to write sustainable prose?" (Bartkevicius and Hussmann 21). Williams employs "sustainable prose" in many passages from *Refuge,* but nowhere more eloquently than in her ecofeminist tribute to the earth and the women who determine to sustain it:

> The women couldn't bear it any longer. They were mothers. They had suffered labor pains but always under the promise of birth. The red hot pains beneath the desert promised death only, as each bomb became a stillborn. A contract had been made and broken between human beings and the land. A new contract was being drawn by the women, who understood the fate of the earth as their own. (288)

If these women can join to protect the earth from nuclear devastation, Williams implies in this utopian passage, perhaps they can also protect humans from at least one source of cancer.

ECOLOGICAL SELVES AND HUMAN RIGHTS

Despite their formal and thematic differences, the environmental narratives of Carson, Steingraber, and Williams contend with issues of cancer and self-representation in several similar ways. First, these writers approach the study of cancer's link to carcinogens via "local excursions" as well as analysis of scientific data and autobiographical revelation. Literary critic John Tallmadge defines local excursions as "ramble[s]" during which "the curious naturalist . . . records observations" (197–98); women writers who adapt this strategy use excursions to acquaint readers with sites of elevated cancer risk. Carson, for example, transports readers to the Miramichi River salmon feeding grounds on the coast of New Brunswick, where in 1954 the Canadian government, in an attempt to save nearby forests from the spruce budworm, sprayed large quantities of DDT that within two days killed not only the salmon but brook trout and songbirds as well (131). Steingraber takes readers to the prairie grasses and polluted streams of Tazewell County, Illinois, her home, a community with unexplained high cancer rates that may be linked to elevated exposure to carcinogens (*Living* 1–6, 57–78). And Williams shares with readers her favorite haunt, Utah's Bear River Migratory Bird Refuge, threatened by an unexpected rising of the Great Salt Lake much as her family is threatened by an apparently arbitrary cancer epidemic that she ultimately connects to nuclear fallout (3–8, 281–87). The narrative goals of such literary excursions include breaking silence about connections between cancer incidences and toxic environments and connecting the personal and political by way of searing case studies.

Each of these three writers constructs in her narrative an authoritative "ecological self" that challenges traditional binaries of culture/nature, human/animal, and male/female. In Brooke Libby's terms, representing the self as ecological involves reconfiguring agency "not as the function of a uniquely human rational consciousness but as belonging to any being or object that evidences energy" (260). In this spirit Carson claims there exists "an ecology of the world within our bodies" even as she strives to protect "the whole stream of life" from what she terms not pesticides but "biocides" (Lear xv). In this spirit Steingraber insists that humans must seek our "ecological roots" as well as genealogical and must recognize that except for our chromosomes, "all the material that is us—from bone to blood to breast tissue—has come to us from the environment" (*Living* 267). And in this spirit Williams declares that "the earth is not well and neither are we," thereby attributing the condition of life-threatening illness to the planet as well as to humans (Bartkevicius and Hussmann 9–10). Environmental narratives bear witness to the integrity of the authors' ecological selves by revealing their view of nature and humanity as interwoven, critiquing inadequate federal environmental policies, challenging scientists' lack of sustained research on cancer's environmental causes, and advocating environmentally focused cancer activism.[16]

Finally, each writer uses her narrative as an opportunity to define cancer as a human rights issue. Carson couches this commitment in terms of humans to come: "Future generations are unlikely to condone our lack of prudent concern for the integrity of the natural world that supports all life" (13). Williams recognizes that to speak out about links between cancer and nuclear contamination is to address "issues of health, justice, and sovereignty" (Bartkevicius and Hussmann 16). Steingraber is most explicit in her use of human rights rhetoric, as seen in her passionate defense of environmental justice and her concern over the pollution of community creeks by leakage from nearby hazardous waste sites: "No one can quantify what the loss of a creek means to a child in Tennessee or measure the grief of parents who must forbid their son or daughter from exploring its banks. But I think we can say with assurance that the transformation of a popular swimming hole into a cancer hazard and child's play into a cancer risk factor is a terrible diminishment of our humanity" (*Living* 269). What we do not know *does* hurt us, these narratives reveal, and humans have a right to know about the environmental causes of cancer.

CONCLUSION

The Cultural Work of
Women's Cancer Literature

As we have seen, contemporary feminist theories of the body and disability theory shed light not only on what women's literary representations of cancer *mean* but also on what they *do*. In this study I have investigated how women's cancer texts make activist as well as aesthetic interventions, thus opening up questions of cultural transformation. Here I wish to argue that, ultimately, women's writing about cancer undertakes four important kinds of work that facilitate cultural change: it foregrounds ill women's agency rather than their victimization; it celebrates feminist themes of affiliation, resistance, and new knowledge; it offers opportunities for healing to both writers and readers; and it provides strategies for mourning and commemorating the women whose lives have been lost to this disease.

The first kind of cultural work that contemporary cancer literature performs is to challenge the "blame the victim" ideology that permeated literary representations of the disease from the nineteenth century to the mid-twentieth. As an alternative to this disturbing ideology, these cancer texts offer empowering representations of ill women's agency that are grounded in the authority of lived experience. As Susan Sontag has demonstrated in *Illness as Metaphor*, cancer has long been portrayed in medical discourse as "a disease following emotional resignation—a bioenergetic shrinking, a giving up of hope" (23). Women cancer patients, in particular, have been represented as being at fault for contracting the disease through their denial of "hidden passions," Sontag notes (49). The ancient physician Galen claimed that a "melancholy woman" was more likely to suffer from breast cancer than a "sanguine" one; the nineteenth-century oncologist Herbert Snow wrote that most breast and uterine cancer patients exhibited "previous mental trouble" or a history of "some debilitating agency"; and the twentieth-century philosopher Wittgenstein viewed cancer as "a gruesome penalty exacted for a lifetime of instinctual renunciation" (*Illness* 49–52). Nineteenth- and early-twentieth-century literary representations of ill women per-petuated similar stereotypes; during these eras, as Diane Price Herndl demonstrates in *Invalid Women,* illness was traditionally gendered femi-nine by U.S. women writers as well as men, and three options existed for representing the figure of the female invalid: she could "die, go mad, or get well" (15). These literary portraits were also class bound: Herndl fur-ther notes that numerous texts exploited "the historical connection between spiritual goodness, material wealth, and illness" to suggest that "a wealthy woman's illness is somehow more important than anyone else's," while texts that represented poor women often "extend[ed] the figure of the working class as sick, and therefore as potentially sicken-ing" (215). Most contemporary women writers, in contrast, question the gendering of illness as feminine and refuse to blame women of any class for their disease. In addition, these writers scrutinize any stigmatization that cancer patients in their narratives may encounter, whether inflicted by the patients themselves, their physicians, or other representatives of a culture of surveillance.

In this way women writers of the 1990s and beyond claim the right to represent and interpret the experience of cancer on their own terms—for as autobiography theorist Joan W. Scott has noted, " 'experience' is dis-cursive, both an interpretation *and* in need of interpretation" (58). Expe-rience as a feminist theoretical concept is closely linked to women's for-mations of subjectivity and sociohistorical consciousness, as this definition by Teresa de Lauretis suggests: "Experience is the process by which, for all social beings, subjectivity is constructed. Through that process one places oneself or is placed in social reality and so perceives and comprehends as subjective . . . those relations—material, economic, and interpersonal—which are in fact social, and, in large perspective, historical" (116). Women's subjectivity, historical consciousness, and consequent agency are central themes in texts that interrogate the politics of cancer treatment, mastectomy, reconstructive surgeries, and prosthe-sis. In *The Cancer Journals,* for example, Audre Lorde uses her constructed identity as a black lesbian and a resistant cancer patient to question "the function of cancer in a profit economy" and the "cosmetic sham" of prosthesis and thus to assert her own agency (49). More than twenty years later Janet Reibstein, in her memoir *Staying Alive,* uses her identity as the inheritor of an Ashkenazi Jewish maternal genealogy of cancer and a carrier of the breast cancer gene BRCA1 to explain her decision to undergo bilateral prophylactic mastectomies: "What I was about to do represented the cutting edge (literally) of what women with an inherited tendency towards breast cancer could do to prevent it" (212). For Reibstein, the choice of elective surgery and reconstruction results in a sense of detachment from the conventional icons of femininity: "These breasts are neither beautiful nor grotesque. They are neither me nor not me. . . . I regard the breasts of the sunbathing women of varying ages and sizes with no longing but also with little identification. I am beyond breasts" (238–39). Texts such as Lorde's and Reibstein's, along with many of the literary works analyzed in this study, represent the experience of cancer through the twin lenses of women's constructed subjectivity and sociohistorical agency, not through the culturally prevalent and stigmatizing lenses of victimization and blame.

The second type of cultural work that women's cancer literature does is to foreground powerful conceptualizations of ill women's affiliations, their resistance to objectification, and the new knowledge they garner from the experience of cancer. Such new knowledge is grounded in what Margrit Shildrick calls a "postmodern feminist ethic" (12). Women's affiliation is emphasized in texts that document the ability of communities of women to provide their members with emotional sustenance in the face of life-threatening illness. Barbara Rosenblum, for instance, pays tribute in *Cancer in Two Voices* to both her life partner, Sandra Butler, and to a "battalion" of friends—"twenty women who would be involved in my healing and caretaking" (12). Women in several performance narratives learn creative strategies for coping with cancer through the support of their relational networks: Sandra in Maxine Bailey and Sharon M. Lewis's *Sistahs* defies the stabs of pain that accompany her uterine bleeding by vigorously stirring and peppering the Trinidadian soup that she is making with and for her partner, her daughter, her sister, and her best friend (43); Wanda in Lisa Loomer's *The Waiting Room* invents feminist revisions of sexist fairy tales to share with her medicalized companions, the foot-bound but resistant Forgiveness from Heaven and the no-longer-corseted Victoria (74–75). These textual representations of women's affiliations demonstrate the power of community to serve as an antidote to the sense of isolation that can accompany grave illness.

Women's resistance appears centrally in texts that critique the medical system in the United States and the United Kingdom, interrogate the prolonged medicalization of the terminally ill, and connect the objectification of cancer patients to other forms of bodily exploitation that women confront globally. Barbara Ehrenreich, for example, trenchantly questions the capitalistic and infantilizing motives of the U.S. "breast cancer marketplace" in "Welcome to Cancerland" (44); Zillah Eisenstein, in *Manmade Breast Cancers,* links the invasiveness of cancer to global human rights abuses: "I write about breast cancer in order to demand a more just world free of the wars in iraq, kosovo, belgrade, rwanda, and pakistan and inside U.S. prisons where bodies are not taken seriously enough" (2). New knowledge is generated in cancer texts that cross formerly taboo boundaries. Diane Price Herndl in "Reconstructing the Posthuman Feminist Body . . . ," for example, embraces rather than stigmatizes the "alien" landscape of her postmastectomy reconstructed breast by representing its "palpable artificiality" as an empowering source of embodied, sociohistorical, and ethical consciousness (151–52). The ways in which these texts promulgate new knowledge is potentially radicalizing in that they develop parallels between women's cancerous or hybrid bodies and women's culturally dislocated or war-ravaged bodies as sites of resistant consciousness.

The third kind of cultural work that cancer literature undertakes is to facilitate the process of healing for writers and readers whose lives have been touched by this disease. For many women whose voices are considered in this book, writing serves as a healing act. "I'm a writer—of poems, essays, reviews . . . but not long ago, I was not a maker of particular texts or a professor or the editor of a venerable magazine but only another woman with cancer," claims Hilda Raz. "Maybe you already know what I learned: a million women, some of whom write and edit, have had breast cancer too, and many have used their writing as a strategy for survival" ("Writing" 121). Just as inscribing the cancer experience can help women to heal, so can reading this literature, for both making art out of illness and engaging with that art are communal endeavors. In "Scenes from a Mastectomy" poet and scholar Alicia Ostriker pays homage to a community of women who explore cancer literature and discuss their bodies, illnesses, and desires in a gender-segregated space:

> We spin our secret filaments, filiations, out of the earshot of men. Men who would be scandalized, men who would be horrified to hear us speak as we do about our bodies. To hear us speak, cackle, whisper, and roar as we do about birth, about sex, about sickness. (189)

While Ostriker views ill women's separate environments as subversive sites, other women with cancer approach writing as a means of communicating with spouses or male partners and with children. As an "autothanatographer," for example, Ruth Picardie addresses directly the husband she anticipates leaving and the children she will not see grow in poignant letters to be delivered posthumously, documents that focus on her experience as Matt's wife and the children's mother and her dreams for their lives rather than on her own role as writer. In theorist Susanna Egan's words, "Autothanatographers experience their deathward dissolution as physical transformations that alter their sense of both who they are and of what matters about their lives. They tend on the whole to be more preoccupied with rendering the impact of death on life than with giving birth to the author of the text" (6). As "the author of the text" that became *Before I Say Goodbye,* Picardie expresses the desire that reading her letters after her death will help her family heal; as she has found release in writing them, readers outside her family circle may also find release through empathic identification with Picardie's determination to record what matters.

Finally, women's cancer literature facilitates individual, familial, and cultural mourning for women who die of this disease and functions as a means of commemorating them. In 2004 more than two hundred thousand women in the United States contracted breast cancer, and more than forty thousand died of it (Gorman 50–52; www.komen.org). Surely the lives of all women and many men and children are affected by these statistics—and by the reality that one hundred thousand additional U.S. women die annually of ovarian, uterine, and other cancers (Proctor 1). Women's writing about cancer pays homage to the ill, the dying, and the dead even as it helps the living cope. Textual representations of dying women often ascribe them with emotional strength; while they are not "survivors," they often respond courageously to their illness and invasive treatments, and they manifest deathbed wisdom and even humor that inspire those who outlive them. To be sure, many cancer texts also represent the anger, fear, and loss with which the dying protagonists and their loved ones struggle, thus posing a needed corrective to facile idealizations. This literature thus explores a complex yet all-too-familiar cultural landscape of grief in the face of an unchecked epidemic and offers vicarious comfort and keen insights to readers who inhabit that terrain.

The power of women's cancer literature to commemorate the dead and dying is evident in Gini Alhadeff's tender depiction of the Princess's failing body in *Diary of a Djinn* and, via a different tonal register, in Mahasweta Devi's furiously ironic depiction of Jashoda's swollen corpse in "Breast-Giver." For me, however, the most moving example of commemorative writing appears in the cancer journal of my friend of seventeen years, Lynda Hart, a lesbian performance theorist who died of inflammatory breast cancer on December 31, 2000. In her July 29, 2000, journal entry, written as she awaited results of the medical tests that would confirm the presence of metastasized cancer, Lynda tracks the power of illness narratives to commemorate both one's beloved others and one's embodied self:

> Now I want to write again—about a lot of things. Another biopsy on Tuesday—it could be positive and I would surely lose my breast and perhaps my life. But I would have time to write. About: Deb, my dearest friend ever, my confidante, my soul-mate, even my guru at times. . . . And about Dom—her beauty is extraordinary. . . . And Stacey—I want to write about how she delights me, astounds me, I want to write about how I love to unroll her shirt sleeves as I put them in the wash—how I see and feel her beautiful forearms in the space where the rolled sleeves have opened. And I want to write about my breasts—memorialize them.

As Lynda writes, dying of cancer but not yet certain of it, she testifies to her desire to commemorate other women and to be commemorated. Such memorializing requires witnesses, a role that every reader of women's cancer literature arguably undertakes. As I bear witness, then, to the notebook pages that Lynda filled, the women she honored, and the beautiful breasts she wanted to memorialize, so do all readers of women's writing about cancer serve as putative agents of commemoration.

Notes

INTRODUCTION

1. Similar accounts of research, risks, and possible cures have abounded since the women's health movement began in the 1970s, when feminists first promoted self-help, organized cancer support groups, challenged paternalistic physicians, and criticized the disabling Halsted mastectomy. Women's cancer advocacy continued in the 1980s, most notably with the establishment of the Susan G. Komen Breast Cancer Foundation in Texas in 1982 and the Mautner Project for Lesbians with Cancer in Washington, D.C., in 1989. However, activism on behalf of and by women with cancer and especially breast cancer entered the U.S. political mainstream with full force during the 1990s. In 1991 Dr. Susan Love, with Susan Hester and Amy Langer, founded the National Breast Cancer Coalition (www.natlbcc.org), a lobbying group dedicated to increasing research funds. In 1992 Congress appropriated $210 million, an unprecedented figure, for breast cancer research. In the 15 August 1993 *New York Times Magazine*, Susan Ferraro analyzed "the anguished politics of breast cancer" and helped to popularize the statistic that one in eight U.S. women will experience this disease in their lifetimes. At the same time, data for the United Kingdom put women's risk there at one in eleven.

In October 1993 U.S. President Bill Clinton hosted a breast cancer symposium at the White House to inaugurate a national action plan. In 1994, after more than a decade of searching, geneticists Mary-Claire King and Mark Skolnick identified the BRCA1 "breast cancer gene"; a second genetic mutation, BRCA2, was identified the next year. But hopes that genetic testing would reduce women's vulnerability became complicated as ethical and economic issues about the efficacy of such procedures surfaced. "Tests to Assess Risks for Cancer Raising Questions," proclaimed Gina Kolata in the 27 March 1995 *New York Times*. An ethical question began to revolve around the increasing demand for prophylactic mastectomies by "high-risk" women who might or might not carry these genes and as of yet had no symptoms. "Study Says Few Women Rue Preventive Breast Operation" read the *New York Times* headline of 17 May 1999. Clearly the "silent epidemic" was no longer silent. See Altman 291–333; Casamayou 63–152; Ehrenreich 47; Lerner 241–90; Love 515–26; Potts 1; Stabiner xii, 3–19.

2. For support of these claims and further analysis of these statistics, see Henschke and McCarthy, 43–98; Proctor 2, 105–10, 253, 293 nn.29, 36; Ravenholt 213–40; Trichopoulos et al. 1697–1701. Based on data provided by the American Cancer Society, Conner and Langford state that 79,200 U.S. women were diagnosed with lung cancer in 2003 and that 65,700 died of this disease. Comparable figures for uterine cancer were 39,300 new diagnoses and 6,600 deaths; for ovarian cancer, 23,300 diagnoses and 14,000 deaths (11–12).

3. For support of these claims and further analysis of these statistics, see Casamayou xiii, 1–18; Ferraro 24–27, 58–62; Love 165–218. For a history of the search for a breast cancer gene, see Angier.

4. The most informative cancer Web sites I have found are those sponsored by the National Cancer Institute (www.cancer.gov), the American Cancer Society (www.cancer.org), and the women's health advocacy organization Imaginis (http://imaginis.com). Regarding breast cancer in particular, see these Web sites as well as those of Breast Cancer Action (www.bcaction.org), the National Breast Cancer Coalition (www.natlbcc.org), and the Breast Cancer Fund (www.breastcancerfund.org). Gilda's Club International offers emotional and social support for cancer patients and their families; see www.gildasclub.org.

5. For a theoretical examination of how women process knowledge about breast cancer, see Fosket.

6. Less than 1 percent of all breast cancers occur in men, however; see Altman 44; Casamayou 15; Love 354–55. The Komen Foundation Web site predicted that 216,000 cases of breast cancer in women would occur in 2004 and that 40,000 would die of it, while 1,450 cases would occur in men and 470 would die of it; see www.komen.org.

7. However, in this study I also discuss texts that address bladder cancer and leukemia. It is interesting to speculate about why women write primarily about breast, uterine, and ovarian cancers given the fact that lung cancer is so prevalent. My working hypothesis is that because of conventional cultural prescriptions of and proscriptions regarding "femininity," many women find "gynecological" cancers especially vexing to their understanding of their gender and sexual identities. I explore this topic further in the chapters to come. Moreover, because lung cancer is often deadly, it could be that few women live long or well enough after diagnosis to reflect on and inscribe their experience of this disease.

8. The term *autopathography* was coined by literary scholar G. Thomas Couser ("Autopathography" 65–75). For analysis of illness narratives, see also Couser, *Recovering*.

9. The phrase "discipline and punish" refers to the title of a study of systemic prison abuses by Michel Foucault.

10. Exceptions to this claim are scholarly works on breast cancer poetry by Hartman and Zeiger, upon whose insights I draw.

11. Theorists of autobiography who have explicitly addressed cancer memoirs include Couser, "Autopathography"; Couser, *Recovering;* Gilmore; Isaak; Knopf-Newman; Libby; Perrault, *Writing Selves;* Potts; Tallmadge.

12. In 1993 the *Boston Globe* published an article titled "Breast Cancer Risk in Lesbians Put at 1 in 3" (cited in *Love* 185), although the research on which the article was based generated and continues to generate considerable debate. Dr. Susan Love explains that research conducted by Suzanne Haynes of the National Cancer Institute on which the *Globe* article drew posited that certain "lifestyle" issues placed lesbians at higher risk, including the findings that one in four lesbians over fifty were heavy drinkers and that more than 70 percent of lesbians had never been pregnant. However, Love notes that further studies are under way that assess risk factors among lesbian populations more extensively (Love 185; Boehmer 3). A 1994 article by Gina Kolata in the *New York Times*, "Deadliness of Breast Cancer in Blacks Defies Easy Answer," explores possible reasons why African American women face significantly higher risks of dying from breast cancer than do white women in the United States, even though African Americans have a lower incidence of this disease—one in nine rather than one in eight. Among the explanations are the high poverty rates among African Americans, inadequate preventative health care, and possible hormonal factors. See Bair and Cayleff 9–10, 13–14; Jacob, Spieth, and Penn 244–56; Love 184.

CHAPTER 1

1. In *AIDS and Its Metaphors*, Sontag reflects on her process of writing *Illness as Metaphor* and considers the extent to which her claims about medical discourse and stigmatization still obtain. Although she argues that "attitudes about cancer have evolved" and that "getting cancer is not quite as much of a stigma" as it once was, she posits that a troubling and similar victim-blaming now occurs in our cultural discourse about AIDS and that this discourse has implications for how cancer is represented today as well (103); see also 93–116.

2. For more information about this poster, see www.breastcancerfund .org; for further analysis of its cultural significance, see Garland Thomson, "Integrating" 13.

3. For more information about Matuschka and her art, see www. songster.net/projects/matuschka.

4. Hammid's photograph of Metzger is reprinted in Yalom 270; information about it can be obtained from TREE, P.O. Box 186, Topanga, CA 90290. For a cultural analysis of women's breast tattoos, see Langellier.

5. Before providing her own analysis of "Breast-Giver," Spivak offers multiple readings by applying Marxist, liberal feminist, and French feminist

lenses. She thus reveals the story's subversive themes and salient fissures but also probes the limitations of these theories for interpreting texts by "third world women" that represent the "gendered subaltern"; see 247–64.

6. I trust that my respect for Spivak and her interpretation of Devi's story are evident in my decision to give her reading the "last word." However, I also see merit in my postmodern feminist reading of the story as an ironic cancer narrative on which the tropes of medicalized, leaky, amputated, prosthetic, and dying bodies can shed light.

CHAPTER 2

1. It is important to point out that these plays address philosophical and feminist topics other than cancer, albeit topics that may be linked to the disease. *Wit* offers a woman educator's passion for metaphysical poetry as a lens for examining mortality, death, and dying: "Nothing but a breath—a comma—separates life from life everlasting" (14). *My Left Breast* traces the bonds of affection between a lesbian and her son: "Now he is twenty and I am still his mother. I am still here. We are still arguing" (215). *Sistahs* celebrates chosen family as a vehicle of resistance: "When I say family, I mean it in the biggest sense. A complex, extended, non-traditional family, with its own secret language, a recipe to survive genocide" (38). And *The Waiting Room* explores how women have joined together to reject the temptation of negative body image: "But the sisters kept saying, 'You're beautiful.' . . . And eventually the women started to buy it" (75).

2. The analyses of Bordo and Rich raise the question of why writing about bodies and *as* bodies has been difficult for many women historically and why such writing remains controversial. The belief in a mind-body dichotomy has characterized Western philosophy from Plato to Descartes to Nietzsche, and church fathers such as Augustine and Jerome have presented the body as the enemy of both spirituality and reason. Augustine railed against the "slimy desires of the flesh," and both he and Descartes provided rules for gaining control over the body and its desires. Moreover, in this conception of body and mind as inimical, women have been identified with the bodily sphere and thus devalued, while men have been posited as rational and superior beings. Because Western thought was founded on this fear of the corporeal, the body has been constructed as the feminine, or "lesser," principle in a pervasive set of binary opposites: passion/reason, Other/self, immanence/transcendence, and of course male/female. Historically, the female body has been seen as fundamentally passive yet paradoxically dangerous, which has led to its social devaluation and, in turn, to the devaluation and oppression of women (Grosz 3–24).

3. Elsewhere I have criticized at greater length Edson's sexist assumptions about Vivian's emphasis on professional over relational identity; see DeShazer, "Walls," 114–16. For a similar critique of *Wit* from the perspective of an academic who has also been a cancer patient, see Vanhoutte.

4. For Christian interpretations of *Wit*, based in part on Edson's claim to interviewer Adrienne Martini that sometimes humans get "the opportunity to experience God in spite of yourself" (25), see Eads; Lamont; Sykes.

5. Vanhoutte 397–98 reads these scenes in which Jason invades Vivian's body as "disturbing" in their humiliation of the protagonist and argues that Edson reproduces stereotypes of "the retributive and the pedagogical nature of cancer" that Sontag critiques in *Illness as Metaphor*.

CHAPTER 3

1. See Pastan; Marilyn Hacker, *Winter Numbers;* Hall; Steingraber, *Post-Diagnosis*. Also see Bryer for a breast cancer sequence by a South African writer.

2. The exception is Ostriker, who focuses primarily on her gender identity in her breast cancer sequence although her Jewish identity is central to many other poems and several of her scholarly works, most notably *Nakedness*.

3. Since the four poets discussed here write autobiographical poems that foreground their own experiences of breast cancer, I use the terms *poet* and *speaker* interchangeably in this chapter to designate the *I* who finds voice in each sequence. I am supported in this decision by Ostriker, who claims in *Stealing the Language* that for many contemporary women poets, the "academic distinctions between the self and what we in the classroom call the 'persona' move to the vanishing point. . . . When a poet today says 'I,' she is likely to mean herself, as intensely as her imagination and her verbal skills permit" (12). Although I do not endorse this generalization fully—after all, many women writers do adopt personae—I believe that most breast cancer poems fit Ostriker's description. In a postmodern era, however, I would also stress that any poetic representation of the *I* or *self* should be viewed as fluid and contingent rather than fixed or monolithic.

4. For a discussion of cancer, African American women, and conjuring, see Epps.

5. In 2004 Clifton published another collection of poems, *Mercy*, that addresses her cancer and includes moving elegies on the deaths of two of her adult children.

6. In an article in *Feminist Studies* that appeared just as this book was going to press, Stephanie Hartman analyzes the scar imagery in breast cancer poetry by Hacker, Lorde, Raz, and Clifton; see esp. 155–65. Her focus, however, is on the contours and prevalence of this imagery in individual poems, while mine is on the position that scar images inhabit in poetic sequences that address cancer as the key theme.

7. On the issue of women's breast prostheses and cultural discourses of the "normate," see Lorde, *Cancer* 16, 49–60; Garland Thomson, *Extraordinary* 8; Garland Thomson, "Integrating" 10.

CHAPTER 4

1. For information about the breast cancer advocacy of the Susan G. Komen Foundation, see www.komen.org.

2. Many authors of women's romance fiction acknowledge these motives: Kathleen Woodiwiss claims as her goal to "make ladies' hearts throb with anticipation," Jude Deveraux creates "enchanted" tales of true love as antidotes to "rape sagas," and Phyllis Whitney writes with the awareness that "women want to love and be made love to as they love babies—that is, in a nurturant fashion" (Radway, "Readers" 569–70).

3. Among the many popular novels published since 1985 that address women's nurturance of cancer patients are Berg, *Never;* Dart; Diamant; Landvik; Winston.

CHAPTER 5

1. Numerous textual clues—most notably, the narrator's meditations on the similarity of Louise's body to her own—suggest a female speaker; hence, I use feminine pronouns in reference to the narrator and I assume a lesbian love affair with Louise. Critics Allen and Burns agree that Winterson's narrator is best read as female; Harris notes, however, as I do, that the narrator assumes a "masculine" subject position in objectifying Louise, and Gilmore warns against ascribing a gender identity to this narrator and uses the pronouns he/she to refer to the narrator.

2. It is noteworthy that none of these three novelists represents her protagonist's cancer as breast or gynecological, as most women writers do; rather, they choose as their focal disease a blood-related cancer (Maso and Winterson) or an unnamed one (Minot). This choice might reflect the fact that cancer in these texts serves as a backdrop for the writers' primary subject of interest, ill or dying women's erotic memories, and for the writers' linguistic experimentation.

3. Maso, Minot, and Winterson have also acknowledged other modernist and early modern writers as influences, including male writers. Both Maso and Winterson pay homage to Gertrude Stein in their essays on writing; see Maso, *Break* 72–104; Winterson, *Art* 45–60. Maso frequently cites the poetry of Federico García Lorca and Paul Celan in *Ava;* recurring most notably are the erotically charged line from Lorca "green, how much I want you green," panted by both Ava and her lovers, and the abject images of drowned hands from Celan. Minot includes in *Evening* an epigraph from William Faulkner's *The Sound and the Fury* and has elsewhere expressed indebtedness to Faulkner (Welch). In *Written on the Body* Winterson riffs comically on D. H. Lawrence as sexual antimuse: "She was not a D. H. Lawrence type; no-one could take Louise with animal inevitability" (20). In addition, she conjures Shakespeare's Caliban as a linguistic authority: "You taught me language and my profit on't is I know how to curse. The red plague rid you / For learning me your language" (9). Nonetheless, while allusions to male literary classics permeate these novels, the governing influences of *Ava* and *Written on the Body* and arguably of *Evening*

remain those of Woolf and the French feminist experimental writers.

4. These three novelists display significant differences in their representations of memory, death, and desire as well as the affinities previously discussed. One critical difference centers on their protagonists' sexual orientations. Although Maso's Ava has had mostly male lovers, she also refers to erotic desire for women, and on her deathbed she evinces an autoerotic consciousness; she thus can best be considered bisexual. Winterson's unnamed narrator, unidentified by gender as well, revels in an apparently lesbian passion for a bisexual woman. Minot's Ann, in contrast, is resolutely heterosexual. Yet these disparate forms of desire resonate comparably and with equal richness in the focal texts. Indebted to Woolf's androgynous notion of great writers as "man womanly and woman manly," as well as to Cixous's articulation of women's "infinite and complex sexuality," Maso's *Ava*, Minot's *Evening*, and Winterson's *Written on the Body* extend readers' knowledge of erotic subjectivity across sexual orientations (Woolf; Cixous 395; see also Cixous and Clément).

5. For a historical and theoretical overview of connections between suffering bodies and the suffering of the world, see Scarry.

6. The narrator's claim that hospitals are no place for sick people recalls Mahasweta Devi's nearly identical claim in "Breast-Giver" in explaining why Jashoda resisted medicalization despite the large lump in her breast.

7. For further discussion of Wittig's influence on Winterson's narrative, see Gilmore 123–24, 137–38.

8. Burns, for example, views Louise's return as the narrator's fantasy, while Allen argues that Winterson encourages readers to interpret this return as "actual."

CHAPTER 6

1. For feminist theories of women's autobiography that foreground gender differences, see Brodzki and Schenck; Friedman, "Women's"; Sidonie Smith, *Poetics*.

2. Gilmore cites as sources that raise these constitutive questions Mason; Sidonie Smith, "Identity's"; Weintraub.

3. The term *autopathography* is taken from Couser, "Autopathography"; for a discussion of illness narratives, see also Kleinman, *The Illness Narratives*.

4. Women's cancer narratives existed long before the twentieth century, however. In an extended letter to her sister, English novelist Fanny Burney became the first writer to recount the circumstances of her mastectomy, conducted in 1811 by Napoleon's physician in her home and without anesthetic. Having consulted three surgeons, Burney described the shock of diagnosis in a manner familiar to many contemporary women: "I was formally condemned to an operation by all Three. I was as much astonished as disappointed—for the poor breast was no where discoloured, & not much larger than its healthy neighbour" (129). Her graphic account of the surgery remains riveting:

When the dreadful steel was plunged into the breast—cutting through veins—arteries—flesh—nerves—I needed no injunctions not to restrain my cries. I began a scream that lasted unintermittently during the whole time of the incision—I almost marvel that it rings not in my Ears still! so excruciating was the agony. When the wound was made and the instrument was withdrawn, the pain seemed undiminished, for the air that suddenly rushed into those delicate parts felt like a mass of minute but sharp and forked poniards, that were tearing the edges of the wound. (135–38)

Miraculously, Burney survived this operation and lived for another thirty years. Yet despite its narrative power and historical significance, her cancer testimony was not published until 1986 due to nineteenth- and early-twentieth-century constraints on discussing female embodiment. For further analysis of Burney's experience and text, see Olson 51–53; Yalom 221–25.

5. See www.komen.org.

6. Information about the Women and Cancer Walk, which sponsored events from 1992 until 1996, can be found at the Web site for Breast Cancer Action, www.bcaction.org. The online literature that recounts its history claims that "before the battle of the corporate walkathons, there was the Women and Cancer Walk."

7. Toxic Tours of the Cancer Industry has become a part of the Toxic Links Coalition, a Bay Area alliance of cancer activists and environmental justice advocates; see www.sfbg.com.

8. A different type of environmental narrative is Cherrie Moraga's play, *Heroes and Saints,* which addresses the theme of a "cancer cluster" in a migrant farmworkers' community in California where children are being born with birth defects and dying of various cancers. I did not include discussion of this powerful play in chapter 2 because its protagonist, Cerezita, did not fit my paradigm of protagonists who are diagnosed with or dying of cancer; rather, Cerezita was born with no body, only a head, because of the environmental pollution to which her pregnant mother had been exposed. For feminist analysis of environmental racism and "at risk" communities, see Fishman.

9. An exception is Marcy Jane Knopf-Newman's *Beyond Slash, Burn, and Poison: Transforming Breast Cancer Stories into Action,* published just as this book was going to press.

10. See, for example, Bernie Siegel, *Peace, Love, and Healing.*

11. Despite the fact that Ruth Picardie's narrative evinces no overt connection to the women's health movement, it is important to note that Picardie and her friend, Beth Wagstaff, another young mother diagnosed with metastasized breast cancer, together launched the Lavender Trust, an organization designed to provide support and age-appropriate information to young women in the United Kingdom with breast cancer. A portion of the proceeds from sales of *Before I Say Goodbye* goes to this organization, and Picardie's family members continued their involvement with it after her death. For more information about

the aftermath of Ruth Picardie's death from the point of view of her sister, a writer and spiritualist, see Justine Picardie, *If the Spirit Moves You*.

12. For documentation of these statistics, see Casamayou; Lerner; Love; Proctor.

13. According to Proctor, Heuper's landmark 1942 study, *Occupational Tumors and Allied Diseases*, which Carson praised as the "Bible" of environmental carcinogens, was neglected by scholarly cancer journals in part because of World War II, in part because of the threat Heuper posed to American industry. In the 1940s the Du Pont Corporation falsely accused him of having Nazi ties; in the 1950s the company claimed that he was a communist. Although tobacco companies vehemently protested his "tobacco theory of cancer," they secretly studied his papers linking cigarette smoking to lung cancer; the asbestos industry, in turn, both objected to and learned from his research connecting its product to the same illness. By the time Carson published *Silent Spring*, however, Heuper had received prestigious awards for his research from the American Association for the Advancement of Science and the World Health Organization; thus, Carson's reliance on his argument in building her own was less controversial than it would have been in earlier decades (Proctor 36–46).

14. For more information on Carson's struggles as a woman scientist, see Lear; Michael Smith.

15. For a more extensive literary account of the emotions that characterized her experience of cancer, see Steingraber's collection of poetry, *Post-Diagnosis*.

16. For further support of the argument that more research into environmental causes of cancer is necessary, see Colborn, Dumanoski, and Myers; www.bcaction.org; www.breastcancerfund.org. To consider the contested landscape of one study designed to evaluate possible environmental factors leading to high incidences of breast cancer among women on Long Island, see Kolata, "Epidemic."

Works Cited

Acker, Kathy. "The Gift of Disease." *Guardian Weekend Supplement,* 18 Jan. 1997, 14–21.

Alhadeff, Gini. *Diary of a Djinn.* New York: Pantheon Books, 2003.

Altman, Roberta. *Waking Up/Fighting Back: The Politics of Breast Cancer.* Boston: Little, Brown, 1996.

Allen, Carolyn. *Following Djuna: Women Lovers and the Erotics of Loss.* Bloomington: Indiana University Press, 1996.

Angier, Natalie. *Natural Obsession: Striving to Unlock the Deepest Secrets of the Cancer Cell.* New York: Houghton Mifflin, 1988.

Armstrong, Nora. Rev. of *The Saving Graces,* by Patricia Gaffney. http://www.likesbooks.com. 19 Nov. 2002.

Artis, Brandyn Barbara. "Titbits." In *The Breast: An Anthology,* ed. Susan Thames and Marin Gazzaniga, 177–81. New York: Global City Press, 1995.

Aston, Elaine. *Feminist Theatre Practice: A Handbook.* London: Routledge, 1999.

Bailey, Maxine, and Sharon M. Lewis. *Sistahs.* Toronto: Playwrights Canada Press, 1998.

Bair, Barbara, and Susan E. Cayleff, eds. *Wings of Gauze: Women of Color and the Experience of Health and Illness.* Detroit: Wayne State University Press, 1993.

Bakare-Yusuf, Bibi. "The Economy of Violence: Black Bodies and the Unspeakable Terror." In *Feminist Theory and the Body: A Reader,* ed. Margrit Shildrick and Janet Price, 311–23. Edinburgh: Edinburgh University Press, 1999.

Bartkevicius, Jocelyn, and Mary Hussmann. "A Conversation with Terry Tempest Williams." *Iowa Review* 27:1 (1997): 1–23.

Bassnett, Susan. "The Politics of Location." In *The Cambridge Companion to Modern British Women Playwrights,* ed. Elaine Aston and Janelle Reinelt, 73–81. Cambridge: Cambridge University Press, 2000.

Belfer, Lauren. Rev. of *Talk before Sleep,* by Elizabeth Berg. http://www.barnesandnoble.com. 19 Nov. 2002.

Belsey, Catherine. "Constructing the Subject: Deconstructing the Text." In *Feminist Criticism and Social Change,* ed. Judith Newton and Deborah Rosenfelt, 45–64. New York: Methuen, 1985.

Benjamin, Jessica. *The Bonds of Love: Psychoanalysis, Feminism, and the Problem of Domination.* New York: Pantheon Books, 1988.

Berg, Elizabeth. *Never Change.* New York: Washington Square Press, 2001.

———. *Talk before Sleep.* New York: Random House, 1994.

Berlin, Monica. "Approaches to Carole Maso's *Ava.*" http://www.centerforbookculture.org/casebooks. 1 Dec. 2002.

Boehmer, Ulrike. *The Personal and the Political: Women's Activism in Response to the Breast Cancer and AIDS Epidemics.* Albany: SUNY Press, 2000.

Bordo, Susan. *Unbearable Weight: Feminism, Western Culture, and the Body.* Berkeley: University of California Press, 1993.

Boston Women's Health Collective. *Our Bodies, Ourselves.* New York: Simon and Schuster, 1976.

Brodzki, Bella, and Celeste Schenck. *Life/Lines: Theorizing Women's Autobiography.* Ithaca: Cornell University Press, 1988.

Bronfen, Elisabeth M. *Over Her Dead Body: Death, Femininity, and the Aesthetic.* New York: Routledge, 1992.

Brownworth, Victoria A., ed. *Coming Out of Cancer: Writings from the Lesbian Cancer Epidemic.* Seattle: Seal Press, 2000.

Bryer, Lynne. *The Cancer Years.* Plumstead, South Africa: Snailpress, 1999.

Burney, Fanny. *Selected Letters and Journals.* Ed. Joyce Hemlow. Oxford: Oxford University Press, 1986.

Burns, Christy L. "Fantastic Language: Jeanette Winterson's Recovery of the Postmodern World." *Contemporary Literature* 37:2 (1996): 278–306.

Butler, Judith. *Bodies That Matter: On the Discursive Limits of "Sex."* New York: Routledge, 1993.

———. "Performative Acts and Gender Constitution: An Essay in Phenomenology and Feminist Theory." In *Performing Feminisms: Feminist Critical Theory and Theatre,* ed. Sue-Ellen Case, 270–82. Baltimore: Johns Hopkins University Press, 1990.

Butler, Sandra, and Barbara Rosenblum. *Cancer in Two Voices.* Duluth, Minn.: Spinsters Ink, 1991.

Carson, Rachel. *Silent Spring.* 1962. Boston: Houghton Mifflin, 2002.

Caruth, Cathy. "Trauma and Experience: Introduction." In *Trauma: Explorations in Memory,* ed. Cathy Caruth, 3–12. Baltimore: Johns Hopkins University Press, 1995.

Casamayou, Maureen Hogan. *The Politics of Breast Cancer.* Washington, D.C.: Georgetown University Press, 2001.

Chodorow, Nancy. *The Reproduction of Mothering: Psychoanalysis and the Sociology of Gender.* Berkeley: University of California Press, 1978.

Cixous, Hélène. "The Laugh of the Medusa." In *The Longman Anthology of Women's Literature*, ed. Mary K. DeShazer, 390–405. New York: Addison Wesley Longman, 2001.

Cixous, Hélène, and Catherine Clément. *The Newly Born Woman*. Trans. Betsy Wing. Minneapolis: University of Minnesota Press, 1975.

Clifton, Lucille. *The Book of Light*. Rochester: BOA Editions, 1992.

———. *Mercy*. Rochester: BOA Editions, 2004.

———. "Simple Language." In *Black Women Writers (1950–1980): A Critical Evaluation*, ed. Mari Evans, 137–38. New York: Anchor Books, 1983.

———. *The Terrible Stories*. Rochester: BOA Editions, 1996.

Coen, Stephanie. "Medicine Show: An Interview with the Playwright Lisa Loomer." *American Theatre* 11:10 (1994): 30.

Colborn, Theo, Dianne Dumanoski, and John Peterson Myers. *Our Stolen Future: Are We Threatening Our Fertility, Intelligence, and Survival?—A Scientific Detective Story*. New York: Penguin, 1996.

Cole, Jenny. *Journeys (with a Cancer)*. London: Pawprints, 1995.

Collins, Patricia Hill. *Black Feminist Thought: Knowledge, Consciousness, and the Politics of Empowerment*. Boston: Unwin Hyman, 1990.

Conner, Kristine, and Lauren Langford. *Ovarian Cancer: Your Guide to Taking Control*. Sebastopol, Calif.: O'Reilly, 2003.

Cooley, Nicole. "Textual Bodies: Carole Maso's *Ava* and the Poetics of Over-Reaching." http://www.centerforbookculture.org/casebooks. 1 Dec. 2002.

Couser, G. Thomas. "Autopathography: Women, Illness, and Lifewriting." *a/b: Auto/Biography Studies* 6:1 (1991): 65–75.

———. *Recovering Bodies: Illness, Disability, and Life Writing*. Madison: University of Wisconsin Press, 1997.

Crowley, Leslie. Rev. of *Talk before Sleep*, by Elizabeth Berg. http://www.storycircle.org. 19 Nov. 2002.

Cummins, Maria. *The Lamplighter*. 1854. New York: Irvington Publishing, 1972.

Daly, Mary, with Jane Caputi. *Webster's First New Intergalactic Wickedary of the English Language*. Boston: Beacon Press, 1987.

Dart, Iris Rainer. *Beaches*. New York: HarperCollins, 1985.

Davies, Kim. *Me, Amazon Woman—LCIS Breast Cancer: The Controversy*. Tampa: Me, Amazon Woman Publishing, 2000.

Davis, Amelia, ed. *The First Look*. Urbana: University of Illinois Press, 2000.

de Lauretis, Teresa. "Eccentric Subjects: Feminist Theory and Historical Consciousness." *Feminist Studies* 16:1 (1990): 115–50.

Delinsky, Barbara, ed. *Uplift: Secrets from the Sisterhood of Breast Cancer Survivors*. New York: Washington Square Press, 2001.

Del Sesto, Christine. Rev. of *Evening*, by Susan Minot. http://www.amazon.com. 1 Dec. 2002.

DeShazer, Mary K, ed. *The Longman Anthology of Women's Literature*. New York: Addison Wesley Longman, 2001.

———. "'Walls Made Out of Paper': Witnessing *Wit* and *How I Learned to Drive*." *Women and Performance: A Journal of Feminist Theory* 13:1 (2002): 107–20.

Diamant, Anita. *Good Harbor*. New York: Scribner, 2002.

Diamond, Elin. *Unmaking Mimesis*. London: Routledge, 1997.

Devi, Mahasweta. "Breast-Giver." Trans. Gayatri Chakravorty Spivak. In *In Other Worlds: Essays in Cultural Politics*, ed. Gayatri Chakravorty Spivak, 222–40. New York: Routledge, 1988.

Dickinson, Emily. *The Complete Poems of Emily Dickinson*, ed. Thomas H. Johnson. Boston: Back Bay Books, 1960.

Douglas, Ann, ed. *Charlotte Temple and Lucy Temple*. New York: Penguin, 1991.

Duncker, Patricia. *Sisters and Strangers: An Introduction to Contemporary Feminist Fiction*. London: Basil Blackwell, 1992.

Dunnivant, Sylvia, ed. *Celebrating Life: African American Women Speak Out about Breast Cancer*. New York: Basic Books, 1995.

Eads, Martha Greene. "Unwitting Redemption in Margaret Edson's *Wit*." *Christianity and Literature* 51:2 (2002): 241–56.

Edson, Margaret. *Wit*. New York: Faber and Faber, 1999.

Egan, Susanna. *Mirror Talk: Genres of Crisis in Contemporary Autobiography*. Chapel Hill: University of North Carolina Press, 1999.

Ehrenreich, Barbara. "Welcome to Cancerland." *Harper's Magazine*, Nov. 2001, 43–53.

Eisenstein, Zillah. *Manmade Breast Cancers*. Ithaca: Cornell University Press, 2001.

Eliot, George. "Silly Novels by Lady Novelists." In *The Longman Anthology of Women's Literature*, ed. Mary K. DeShazer, 248–63. New York: Addison Wesley Longman, 2001.

Epps, Janice Coombs. "On Cancer and Conjuring." In *The Black Women's Health Book: Speaking for Ourselves*, ed. Evelyn C. White, 38–43. Seattle: Seal Press, 1990.

Eskenazi, Loren. "Breast Reconstruction." In *The First Look*, ed. Amelia Davis, 75–82. Urbana: University of Illinois Press, 2000.

Faulkner, William. *The Sound and the Fury: The Corrected Text*. 1929. New York: Vintage Books, 1990.

Ferraro, Susan. "The Anguished Politics of Breast Cancer." *New York Times Magazine*, 15 Aug. 1993, 24–27, 58–62.

Fishman, Jennifer. "Assessing Breast Cancer: Risk, Science, and Environmental Activism in an 'At Risk' Community." In *Ideologies of Breast Cancer: Feminist Perspectives*, ed. Laura K. Potts, 181–204. London: Macmillan, 2000.

Forcey, Linda Rennie. "Feminist Perspectives on Mothering and Peace." In

Mothering: Ideology, Experience, and Agency, ed. Evelyn Nakano Glenn, Grace Chang, and Linda Rennie Forcey, 355–75. New York: Routledge, 1994.

Forte, Jeanie. "Focus on the Body: Pain, Praxis, and Pleasure in Feminist Performance." In *Critical Theory and Performance*, ed. Janelle G. Reinelt and Joseph R. Roach, 248–62. Ann Arbor: University of Michigan Press, 1992.

Fosket, Jennifer. "Problematizing Biomedicine: Women's Constructions of Breast Cancer Knowledge." In *Ideologies of Breast Cancer: Feminist Perspectives*, ed. Laura K. Potts, 15–36. London: Macmillan Press, 2000.

Foucault, Michel. *Birth of a Clinic*. Trans. Alan Sheridan. New York: Tavistock Publications, 1973.

———. *Discipline and Punish: The Birth of the Prison*. Trans. Alan Sheridan. London: Allen Lane, 1977.

Freedman, Barbara. "Frame-Up: Feminism, Psychoanalysis, Theatre." In *Performing Feminisms: Feminist Critical Theory and Theatre*, ed. Sue-Ellen Case, 54–76. Baltimore: Johns Hopkins University Press, 1990.

French, Marilyn. *A Season in Hell*. New York: Ballantine Books, 1998.

Friedman, Susan Stanford. "Craving Stories: Narrative and Lyric in Contemporary Theory and Women's Long Poems." In *Feminist Measures: Soundings in Poetry and Theory*, ed. Lynn Keller and Cristanne Miller, 15–42. Ann Arbor: University of Michigan Press, 1994.

———. "Women's Auto-Biographical Selves: Theory and Practice." In *The Private Self*, ed. Shari Benstock, 34–42. Chapel Hill: University of North Carolina Press, 1988.

Fuss, Diana. *Essentially Speaking: Feminism, Nature, and Difference*. New York: Routledge, 1989.

Gabbard, Andrea. *No Mountain Too High: The Story of the Women of Expedition Inspiration—A Triumph over Breast Cancer*. Seattle: Seal Press, 1998.

Gaffney, Patricia. *The Saving Graces*. New York: HarperCollins, 1999.

Garland Thomson, Rosemarie. *Extraordinary Bodies: Figuring Physical Disability in American Culture and Literature*. New York: Columbia University Press, 1997.

———. "Integrating Disability, Transforming Feminist Theory." *NWSA Journal* 14.3 (Fall 2002), 1–32.

Gilbert, Sandra M., and Susan Gubar, eds. *The Norton Anthology of Literature by Women*. New York: W. W. Norton, 1985.

Gilman, Sander. *Difference and Pathology: Stereotypes of Sexuality, Race, and Madness*. Ithaca: Cornell University Press, 1985.

Gilmore, Leigh. *The Limits of Autobiography: Trauma and Testimony*. Ithaca: Cornell University Press, 2001.

Glacel, Barbara Pate. *Hitting the Wall: Memoirs of a Cancer Journey*. Seattle: Hara Publications, 2001.

Goodman, Lizbeth. *Contemporary Feminist Theatres: To Each Her Own*. London: Routledge, 1993.

Gorman, Christine. "Rethinking Breast Cancer." *Time,* 18 Feb. 2002, 50–58.

Granger, Susan. Rev. of *One True Thing* (film) http://www.allreviews.com. 18 Nov. 2002.

Grealy, Lucy. *Autobiography of a Face.* Boston: Houghton Mifflin, 1994.

Grosz, Elizabeth. *Volatile Bodies: Toward a Corporeal Feminism.* Bloomington: Indiana University Press, 1994.

Hacker, Marilyn. "Journal Entries." In *Living on the Margins: Women Writers on Breast Cancer,* ed. Hilda Raz, 201–41. New York: Persea Books, 1999.

———. *Winter Numbers: Poems.* New York: W. W. Norton, 1994.

Hacker, Roberta L. "As Luck Would Have It." In *Coming Out of Cancer: Writings from the Lesbian Cancer Epidemic,* ed. Victoria A. Brownworth, 72–81. Seattle: Seal Press, 2000.

Hall, Judith. *Anatomy, Errata.* Columbus: Ohio State University Press, 1998.

Harris, Andrea. *Other Sexes: Rewriting Difference from Woolf to Winterson.* Albany: SUNY Press, 2000.

Hart, Lynda. *Between the Body and the Flesh: Performing Sadomasochism.* New York: Columbia University Press, 1998.

———. Unpublished journal. August 2000.

Hartman, Stephanie. "Reading the Scar in Breast Cancer Poetry." *Feminist Studies* 30:1 (2004): 155–77.

Henschke, Claudia I., and Peggy McCarthy. *Lung Cancer: Myths, Facts, Choices—and Hope.* New York: W. W. Norton, 2002.

Herndl, Diane Price. *Invalid Women: Figuring Feminine Illness in American Fiction and Culture.* Chapel Hill: University of North Carolina Press, 1993.

———. "Reconstructing the Posthuman Feminist Body Twenty Years after Audre Lorde's *Cancer Journals.*" In *Disability Studies: Enabling the Humanities,* ed. Sharon L. Snyder, Brenda Brueggemann, and Rosemarie Garland Thomson, 144–55. New York: Modern Language Association of America, 2002.

Hirsch, Marianne. *The Mother/Daughter Plot: Narrative, Psychoanalysis, Feminism.* Bloomington: Indiana University Press, 1989.

Holmes, Martha Stoddard. Rev. of *Evening,* by Susan Minot. http://endeavor.med.nyu/lit-med/lit. 1 Dec. 2002.

Hull, Akasha (Gloria). "Channeling the Ancestral Muse: Lucille Clifton and Dolores Kendrick." In *Feminist Measures: Soundings in Poetry and Theory,* ed. Lynn Keller and Cristanne Miller, 96–116. Ann Arbor: University of Michigan Press, 1994.

Irigaray, Luce. "This Sex Which Is Not One." In *New French Feminisms,* ed. Elaine Marks and Isabelle de Courtivron, 99–106. New York: Schocken Books, 1981.

Isaak, Jo Anna. "In Praise of Primary Narcissism: The Last Laughs of Jo Spence and Hannah Wilke." In *Interfaces: Women/Autobiography/Image/Performance,* ed. Sidonie Smith and Julia Watson, 49–68. Ann Arbor: University of Michigan Press, 2002.

Jacob, Teresa C., Leslie E. Spieth, and Nolan E. Penn. "Breast Cancer, Breast Self-Examination, and African-American Women." In *Wings of Gauze: Women of Color and the Experience of Health and Illness,* ed. Barbara Bair and Susan E. Cayleff, 243–56. Detroit: Wayne State University Press, 1993.

Jaffee, Annette Williams. "The Good Mother." In *Living on the Margins: Women Writers on Breast Cancer,* ed. Hilda Raz, 46–56. New York: Persea Books, 1999.

Kallet, Marilyn. "Doing What You Will Do: An Interview with Lucille Clifton." In *Sleeping with One Eye Open: Women Writers and the Art of Survival,* ed. Marilyn Kallet and Judith Ortiz Cofer, 80–85. Athens: University of Georgia Press, 1999.

Karten, Harvey. Rev. of *One True Thing* (film). http://www.allreviews.com. 18 Nov. 2002.

Kasper, Anne S., and Susan J. Ferguson, eds. *Breast Cancer: Society Shapes an Epidemic.* New York: Palgrave Press, 2000.

Keller, Lynn. *Forms of Expansion: Recent Long Poems by Women.* Chicago: University of Chicago Press, 1997.

Kimmich, Allison. "Writing the Body: From Abject to Subject." *Auto-Biography Studies* 13:2 (1998): 223–34.

King, Greg. Rev. of *One True Thing* (film). http://www.allreviews.com. 18 Nov. 2002.

Klausner, Harriet. Rev. of *The Saving Graces,* by Patricia Gaffney. http://www.silcom.com. 18 Nov. 2002.

Klawiter, Maren. "Racing for the Cure, Walking Women, and Toxic Touring: Mapping Bay Area Cultures of Action." In *Ideologies of Breast Cancer: Feminist Perspectives,* ed. Laura K. Potts, 63–97. London: Macmillan Press, 2000.

Kleinman, Arthur. *The Illness Narratives: Suffering, Healing, and the Human Condition.* New York: Basic Books, 1988.

Knopf-Newman, Marcy Jane. *Beyond Slash, Burn, and Poison: Transforming Breast Cancer Stories into Action.* New Brunswick, N.J.: Rutgers University Press, 2004.

Kolata, Gina. "Deadliness of Breast Cancer in Blacks Defies Easy Answer." *New York Times,* 3 Aug. 1994, C10.

———. "Epidemic That Wasn't." *New York Times,* 29 Aug. 2002.

———. "New Approach about Cancer and Survival." *New York Times,* 1 June 2004, A1, 14–15.

——— "Study Says Few Women Rue Preventive Breast Operation." *New York Times,* 17 may, 1999, A1.

———. "Tests to Assess Risks for Cancer Raising Questions." *New York Times,* 27 Mar. 1995, A1.

Kristeva, Julia. *Powers of Horror: An Essay on Abjection.* Trans. Leon S. Roudiez. New York: Columbia University Press, 1982.

Kuebler, Carolyn. "Reading Carole Maso." http://www.centerforbookculture.org. 1 Dec. 2002.

Kuner, Susan, Carol Matzkin Orsborn, Linda Quigley, and Karen Leigh Stroup, eds. *Speak the Language of Healing: Living with Breast Cancer without Going to War.* Berkeley, Calif.: Conari Press, 1999.

Kushner, Rose. *Breast Cancer: A Personal History and an Investigative Report.* New York: Harcourt Brace, 1975.

Lamont, Rosette C. "Coma versus Comma: John Donne's Holy Sonnets in Edson's *Wit.*" *Massachusetts Review* 40:4 (1999–2000): 569–75.

Landvik, Lorna. *Patti Jane's House of Curls.* New York: Ballantine Books, 1996.

Langellier, Kristin M. " 'You're Marked': Breast Cancer, Tattoo, and the Narrative Performance of Identity." In *Narrative and Identity: Studies in Autobiography, Self, and Culture,* ed. Jens Brockmeier and Donal Carbaugh, 145–84. Amsterdam: John Benjamins Publishing, 2001.

Laub, Dori and Shoshana Felman. *Testimony: Crises of Witnessing in Literature, Psychoanalysis, and History.* New York: Routledge, 1992.

Lazarre, Jane. *Wet Earth and Dreams: A Narrative of Grief and Recovery.* Durham, N.C.: Duke University Press, 1998.

Lear, Linda. *Rachel Carson: Witness for Nature.* New York: Henry Holt, 1997.

Leopold, Ellen. *A Darker Ribbon: Breast Cancer, Women, and Their Doctors in the Twentieth Century.* Boston: Beacon Press, 1999.

Lerner, Barron H. *The Breast Cancer Wars: Fear, Hope, and the Pursuit of a Cure in Twentieth-Century America.* Oxford: Oxford University Press, 2001.

Libby, Brooke. "Nature Writing as *Refuge:* Autobiography in the Natural World." In *Reading under the Sign of Nature: New Essays in Ecocriticism,* ed. John Tallmadge and Henry Harrington, 251–64. Salt Lake City: University of Utah Press, 2000.

Lifshitz, Leatrice H., ed. *Her Soul beneath the Bone: Women's Poetry on Breast Cancer.* Urbana: University of Illinois Press, 1988.

Linton, Simi. *Claiming Disability: Knowledge and Identity.* New York: New York University Press, 1998.

Loomer, Lisa. *The Waiting Room.* New York: Dramatists Play Services, 1998.

Lorde, Audre. *A Burst of Light.* Ithaca, N.Y.: Firebrand Books, 1988.

———. *The Cancer Journals.* San Francisco: Spinsters Ink, 1980.

———. *The Marvelous Arithmetics of Distance: Poems, 1987–1992.* New York: W. W. Norton, 1993.

———. *Sister Outsider: Essays and Speeches.* Freedom, Calif.: Crossing Press, 1984.

Love, Susan M., with Karen Lindsey. *Dr. Susan Love's Breast Book.* 2nd ed. New York: Addison Wesley Publishing, 1995.

Martini, Adrienne. "The Playwright in Spite of Herself." *American Theatre* 16:8 (1999): 22–25.

Maso, Carole. *Ava.* Normal, Ill.: Dalkey Archive Press, 1993.

———. *Break Every Rule: Essays on Language, Longing, and Moments of Desire.* Washington, D.C.: Counterpoint, 2000.

Mason, Mary. "The Other Voice." In *Autobiography: Essays Theoretical and Critical,* ed. James Olney, 207–35. Princeton: Princeton University Press, 1980.

Masse, Michelle A. *In the Name of Love: Women, Masochism, and the Gothic.* Ithaca: Cornell University Press, 1992.

McLeese, Don. Rev. of *MotherKind,* by Jayne Anne Phillips. www.barnesand-noble.com. 1 Dec. 2002.

Metzger, Deena. *Tree* and *The Woman Who Slept with Men to Take the War Out of Them.* Culver City, Calif.: Peace Press, 1978.

Middlebrook, Christina. *Seeing the Crab: A Memoir of Dying before I Do.* New York: Doubleday, 1996.

Miller, Susan. *My Left Breast.* In *The Breast: An Anthology,* ed. Susan Thames and Marin Gazzaniga, 214–36. New York: Global City Press, 1995.

Minot, Susan. *Evening.* New York: Vintage Books, 1998.

———. Interview. http://www.randomhouse.com/boldtype/1098/minot/interview.htm. 1 Dec. 2002.

———. *Rapture.* New York: Vintage Books, 2002.

Mitchell, David T., and Sharon L. Snyder. *Narrative Prosthesis: Disability and the Dependencies of Discourse.* Ann Arbor: University of Michigan Press, 2000.

Mohanty, Chandra Talpade, Ann Russo, and Lourdes Torres, eds. *Third World Women and the Politics of Feminism.* Bloomington: Indiana University Press, 1991.

Moore, Steven. "An Interview with Carole Maso." http://www.centerfor bookculture.org/interviews. 1 Dec. 2002.

Moraga, Cherrie. *Heroes and Saints and Other Plays.* Albuquerque: West End Press, 1994.

Morgan, Kathryn Pauly. "Contested Bodies, Contested Knowledges: Women, Health, and the Politics of Medicalization." In *The Politics of Women's Health: Exploring Agency and Autonomy,* ed. Feminist Health Care Ethics Research Network, 83–121. Philadelphia: Temple University Press, 1998.

Mulvey, Laura. "Visual Pleasure and Narrative Cinema." *Screen* 16 (1975): 6–18.

Nestle, Joan. *A Fragile Union: New and Selected Writings.* San Francisco: Cleis Press, 1998.

Newmark, Kevin. "Traumatic Poetry: Charles Baudelaire and the Shock of Laughter." In *Trauma: Explorations in Memory,* ed. Cathy Caruth, 236–55. Baltimore: Johns Hopkins University Press, 1995.

Nielsen, Jerri, with Maryanne Vollers. *Ice Bound: A Doctor's Incredible Battle for Survival at the South Pole.* New York: Talk Miramax Books/Hyperion, 2001.

Noble, Marianne. *The Masochistic Pleasures of Sentimental Literature.* Princeton: Princeton University Press, 2000.

Olson, James S. *Bathsheba's Breast: Women, Cancer, and History*. Baltimore: Johns Hopkins University Press, 2002.

Ostriker, Alicia Suskin. *The Crack in Everything*. Pittsburgh: University of Pittsburgh Press, 1996.

———. *The Nakedness of the Fathers: Biblical Visions and Revisions*. New Brunswick: Rutgers University Press, 1994.

———. "Scenes from a Mastectomy." In *Living on the Margins: Women Writers on Breast Cancer*, ed. Hilda Raz, 175–200. New York: Persea Books, 1999.

———. *Stealing the Language: The Emergence of Women's Poetry in America*. Boston: Beacon Press, 1986.

Pastan, Linda. *A Fraction of Darkness*. New York: W. W. Norton, 1985.

Perloff, Marjorie. "From Image to Action: The Return of Story in Postmodern Poetry." *Contemporary Literature* 23 (1982): 411–27.

Perrault, Jeanne. "'That the Pain Not Be Wasted': Audre Lorde and the Written Self." *Auto/Biography Studies* 4:1 (1988): 1–16.

———. *Writing Selves: Contemporary Feminist Autobiography*. Minneapolis: University of Minnesota Press, 1995.

Phillips, Jayne Anne. Interview. www. jayneannephillips.com. 1 Dec. 2002.

———. *MotherKind*. New York: Random House, 2000.

Picardie, Justine. *If the Spirit Moves You: Life and Love after Death*. New York: Penguin, 2002.

Picardie, Ruth. *Before I Say Goodbye: Recollections and Observations from One Woman's Final Year*. New York: Henry Holt, 2000.

Plath, Sylvia. *Collected Poems*. Ed. Ted. Hughes. New York: Harper and Row, 1981.

———. *Johnny Panic and the Bible of Dreams: Short Stories, Prose, and Diary Excerpts*. New York: Harper and Row, 1979.

———. *The Journals of Sylvia Plath*. Ed. Ted Hughes and Frances McCullough. New York: Ballantine Books, 1983.

Potts, Laura K. "Publishing the Personal: Autobiographical Narratives of Breast Cancer and the Self." In *Ideologies of Breast Cancer: Feminist Perspectives*, ed. Laura K. Potts, 98–127. London: Macmillan Press, 2000.

Proctor, Robert N. *Cancer Wars: How Politics Shapes What We Know and Don't Know about Cancer*. New York: Basic Books, 1995.

Quindlen, Anna. *One True Thing*. New York: Dell Publishing, 1994.

Radner, Gilda. *It's Always Something*. New York: 1988.

Radway, Janice. "The Readers and Their Romances." In *Feminisms: An Anthology of Literary Theory and Criticism*, ed. Robyn R. Warhol and Diane Price Herndl, 551–92. New Brunswick, N.J.: Rutgers University Press, 1991.

———. *Reading the Romance: Women, Patriarchy, and Popular Literature*. Chapel Hill: University of North Carolina Press, 1984.

Ratzan, Richard M. Rev. of *Talk before Sleep*, by Elizabeth Berg. http://endeavor.med.nyu/lit-med. 18 Nov. 2002.

Ravenholt, R. T. "Tobacco's Global Death March." *Population and Development Review* 16 (1990): 213–40.

Raz, Hilda. *Divine Honors.* Hanover, N.H.: Wesleyan University Press, 1997.

———. "Introduction: Writing on the Margins." In *Living on the Margins: Women Writers on Breast Cancer,* ed. Hilda Raz, vii–xvii. New York: Persea Books, 1999.

———. "Writing the Impossible." In *Sleeping with One Eye Open: Women Writers and the Art of Survival,* ed. Marilyn Kallet and Judith Ortiz Cofer, 121–25. Athens: University of Georgia Press, 1999.

Reibstein, Janet. *Staying Alive: A Family Memoir.* New York: Bloomsbury, 2002.

Renner, Pamela. "Science and Sensibility." *American Theatre* 16:4 (1999): 34–36.

Rich, Adrienne. "Notes toward a Politics of Location." In *Blood, Bread, and Poetry: Selected Prose, 1979–1985.* New York: W. W. Norton, 1986.

———. *Of Woman Born: Motherhood as Experience and Institution.* New York: W. W. Norton, 1976.

———. *On Lies, Secrets, and Silence: Selected Prose 1966–1978.* New York: W. W. Norton, 1979.

———. "A Woman Dead in Her Forties." In *The Fact of a Doorframe: Poems Selected and New, 1950–1984,* 250–55. New York: W. W. Norton, 1984.

Rich, Katherine Russell. *The Red Devil: A Memoir about Beating the Odds.* New York: Three Rivers Press, 1999.

Robson, Ruthann. "not // a story." In *Coming Out of Cancer: Writings from the Lesbian Cancer Epidemic,* ed. Victoria A. Brownworth, 47–53. Seattle: Seal Press, 2000.

Rodgers, Joni. *Bald in the Land of Big Hair.* New York: HarperCollins, 2001.

Rollin, Betty. *First, You Cry.* 1976. New York: Quill Press, 2000.

Rowson, Susanna. *Charlotte Temple.* Ed. and intro. Cathy N. Davidson. 1791. New York: Oxford University Press, 1986.

Rukeyser, Muriel. "Kathe Kollwitz." In *Out of Silence: Selected Poems,* ed. Kate Daniels, 129–33. Evanston, Ill.: TriQuarterly Books, 1992.

Scarry, Elaine. *The Body in Pain: The Making and Unmaking of the World.* New York: Oxford University Press, 1985.

Schmidt, Maia Saj. "Literary Testimonies of Illness and the Reshaping of Social Memory." *a/b: Auto/Biography Studies* 13:1 (1988): 71–91.

Schneider, Rebecca. *The Explicit Body in Performance.* London: Routledge, 1997.

Scott, Joan W. "Experience." In *Women, Autobiography, Theory: A Reader,* ed. Sidonie Smith and Julia Watson, 57–71. Madison: University of Wisconsin Press, 1998.

Sedgwick, Eve Kosofsky. "White Glasses." In *Tendencies,* 252–66. Durham, N.C.: Duke University Press, 1993.

Segrave, Elisa. *The Diary of a Breast.* London: Faber and Faber, 1995.

Shea, Suzanne Strempek. *Songs from a Lead-Lined Room: Notes—High and Low—from My Journey through Breast Cancer and Radiation*. Boston: Beacon Press, 2002.

Shildrick, Margrit. *Leaky Bodies and Boundaries: Feminism, Postmodernism, and (Bio)Ethics*. London: Routledge, 1997.

Shildrick, Margrit, with Janet Price. "Openings on the Body: A Critical Introduction." In *Feminist Theory and the Body: A Reader*, ed. Margrit Shildrick and Janet Price, 1–14. Edinburgh: Edinburgh University Press, 1999.

Siegel, Bernie. *Peace, Love, and Healing: Bodymind Communication and the Path to Self-Healing: An Exploration*. New York: HarperCollins, 2001.

Simmonds, Felly Nkweto. "A Remembering." In *Cancer: Through the Eyes of Ten Women*, ed. Patricia Duncker and Vicky Wilson, 35–51. London: Pandora, 1996.

Smith, Michael B. "'Silence, Miss Carson!': Science, Gender, and the Reception of *Silent Spring*." *Feminist Studies* 27:3 (2001): 733–52.

Smith, Sidonie. "Identity's Body." In *Autobiography and Postmodernism*, ed. Kathleen Ashley, Leigh Gilmore, and Gerald Peters, 266–92. Amherst: University of Massachusetts Press, 1994.

———. *The Poetics of Women's Autobiography*. Bloomington: Indiana University Press, 1987.

Smith, Sidonie, and Julia Watson. "Introduction: Mapping Women's Self-Representation at Visual/Textual Interfaces." In *Interfaces: Women/Autobiography/Image/Performance*, ed. Sidonie Smith and Julia Watson, 1–46. Ann Arbor: University of Michigan Press, 2002.

———. "Introduction: Situating Subjectivity in Women's Autobiographical Practices." In *Women, Autobiography, Theory: A Reader*, ed. Sidonie Smith and Julia Watson, 3–52. Madison: University of Wisconsin Press, 1998.

Smith-Rosenberg, Carroll. "The Female World of Love and Ritual: Relations between Women in Nineteenth-Century America." *Signs* 1:1 (1975): 1–30.

Sontag, Susan. *AIDS and Its Metaphors*. 1988. New York: Picador, 2001.

———. *Illness as Metaphor*. New York: Farrar Straus Giroux, 1977.

Sova, Cathy. Rev. of *The Saving Graces*, by Patricia Gaffney. http://www.theromancereader.com. 18 Nov. 2002.

Spence, Jo. *Cultural Sniping: The Art of Transgression*. London: Routledge, 1995.

Spivak, Gayatri Chakravorty. *In Other Worlds: Essays in Cultural Politics*. New York: Routledge, 1988.

Stabiner, Karen. *To Dance with the Devil: The New War on Breast Cancer*. New York: Delacorte Press, 1997.

Stacey, Jackie. *Teratologies: A Cultural Study of Cancer*. London: Routledge, 1997.

Steingraber, Sandra. *Living Downstream: An Ecologist Looks at Cancer and the Environment*. New York: Addison Wesley Publishing, 1997.

———. *Post-Diagnosis*. Ithaca, N.Y.: Firebrand Books, 1995.

Sykes, John D., Jr. "*Wit*, Pride, and the Resurrection: Margaret Edson's Play and John Donne's Poetry." *Renascence* 55:2 (2003): 163–74.

Tallmadge, John. "Beyond the Excursion: Initiatory Themes in Annie Dillard and Terry Tempest Williams." In *Reading the Earth: New Directions in the Study of Literature and Environment,* ed. Michael P. Branch, Rochelle Johnson, Daniel Patterson, and Scott Slovic, 197–207. Moscow: University of Idaho Press, 1998.

Thames, Susan, and Marin Gazzaniga, eds. *The Breast: An Anthology.* New York: Global City Press, 1995.

Tompkins, Jane. "Sentimental Power: *Uncle Tom's Cabin* and the Politics of Literary History." In *Feminisms: An Anthology of Literary Theory and Criticism,* ed. Robyn R. Warhol and Diane Price Herndl, 20–39. New Brunswick, N.J.: Rutgers University Press, 1991.

Trichopoulos, Dimitrios, et al. "Active and Passive Smoking." *Journal of the American Medical Association* 268 (1992): 1697–1701.

Vanhoutte, Jacqueline. "Cancer and the Common Woman in Margaret Edson's *Wit*." *Comparative Drama* 36:3–4 (2002): 391–410.

Wachsmith, Maudeen. Rev. of *The Saving Graces,* by Patricia Gaffney. http://www.silcom.com. 18 Nov. 2002.

Wadler, Joyce. *My Breast: One Woman's Cancer Story.* London: Women's Press, 1994.

Warner, Susan. *The Wide, Wide World.* 1851. New York: Feminist Press, 1987.

Weintraub, Karl. *The Value of the Individual.* Chicago: University of Chicago Press, 1978.

Welch, Dave. "Back in Bed with Susan Minot." 2002. http://powells.com/authors/minot.htm. 1 Dec. 2002.

Welter, Barbara. "The Cult of True Womanhood, 1820–1860." *American Quarterly* 18:2, pt. 1 (1966): 151–74.

Wilkinson, S., and C. Kitzinger. "Toward a Feminist Approach to Breast Cancer." *In Women and Health: Feminist Perspectives,* ed. S. Wilkinson and C. Kitzinger. London: Taylor and Francis, 1994.

Williams, Terry Tempest. *Refuge: An Unnatural History of Family and Place.* New York: Random House, 1991.

Wills, David. *Prosthesis.* Stanford, Calif.: Stanford University Press, 1995.

Winston, Lolly. *Good Grief.* New York: Warner Books, 2004.

Winterson, Jeanette. *Art Objects: Essays on Ecstasy and Effrontery.* Toronto: Vintage Canada, 1995.

———. Home page. http://www.jeanettewinterson.com. 1 Dec. 2002.

———. *Written on the Body.* New York: Alfred A. Knopf, 1993.

Wittig, Monique. *The Lesbian Body.* Trans. David Le Vay. Boston: Beacon Press, 1986.

Woodman, Marion. *Bone: Dying into Life.* New York: Viking, 2000.

Woolf, Virginia. *A Room of One's Own.* 1929. New York: Harcourt Brace Jovanovich, 1989.

290 ->   WORKS CITED

Yalom, Marilyn. *A History of the Breast*. New York: Ballantine Books, 1997.

Zeiger, Melissa F. *Beyond Consolation: Death, Sexuality, and the Changing Shapes of Elegy*. Ithaca: Cornell University Press, 1997.

Zinman, Toby. "Illness as Metaphor." *American Theatre* 16:8 (1999): 25.

Index

INDEX